During the Napoleonic Wars it was customary for British troops ordered on active service to take some of their wives with them. The usual proportion was six women per hundred men. The wives who were to accompany their husbands were chosen by ballot: excitement for the lucky ones and anguish for those left behind. The latter often marched with the regiment to the port of departure, desperate to remain with their men till the last moment, and there were harrowing scenes as families were separated, perhaps forever.

The women who were to accompany their husbands had to endure all the hazards of the high seas, often in slow and leaky transports. In bad weather, conditions resembled a slave ship, with men and women battened down below, rolling about and seasick in the darkness. There were storms, fires, childbirth and sometimes shipwreck to contend with.

Once landed in the theatre of war, the women faced a life of almost constant marching in summer heat and winter cold. Most of them managed to acquire a donkey to carry their few possessions. There were no tents until late in the war, and regiments were either quartered in whatever buildings were available, or bivouacked in the open. Clothing and especially shoes wore out, and women often had to supply their wants by stripping the dead. Food was frequently in short supply, and, as they were entitled only to half a man's ration, they were notorious plunderers. This frequently resulted in brutal punishment from the provost marshals.

After battles or sieges, soldiers' wives tended the wounded, but they were also determined looters and shared the army's besetting sin of drunkenness. Occasionally they were taken prisoner, and were sometimes involved in the actual fighting. More often they had to search a battlefield for a wounded husband or his mutilated remains. Many women were widowed, and solved the problem by quick remarriage to another soldier, some of them several times.

After the war, the survivors came home to an uncertain future. Some prospered; others slipped into penury. Some had a surprising later life, and a few earned themselves permanent memorials. Most vanished from the record. This book is an attempt to shed some light on these forgotten heroines and their part in the country's long war against the French.

David Clammer was born and brought up in Dorset. He taught history for more than 30 years. Since retirement, he has given history lectures aboard expedition ships in the Polar regions. He is the author of several books on Victorian military campaigns, and articles on textbook research, arctic cartography and local history. More recently, he has written extensively on the Napoleonic invasion threat, and was elected to the Royal Historical Society. He lives with his wife in a village in Cambridgeshire.

Ladies, Wives and Women

British Army Wives in the Revolutionary and Napoleonic Wars 1793–1815

David Clammer

 Helion & Company

Helion & Company Limited
Unit 8 Amherst Business Centre
Budbrooke Road
Warwick
CV34 5WE
England
Tel. 01926 499619
Email: info@helion.co.uk
Website: www.helion.co.uk
Twitter: @helionbooks
Visit our blog at http://blog.helion.co.uk/

Published by Helion & Company 2022
Designed and typeset by Mach 3 Solutions Ltd (www.mach3solutions.co.uk)
Cover designed by Paul Hewitt, Battlefield Design (www.battlefield-design.co.uk)
Text © David Clammer 2022
Illustrations © as individually credited.
Maps by George Anderson © Helion & Co. 2022

Cover: British light dragoon in taking leave of his sweetheart. Mezzotint by J. Murphy after Wheatley. (Anne S.K. Brown Military Collection)

Every reasonable effort has been made to trace copyright holders and to obtain their permission for the use of copyright material. The author and publisher apologise for any errors or omissions in this work, and would be grateful if notified of any corrections that should be incorporated in future reprints or editions of this book.

ISBN 978-1-915113-90-0

British Library Cataloguing-in-Publication Data.
A catalogue record for this book is available from the British Library.

All rights reserved. No part of this publication may be reproduced, stored in a retrieval system, or transmitted, in any form, or by any means, electronic, mechanical, photocopying, recording or otherwise, without the express written consent of Helion & Company Limited.

For details of other military history titles published by Helion & Company Limited, contact the above address, or visit our website: http://www.helion.co.uk

We always welcome receiving book proposals from prospective authors.

Contents

List of Maps and Illustrations		vi
Acknowledgements		viii
A Chronology of the Wars		ix
1	Following the Drum	13
2	Drawing Lots	23
3	Before The Mast	47
4	On the March	63
5	The Bare Necessities	82
6	Hazards	104
7	Corunna	123
8	Under Fire	145
9	The Fatal Field	162
10	Bad Behaviour	175
11	Marriage à la Mode	190
12	Going Home	208
13	Survivors	225
Bibliography		239
Index		249

List of Maps and Illustrations

The Charms of a Red Coat. An officer talks with a lady on horseback while two others take tea in a tent. Coloured mezzotint published by Robert Sayer, 1 November 1782. (Anne S.K. Brown Military Collection, Brown Univeristy) — 19

Selling a Wife by Thomas Rowlandson, 1812. A man whose wife is tied with a rope offers her for sale, while a soldier holds out his money. The woman seems quite happy with this transaction. (Public domain) — 21

War. A Wealthy officer bids farewell to his family and servants in a grand house. A soldier holds his charger ready while transports wait in the bay. Stipple engraving after Henry Singleton. (Anne S.K. Brown Military Collection, Brown University) — 31

Deserter taking leave of his wife. A young man's distraught wife embraces him at their cottage door while soldiers prepare to march him away. Perhaps he had enlisted while drunk. (Anne S.K. Brown Military Collection, Brown University) — 36

Rosabell. A popular song sheet depicting a woman with a child on a quay waving farewell to soldiers boarding transports in longboats. By John Mayne 12 December 1806. (Anne S.K. Brown Military Collection, Brown University) — 44

The landing of the British Army at Figueria da Foz in early August 1808. A number of women and children can be seen amongst the troops. Engraving after Henri Leveque, 1812. (Anne S.K. Brown Military Collection, Brown University) — 64

Cartoon by Thomas Rowlandson, 1798. A detachment of troops have commandeered several carriages. One woman is riding on a waggon, another is running after a cart. Aquatint by Ackermann. (Anne S.K. Brown Military Collection, Brown University) — 67

Watercolour by Thomas Rowlandson, 1800. Cavalry troops escort a baggage waggon with a woman perched on top. Not always a safe ride. (Anne S.K. Brown Military Collection, Brown University) — 74

Somewhere on campaign a group of redcoats are cooking under a tree, while two women do the laundry in the stream and another hangs it up to dry. Aquatint after Thomas Rowlandson, 1 April 1798. (Anne S.K. Brown Military Collection, Brown University) — 85

A watercolour by Edward Eyre c.1780 showing a camp in in Green Park, London. The women are busy with the laundry, using a wheelbarrow to move the tub. (Anne S.K. Brown Military Collection, Brown University) — 98

'To pack up her tatters and follow the drum.' A satirical cartoon by Thomas
    Rowlandson, published April 1811, in which the women are depicted carrying the
    men across a stream. (Anne S.K. Brown Military Collection, Brown University)   111

The allied army crossing the Mondego river, 21 September 1810 by Thomas St Clair.
    The troops marched into the ford, here narrow and shallow. However, deep and
    fast flowing crossings were a great hazard for the women especially. (Anne S.K.
    Brown Military Collection, Brown University)   117

The British lines before Alexandria, June 1801. An aquatint after Captain Walker, 3rd
    Guards. Soldiers and their wives can be seen sheltering from the Egyptian sun in
    the middle tent. (Anne S.K. Brown Military Collection, Brown University)   120

The retreat to Corunna.   125

Regimental baggage on the march in mountainous country. Two women can be seen,
    one with a child on her back, the other on a mule. Aquatint by Thomas St Clair,
    1812. (Anne S.K. Brown Military Collection, Brown University)   133

The Battle of Vimeiro. As the troops advance a woman and child can be seen hurriedly
    seeking a place of safety. Engraving after Henri Leveque, 1812. (Anne S.K. Brown
    Military Collection, Brown University)   150

The field of Waterloo after the battle. Several women can be seen searching for the dead
    or wounded, and one is overcome with horror and emotion. Aquatint after John
    Heaviside Clark, 1817. (Anne S.K. Brown Military Collection, Brown University)   166

A cavalry barrack room. A woman is peddling refreshments, but the other two,
    one with a child and the other washing, appear to be soldiers' wives. Aquatint
    by Thomas Rowlandson, 1788. (Anne S.K. Brown Military Collection, Brown
    University)   177

Divine service in the field. The padre has his Bible or sermon laid out on the drums.
    The soldiers and officers listen attentively as do the four women, three of them
    with babies. A rather idealised scene by Thomas Rowlandson, 1798. (Anne S.K.
    Brown Military Collection, Brown University)   194

A long column of troops marching into the distance. Two of the women, one smoking
    a pipe, tramp along with their children while two more are sharing a donkey.
    Aquatint by Thomas Rowlandson, 1798. (Anne S.K. Brown Military Collection,
    Brown University)   212

A British bivouac in Paris. The women may be British wives, or possibly French
    prostitutes. Engraving by Jean Baptiste Genty, 1815. (Anne S.K. Brown Military
    Collection, Brown University)   214

The Ballad Singers. A disabled veteran soldier with his wife and children, playing and
    singing and begging for alms in the street. Aquatint, 1820. (Anne S.K. Brown
    Military Collection, Brown University)   230

Acknowledgements

Many people have assisted my research, and without their help this book could not have been written. First, I wish to thank the staff of the Munby Rare Books Room in the Cambridge University Library, especially Claire Welford-Elkin for her friendly help over a good many years. Also in Cambridge, the librarians of Queens' College Old Library, St John's and Trinity have granted me access to volumes in their collections.

The staff of Cheshire Archives and Local Studies, Dorset History Centre, East Riding Archives, Huntingdon Record Office, Lancashire Infantry Museum, Nottinghamshire Archives, Surrey History Centre, and Shropshire Archives have answered queries and provided copies of material in their archives. David Blake of the Museum of Army Chaplaincy, Ruth Evans of the Inniskilling Fusiliers Museum, Dr Lucinda Lax of the National Galleries of Scotland, Emma Mawdsley of the National Army Museum, Rob McIntosh of the Museum of Military Medicine, and Mike Tanner of the Pontypool Museum, have all taken the time to answer queries or send me copies of information. Thanks also to Dr Anna Ritchie for checking material in the National Library of Scotland, and, as always, for her hospitality.

I wish to thank the editors of the family history journals who published my article on army wives, and the people who contacted me with such fascinating information about their ancestors (including those in Australia, New Zealand and the United States): Steven Bumstead, Ian Cameron, Andrew Campbell, Janetta Condon, Trevor Cooper, Sally Gale, John Hynes, Philip Martin, David Patterson, Sarah Riley, Sandra Robertson, Robert Pauling, and Graham Robertson. Many others emailed me with information I have been unable to incorporate, and they too deserve thanks for sharing their personal researches.

Susan Bickley gave me a valuable lead on Mary Ann Wellington and Richard Cobbold; Andrew Cormack, editor of the *Journal of the Society for Army Historical Research,* published a query regarding women and courts martial; John Ellis shared his thoughts on Sir Walter Scott and the flogging controversy; Sally Howard-Vyse graciously provided me with private copies of the Norcliffe correspondence; and Zack White generously shared information on courts martial from his PhD thesis *Plunder, Provost and Punishment: Discipline under Wellington's Command, 1808–1818*. Especial thanks are due to Andrew Bamford, for his calm and reassuring support during the preparation of the manuscript, and to Rob Griffith, whose meticulous copy-editing has eliminated a number of errors and improved the text. Above all, and as always, my love and thanks to my wife Liz.

A Chronology of the Wars

Readers unfamiliar with the wars against Revolutionary and Napoleonic France may find an outline chronology useful. Naval events are not included, and political developments only where relevant. The list contains the principal actions of the British Army against the French or their allies. The regimental wives would have been present at most of them.

1793
1 February: France declares war on Britain
14 February: Tobago captured
25 February: British troops sail for Flanders
18–21 March: Battle of Neerwinden. British troops under the Duke of York, with Austrian allies, drive the French from the Netherlands.
April: Attacks on Martinique and San Domingo in the West Indies, Pondicherry (India) and Miquelon (Newfoundland)
15 August: Duke of York leads troops to attack Dunkirk
8 September: Battle of Hondschoote. French defeat British and Hanoverian troops and raise the siege of Dunkirk

1794
7 February: British troops land on Corsica
22 March: Martinique captured
4 April: St Lucia captured (subsequently lost and recaptured May 1796)
26 June: French defeat the allies at Fleurus. British and Dutch retire to Holland

1795
14 April: British troops evacuated from Bremen
16 May: The United Provinces make terms with France
17 August: Malacca captured from the Dutch
30 August: Trincomalee captured from the Dutch
16 September: Capture of the Cape of Good Hope

1796
31 August: Corsica evacuated
8 October: Spain declares war on Britain

1797
18–30 April: British attack on Puerto Rico fails

1798
14 November: British forces capture Minorca

1799
27 August: Joint Anglo-Russian landing in Holland
19 September: British troops commanded by the Duke of York win the Battle of Bergen
18 October: York, short of supplies, signs armistice and agrees to evacuate Holland
9 November: Bonaparte becomes First Consul

1800
5 September: Surrender of French troops on Malta to British force under Brigadier General Graham

1801
8 March: British army under Lieutenant General Abercromby lands in Aboukir Bay, Egypt
21 March: French defeated at the Battle of Alexandria
1 October: Preliminaries of the Peace of Amiens agreed between Britain and France

1802
25 March: Peace of Amiens concluded. The French Revolutionary Wars come to an end

1803
18 May: Britain declares war on France. Napoleonic Wars begin
May: British troops reconquer Tobago, St Lucia, Demerara, Essequibo and Berbice but lose San Domingo

1804
18 May: Bonaparte declares himself Emperor of the French
2 December: Coronation of Napoleon at Notre-Dame
12 December: Spain declares war on Britain

1805
11 January: Britain declares war on Spain
20 November: Anglo-Russian force reaches Naples
12 December: Large British force under Lord Cathcart lands in north Germany but is withdrawn the following month

1806
10 January: Sir David Baird's force recaptures Cape of Good Hope
19 January: British forces withdrawn from Naples and sent to Sicily
15 February: Lieutenant General Craig's troop reach Messina and occupy forts
28 June: Beresford's troops capture Buenos Aires

4 July: British troops defeat French at the Battle of Maida in southern Italy

1807
3 February: Brigadier General Auchmuchty's force captures Montevideo
17 March: British force defeated at Rosetta in Egypt
10 July: Lieutenant General Whitelock's attack on Buenos Aires ends in disaster
16 August–7 September: British attack on Copenhagen
7 November: Russia declares war on Britain

1808
27 February: French troops invade Spain
2 May: Spanish revolt in Madrid against the French
June: Various Spanish delegations arrive in London seeking British aid
1 August: Lieutenant General Sir Arthur Wellesley lands in Portugal with 9,000 British troops
17 August: Wellesley defeats French at Roliça
21 August: Wellesley defeats Junot at the Battle of Vimeiro
6 October: Lieutenant General Sir John Moore's advance into Spain begins

1809
9 January: Anglo-Spanish treaty of alliance signed
16 January: Battle of Corunna and British troops evacuated
22 April: Wellesley assumes command of British forces in Portugal
12 May: French under Soult driven out of Oporto
27/28 July: Wellesley wins the Battle of Talavera. He is made Viscount Wellington
28 July: British expedition to Walcheren sails
23 December: Final evacuation of Walcheren

1810
6 February: Guadeloupe captured
February: British troops reinforce the garrison of Cadiz
9 July: British capture Réunion in the Indian Ocean
27 September: Wellington defeats Masséna at Busaco
12 October: French army halted by the Lines of Torres Vedras
14 November: French begin their retreat from the Lines

1811
5 March: Graham defeats French at Battle of Barrosa
3–5 May: Wellington beats Masséna at Fuentes de Oñoro
16 May: Beresford fights Battle of Albuera
4 August: British assault on Java
18 September: Java surrenders
25 September: Action at El Bodon
28 October: Action at Arroyomolinos

1812

8–19 January: British besiege and capture Ciudad Rodrigo
17 March–6 April: Siege and capture of Badajoz
24 June: Napoleon invades Russia
22 July: British victory at the Battle of Salamanca
23 July–late November: British advance to Madrid and Burgos but retire to Portugal

1813

21 June: Wellington's victory at Vitoria
25 July: The actions at Roncesvalles and Maya
28 and 30 July: Battles of Sorauren
7 July–8 September: Siege of San Sebastian
31 August: Actions at San Marcial and Vera
7 October: Passage of the Bidasoa. France invaded
10 November: Battle of the Nivelle
9–10 December: Battle of the Nive
13 December: Battle of St Pierre
December to April 1814: Investment of Bayonne

1814

27 February: Battle of Orthez
8–9 March: Graham defeated at Bergen-op-Zoom
6 April: Napoleon abdicates
10 April: Wellington wins the Battle of Toulouse

1815

1 March: Napoleon lands in France having escaped from Elba; start of the Hundred Days
16 June: Battle of Quatre Bras
18 June: Battle of Waterloo

1

Following the Drum

Little thinks the townsman's wife
Whilst at home she tarries,
What must be the lassie's life
Who a soldier marries[1]

Officially, the Army did not approve of wives.

The *Rules and Regulations for the Cavalry* issued by the Adjutant General's Office on 1 October 1795, early on in the great war with France, spelt out the official view very clearly: 'Marriage must be discouraged as much as possible ... Officers must explain to the men the many miseries that women are exposed to, even in England, when there are too many of them, and particularly on service; and, by every sort of persuasion, they must prevent their marrying, if possible.'[2]

The fact was of course that wives were an unavoidable nuisance. Soldiers had had wives and women of one sort or another since antiquity, and since there was no way of actually preventing marriage when a man was determined on it, the next best thing was to do everything possible to discourage it. So, if a soldier persisted in his wish to marry, his officers were to enquire into the circumstances of the woman concerned and refuse consent if she appeared unable to support herself independently because of idleness or for any other reason. This was to ensure that she did not 'encroach on the man's subsistence', and in such a case the man would be ordered to eat in his mess, since his welfare was paramount from the regiment's point of view. And there was more. 'No man who presumes to marry an improper woman, [whatever that meant] or to marry at all against the consent of the Commanding Officer of his Troop, is to be allowed separate lodgings, or be out of Quarters.' The soldier concerned would be obliged to live in his billet or barrack, and mess with his comrades. In other words, normal married life would simply be made impossible. Moreover, the *Regulations* went on to state that 'a bad Soldier's wife must be got rid of as soon as possible.' Quite how that was to be done was not explained.

But naturally, soldiers did get married, and having done so, it was the accepted practice that a proportion of wives should go with the troops when they sailed on active service. And

---

1   Traditional.
2   Anon., *Rules and Regulations for the Cavalry* (London: Adjutant General's Office, 1795), p.74.

the best that the authorities could do in the circumstances was to restrict the number of wives allowed, and issue more instructions: 'They should be carefully selected, as being of good Character and having the inclination and ability to render themselves useful; it is very desirable that those with children should be left at home.'³ Precisely how suitable women were to be selected was presumably to be left to the discretion of commanding officers, and the reality was that apart from the question of numbers, none of these official strictures were ever fully implemented.

This anxiety about wives was really concerned with regiments or other units in the field. Stationary garrisons were regarded differently. Here, 12 women and their children per troop or company were allowed. In the case of royal veteran battalions, there were virtually no restrictions. Veteran and Garrison battalions were composed of older soldiers, pensioners and invalids who manned fortifications, or worked depots, stores and other forms of not very arduous support work to release able-bodied troops for active service. The War Office had to recognize that a large number of such mature men would be married, and in these cases the order was that 'Women and children of Royal Veteran Battalions are to be victualled to the full number which may be in the regiment.'⁴

The War Office was not alone in thinking that soldiers were better off unmarried, or that it was undesirable for women to go on active service. A minority of soldiers, both officers and men, held the same view, and for a variety of reasons. To some, the terrible misery of parting, the anguished scenes between soldiers and wives and families being left behind at the time of embarkation, was enough to convince them that a soldier was better off single. An anonymous officer of the 81st Foot, embarking from Ramsgate on the Walcheren expedition in July 1809 for instance, found these scenes harrowing. 'The place is full of the wives, friends, and daughters of the officers about to embark. We hourly meet many lovely faces either actually suffused in tears, or with evident marks that they have but just taken the last embrace of some beloved object.' Writing to a friend, he went on to describe the crowds of women assembled to watch the ships set sail, most of them in tears, and hoping against hope to see their husbands, fathers and lovers return safely. 'The more I see of this interesting spectacle, the more do I become a convert to Sir John Moore's maxim – that a soldier should have nothing to do with a wife.'⁵

Others, inured to such harrowing scenes perhaps, simply believed that a soldier had no business with a wife and family because they would be a constant worry and distraction, which no doubt they often were even when they were not with the regiment. This was certainly the position of Major John Patterson of the 50th Foot:

> In time of war, matrimony is a serious draw-back to a soldier. Constant uneasiness about the family he has left at home, when he himself is called abroad, and their

---

3   General Order for Troops destined for Continental Service, War Office, 15 April 1807, in Richard Glover, *Britain at Bay* (London: Allen & Unwin, 1973), p.130.
4   J. Gurwood (ed.), *The General Orders of Field Marshal the Duke of Wellington in Portugal, Spain and France from 1809 to 1814, in the Low Countries and France in 1815, Army of Occupation from 1816 to 1818* (London: Parker, 1837), p.333.
5   Anon., *Letters from Flushing; containing an account of the Expedition to Walcheren, Beveland and the mouth of the Scheldt by an Officer of the Eighty-First Regiment* (London: Phillips, 1809), p.2.

anxiety for him, are painful things to think of; his happiness and peace of mind are marred, and all his best exertions paralyzed, by reflecting on their situation.[6]

Although there is little evidence that Patterson was right in believing that men's fighting efficiency was actually undermined in this way, there were others who held similar views. Peter Le Mesurier, an ensign in the 9th Foot, was on board a transport in Falmouth roads waiting to sail for the Peninsula. He had, he wrote to tell his father in September 1808, been walking the deck with Captain Louzern, a pleasant officer who was married with four children. He had left them behind, which Le Mesurier thought was very wise in view of the hardships to be faced during a voyage. And he added, with all the wisdom of a 19 year old, 'please tell my good Sister Ann that I do not intend to Marry before I am totally unfit for His Majesty's service.'[7] Young Le Mesurier was right about the hardships which women would have to face on board ship, but there were others who deprecated the presence of women and children on active service simply because of the even worse hardships they were often forced to undergo while on campaign. When Charles Steevens of the 20th Foot came to write his reminiscences, he particularly remembered the plight of the women during the retreat to Corunna in 1808, especially one whom he described as 'particularly well-conducted' and who had been with the regiment 11 years. Despite this, she lacked the tough constitution required to survive the Corunna campaign. 'She was missed during the retreat; it appeared that her daughter – quite a young girl – lost her mother in the dark one night, and never heard of her again.'[8] Nor was she the only one.

The dilemma for married people was that if going on active service with the troops was a bad option for everyone concerned, the breaking up of family life if the wife and children remained behind was no better. 'It makes both the Husband & Wife wretched. When the Regiment is under orders for Service she is affraid of loosing him & he dreads the consequences, should he have the misfortune to lose his life, of leaving a beloved wife and family with perhaps a wretched pitance' was the way one officer put it.[9] He might have added that the pain of indefinite separation, with the real possibility that the husband might never come home at all, must itself have been hard to bear. A sobering example of such a situation concerned Major William Harness of the 80th Foot. On 9 April 1796 the regiment embarked for the Cape on their way east in response to French machinations in India. He left behind his beloved wife Bessy and his children. There followed several years of service in India, during which his letters are full of a painful yearning to return to England. In 1801 the 80th was posted to Egypt however, to take part in Abercromby's campaign against the French army abandoned there by Bonaparte. Harness was sure they would be posted home, but in September they were ordered back to India to fight against the Marathas. Harness

---

6   John Patterson, *Camp and Quarters. Scenes and Impressions of Military Life* (London: Saunders & Otley, 1840), vol.1, p.114.
7   A. Greenwood (ed.), *Through Spain with Wellington. The Letters of Lieutenant Peter Le Mesurier of the 'Fighting Ninth'* (Stroud: Amberley, 2016), p.10.
8   Charles Steevens, *Reminiscences of my Military Life from 1795 to 1815* (Winchester: Warren, 1878), p.71.
9   Greenwood (ed.), *Letters*, p.58.

died suddenly after a short illness in June 1804. After a separation of eight years, he, his wife and children never saw each other again.[10] Such a situation must have been commonplace.

William and Bessy Harness were at least able to correspond, though painfully slowly. On 10 January 1802, for instance, William, then at Alexandria in Egypt, received a letter which Bessy had written on 15 November 1800. If the ordinary soldier was a letter-writer, as many were, his wife might at least have known something of his whereabouts and welfare. For the literate, the army's postal service worked very efficiently in the Peninsula and the Low Countries; further afield it was often a different matter. But since the rate of literacy amongst working women was considerably lower than for men, it seems likely that many soldiers abroad on active service may never have received news from home, and that both parties must often have existed in a state of unknowing silence.

Indeed, the separation inevitable in the military life presented an unhappy prospect. After the Danish campaign of 1807, William Surtees, a quartermaster sergeant in the 2/95th Foot, got leave to return to his home village of Corbridge in Northumberland, where he took the opportunity to get married. His bride was a girl he had known since schooldays, but despite this old and comfortable familiarity, things did not turn out well: 'I cannot say that I enjoyed in the marriage state that happiness which I expected from it, partly owing to the frequent and long separations which my calling rendered unavoidable ... I believe, during the eight years which my wife lived after our union, I spent more than six of these absent from her.'[11] When he was home again after the Corunna retreat in January 1809, Surtees, who had been commissioned as quartermaster in the newly raised third battalion of the 95th, was again joined by his wife, 'the child to which she gave birth in my absence having died when six weeks old' as he put it dispassionately.[12] She never had another, and this he thought was probably as well, as she was in a very delicate state of health. After a few months they were separated again, and we are not even told her name. A bleak account of a bleak relationship, but probably not untypical.

It is not surprising that some army marriages came to grief. Major Patterson remembered one such. The regiment was joined by a new officer who at the venerable age of 40 was still an ensign. He had however just acquired a wife, who arrived 'with all her blushing honours thick upon her.' It was not destined to last. 'Placed between two fires,' as Patterson put it dryly, 'matrimony and campaigning, his Scylla and Charybdis, shipwreck ensued.'[13]

Then there were those men who took a particularly jaundiced view of the 'very reprehensible custom of allowing soldiers' wives to follow the army' on moral grounds. Despite all the evidence to the contrary, the private Scottish soldier of the 71st Foot who wrote his memoirs anonymously, held that the women of the regiment, who might have been expected to wash and sew for their husbands, did nothing useful at all. Worse still, in his puritanical view, 'Their profligate lives were not only the detestation of their own husbands, but even of many other soldiers.'[14] He seems to have had some unfortunate experiences. Few soldiers

---

10   Caroline Duncan-Jones (ed.), *Trusty and Well Beloved. The Letters Home of William Harness an Officer of George III* (London: SPCK, 1957), p.90.
11   William Surtees, *Twenty-Five Years in the Rifle Brigade* (London: Muller, 1973), p.75.
12   Surtees, *Twenty-Five Years*, p.101.
13   Patterson, *Camp and Quarters*, vol.1, p.126.
14   Anon. *Vicissitudes in the Life of a Scottish Soldier Written by Himself* (London: Colburn, 1827), p.79.

were this censorious. Some men were clearly attracted to the idea of marriage, but thought better of it in the event. The old hussar who wrote his memoirs under the pseudonym of 'Chelsea Pensioner' described how, when quartered near London, he had been smitten by the daughter of a respectable tradesman. The liaison was discovered however, and there was a considerable row. This, he felt in retrospect, was all for the best, and for the rest of his military career 'I eschewed all thoughts of the noose matrimonial.'[15]

Private Wheeler of the 51st Light Infantry took a thoroughly balanced view of the matter. A prolific letter writer, he described in detail the life he was leading in Belgium in May 1815 as the allied army concentrated before Waterloo. The local people were hospitable, the food good and grog plentiful. The local girls were pretty, and becoming attached to some of his comrades, and no doubt shortly to the regiment as well. But Wheeler went on:

> I must here observe that your humble servant does not intend to get entangled with any of them. It might be all very fine in its way and no doubt there are many sweets in having a pretty lovely young woman for a comrade, but then, I know from observation that there is an infinite number of bitters attending it, a soldier should always be able to say when his cap is on, his family is covered, then he is free as air.[16]

It has to be said that there was at least one more encouraging view of married military life. The *Regulations of the Rifle Corps*, written by Lieutenant Colonel William Stewart in 1801 for the regiment that became the famous 95th Rifles, took a positive view of the virtues of well-managed wedlock: 'The marriage of soldiers being a matter of benefit to a regiment, of comfort to themselves, or of misery to both, exactly as it is under good or bad regulation'. Standards were set out which were to apply in the new unit: 'The Rifle Corps shall be a home of comfort to those who are entitled to feel its benefits, but shall not be a source, as is too often the case, of multiplying misery and prostitution among those who should be under every good soldier's peculiar care and protection.'[17] These ideas were enlightened, and may been ahead of their time and may have been shared by Sir John Moore when he commanded one of the 95th's battalions at Shorncliffe. The regulations even envisaged a system of providing a regimental welfare fund which could be used to assist soldiers' wives who were lying-in or were ill to be administered by the regimental surgeon.[18] This enlightened regime may well account for the fact that within the 95th it was possible for private soldiers to celebrate marriage in some style. Lieutenant Robert Fernyhough, who had exchanged from the Royal Marines into the 95th, noted that while they were quartered at Shorncliffe in May 1812 'a rifleman of ours was married the other day, and the regimental band played the new couple to and from the church.'[19]

---

15   Chelsea Pensioner, *Jottings from my Sabretasch* (London: Bentley, 1847), p.120.
16   B.H. Liddell Hart (ed.), *The Letters of Private William Wheeler 1809–1828* (London: Michael Joseph, 1952), p.162.
17   J.F.C. Fuller, *Sir John Moore's System of Training* (London: Hutchinson, 1924), p.159.
18   J.F.C. Fuller, *Sir John Moore's System*, p.159.
19   Thomas Fernyhough, *Military Memoirs of Four Brothers by the Survivor* (Staplehurst: Spellmount, 2002), p.119.

The fact was that despite both personal and official disapproval, and the obstacles placed in their way, thousands of women not only became soldiers' wives, but sailed away to war as women of the regiment and faced lives of adventure and hardship difficult for the modern imagination to grasp. Given the dangers and uncertainties of military life, the risk of being left behind at home on the one hand and the hardships of campaigning on the other, one may well ask why it was that women married soldiers in the first place. No doubt there was a variety of answers. It may have seemed a better option than the drudgery of domestic service. Some women perhaps saw it as a way of escaping the back-breaking toil of agricultural labour. Perhaps it offered an alternative to the remorseless discipline of factory work. And to women whose lives may have offered only hardship whatever they did, perhaps army life seemed to promise a life of movement, adventure and colour as it undoubtedly did for many men who volunteered to fight for King and Country. There is some evidence to suggest that the 'old red rag' actually did indeed attract the women and girls. We might take events in south Dorset as an example.

During the early part of the war, George III and his family were in the habit of taking their summer holidays at Weymouth, and since this was the period when the French invasion scare was at its height, the area of south Dorset was strongly garrisoned. In some cases, the troops outnumbered the local inhabitants, whose social and economic lives were considerably affected. One result was the striking number of marriages which took place between soldiers and local women, as the parish records attest. At All Saints at Wyke, on the outskirts of Weymouth, more than 40 military weddings took place during the war, most of which involved men from militia regiments or infantry of the line. In the winter of 1796–1797 for example, men of the 29th Foot married five local women, and the 39th were even busier, finding themselves nine brides.[20] Wareham on the other hand comprised three parishes, and they all saw marriages to a variety of regiments. In 1806 and 1807, Hannah Budden, Elizabeth Ash and Mary Bartlett found husbands in the Royal Horse Artillery. Further north, in Shaftesbury, Sarah Pond married into the 11th Foot, and Ruth Hopkins and Lucy Oram marched away with the 43rd.[21]

As Dorchester was largely a cavalry base, it is not surprising to find that the majority of the marriages at Holy Trinity and St George's in Fordington were between local women and dragoons. On 20 March 1797 for instance, Sarah Amey married John Roger of the Scots Greys, the 2nd (Royal North British) Dragoons as they were properly known at the time, and Hugh Valiance of the same regiment wed Agnes Buncle on 31 August 1801. The 10th, 12th, 14th, and 15th Light Dragoons all appeared in the registers, as did the 1st and 2nd Dragoons and the 3rd Dragoon Guards. But by far the most successful campaign for the hearts of Dorchester girls was waged by the troopers of the 11th Light Dragoons. In three months in 1798 and six months in the following year, they carried off 10 local girls, five of them in the single month of February 1799. Joseph Taylor married Sarah Fowler; Thomas Ward carried off Rachel Stead; Mary Bond allied herself to Robert Wiltshire, and Anne Hiscock became the wife of James Horsfull.[22] Romance spread to neighbouring villages such as Charminster,

---

20 David Clammer, 'Soldiers and Civilians. Troops in Dorset 1793–1805', *Journal of the Society for Army Historical Research*, vol.98, Autumn 2015, p.228.
21 Clammer, 'Soldiers and Civilians', p.227.
22 Clammer, 'Soldiers and Civilians', p.227.

The Charms of a Red Coat. An officer talks with a lady on horseback while two others take tea in a tent. Coloured mezzotint published by Robert Sayer, 1 November 1782. (Anne S.K. Brown Military Collection, Brown Univeristy)

where John Drysdale of the 2nd Dragoons found Sarah Fox a willing partner in the summer of 1802. Sarah Tizard was carried away by William Clark of 'ye Royal Regiment of Horse Guards commonly called the Blues' in the following April, Robert Lanshard of the 20th Light Dragoons found a bride in the person of Bathsheba Drake.[23]

This pattern of military marriages was probably quite usual in places where there were considerable numbers of troops, and despite official discouragement and all the likely hazards and heartbreak entailed, there were evidently plenty of women willing to follow the drum. So perhaps John Malcolm, a lieutenant in the 42nd Foot, was not too far wrong when he wrote 'There is a charm in the gorgeous array, the nodding plume, and the martial air of the soldier – in the unrestrained freedom which is supposed to belong to the military life.'[24] There were to be sure occasions when a soldier acquired a wife under rather different circumstances. On 15 March 1805, the *Kentish Gazette* informed its readers that the wife of one of the navvies employed in digging the Royal Military Canal 'was conducted by her husband to the market place, at Hythe, with a halter round her neck and tied to a post 'for the purpose of selling her. She was about twenty, 'and of a likely form and figure.' She was bought for sixpence by a drummer belonging to the band of the 4th Foot, who seemed well pleased with his bargain despite the woman's two black eyes.[25]

Whether the soldier actually married her was not recorded, and one wonders what their subsequent adventures were. This was not the only case of its kind. James Aytoun, stationed in the Caribbean with the 58th Foot recalled a man named Daws selling his wife ('anything but a vestal') to another soldier, Robert Lee, for 14 dollars and a pair of silver buckles.[26]

In February 1793, Revolutionary France declared war on Britain, so beginning the longest and most expensive war the country had ever been involved in. It went on, with the brief intermission at the time of the Treaty of Amiens in 1802–1803, and a pause after Napoleon's first abdication in 1814, until Napoleon's final defeat at Waterloo in June 1815: 22 years. This was the conflict that before 1914–1918 was often referred to as The Great War. It was an apt description, not only because of its duration but because of its scale. British troops were deployed from Canada to India; from Denmark to South America; from Italy to the West Indies; from the Low Countries to Egypt; and most famously in Portugal and Spain. And wherever British regiments went, they took some of their women with them.

This great struggle produced a remarkable amount of writing on the part of soldiers of almost every rank from private to general. Much of this was written on the spot, often under very difficult circumstances. Many men wrote letters home, and many kept diaries. Some of the men who put pen to paper, whether private soldiers or commissioned officers, never mentioned the regimental wives at all. It may be that they were simply not interested, or perhaps the presence of women was so much a part of everyday life as to need no comment. But on some soldiers, the women and their experiences made a deep and lasting impression, and a large number of them did think it worthwhile to include the women in their

---

23 Clammer, 'Soldiers and Civilians', p.227.
24 J. Malcolm, 'Reminiscences of a Campaign in the Pyrenees and South of France in 1814', in Anon., *Memorials of the Late War* (Edinburgh: Constable, 1828,), p.235.
25 Cited in P.A.L. Vine, *The Royal Military Canal*, (Newton Abbot: David & Charles, 1972), p.60.
26 Martin R. Howard, *Death before Glory! The British Soldier in the West Indies in the French Revolutionary and Napoleonic Wars 1793-1815* (Barnsley: Pen & Sword, 2015), p.173.

Selling a Wife by Thomas Rowlandson, 1812. A man whose wife is tied with a rope offers her for sale, while a soldier holds out his money. The woman seems quite happy with this transaction. (Public domain)

observations, many of which show the writers to have been deeply interested and sympathetic eye-witnesses. The diaries and letters, all written independently of each other, have an immediacy which takes the reader close to the events described. So does the fact that we sometimes find incidents being recorded by more than one eye-witness. The harrowing scenes of women dying in childbirth in the snow during the Corunna retreat, for instance, were described by a number of observers, and the cumulative effect is not easily forgotten. It is however a striking fact that soldiers in the field, suffering very often from exhaustion, wounds, hunger, thirst, appalling weather conditions or the trauma of battle, should have thought to have mentioned the regimental women at all.

After the war was over there was a fashion for memoir-writing which extended well into the nineteenth century. Here, the old soldiers had to rely to a large extent on memory, though many of them appear to have been based their writings on notes, diaries or correspondence kept at the time. Some of these veterans allowed themselves to colour their narratives with the purple prose of Victorian sentimentality, and some discovered an almost novelistic talent for vivid invented dialogue, especially of the Irish variety, and of this we need to be careful. But it is noteworthy that in recollecting in later years their part in The Great War, with its triumphs and disasters, its personal dangers, hardships and adventures, they should have included so memorably the doings of the women of the regiment.

Unfortunately, only a tiny number of army wives are known ever to have put pen to paper to record their own experiences, and of these only two recorded events on the battlefields. The remainder are mostly concerned with life in barracks, or on board naval transports or the experience of being in Brussels during the Waterloo campaign. We therefore have to rely almost entirely on the evidence left us by the men, and on the regulations, despatches and orders issued by the masculine official hand. This is at least better than nothing, and it is a rich body of material which allows the regimental women to emerge from the historical shadows, enabling us to witness something of their lives, adventures and sufferings. A few emerge onto the stage as vivid individuals in real situations.

Mrs Howans of the 95th for example, who watched her husband's flogging on the route to Vigo, and carried his rifle and equipment for him afterwards to spare his bloody back. Mrs Maguire saved the colours of the 4th Foot when they were in imminent danger of capture. Or there was Mrs Retson of the 94th, who fetched water for the wounded at Fort Matagorda under heavy fire when the drummer-boy ordered to do so was too frightened to move. Mrs Currie, whose husband was aide-de-camp to Lieutenant General Hill, made tea for the 2nd Division staff, and held elegant little receptions. Mrs Maibee of the 51st was killed by a cannon ball in the act of making chocolate for her husband's breakfast. Nance M'Dermot of the 85th ran mad with grief when her man was killed at Bayonne. Eliza Tolmie, heavily pregnant, dragged her wounded husband off the field of Waterloo – he was in the Scots Greys – and having dressed his wounds went into labour and gave birth on the spot.

How many women had experiences like these during the great French wars will never be known. A fair number can be identified by name, but most remain amongst the invisible people of the past, who enacted their brief roles and vanished from the scene without voices or faces. What follows is an attempt to tell their story: the doughty women who followed the drum.

2

Drawing Lots

But chance denied the wish'd- for prize,
The envied lot another drew;
Now sorrow dim'd her sleepless eyes,
And to despair her sorrow grew[1]

Since the army could not actually prevent soldiers from marrying, the next best thing was to restrict the number of women who would be allowed to accompany the troops when sent abroad on active service. This was sensible, and the official position was expressed in the *General Order for Troops destined for Continental Service* which was promulgated on 15 April 1807:

> Women only in the proportion of Six to every Hundred Men will be permitted to embark. They should be carefully selected, as being of good Character and having the inclination and ability to render themselves useful; it is very desirable that those who have children should be left at home.[2]

In 1811, the Adjutant General issued a fresh order amplifying the position: 'Except on Occasions, when circumstances may render it necessary for Troops to embark entirely without Women, (which will be particularly notified), *the lawful Wives of Soldiers* are permitted to embark in the proportion of *Six to One Hundred Men,* including Non-commissioned Officers.'[3] On those simple words depended a great deal more human happiness and misery than perhaps the Adjutant General could well imagine.

What this amounted to in practice was half a dozen women per company of 100 men, or about 60 to a full infantry battalion. The situation was somewhat different in the cavalry, where the *Rules and Regulations for the Cavalry* stated that three or four women to a troop were sufficient.[4] The establishment of cavalry regiments was altered a number of times during the great French war. In 1800 it was raised to 10 troops (eight of which were to go on active service) each with a strength of 90 rank and file. That would have given a strength of

---

1 Contemporary ballad.
2 Glover, *Britain at Bay*, p.130.
3 Anon., *General Regulations and Orders for the Army* (London: Adjutant General Office, 1811), p.255.
4 Anon., *Rules and Regulations for the Cavalry*, p.74.

over 700 men, though the reality was that the average regimental strength in the field during the period was about 400.[5] In that case, it seems likely that the number of women accompanying a cavalry regiment may have been somewhere between 24 and 32.

Whatever the general order may have stated, there never seems to have been any question of selecting wives on the basis of character or usefulness, which would have imposed an impossible burden on the officers and could never have been accepted as fair by the private soldiers. Instead, there was a drawing of lots, of which George Gleig, then a young subaltern in the 85th Foot said 'There are not many scenes in human life more striking or more harrowing to the feelings of him who regards it for the first time.' In the case of the 85th, about to march for embarkation for the Peninsula, the drawing of lots had been left to the last possible moment, 'probably with the humane design of leaving to each female, as long as it can be left, the enjoyment of that greatest of all earthly blessings, hope.'[6] In reality there was no way of avoiding the anguish involved on such occasions. Robert Butler, who was a fife-major in the second battalion of the 1st Foot (Royal Scots) witnessed just such a drawing of lots when his battalion was ordered to Portsmouth from Hastings in the spring of 1807, to embark for India. The battalion was 1,000 strong, which meant that 60 women would be allowed to go, but Butler thought that between two and three hundred of the men were married. There now came, as he put it, 'the tug of war for the married people' as the lots were drawn. What was especially traumatic was that as the battalion was bound for India, they were going to be gone for a period of years (actually seven). 'You may conceive what barrack-rooms we had after it was over.'[7] The likelihood was that given the probable length of such a posting, and the dangers of both war and climate, that many of these married couples would never meet again. In some cases at least, these regiments appear to have been allowed extra wives. Mrs Sherwood recorded that when she sailed for India with the 53rd Foot, 10 women per company were permitted to embark.[8] Nor was the burden of this separation only felt by the women left behind. Butler noted this little tragedy in his diary: 'At sea, Ship *Coutts,* May 1st. William Troop departed this life. He was one of those unhappy creatures who left his wife behind, and died of a broken heart ... his feelings being unable to stand the separating stroke, he sunk under this insurmountable load of sorrow.'[9] Did Mrs Troop ever know of her husband's death and burial at sea?

Sergeant Joseph Donaldson of the 94th Foot penned a vivid account of the drawing of lots years later when he was back in Glasgow. Like Gleig, he never forgot the scenes he had witnessed. In 1810 the regiment was in Jersey when it was ordered to Portugal. As usual, there were far more women in Donaldson's company than could go, and they and their husbands, and a crowd of spectators, assembled in the pay sergeant's room for the drawing of lots. Folded pieces of paper had been prepared with 'To go' or 'Not to go' written on them, and put in a hat. The sergeant stood in the middle of the room, and called on the women in order of the seniority accorded to them by their husband's rank to step forward

---

5   Philip Haythornthwaite, *The Armies of Wellington* (London: Arms & Armour, 1994), p.101.
6   G.R. Gleig, *The Subaltern* (London: Blackwood, 1823), p.6.
7   R. Butler, *Narrative of the Life and Travels of Sergeant Butler Written by Himself* (Edinburgh: David Brown, 1823), p.36.
8   Sophia Kelly (ed.), *The Life of Mrs Sherwood* (London: Darton, 1854), p.270.
9   Butler, *Narrative,* p.40.

and draw a ticket. The atmosphere was tense. The first woman was the sergeant's own wife. She drew a 'Not to go' ticket, but neither she nor her husband appeared much concerned. Next was a corporal's wife, who drew a 'To go' ticket. Neither of them were much liked in the company, and this provoked as little reaction as the first. The next woman was an old campaigner, 'a most outrageous virago' according to Donaldson, 'who thought nothing of giving her husband a knock down when he offended her.' She was the cause of frequent disturbances around the cooking fire, and there was general disappointment when she drew a lucky ticket. 'Hurra' she said, 'old Meg will go yet, and live to scald more of you about the fireside.' A particularly harrowing scene followed, when it came to the turn of the young wife of a popular soldier named Sandy. She drew a ticket, but in her anxiety could not open it. She gave it to another soldier to open for her. Everyone hoped she would be lucky, but it was a 'not to go' ticket, and she fainted in her distress. And so it went on, and the barrack was filled with cries of anguish and especially the keening of the Irish women, of whom there were many in the regiment.[10] Somehow the process seemed worse when the women concerned were popular or regarded as especially respectable. The old hussar writing under the name 'Chelsea Pensioner' described the departure of his regiment for the Peninsula in 1808, and the painful separation of man and wife. 'The corps numbered amongst the latter many respectable females, who would have done credit to a domestic circle comprising far superior elements than the usual occupants of a barrack-room.'[11] Not all the women were hard cases like old Meg.

On one occasion at least, women to go were chosen by the casting of dice, a scene witnessed by a young midshipman some time during the period when Bonaparte was First Consul between 1799 and 1804. Troops were assembled at Northfleet ready to go aboard an East Indiaman. At this particular moment there was a group of soldiers formed in a circle round a drum, with some officers in the centre. In this case the women stood behind, and an unusual silence fell on the scene. It looked like a court martial. The men stepped forward in turn, and in the silence the rattling of dice on the drum-head could be heard. There were gasps of satisfaction or of despair as the process went on and 'every moment seemed to produce an increased excitement … By some it was treated as a matter of indifference, but those were generally the successful parties; but to others it seemed the issue between life and death.' This 'novel species of gambling' as the midshipman put it, went on until all the wives to go had been chosen. There was one girl in particular who attracted his notice by her anguish when not chosen. As it happened, there were some civilians who had witnessed these strange proceedings, and moved by the young woman's plight, had raised a sum of money sufficient to pay her passage as an extra woman. This must have been a unique event, and possible only because the ship was an East Indiaman. It would not have been permitted aboard either a Royal Navy ship or a hired transport.[12]

There were a number of occasions when official reasons were found either for not allowing any wives to accompany the troops at all, or to restricting their numbers. Sometimes this

---

10 Joseph Donaldson, *Recollections of the Eventful Life of a Soldier by the late Joseph Donaldson, Sergeant in the Ninety-Fourth Scots Brigade* (Edinburgh: Tait, 1838), p.51.
11 Chelsea Pensioner, *Jottings*, p.58.
12 Flexible Grummet, 'Leaves from my Log-Book No 1', in *United Services Journal and Naval and Military Magazine* (London: Colburn, 1834), p.487.

seems to have been because of the particular nature of the service, and it happened twice to the 92nd. In August 1799 when the regiment embarked at Ramsgate for Holland women were not allowed on board the transports. On this occasion there were some well-wishers present and some gentlemen offered to pay the soldiers' wives passage back to London, and to give them half a crown as well.[13] In May the following year the regiment embarked for what was initially a secret destination – it was actually an attack on Belle Isle in Quiberon Bay. This time all the women were left behind at Newport on the Isle of Wight, as was the heavy baggage.[14] And in June 1809, when William Thornton Keep, a 17-year-old ensign in the 77th found himself bound for war, he wrote to his mother to tell her that 'we have the satisfaction of knowing that we are about to be sent somewhere on actual service, as no women and children may accompany us.'[15] Their destination was in fact Walcheren, and the women and children were very lucky not to be exposed to the disastrous fever which decimated the entire British force. Sometimes it seems that a commanding officer would decide on an arbitrary number. In September 1810 Ensign Bakewell was part of a detachment of 200 men sent from Ballyshannon in Ireland to reinforce the third battalion of the 27th Foot in Spain. 'Major Neynoe had informed this detachment that one man out of every twenty would be permitted to take his wife to the Peninsula.'[16] Since that was almost the equivalent of the official allowance, there appears to be no reason why the number should have been varied.

Bakewell states that in the reinforcement for the 3/27th he thought that about a third of the men were married, but it is not easy to know whether that was a typical figure. Sometimes the number of wives accompanying the regiments appears to be surprisingly low, and it is not clear whether this was because relatively few of the soldiers were married, or whether the commanding officer had some reason for applying restrictions. It is hard to see why that should have been the case with a brigade sailing for Portugal under the command of Major General Sherbrooke in January 1809, early in the Peninsular War. The brigade was composed of four strong battalions: The 1st Coldstream Guards had 1,120 rank and file, yet they only took 17 women with them when they might very well have taken more than 60. The 1/3rd Guards were even stronger, with 1,361 other ranks, and only 19 wives instead of the 70 or so they might have had. The two line battalions were not so strong, but the pattern was repeated: The 87th Foot had only 15 women instead of more than 40, and the 88th Foot with 842 men was accompanied by only 22 wives rather than the 50 or so they might have had. Put another way, Sherbrooke's brigade of 4,114 men took only 73 women to war, or about one-third of the number which might have been expected.[17]

There were occasions when individual officers were prepared to turn a blind eye to the regulations and use their own initiative, or when an exception was made in the case of an

---

13 C.G. Gardyne, *The Life of a Regiment. The History of the Gordon Highlanders from its foundation in 1794 to 1816* (Edinburgh: Douglas, 1901), vol.1, p.62.
14 Anon., *Narrative of a Private Soldier in His Majesty's 92nd Regiment of Foot Written by Himself* (Uckfield: Naval & Military, nd.), p.54.
15 I. Fletcher (ed.), *In the Service of the King. The Letters of William Thornton Keep at Home, Walcheren, and in the Peninsula, 1808–1814* (Staplehurst: Spellmount, 1997), p.27.
16 Ian Robertson (ed.), *The Exploits of Ensign Bakewell. With the Inniskillings in the Peninsula, 1810–11* (London: Frontline, 2012), p.7.
17 D. Mackinnon, *Origins and Services of the Coldstream Guards* (London: Bentley, 1833), vol.2, p.103.

individual who was especially favoured for some reason. When the 1st Foot embarked for India in April 1807, Mrs Allen, the wife of one of the bandsmen had been unlucky in the drawing of lots. But Robert Butler managed to speak to the colonel on the woman's behalf. The colonel must have had a high opinion of Butler's talents, because he sent for the woman and asked if her husband would not be jealous of the fife-major who had spoken so warmly on her behalf. But he did agree: 'That is right; give my compliments to Captain Glover, and desire him from me to put down your name to go with his company.'[18] Neither Butler nor Mrs Allen had any idea what an impact this decision was to have on their lives. Another example concerned Catherine Exley who was with the 34th at Chichester when the regiment was posted to Jersey and then ordered to Portugal. Catherine wished to go, despite the fact that she had a comfortable position as companion to a sea captain's widow. In this case she was not required to draw lots: the colonel wrote to the commanding general, who gave his consent. Unfortunately, this was not a lucky move. The regiment arrived in Portugal in July 1809 and were encamped at Alcantara near Lisbon, and here her child, a little boy, contracted measles and died.

More is known about Catherine than most army wives. She was born in Leeds in 1779. Her father was a comber in the worsted industry. Her mother came from a Quaker family in Appleby, but died when Catherine was an infant. Her father remarried but died when she was 12, leaving her to be brought up by her stepmother. At the age of 19 she became a domestic servant. In 1805 she met and married Joshua Exley, a corporal in the 34th Foot, and her military career began a month later. Catherine is a uniquely important eyewitness because she is the only private soldier's wife known to have written an account of her experiences during the war in the Peninsula. This in itself is remarkable, because at the time of her marriage she was illiterate, and had to make her mark in the church register. The narrative itself had a curious career. She is believed to have written it in the 1830s, possibly in order to earn some money. But it did not see the light of day until 1857, the year of her death, when it was published by a local printer in Batley. Copies must have been rare, but it was rediscovered in 1923, when the *Dewsbury Reporter* ran the story under the title *Batley Woman's Wonderful History*. Wonderful it is and was at last made generally available in 2014 when it was published as *Catherine Exley's Diary*.[19]

When it came to the final crisis of the wars, the campaign of Waterloo, Wellington was particularly anxious to limit the number of women present. The Coldstream Guards anticipated Wellington's instructions, as Captain Bowles explained in a letter to Lord Fitzharris written from Brussels on 18 March: 'Every preparation is made or making for our taking the field at a moment's warning. Our heavy baggage, supernumerary women and children, etc, go off tomorrow for Ostend.'[20] The General Order enforcing this appeared four days later, on 22 March, three months before the battle.[21] There was more than enough to do during the

---

18 Butler, *Narrative*, p.36.
19 R. Probert (ed.), *Catherine Exley's Diary. The Life and Times of an Army Wife in the Peninsular War* (Kenilworth: Brandrum, 2014), p.25. This is actually a memoir rather than a diary.
20 Earl of Malmsbury (ed.), *A Series of Letters of the First Lord Malmsbury His Family and Friends from 1745 to 1820* (London: Bentley, 1870), vol.2, p.431.
21 J. Gurwood (ed.), *General Orders in Portugal, Spain and France from 1809 to 1814 and the Low Countries and France 1815* (London: unknown, 1832), Bruxelles, 22 March 1815, pp.427–428.

period when the Allied army was being hastily assembled, and British troops, in particular, were being scraped together from every possible source without worrying about wives: 'All women belonging to British regiments, beyond one for each twenty-five men, including serjeants, drummers, trumpeters, and rank and file, are immediately to be sent from their regiments to Ostend, for the purpose of being forwarded to their respective homes.' At Ostend, arrangements were in place to ship these extra women over to England, and those women who were entitled were to be given the appropriate allowance to get them to their homes. Those so entitled would be the women whose names appeared in the paymasters' lists, and would receive the commanding officer's signature. These regulations were to be strictly enforced, and the order went on to state that 'Rations are not to be allowed for more than one woman for every twenty-five men. This applies to all descriptions of troops.'[22]

Even so, it appears that some regiments felt that Wellington's orders were open to interpretation. When the Royal Welch Fusiliers were disembarking in Belgium, Jenny Griffiths, the 17-year-old wife of Lewis Griffiths, a private in No. 7 company, was told by Colonel Ellis, mindful of Wellington's order to restrict the number of women, to remain on board. But she refused, saying that she and her six-month-old baby should be with her husband. Private Lewis also refused to disembark without his wife. This was a court martial offence, but the colonel, moved perhaps by this show of family solidarity, relented, and the little family disembarked together.[23] Not all officers felt able to show this degree of flexibility. The colonel of the 1/95th had made it clear that on this occasion no women at all were to be allowed to go with the battalion. When they landed at Ostend on 27 April, he was therefore angered to see Corporal Pitt on the quay-side with his wife, and ordered her to be put back on board the ship immediately. Pitt however refused, saying 'Sir, my wife was separated from me, when I went to the Peninsular War and I had rather die than be parted from her again.'[24] This could not be tolerated. A drum-head court martial was immediately held, which reduced Pitt to a private soldier and sentenced him to 300 lashes. Pitt was a good soldier and a good man, and nobody wished the sentence to be carried out, but he was tied up and the troops drawn up in the usual fashion to witness the punishment. However, it happened that there was no surgeon present to superintend, and Lieutenant Simmons was ordered to act instead. It occurred to Simmons that he was therefore in a position to abridge the punishment, so after 100 lashes he stepped forward and declared that in his opinion the man had taken enough. This was accepted at once, and afterwards the colonel congratulated Simmons on doing exactly the right thing. He had hated to have Pitt punished, but felt that he had had no alternative. What happened to Pitt's wife Simmons did not record.

Some commanding officers decided that attempting to enforce the unenforceable would only lead to trouble and be bad for morale. In the event, two or three women per company seems to have been the usual allowance. Even this produced unpleasant difficulties, not least in the 2/27th Foot, the Inniskillings, which was stationed at Portsmouth and which, as an Irish regiment, had a large contingent of wives. The 2nd battalion was ordered to provide a draught of men to reinforce the 1st battalion in Belgium, and when they came to embark

---

22   Gurwood, *General Orders*, Bruxelles, 22 March 1815, p.428.
23   Personal communication from Mike Tanner, Pontypool Museum.
24   George Simmons, 'Journal of First Lieutenant George Simmons', in G. Glover (ed.) *Waterloo Archive* (Barnsley: Frontline, 2012), vol.4, p.204.

for Spithead, it was realized that a large number of women were already aboard the transports, and that few of the wives who were left could be allowed to go. Colonel John MacLean therefore ordered lots to be drawn for each company. In order to enforce this, Lieutenant Charles Crowe, the 2nd battalion adjutant, posted a sergeant's guard at the approach to the jetty where the men climbed down into the boats to be rowed out to the ships riding at the Spithead anchorage.

> I was deeply engaged at the extreme of the jetty, when a shout of horror made me look to the rear. A lovely young woman with a baby in her arms had forced through the guard, and was rushing with the frenzy of desperation to throw herself and babe into the boat below to her husband! She was not ten yards distant; but instantly I ran, and grasped her in my arms and having given myself a rotary motion to check her impetus, the woman, baby, and Adjutant were sprawling on the jetty!![25]

The disconsolate woman had no alternative but to return to Ireland with the large number of other wretchedly unhappy wives, though they did at least receive an allowance per mile to enable them to do so.

When the 43rd were summoned from Ireland at the beginning of the campaign they had been allowed to take four women per company, but when they arrived at Ostend in Belgium, and began to embark on the canal barges which were to convey them to Bruges, an order was received that only two women in each company were to be allowed to proceed. This naturally caused a storm of grief and consternation 'to those who had to return without any preparation for such an unexpected separation, or any provision but that which the liberality of their country might allow.'[26] The unlucky ones were placed under guard and taken to a barrack, weeping and wailing. But the army was no match for these wives. The regiment had only been two days at Ghent when these tough and resourceful women turned up. They were forced to return to Ostend, to be re-embarked for England, but after a couple of weeks they again managed to evade the authorities and somehow to find and rejoin the regiment. By this time the army had more pressing problems, and the women were allowed to go right through the climactic campaign of the long war.

There were indeed many army wives at Ostend as increasing numbers of troops arrived to disembark. Amongst the fresh arrivals was Captain Mercer's G Troop, Royal Horse Artillery. Their transport ran right into the harbour until it grounded on the sand, and sailors swarmed on board to begin the tricky task of unloading guns, limbers, ammunition and horses. As the ebb tide lowered the depth of water, equipment was heaved onto the sand, and horses swung outboard. As the artillerymen struggled to calm their horses and rescue items of equipment, there were groups of women everywhere: 'Disconsolate-looking groups of women and children were to be seen here and there sitting on their poor duds, or roaming about in search of their husbands, or mayhap of a stray child, all clamouring, lamenting, and materially increasing the babel-like confusion, amidst which Erin's brogue

---

25 G. Glover (ed.), *An Eloquent Soldier. The Peninsular War Journals of Lieutenant Charles Crowe of the Inniskillings 1812–1814* (London: Frontline, 2011), p.305.
26 James Anton, *Retrospect of a Military Life during the most eventful periods of the Last War* (Edinburgh: Lizars, 1841), p.179.

was everywhere predominant.'27 It took Mercer and his officers most of the following day, the 14th, to sort out the chaos and get the troop assembled with all its guns, horses and impedimenta, and while this was still being unloaded from the transport he had time to note the local boatmen watching with amusement:

> ... the bustling anxiety of a score of soldiers' wives, who, loaded with children or bundles, their ample grey or faded red cloaks flying out loosely behind them, struggled through all impediments opposed to their progress with an activity, perseverance, and volubility which seemed highly diverting to the mariners, many of whom, in broken English, were bantering these amazons, or exchanging coarse jokes with them; at which play, however – the ladies being mostly from the Green Isle – the gentlemen came off second best.28

However many women were to go with their men on any particular occasion, the moment of departure finally arrived, and the scene which followed was always the same, and described as such by many eyewitnesses. 'The morning soon began to dawn,' recalled George Wood, when 82nd Foot left Uxbridge on their way to Ireland in early 1807, 'the baggage already towered on the creaking waggons: the women and children scaled the massive pile, – where seated, they might enjoy their short pipe and little bottle, as they slowly moved along the weary way.' This sounds exactly like the scenes depicted by W.H. Pyne in the *Camp Scenes* pictures produced in 1805. The bugles sounded the general (the morning signal that a march was about to begin), the column swung into motion, and the wives and sweethearts who were being left behind tried to cling to their men, many of them imploring, crying and fainting. As the battalion passed over a bridge, sentries were posted to prevent the women trying to follow, but one distraught girl threw herself off the parapet into the water, trying to swim after the men. She almost drowned. Scenes like these were a commonplace of military life, Wood discovered, 'but certainly their first appearance was not calculated to give me any very favourable impression of it.'29 Indeed not, and they by no means always involved regimental wives. In August 1807 the 1st West Yorkshire Militia was given a route from where it was based in Yorkshire to Hull. On the morning of departure the band struck up, which 'was a signal for windows to be hastily open by many fair ladies en déshabille, waving their white handkerchiefs and delicate hands, until a wind in the road concealed them from our admiration.'30 When the 9th Foot marched out of Canterbury in July 1809, on route for Deal and the expedition to Walcheren, with drums beating and colours flying, the streets were crowded with people waiting to bid them farewell, 'as were many young women with watery eyes, who were then deprived of their fancy men.'31

---

27 Cavalié Mercer, *Journal of the Waterloo Campaign kept throughout the Campaign of 1815* (London: Greenhill, 1985), p.8.
28 Cavalié Mercer, *Journal of the Waterloo Campaign*, p.15.
29 George Wood, *The Subaltern Officer: A Narrative* (London: Prowsett, 1825), p.7.
30 E. Hathaway (ed.), *A True Soldier Gentleman. The Memoirs of Lt. John Cooke 1791–1813* (Swanage: Shinglepicker, 2000), p.43.
31 James Hale, *Journal of James Hale, late Sergeant in the Ninth Regiment of Foot* (London: Longman, 1826), p.40.

War. A Wealthy officer bids farewell to his family and servants in a grand house. A soldier holds his charger ready while transports wait in the bay. Stipple engraving after Henry Singleton. (Anne S.K. Brown Military Collection, Brown University)

On 16 January 1809 the 23rd Foot, based for the winter in Colchester, suddenly received orders to march the following day for Portsmouth, bound for foreign service, which turned out to be Nova Scotia. 'The whole night was of course spent in bustle of every description, and at day-light the 1st division was under arms, baggage waggons loaded, and the usual wailings of sweet-hearts and wives, who were not allowed to accompany their husbands on foreign service, resounded in the barrack yard.'[32] These scenes were made more poignant by the fact that that regimental bands always seemed to play the same heart-wrenching tunes. On 1 January 1811, 320 men of the 2nd Battalion of the 43rd Light Infantry marched for Portsmouth to join the 1st Battalion in Portugal. Those who were not to go accompanied the column as far as the first halt. Then as Lieutenant Cooke recalled, 'The merry notes of the horns struck up "Over the hills and far away", the signal for wives to be torn from their husbands, children from their fathers, and friends from their companions.'[33] And as Elizabeth Ham remembered the departure of the 67th Foot from Guernsey bound for the war in Spain, 'It was a melancholy sight that, marching with colours flying and the band playing the everlasting tune, the "Girl I left behind me", the poor wives and children running crying by the sides of their husbands and fathers for a last look – a last look it proved to many of them, poor creatures.'[34]

It was the same when the day came for 85th Foot came to depart for the theatre of war. The battalion fell in at 4:00 a.m., as the light of the moon was slowly giving way to the first streaks of dawn, and as the companies assembled, Gleig could see in the wan light the forms of women gathered round the lines, and hear the half suppressed shrieks and sobs. The six women per company had been drawn, leaving perhaps a couple of dozen, and this had produced 'in many instances, a violence of grief, the display of which it is impossible to witness with any degree of indifference.'[35] Gleig certainly never forgot what he had witnessed.

In October 1812 the 28th Foot, stationed at the Berry Head fort near Brixham were ordered to Plymouth to embark for Spain. With them marched William Thornton Keep, who had transferred from the 77th. Writing to his brother from the *Hero* transport, waiting to sail, he described the regiment's leave-taking with the many friends they had made in the town, and then went on:

> You would have laughed to see one poor creature ... who has been for years in the Regiment, perched upon a rock and giving vent to her lamentations as we filed down the road before her on the way to Brixham, the tears rolling over her weather beaten features, and her fists clenched in a wild paroxysm of grief and heroism, crying out 'fight 28th – fight boys – fight 'em.[36]

---

32 R.N. Buckley (ed.), *The Napoleonic War Journal of Captain Thomas Henry Browne 1807–1816* (London: Bodley Head, 1987), p.69.
33 Hathaway, *A True Soldier*, p.68.
34 E. Gillet (ed.), *Elizabeth Ham by Herself* (London: Faber, 1945), p.170.
35 Gleig, *The Subaltern*, p.6.
36 I. Fletcher (ed.), *In the Service of the King. The Letters of William Thornton Keep at Home, Walcheren and in the Peninsular War 1808–1814* (Staplehurst: Spellmount, 1997), p.102.

Keep was a young ensign. Had he been more experienced, perhaps he would have regarded this old woman with a little more understanding. Somehow, she seems representative of a whole host of old regimental women.

It comes a relief to know that these unhappy, even desperate women left behind in barracks or at the quay-side were not actually abandoned by the army. With the large numbers of troops being posted abroad, Parliament had realized that the considerable numbers of women left behind could not be left entirely to their own devices. Even a single regiment could create a significant difficulty. In 1808 for instance, when the 18th Hussars embarked at Northfleet, 745 all ranks strong, bound for the Peninsula, they left 91 women behind.[37] Legislation was accordingly passed to issue allowances to wives to enable them to make their way to their homes or wherever they intended to live while their husbands were away on service. The result was a comprehensive set of regulations which by the standards of the day was remarkably humane.

When any 'Regiment, Battalion, Corps, or Detachment' was to embark for foreign service, the commanding officer was to have a list made of all the wives and children who were to be left behind, and who wished to claim the allowance to enable them to return home. Presumably, they all did. Each woman was to be given a duplicate of the part of the list which applied to her, countersigned by the commanding officer stating that she was the wife 'or reputed wife' of a soldier in his unit. The list itself was to be forwarded to the Secretary at War. The woman concerned had to take her part of the form to 'some neighbouring Justice or Magistrate' who was required to fill up his part of the document specifying the woman's destination and assigning the route which she was to follow. (There was no doubt a great deal of poring over maps). This would enable her to claim the authorised allowance, which was not to exceed two pence per mile.

As the woman set out on her journey, she had to present herself to the overseer of the poor of each parish she marched through. Dipping into the monies he held for the relief of the parish poor, the overseer then gave the woman sufficient cash to get her to the next place specified on her route, though this was not to exceed a distance of 18 miles. Having satisfied himself that the woman was genuine, he endorsed the certificate and took a receipt from the woman, 'signed with her Hand or with her Mark'. This naturally left a hole in the parish funds, and the overseer recovered the money by sending the woman's receipt, together with one of his own, to the district Collector of Excise. He reimbursed the overseer and reclaimed the money from the agent of the regiment concerned. With significant numbers of wives on the move in this way, it is not hard to imagine that the financial and administrative burden on the parish overseers across the country was considerable. And so the deserted wife at last made her way to the final place on her prescribed route 'antecedent to her Arrival at her Home or Place of Settlement.' Here she handed her certificate over to the overseer of the poor in exchange for the pittance to see her to her journey's end. It was then sent to the Collector of Excise, who in turn sent it to the War Office. There was a final sting in the

---

[37] Eric Hunt (ed.), *Charging Against Napoleon. Diaries and Letters of Three Hussars 1808–1815* (London: Leo Cooper, 2001), p.7.

tail. 'Wives of Soldiers not complying with the Regulations hereinbefore prescribed shall be treated as Vagrants.'[38]

The following year, it was realised that there was a loophole in these arrangements. Many regiments were posted abroad directly from Ireland, which meant that considerable numbers of women who had not been lucky in the ballot were stranded on the wrong side of the Irish Sea and unable to afford a passage back to elsewhere in Great Britain. In April 1812 therefore, *An Act for enabling the Wives and Families of Soldiers embarked in Ireland for Foreign Service to return to their Homes* was passed.[39] This was similar to the previous Act, but there were some differences. The woman would, as before, get her certificate from the commanding officer of the regiment, and take it to a justice of the peace who would give her the route she was to take home. Instead of going to the overseers of each parish to obtain her daily allowance however, she had to report to the postmaster of each place. If a naval transport was available when she reached the designated port, the woman and her children were given a free passage to any convenient port in Britain. If only commercial vessels were available, the woman was to be found a passage the price of which was not to exceed the cost allowed for transporting a soldier. It was also foreseen that once at the port there might be 'delays arising from unavoidable causes.' Sailing might be delayed by contrary winds or storms, or there was the possibility that she or her children might be ill and unable to embark. In such cases, extra money would be made available – 6d a day for the woman and 3d a day for each child. It was an enlightened piece of legislation, though parliament probably considered that the alternative of having numbers of stranded and homeless women and children on the hands of local authorities might have cost a good deal more.

In some cases, women left behind had at least the prospect of a home and family to return to. Quartermaster Sergeant William Surtees, who had married his wife in Corbridge, his native village, while on leave after the Danish campaign of 1807, as we saw previously. But on the expiration of his leave, they had to rejoin his battalion (the 2/95th) at Hythe. While there, orders came for the battalion to embark for the Corunna campaign and 'it became indispensible that my poor wife should return to Northumberland, and under the protection of her parents, till my return, should it please God to spare me.'[40] As a quartermaster sergeant, Surtees was probably able to send his wife home by coach, but even so it must have been a trial, alone and in an advanced state of pregnancy. At least she had a home to go to.

The plight of a woman 'not to go' who was left behind while pregnant was appalling, and George Gleig, who had witnessed the drawing of lots for the first time when the 85th was ordered on active service, described the tragedy that befell one of his men and his wife. Gleig told the story at length, originally for *Blackwood's Magazine*, enlivened with plenty of vivid dialogue, not all of which can have been recalled accurately. The situation itself was still vivid in his mind when he came to put his memoirs into book form in 1825, and however embroidered, gives a vivid picture of a situation which cannot have been unusual.

One of the recently joined men of the 85th was a Highlander, Duncan Stewart, a farmer's son from Balquidder. Against his father's wishes, he had fallen for a girl named Mary, and as

---

38   51 Geo III cap.106. *An Act for enabling the Wives and Families of Soldiers embarked for Foreign Service, to return to their Homes.*
39   52 Geo III cap.27.
40   Surtees, *Twenty Five Years*, p.73.

Gleig puts it, 'Duncan was assured of becoming a father, before he was a husband.' The pair married in secret, but soon after this, while driving a flock of sheep to market, Duncan fell in with a party of soldiers who were on the look-out for recruits. It was the old story. Plied with drink, and the King's shilling pressed into his hand, he found himself in Edinburgh and put aboard a ship for the south without time even to inform his father. Somehow, Duncan managed to send for his young wife, who somehow or other managed to reach Hythe just a week before the regiment received orders to embark for foreign service. Mary, heavily pregnant, was unlucky with the lot-drawing, and overcome with grief, appealed to the officers to let her go, but in vain.

Duncan agreed that Mary should accompany the battalion as far as Dover, where they were to embark. 'The band now struck up, and the column began to move, the men shouting, partly to drown the cries of the women, and partly to express their own willingness to meet the enemy. Mary walked by the side of her husband; but she looked more like a moving corps than a living creature.' They had hardly gone three miles when she was seized with labour pains. Military discipline was mercifully relaxed in order that Duncan might take care of his wife. He undertook to rejoin as soon as possible, and was allowed to fall out of the ranks. He and a sergeant called M'Intyre helped Mary into a wayside cottage, where according to George Gleig, she was kindly received. The battalion marched on to Dover, where the transports were waiting at the pier, and where the rest of the day was spent laying in the necessary provisions. Gleig could not get the plight of Duncan Stewart and his wife out of his mind, and walked some way back towards Hythe until he saw two soldiers coming towards him. It was Stewart and M'Intyre. Gleig asked how Mary Stewart was, but Duncan saluted and marched past without stopping or speaking. Gleig asked M'Intyre, who stood still and burst into tears. 'She is at rest, sir' was all that he could say. Mary had died within minutes of entering the cottage, and all attempts to save her baby had failed. The officer commanding the depot at Dover took it upon himself to allow Stewart to remain behind to bury his wife and child, but he refused, too stunned perhaps to think clearly. 'All that he desired was a solemn assurance from the officer that he would see his dear Mary decently interred; and as soon as the promise was given, the young widower hastened to join his regiment. He scarcely spoke after; and he was one of the first who fell after the regiment landed in Spain.' Gleig, who after the war took Holy Orders, added that this story might have been taken from a tale of romance, had it not been known to the officers and men of his regiment.[41]

Charles O'Neil was in Ireland with the 28th Foot when they were ordered to proceed to England, whence they sailed for the Peninsula. When the time came for the regiment to march, he witnessed a small personal tragedy: 'A woman, pale and sickly looking, worn to premature old age by incessant toil and suffering, and the mother of five little children, was bidding farewell to her husband.' The wretched man had enlisted while drunk, and had lost or spent all his money. He was the sole support of his family, and now that he was sober, the appalling nature of the situation had come home to him. But his regiment was marching for the wars, and there was no remedy. 'The money was gone, he had pledged himself, and he

---

41   Gleig, *The Subaltern*, pp.7–19.

Deserter taking leave of his wife. A young man's distraught wife embraces him at their cottage door while soldiers prepare to march him away. Perhaps he had enlisted while drunk. (Anne S.K. Brown Military Collection, Brown University)

must go, and leave his family to starve or live on the bread of charity.'42 How often was such a scene acted out in the long war against France?

Sometimes the women's predicament could be distressing in other ways. In November 1813 for instance, the 73rd Foot was returning in a storm from Rostock at the conclusion of its very limited part in the north German campaign, expecting to land at Yarmouth. Despite the usual practice, peremptory orders were issued that all the women and children were to be put ashore at Yarmouth, while the troops were diverted to Holland. Thus, the women were in effect abandoned in a completely strange place. 'These orders were a sad disappointment to most of us; but it was particularly distressing to the married people, to be separated this suddenly – the women and children landed in a strange place, perhaps hundreds of miles from their home, and no resources.'43 Another example of women being left behind occurred in May 1800 when the 92nd Foot was stationed on the Isle of Wight. They were suddenly ordered to embark on two transports for an unknown destination, which turned out to be an attack on Belleisle. 'We left all our women and heavy baggage in the Isle of Wight' recorded an anonymous private soldier.44 What became of the women, stranded on an island, he did not say. Perhaps they remained with the regimental cardre.

How exactly soldiers' wives manage to make these journeys is something of a mystery. Not long after Catherine's marriage to Joshua Exley in 1805, the 34th Foot was posted first to Jersey, then the Isle of Wight, prior to being sent to Madeira. But as Catherine was pregnant she was not permitted to accompany the regiment, and had to return to her home parish at Batley, near Leeds. This was a distance of more than 260 miles, but she does not mention in her account how she made the journey, and stated only that once she arrived 'the overseers there kindly recommended me to the poor-house, which in my case was only such in name, for every comfort was afforded me.' The 34th however was delayed by storms and put into harbour somewhere in Ireland, and was then sent back to England, landing at Chichester, from where Joshua wrote, asking her to join him. This seems to refer to late 1808, because the battalion finally arrived in Portugal in 1809. So Catherine set out from Batley, this time with her baby, and this time she did receive some assistance. 'Through the kind contributions of my neighbours I did not set out penniless, and was enabled to travel by waggon from Leeds for the sum of 15s.' Her diary is tantalisingly short on details; she gives no dates, or say how far she rode in the waggon, or where she stayed on the journey, which was if anything longer that her trek back to Batley. But somewhere she met an innkeeper whom she had known in Leeds, who recognised her and kindly sent her in a chaise which was returning to a point within 12 miles of where her husband was stationed. She now spent her last remaining sixpence on forwarding her luggage by coach (she had her baby to carry) and set off to walk the last part of the journey. She called at an inn to warm the baby where a kindly gentleman gave her a shilling and bought her some food. Here she was joined by another woman also walking to join her husband. By eight that night, they were still eight miles from their destination and lay down by the roadside to sleep on some straw. And here their husbands found them, having somehow got word of their whereabouts. This was no

---

42   Charles O'Neil, *The Military Adventures of Charles O'Neil* (Worcester: Livermore, 1851), p.30.
43   Thomas Morris, *Recollections of Military Service in 1813, 1814 and 1815* (London: Longman, 1967), p.25.
44   Anon., *Narrative of a Private Soldier in His Majesty's 92nd Regiment*, p.54.

doubt typical of the experience of many army wives, and Catherine Exley seems to have thought the experience quite normal.[45]

There were exceptions to this sort of hardship; some non-commissioned officers were certainly in a position to pay for their wives to travel by coach, although this in itself was an uncomfortable experience. William Tennant was a pay sergeant in the 3/1st Guards, and when in April 1815 the battalion was ordered to Belgium he and his wife had been married only a few months. As Ann was pregnant, it was decided that she should return from the depot in London to her parent's home at Presteigne, then in Radnorshire. She was able to go by coach, and she wrote to William on 24 April to tell him she was safely home: 'I have the happiness to inform you that I had a very good journey into the country.' The weather had been fine, followed by some snow which had then cleared away. 'I took my place on the outside of the coach but had the luck to be inside all night and that was very comfortable as I was very much fatigued.'[46] She did not say how long the journey from London to Wales had taken, and we might wonder at her ideas of comfort, but at least she was not walking.

Army wives tramping the roads, often with their children, must have been a familiar sight to travellers, and no doubt a kindly carter or carrier would sometimes give them a lift for a few miles. Sometimes there were acts of generosity of a different kind. Lord Cranley, Lord Lieutenant and Colonel of the 2nd Surrey Militia was an eccentric character whose dress and deportment sometimes caused him to be mistaken for his own coachman. One day he was seen to drive back into Canterbury after a field-day with his carriage completely crammed with soldiers' wives whom he had picked up on the road.[47] Another such example occurred sometime after the Battle of Albuera in 1811, when Major Tidy (as he then was) of the 14th Foot, was returning to England with despatches. Having landed at Portsmouth he took a post-chaise to London. At some point on the way he saw a poor woman sitting by the roadside with her little bundle. Tidy stopped his coach and asked if he could help, intending to give her money. She turned out to be a soldier's wife, making her way back to London. So the 'bearer of His Majesty's despatches opened the chaise door, and taking the tired and shabby wanderer in, he carried her all the way to Town beside him.'[48] This anecdote was proudly recorded by his daughter.

But the reality, despite individual acts of charity and the official scheme to enable women left behind to reach their homes, was that there was considerable hardship. In April 1798, a poem appeared in the *Cambridge Intelligencer* called *The Soldier's Wife*. In it, the poet laments in bitter terms the hardship faced by army wives trekking across country in winter weather. He describes them as 'weary way-wanderers' as they travel painfully over the rugged roads, 'languid and sick of heart' and wild in appearance. The poet was Robert Southey, who became Poet Laureate in 1813, and the fact that the verses appeared in a provincial newspaper suggests that the scene he was describing was a familiar one across the country. Southey was interested in the Napoleonic wars; he wrote an early history of the war in the

---

45 Probert (ed.), *Exley Diary*, pp.24–25.
46 Nottinghamshire Archives: M24,299: Letters of Sergeant William Tennant 1/3rd Guards and his wife Ann.
47 Liddell Hart (ed.), *Letters*, p.17.
48 Mrs Ward, *Recollections of an Old Soldier. A biographical sketch of the late Colonel Tidy, CB. 24th Regiment* (London: Bentley, 1849), p.78.

Peninsula, and a life of Nelson. He was also angry about the state of the poor, including soldiers' wives. In a poem entitled *The Complaints of the Poor,* a rich man asks the poet why the poor are always complaining. The poet takes him for a walk and points out several poor people including a homeless man, a begging child and a young prostitute. Then they come to a soldier's wife sitting exhausted on a stone with her two babies in the bitter wind. What was she doing? 'She told us that her husband served/ A soldier, far away,/ And therefore to her parish she/ Was begging back her way.'[49] She was in fact what the rich man and the Adjutant General would have regarded as a vagrant.

Sometimes a few women managed to get around the regulations with the help of a sympathetic officer's wife. When the 67th Foot was ordered from Guernsey to Gibraltar, bound for the Peninsula, in 1809 or 1810, the wife of Lieutenant Cassidy was besieged with women who were not to go, begging to be taken as her cook or laundress, and Mrs Cassidy, anxious to help, sailed 'with as large an establishment of this kind as decency would allow.'[50] When the 53rd sailed for India aboard the *Devonshire,* Mrs Sherwood, one of the officer's wives, 'had the privilege of choosing one who was to be my servant on the voyage, and of course I could do no other than choose our man-servant's wife Betty. By this, Betty Parker was assured of her passage as my servant.'[51] Some regimental officers at least were well aware of the plight of women who were to be left behind, and did what they could to remedy it. William Warre, a captain in the 23rd Light Dragoons was one such. Warre was in Ireland awaiting a posting to Portugal as ADC to Major General Fergusson, (he was a fluent Portuguese speaker) and on 22 June 1808 he wrote to his father from Cove: 'We have been endeavouring to establish a ball here this evening for the relief of the poor distressed wives of the Soldiers, but it is a very bad day and I fear we shall have but a thin attendance.'[52] However, it was better than he feared, and five days later Warre was able to inform his mother

> We had a gay ball here on Friday, in a storehouse fitted up with flags, for the relief of the distressed soldiers' wives. We had a good many people, and collected about £50 free of expenses, little enough among so many objects. I have had a good deal of trouble, but who would grudge it in such a cause?[53]

Something similar happened in Guernsey when the 67th left for active service. Elizabeth Ham, a Dorset girl who was staying on the island at the time recorded how she attended the theatre for an amateur production staged for the benefit of the soldiers' wives who were not to go. It seems to have been regarded as an important occasion. She was one of the party accompanying the general officer commanding, and sat in the Government box accompanied by the general's staff officers. It was, she wrote, 'all very grand, and very dull.'[54] But no doubt it raised a considerable sum of money.

---

49 R. Southey, *The Complaints of the Poor*, <https://www.poetryfoundation.org/poems/57952/the-complaints-of-the-poor>, accessed November 2019.
50 Gillet (ed.), *Elizabeth Ham*, p.170.
51 Kelly (ed.), *Life*, p.270.
52 E. Warre (ed.), *Letters from the Peninsula 1808–1812* (London: Murray, 1909), p.13.
53 Warre, *Letters*, p.15.
54 Gillet (ed.), *Elizabeth Ham*, p.40.

Many men going abroad must have been aware that the wives they were leaving behind faced a difficult financial future, but the army seems to have had no official system by which a soldier could remit a part of his pay home, and there are very few references to individual men trying to do so. In 1814, when the Coldstream Guards were embarking for Holland, Thomas Jackson, being a sergeant, and paid more money than a private, 'allowed one half of it to my beloved wife in England, although I knew she could, if friendless, get her living at her business, a dress-maker.'[55] And Sir Alexander Dickson, commanding the Royal Artillery in Spain in April 1813, mentioned in a letter that a soldier named Marshall had applied to have £1 10s deducted from his pay so that his wife could receive it in England. Dickson had given the man the necessary certificate.[56] Such cases were certainly the exception to the rule, and with the best will in the world, it would have been difficult for men to survive the hardships of campaigning without the pittance they received, frequently months in arrears.

Sometimes it happened that a regiment had so many women attached that they were sent back to whence they came *en masse*. Such a case occurred in 1799 to the Tarbert Fencibles. The regiment had been quite some time in Ireland, where it had acquired a very large number of women, and these had accompanied the men when they were transferred to southern England. When the regiment marched from Poole to Botley, they were inspected by Lieutenant General Whitlock, who was displeased that they had almost as many women as men, which was then generally the case with Irish regiments, or in this case had been stationed in Ireland. Whitlock consulted higher authority, and in due course an order arrived from the Commander-in-Chief directing that all the women, except for the six per company regulations allowed, were to be sent back to Ireland immediately, and that they were to be marched to Bristol to embark. This involved nearly 400 voluble Irish women. 'It was really distressing to behold the misery of these poor creatures on being thus separated from their husbands. The greater number of them had been married but a short time, and many of them having displeased their friends by marrying soldiers had not a home to return to.'[57] So wrote Lieutenant John Harley (who later transferred to the 54th) who was given the unenviable task of supervising this journey

At least the allowances granted by the government for this operation were generous – no doubt because of fear of what might otherwise happen. Lieutenant Harley was instructed to pay each woman a shilling a day, with sixpence for each child during the march, and when they embarked at Bristol, a further guinea for each woman and a half-guinea per child. Given the numbers involved, the march assumed the character of the military operation which it was. It was necessary to have an official route agreed on beforehand, and Harley had to travel to Winchester to consult Major General St John, in order that the women would be entitled to billets. When the route was allocated, the next difficulty as to what this body of women were to be called. Were they a regiment, or a detachment, or a party? The

---

55 E. O'Keeffe (ed.), *Narrative of the Eventful Life of Thomas Jackson Militiaman and Coldstream Sergeant, 1803–15* (Solihull: Helion, 2018), p.56.
56 J. Leslie (ed.), *The Dickson Manuscripts being Diaries, Letters, Maps, Account Books with various other Papers of the Late Major-General Sir Alexander Dickson* (Woolwich: Royal Artillery Institution, 1908), vol.5, p.861.
57 John Harley, *The Veteran or Forty Years in the British Service* (London: Colburn, 1838), vol.1, p.70.

general suggested they should be styled 'useless baggage', but Mrs St John, who was present at the discussions, objected to such a term, and it was decided that the women of the Tarbet Fencibles should be designated a detachment.

'Every necessary arrangement having been made, I proceeded, in full regimentals, with my battalion of women, accompanied by a sergeant, who was to assist me in procuring billets for them on the march' wrote John Harley.[58] Unsurprisingly, the journey was not without incident. At Romsey, at the end of the first day's march, the constable refused to provide billets on the grounds that women were not entitled to them, and Harley and his sergeant would have been in difficulties had not the innkeeper's wife taken pity on the women and allowed them to sleep in her out-houses. As they proceeded through Hampshire and Wiltshire the lieutenant was 'not a little annoyed by the ribald jests and impertinent remarks of every low fellow, upon my regiment of *she soldiers*'.[59] It was all very humiliating, and worse was to follow. As the column approached Bath, where Harley had many friends and acquaintances, he decided that he could simply not face the ridicule he would be exposed to marching through with this '*corps des femmes*' as he put it. So, a mile or so out of town he handed the women into the care of the sergeant, giving him the day's pay to distribute. He then made for the White Hart inn, where he was just settling down to dinner when one of the waiters came in to announce 'Colonel, some of your women are below in the hall, and want to speak to you.'[60] However, the women were too impatient to wait and 40 or 50 of them burst in amongst the startled diners, headed by the wife of one of the drummers. They demanded their day's allowance, which the sergeant had apparently not given them, and threatened that if it was not forthcoming, they would all set off back to their husbands. Harley, covered with confusion, ran from the room pursued by the women, but made good his retreat to York House. He then ordered the sergeant to inform the women that if there was any repetition of this behaviour, he would abandon them at once, and leave them without further assistance.

Arrived at last at Bristol, Harley succeeded in chartering a vessel, and with the help of a sympathetic banker, who cashed his bills without charging a discount, and assisted him in obtaining three days' rations for the women and children for the voyage home. After a further difficulty with the Custom House officers regarding the permit to sail, John Harley finally 'had the gratification of seeing the poor women and children sail the same evening, with a fair breeze for old Ireland.'[61]

Once arrived at the port from which the troops were to sail on foreign service, the final, terrible moment of parting could be postponed no longer. And here the private agonies of individual men, women and children became a disquieting public spectacle. When the 29th went on board their transports in December 1807, Lieutenant Leslie recorded in his journal that the men 'embarked amidst the cheers of an immense multitude and the sounds of martial music, to which they cheerfully responded.' But it was, he added, 'distressing to hear the wailings of many poor women and children, who were thus suddenly separated

---

58 Harley, *The Veteran*, p.72.
59 Harley, *The Veteran*, p.73.
60 Harley, *The Veteran*, p.73.
61 Harley, *The Veteran*, p.75.

from their husbands and fathers, and left destitute on the beach.'[62] Leslie's description may have been written later, but was clearly based on a vivid recollection of events at the time. as were many memoirs, written in some cases decades after the event, when the memory of what had been witnessed was still green half a lifetime later. James Archibald Hope was an officer in one of the Highland regiments, and when they embarked for Walcheren in July 1809. When he wrote his anonymous memoirs more than 20 years after the event, he had not forgotten the scenes he had witnessed:

> At the embarkation of some of the battalions, it was truly heart-rending to see the poor women taking leave of their husbands – many of them to meet no more. The agonizing cries, – the piteous lamentations, and the tears which flowed in copious streams down their care-worn cheeks, were more than sufficient to penetrate the hardest heart that ever lay incased in the breast of man ... The parting words of the distressed couples, no one could hear without being sensibly affected. – 'God bless you Mary; be kind to our babes,' or 'Farewell, Betsy; think of me till I return; 'were very generally the requests made by the soldiers, when they grasped the hands of their afflicted partners, to bid them adieu.[63]

Another witness to such scenes was William Lawrence, a Dorset lad who had only recently run away from home and his apprenticeship to join the army. Years later, when he was keeping a pub at Studland, he wrote his autobiography, and included a vivid description of just such a scene. His regiment, the 40th Foot, 1,000 strong, embarked at Portsmouth to sail for South America to join Sir Samuel Auchmuty's ill-fated operations around Monte Video. This was in 1806. 'I had not one to throw so much as a parting glance at myself,' he remembered rather thankfully. The band played *The Girl I Left Behind Me* as they always seem to have done, and how cruelly inappropriate that jaunty tune must have sounded. Young as he was, he was deeply affected by what he saw at the quayside:

> When the order was given to embark, the scene was quite heartrending; I could not see a dry eye in Portsmouth, and if tears could have been collected, they might have stocked a hospital in eye-water for some months. Husband and wife, father and child, young man and sweet-heart, all had to part, and perhaps none were more affected than the last, though with least cause: it was indeed dreadful to view.[64]

It was often impossible for a battalion to shake off the women and children who had resolutely followed the line of march all the way to the harbour or beach, and sometimes not even then, for the women in their desperation would often manage to get into the boats which took the troops out to transports laying at anchor, and even onto the decks of the ships themselves. One such occasion took place at Ramsgate, where boats were moored by

---

62 C. Leslie, *Military Journal of Colonel Leslie, K.H., of Balquhain Whilst Serving with the 29th Regt. in the Peninsula and the 60th Rifles in Canada 1807–1832* (Aberdeen: Aberdeen University Press, 1887), p.7.
63 Anon., *Military Memoirs of an Infantry Officer 1809–1816* (Edinburgh: Anderson, 1833), p.15.
64 G.N. Banks (ed.), *The Autobiography of Sergeant William Lawrence* (London: Sampson Low, 1886), p.17.

the pier-head waiting to take the troops out to the vessels moored in the Downs. 'Several women insisted in going with their husbands into the boats, and actually did so' remembered a sergeant of the 43rd as the regiment prepared to sail on the expedition to Denmark in August 1807. 'Father,' I heard a little child say, 'shall I never see you again!' The grief of separation was inevitable; and on nearing the ship's side, (a transport named the *Sally*) I saw many an embrace, destined by the frightful chances of war to be the last indulged in on earth.'[65] There were of course some men who reported all of this is in a much more matter of fact way. Sergeant Archibald Johnston embarked at Northfleet with the Scots Greys in April 1815 at the start of the Waterloo campaign. He wrote about the tearful women on the quay, one of whom had one child on her back and one on each hand, and all of them calling out to the men aboard the *Fame* transport. But as far as he himself was concerned, he recorded laconically that 'I amongst others left a wife and three children, and parted with them at this time.'[66] At least he was a survivor.

When the 94th Foot, having drawn the women's lots described by Sergeant Donaldson, marched early the next morning to embark at St Helier, the unlucky young wife of the soldier he identifies as Sandy, marched with them, her child in her arms. She went out to the transport in the boat with her husband, till one of the sergeants came to tell her the time had come for her to go ashore. She begged the commanding officer to be allowed to go, but it was no use. He had to obey the regulations. She stepped with the child into the boat, crying that they would never meet again, and the ship moved away from the pier. Her husband was killed in the assault on Ciudad Rodrigo in January 1812.[67] To have got as far as the transport and be turned away at the last moment seems a particularly brutal fate, but it was probably all too common. When the 53rd embarked for India at Portsmouth, it was discovered that (despite the extra number of wives allowed on this occasion) that there was one woman too many. There was only one way of solving the problem: a fresh drawing of lots then and there on the deck. Mrs Sherwood, as an officer's wife, confided her feelings to her diary: 'I saw the agony of the poor woman that was to be carried back to shore. I saw her wring her hands, and heard her cries, and I saw her put in a boat and sent back to Portsmouth, and I felt, whatever my hardships might be, my trials were nothing to hers.'[68]

Stories of young women disguising themselves in uniform in order to follow their lovers are as old as the hills, and probably belong to folk-lore rather than history. But in February 1794 something very like it actually occurred, although in this case the girl was seeking her brother. The 80th Foot, then in Guernsey, had received a draft of new recruits, and as Major Harness explained in a letter to his wife, 'one of them, who appeared to be a very pretty Lad, proved to be a woman.' She had been turned out of her father's house after a disagreement, and had decided to put on men's clothes and go on board a transport vessel. But 'she fell in with a Sergeant, who made her so handsome offers that she changed her

---

65 Anon., *Memoirs of a Sergeant of the 43rd Light Infantry, previous to and during the Peninsular War, including an account of his Conversion from Popery to the Protestant Religion* (Stroud: Nonsuch, 2005), p.25.
66 A. Johnson, 'Journal of Sergeant A. Johnson', in Glover (ed.), *Waterloo Archive*, vol.1, p.34.
67 Donaldson, *Recollections*, p.50.
68 Kelly (ed.), *Life*, p.270.

Rosabell. A popular song sheet depicting a woman with a child on a quay waving farewell to soldiers boarding transports in longboats. By John Mayne 12 December 1806. (Anne S.K. Brown Military Collection, Brown University)

plan and entered [enlisted] without any Bounty; it was not till she found it impossible to conceal that she acknowledged her sex.'[69] Unfortunately, the major did not go on to say what happened to her.

At the start of the Walcheren expedition in 1809, some of the 95th Rifles were embarking in the *Superb* (74), and it had been ordered that the usual proportion of women was to be cut. Some of the frantic wives clung so desperately to their husbands that the officers were obliged to order them to be separated by force. And 'even after we were in the boats and fairly pushed off, the screaming and howling of their farewells rang in our ears far out to sea.'[70] Unsurprisingly, desperation could turn to anger. When the 1st Foot embarked in the

---

69   Duncan-Jones, *Letters*, p.38.
70   C. Hibbert (ed.), *The Recollections of Rifleman Harris* (London: Leo Cooper, 1970), p.114.

spring of 1810, bound for Gibraltar, one woman in private John Douglas's company, Mrs Clarke, was sent ashore at the last moment. As she went down the side of the *Francis and Harriot,* she cried out 'I wish the bloody ship and all that's in it may go to the bottom!'[71] Mrs Clarke however was a resourceful and determined woman, and later in the war managed to smuggle herself out to Spain and rejoin the regiment.

Scenes like these certainly caused some soldiers to be heartily glad that they were not married. John Green, who had joined the 68th Foot at the tender age of 16 in October 1806, after running away from home and trying the life of a privateer, which was not to his liking, found himself in the midst of just such a scene of departure, with hysterical women and distraught children, when his regiment sailed for Walcheren in July 1809. 'On this occasion my feelings nearly overcame me, and I really could not help rejoicing that I was a single man.'[72] Nor was he the only one to feel this as they embarked. Another soldier called Green, a William this time, destined for the Peninsula with the 95th, in May 1809, put it in much the same way. The scene was so upsetting, with women clinging round their husband's necks, wringing their hands and tearing their hair and crying, and the officers forcibly parting them, 'that I was glad to jump into the boat; and felt thankful that I had no wife to bewail my loss.'[73]

Sometimes, no doubt, a sympathetic officer might turn a blind eye to the presence of an extra wife, and once in a while, a woman, luckier or more determined than the others, did manage to circumvent the regulations in plain view. In September 1799, Lady Bessborough was on the pier at Margate watching troops embark for Den Helder when she noticed a woman who was to be left behind. The woman, who was in an almost hysterical state, had a small child at her side and a baby tied to her bosom.

> As soon as they were all in, and the Anchor drawn up, she kept her eyes stedfastly fixed on the transport as it moved slowly up the Harbour. The soldiers were drawn up on the side waving their hands to their friends. Just as it turn'd round the Pier head she darted forward, threw the eldest child into the Arms of her Husband, and jump'd herself, with the other in her arms, amidst the shouts and acclamations of the Mob. The Soldiers received her and laid her gently on the deck, and the officer on board was so touch'd by her perseverance and despair that he permitted her to go. I cannot tell you how much this has struck my fancy; but we are in the midst of adventures here.[74]

Public awareness of such harrowing situations is evident from the number of poems on the subject published in the newspapers. *Rosabell A Ballad* by one John Mayne, appeared in *The Morning Chronicle* on 28 October 1806, one verse of which gives the flavour:

---

71 S. Monick (ed.), *Douglas's Tales of the Peninsula and Waterloo by John Douglas, former Sergeant, 1st Royal Scots* (London: Leo Cooper, 1997), p.15.
72 John Green, *The Vicissitudes of a Soldier's Life or a series of occurrences from 1806 to 1815* (Louth: Green & Jackson, 1827), p.26.
73 J & D Teague (eds), *Where Duty Calls Me. The Experiences of William Green in the Napoleonic Wars* (West Wickham: Synjon, 1975), p.22.
74 Countess Granville (ed.), *Private Correspondence 1781–1821* (London: Murray, 1916), vol.1, p.261.

> The troops were all embark'd on board;
> The ships were under weigh;
> And loving wives, and maids ador'd
> Were weeping round the Bay.

The particular incident described by Lady Bessborough seems to have been the origin of a ballad entitled *William and Mary,* which was a take-off of a ballad of the same title written by Harriett Abrams the same year. It tells the same story of a departing soldier and his lover, and ends with the girl leaping into the ship at the quay-side:

> The sails unfurl'd, as gliding round,
> The parting cheers still louder grew,
> She flew, and with a fearful bound
> Drop'd in her William's arms below.

The song was said to have been written 'to commemorate an interesting incident' by a Lady of Fashion. Was it perhaps Lady Bessborough herself? At all events, the fact that it was published as sheet music does suggest that it was popular, and reflected public concern about the plight of wives left at the quay-side.[75] Whether or not Lady Bessborough was the author of the ballad, she was certainly drawn back to the scenes described. In another letter, undated but written on a Monday in September 1799, she described how she had gone again to witness the embarkation of troops, and had almost been reduced to tears by the scenes of parting she witnessed. She strongly identified with one woman she spoke to just as she was getting into a boat. How could she think of going, somebody asked? 'I could not think of staying' the woman replied. 'I have been moving heaven and earth ever since I heard of it, and if I had not succeeded in getting leave to go with him, I would have follow'd him in the first fishing boat that would take me.' Despite the immense divide of wealth and social status which divided her from the common soldiers' wives, Lady Bessborough was deeply moved. 'I do not think I could bear to stay behind' she told Levenson Gower, 'I would go too.'[76]

But nevertheless, there could be mixed feelings. The officer of the 81st, writing to a friend from Holland in the same month, gave it as his opinion that Sir John Moore had been right when he said that a soldier had no business with a wife. And yet he added wistfully, 'I think that some of these wives are too precious luxuries for us contentedly to give the monopoly of them to you non-military gentlemen.'[77]

---

75 K. McAulay & B. Robinson-Kirkland, 'My Love to the War is Going: Women and Song in the Napoleonic Era', in *The Trafalgar Chronicle New Series* (London: Seaforth, 2018), pp.202–212. The copy of the music in the St Andrews University library (M1.A4M6,40) says that the ballad was 'Founded upon an interesting incident which took place on the embarkation of the 85th Regiment for Holland at Ramsgate, August 10, 1799'. The place and date are different, but it seems the two incidents may have been conflated.
76 Granville (ed.), *Private Correspondence*, vol.1, p.263.
77 Anon., *Letters from Flushing*, p.19.

3

Before The Mast

Loud sounds the tempest – peals of thunder roar,
Tremendous lightnings flash from shore to shore.
Seas dash the shaking rocks, seas mount the flaming sky,
And elements convuls'd – speak dissolution nigh[1]

Cables slipped and anchors weighed, the transports moved slowly out to sea. Whichever theatre of operations they were bound for, the women who had been lucky in the ballot, as well as the troops they sailed with, had now to face the perils and hardships of the sea common to all in the age of sail.

If they were lucky, they may have sailed in Royal Navy warships which had been converted to troop transports. These at least were of reasonable size – 900 tons or more. The majority of vessels however were chartered by the Transport Board from the ever-growing merchant fleet. These vessels were not so large, varying between 150 and 400 tons. It was discovered that colliers made excellent troop transports, being broad in the beam, relatively roomy and of shallow draught, which enabled them to get close inshore. But they were slow, and at night or in heavy weather often found it impossible to keep station with the convoys in which they sailed as a protection against French privateers. The Transport Board insisted that the vessels it chartered were well equipped and fully manned, but there were numerous complaints from army officers not only that the ships' captains were sometimes incompetent or drunk, or both, but that vessels were frequently over-crowded and unseaworthy.

John Patterson of the 50th Foot was one such. 'The transport in which I was embarked, I had almost said *entombed*,' he wrote, 'originally flourished in the occupation of a collier, trading from Newcastle to the Thames, the worst, or most unseaworthy of which, after being pensioned off that service, were hired by Government for the shipment of troops.'[2]

J. S. Cowell, a subaltern in the Guards, would have agreed with this when in the summer of 1810 he found himself bound for the Peninsula in the old and creaky *Lord Eldon,* a 300-ton ex-collier. The skipper, he remembered, was a drunken Northumbrian familiar only with the North Sea, 'and his vessel…an ugly, slow, and leaky drowning machine – always going to leeward like a haystack.'[3]

---

1 From *An Elegy on my Sailor* by John Gabriel Steadman, in *The Weekly Entertainer*, 1795.
2 W.H. Maxwell (ed.), *Peninsular Sketches by Actors on the Scene* (London: Colburn, 1845), vol.1, p.21.
3 Anon., *Leaves from the Diary of an Officer of the Guards* (London: Chapman Hall, 1854), p.4.

One of the hardships faced by women and their children, especially on long voyages, was that they were expected to subsist on reduced rations. Normally, while the army was campaigning, wives were allocated half of a soldier's rations, and children a quarter. At sea however this rule did not apply. Food and water for the voyage were supplied by the Victualling Board, paid for in Navy bills drawn on the Treasury, and issued jointly by the ship's master and an army officer. The troops were generally fed at two-thirds of a seaman's allowance, which meant that six soldiers were allocated the rations of four seamen. Perhaps it was considered that soldiers, being passengers, did not require as much food as working sailors. At the beginning of the French wars, women and children on board ship were given the same allowance as their men. During 1794 however, the children's ration was reduced to half a full allowance. In August 1799, in another effort at economy, the women's ration was cut to one-half and the children's to a quarter of the whole allowance, although the troops continued to be supplied at two-thirds of a seaman's ration.[4] There must have been some very under-nourished women and children on long voyages.

This was a state of affairs which could lead to difficulties, as Lieutenant Harry Ross-Lewin of the 32nd discovered. In 1798 he was sent to Jersey with a detachment of men for the 88th, the Connaught Rangers. They were an undisciplined lot, not yet fully trained; they fought each other over everything, including food, and their women were just as unruly:

> On our way we anchored in the Downs, and sent ashore for fresh meat; but it was not long on deck, when a woman burst into the cabin to make a complaint to me, as commanding officer. 'Oh! my sheep's head!' she roared out; 'sure I had as good a right as the best of them to get some of the meat;' and certainly her face, which was streaming with blood, testified that she had defended her right to the last extremity.[5]

Women could indeed cause trouble on board, as Lieutenant George Woodberry of the 18th Hussars discovered while on passage for the Peninsula in January 1813. There was trouble in the hold, caused by a trooper breaking a bottle over his wife's head. He was confined in the foc'sle and his grog stopped. When the officers looked into the quarrel, they found that the woman had provoked her husband by allowing the black cook to take liberties with her, so her grog was also stopped. 'The more I see of the world' wrote young Woodberry in his diary, 'the more I am disgusted with man and woman of the lower order.'[6]

Wives could also be downright mutinous. Captain George Landmann of the Royal Engineers had embarked on the *Loyal Briton* transport lying in the Solent in January 1806 bound for Gibraltar. The ship had already made a slow passage from the Thames with a large number of women and children on board. They had not been on deck for weeks, with the result that the space between decks was in a filthy and insanitary state. Landmann decreed that they must all be on deck by eight each morning to allow for the cleaning and fumigation

---

4   M.E. Condon, 'Living Conditions on board Troopships during the war against Revolutionary France 1793–1802' *Journal of the Society for Army Historical Research*, vol.49, 1971, pp.13–19.
5   J. Wardell (ed.), *With the Thirty Second in the Peninsula and other Campaigns* (Dublin: Hodges, 1904), p.43.
6   G. Glover and C. York, (eds.), *With Wellington's Hussars in the Peninsula and Waterloo. The Journal of Lt. George Woodberry, 18th Hussars* (Barnsley: Frontline, 2018), p.7.

of their quarters. Many of the women were reluctant to do so, and Mrs McSheen of the Royal Military Artificers, absolutely refused to comply. She claimed to be ill, and said that 'no power upon earth should move her from that place; "neither officer, non-commissioned officer, nor private soldier" had a right to interfere with her; and, in order to add force and solemnity to this determination, she wound up with the closing words of an oath.' She also started to throw sticks, shoes and old potatoes and followed this by screaming that she was being murdered. She then pretended to faint. Landmann seized the moment to order her husband and three other men to carry her up on deck and throw a bucket of water over her. Mrs McSheen however was not prepared for this. She sat up, and as Landmann put it, 'with a countenance most serene, yet full of dignity, she gracefully quitted her couch, advanced with measured step, and joined the other women upon deck without uttering a single word.'[7]

Short commons apart, and whether embarked in transports or warships, conditions on board were of a very basic kind. In theory, army personnel were to be accommodated in a mixture of births and hammocks, though for coastal voyages or short crossings, such as to the Channel Islands, this apparently was not thought necessary. The result was great discomfort.[8] This was certainly not the intention of the Horse Guards. The Adjutant General's orders laid down that married people were 'to be confined in regard to their births to one particular part of the ship'. They also made it clear that 'The married People are not to be intermixed with the single Men, but should have a part of the Deck allotted particularly for their accommodation.'[9] These orders seem seldom to have been observed, with everyone usually packed into whatever space was available without regard to the niceties. It must have come as an unpleasant shock to some of the wives.

At the conclusion of the war in the Peninsula, the 7th Fusiliers were put aboard the *Clarence* (74) for transport back to England. The regiment then numbered about 600, and with them went their women, children and baggage. One deck had been cleared of guns to provide accommodation, but there were no hammocks, so 'we had only the deck, therefore at night we lay like a flock of sheep on a common.' In the Bay of Biscay the ship rolled a great deal, there was much rolling and squeezing and crushing amongst men, women and children.[10] Conditions like these were commonplace. During the evacuation of what was left of the British force which took part in the Walcheren expedition, and with fever still raging amongst the troops being evacuated, conditions on board resembled those on a slave ship, as an officer of the 81st recorded in a letter to a friend:

> The Captains think they perform their contract if they stow our men like so many goods wherever they will lie; they are accordingly thrown together like so many packages, and the motion of the sea, and the consequent commotion of the stomachs, render them as motionless and inanimate. Nothing can possibly be more miserable than the spectacle which is presented in a crowded transport. Imagine some hundreds of human creatures lying as thick together as tamarinds in a jar;

---

7 G.T. Landmann, *Recollections of my Military Life* (London: Hurst, 1854), vol.1, p.5.
8 Condon, 'Living Conditions', p.15.
9 Anon., *General Regulations*, p.251.
10 J.S. Cooper, *Rough Notes on Seven Campaigns in Portugal, Spain, France and America* (Carlisle: Smith, 1869), p.120.

here a hand, there a foot, there a face forcing itself above the shoulders of the crowd, in order to collect a breath of air, and there the uplifted hands of another plucking him down, in order that his own face may have a turn; when suddenly the vessel gives a roll, and every one is seized in an instant with the most horrible sickness … The cries of the women and children, for we have but too many of them, add to the horror of the scene.[11]

Small wonder that he later observed that a voyage was as bad as a battle.

This kind of thing was not unusual. In the summer of 1809 for instance, when the 94th embarked in four transports bound for garrison duty on Jersey, Joseph Donaldson reported that they were stowed with 18 inches per man to lie in, and hardly room to move, which was especially harrowing with many of them becoming sea-sick. 'The women particularly suffered much' he wrote, 'being crammed in indiscriminately amongst the men, and no arrangement made for their comfort.'[12] Sea sickness indeed could be a serious matter for both the troops and their women. Lieutenant Woodberry's transport, the *London,* had sailed from Portsmouth on 19 January. The following day he recorded in his diary that everyone on board 'except the crew and me' was seasick. By the 21st he was concerned that one of his fellow officers, Lieutenant Hesse, was so ill 'I did not expect him to last the night.' Two days later two of the wives were so ill they were suicidal. One was brought up on deck in a state of collapse, and Woodberry gave her some of his private supply of brandy and oatmeal. But they were in such distress that as he noted rather confusedly in his diary 'One of them tried to throw themselves over the edge. Great tumult!!' He may have been a bit of a prig, but by the time they sighted the Rock of Lisbon and supplies were running low, he very generously gave a chicken he still had to Mrs Sweeney, wife of one of the troop sergeant majors, because 'poor woman, she is still very ill.'[13]

Occasionally some basic efforts were made to improve the women's accommodation. John Patterson (who was one of those opposed to the presence of women on active service) saw women on board a troopship crammed into what he described as a 'wretched, loathsome, murky, and abominable hole' – a small space six feet square, but which had at least been partitioned off by a few dirty planks nailed up and tarred. There was also what he described as 'the drop scene', which consisted of 'a ragged piece of sail cloth, which seemed as if it were often used to sift the biscuit, was hung across the cabin to hide the ladies, as well as to veil their blushes.' But inevitably, especially in heavy weather, the sail cloth fell at embarrassing moments, to the loud consternation of the women.[14]

Conditions for officers' ladies were sometimes relatively comfortable, though this was by no means always the case, and they could often have their embarrassments as well. In June 1805, the 53rd, then at Morpeth, received orders to march to Shields and embark for Ramsgate. The battalion was put aboard two transports. Mrs Sherwood, wife of a captain of the regiment, and another officer's wife, decided that they too would go south by sea. 'Anything was preferable for ladies than a transport filled with officers and soldiers' as

---

11   Anon., *Letters from Flushing*, p.249.
12   Donaldson, *Recollections*, p.48.
13   Glover & York (eds), *With Wellington's Hussars*, pp.4–5.
14   Patterson, *Camp and Quarters*, vol.1, p.122.

she put it, so the two wives took passage on a collier, *The Charming Peggy,* which when cleaned after loading provided reasonable accommodation. They had a spacious cabin with stern windows with a table fixed in the centre and a bed placed either side of the door. This she shared with the captain's wife and daughter. They had an uneasy eight-day passage to the mouth of the Thames. Then, while Mrs Sherwood was lying down, there was a disturbance overhead, the door of the cabin flew open and one of the seamen dashed in and hid under her bed. The captain's wife told her the fellow was hiding from the press-gang which had come on board. There was a commotion outside and some of the gang peered through the door. Mrs Sherwood had the presence of mind to keep quite still, and the gang, confronted with a lady lying on her bed, beat a retreat, 'and we all gloried in having saved the poor fellow.'[15]

Nor was this the end of Mrs Sherwood's trials and tribulations. At Easter 1805 the 53rd was placed under orders for India and directed to embark at Portsmouth. She and her husband were allocated to the *Devonshire* but arrived late to find every cabin taken. They bribed the carpenter to give up his and found themselves in possession of a tiny space 'worse than a dog-kennel' near the main mast and the pump handles. Most of the space was occupied by a cannon with just room for a small table and chair. The hammock was slung over the gun. When the pumps were in use bilge water flowed through this apartment, but the worst feature was that it was separated only by a canvas partition from the deck where the troops lived, 'so it was absolutely necessary for me in all weathers to go down to this shocking place before any of the men were turned down for the night.'[16]

Privacy consisting only of a canvas screen was not unusual. Sir Richard Henegan, a military commissary, who had an ear for dialogue, an eye for the ladies and a keen sense of the absurd, described in his memoirs the sort of situations which occurred when he was on the way to Portugal in the *Cora* transport. Unfortunately, he did not record the date. Accommodation was short as usual and the very limited cabin space had been divided by a canvas screen. On one side lived General and Mrs Hay and their two daughters. 'Nice unaffected girls,' thought Henegan, 'and a raw boned Scotch servant, the very personification of Meg Merrilies.' On the other side of the screen lived Henegan, a staff surgeon, Colonel Coghlan of the 61st, a deputy commissary general, three Royal Artillery officers, a Royal Engineer, and a Captain Lancaster, who was paymaster to a battalion of the King's German Legion.[17]

Not that this sort of crowding was unusual. In November 1811 Captain George Bowles of the Guards was aboard a vessel called the *Kingston* sailing from Portsmouth to Lisbon. There was a none too large communal cabin shared by Bowles and four other Guards officers, a German hospital mate, an officer of the waggon train, the veterinary surgeon of the 13th Light Dragoons, a commissary, a gentleman who had been turned out of the British army and was going out to join the Portuguese service, three or four officers of the line, and the wife and daughter of a major in the waggon train. Quite how they all slept Bowles did not mention. But if this lack of privacy for the ladies was not enough to endure,

---

15 Kelly (ed.), *Life*, p.25.
16 Kelly (ed.), *Life*, p.269.
17 Richard Hennegan, *Seven Years Campaigning in the Peninsula and the Netherlands 1808–1815* (Stroud: Nonsuch, 2005), vol.1, p.139.

the gentleman candidate and the waggoner got extremely drunk, and after beating up the commissary offered them 'very improper solicitations'.[18] They were promptly placed under arrest by the senior officers.

Bowles and his companions were at least on a short voyage. In the same year that he was making for Lisbon, others were bound for the Malta garrison. A reinforcement of 12 officers and 300 men of the 1/35th were delayed at Spithead for a month waiting for a convoy to assemble, which was an all-too-common experience. The following voyage, with light airs mixed with storms, took three months. Lieutenant John Hildebrand did not record his recollections of the soldiers' wives, but he was concerned about the lack of privacy endured by the married officers and their ladies. The headquarters ship had a 'state cabin' which measured about six feet square, and this was appropriated by the senior officer and his wife who, luckily, was a high-spirited woman. She needed to be, as this space was separated from that of the other officers only by a screen, so that every word spoken was audible on both sides. The vessel in which Hildebrand himself was sailing was if anything worse, with 'two married officers with their wives ... separated from each other and from the cabin of the bachelors by carpets hung up in a very rough way ... and forming a very imperfect and incomplete screen from sight and none from conversation.'[19] Fortunately, both the ladies and their husbands endured it all with great forbearance. It must have been a difficult three months.

Crammed into inadequate accommodation between decks and not well provided with food, conditions for women and children, as well as the troops, were often aggravated by delays which kept them cooped up on board ship before sailing. In the summer of 1798 Private Samuel Wray of the 61st was aboard the East India transport *Santa Christiana* with the rest of his regiment and their women under orders for Cape Colony which had been wrested from the Dutch. They were delayed six weeks at Spithead before setting sail with a convoy.[20] Lieutenant Cowell aboard the *Lord Eldon* bound for Spain, had a similar experience at Spithead. 'After a month's tugging at our anchor, and bobbing up and down at Spithead, where contrary winds and foul weather detained us, at last on the 31st August 1810 we weighed anchor.'[21] There were further delays at Falmouth, and they arrived too late for the Battle of Busaco.

A month to reach Spain or Portugal was not unusual, but even voyages in home waters could take weeks. After Waterloo, the 40th, having been part of the army of occupation in France, were eventually ordered to Scotland. The regiment embarked at Calais for Leith, which should have taken three days in favourable conditions. Sergeant William Lawrence recorded that it actually took seven weeks. Lawrence had married a Parisienne, and she had never before seen the sea. She was sea-sick and found the experience long and tedious. They were forced into Bridlington where they were detained for three weeks by the weather. 'The first night we were there, the mayor invited the officers to dine with him, and sent a quart of

---

18 Malmesbury, *Letters*, vol.2, p.231.
19 G. Glover (ed.), *The Recollections of Lieutenant John Hildebrand 35th Foot in the Mediterranean and Waterloo Campaign* (Barnsley: Frontline, 2016), p.15.
20 G. Glover (ed.), *The Military Adventures of Private Samuel Wray, 61st Foot 1796–1815* (Huntingdon: Trotman, 2009), p.4.
21 Anon., *Leaves from the Diary of an Officer of the Guards* (London: Chapman Hall, 1854), p.2.

beer on board for each man, and half that quantity for each woman.' They were tied up so long that it was decided that the troops could go ashore during the day provided that they were back on board by 9:00 p.m. 'The inhabitants were particularly kind to us, amongst other things offering our women their houses to wash their clothes in, which offer many accepted.'[22] After this delay they were able to sail northwards again only to be driven back to Bridlington for a further 10 days, the ship rolling so violently that the women especially began to despair.

With troops and their wives and children confined on board for long periods, it was important to do everything possible to maintain health and morale. Troops were sometimes divided into three watches, with one watch on deck and ready if necessary to assist the ship's crew. This would at least help reduce the unhealthy over-crowding between decks and afford some fresh air. The General Orders issued by the Adjutant General's office included 'Regulations to be strictly observed by Troops embarked on board Transports for Service abroad'. These specified that bedding was to be brought on deck every morning to be aired, and 'This order applies equally to the Married People, who are to be confined in regard to their births to one particular part of the ship.' When East Indiamen were employed in moving troops, the regulations were even more specific. The married couples, who were supposed to have their own area of the deck allocated to them, were particularly instructed not to 'obstruct the circulation of the Air by putting up Blankets during the day-time,' presumably a reference to the natural desire of married people to enjoy a little privacy. The orders went on to state that 'the Women, as well as the Men must rise at Six in the Morning, when all their partitions must be removed for the day.'[23] When the sea-state permitted, parades were held on deck to keep everyone on their toes. Similarly, weather permitting, morning periods were set aside for the troops and their wives to wash themselves on deck. In January 1796, the 25th Foot were on their way across the Atlantic to Barbados, and Lieutenant Colonel Dyott was very concerned with cleanliness. He arranged for tubs of seawater to be fixed on the fo'c'sle for the purposes of washing. He also ensured that the decks where the troops and the women slept were 'thoroughly scoured and cleansed.'[24] Sometimes similar arrangements were made for clothes to be washed. This was done by companies, with the wet garments hung in the shrouds and guarded by a sentry. This must have been difficult, and with indifferent results. On one occasion at least, an officer's wife expressed the wish that the colonel would order the soldiers' wives to keep their distance because of the unpleasant smell of their clothes.[25]

Many voyages were of course made in calm conditions. Sir Edward Packenham, commanding the 64th, recorded a passage of 53 days to Halifax, Nova Scotia, in the spring of 1801, which apart from a couple of boisterous days near Bermuda were completely calm.[26]

---

22 Banks (ed.), *Autobiography*, p.231.
23 Anon., *General Regulations 1811*, pp.237–251.
24 R. Jeffery (ed.), *Dyott's Diary 1781–1845. A Selection from the Journal of William Dyott, sometime General in the Brtitish Army and Aide-de-Camp to His Majesty King George III* (London: Constable, 1907), p.86.
25 R. Roy, 'Memoirs of Private James Gunn', *Journal of the Society for Army Historical Research*, vol.49, 1971, p.93.
26 Lord Longford (ed.), *Packenham Letters 1800 to 1805* (London: Bumpus, 1914), p.13.

But storms were a nightmare. They could spring up with little warning and last for days. In the Channel, transports were often driven back to seek shelter. In the Bay of Biscay or the Atlantic, they had to be ridden out. To landlubbers especially, waves could appear – and sometimes were – mountainous, and passengers had the alarming experience of wallowing in the troughs so that other vessels in the convoy were lost from view. Sails were torn away, so that ships drove on under staysails or bare poles. Vessels were dismasted. Ships could be pooped, and the cabin windows smashed, letting in tons of icy water, or waves might break over the fo'c'sle, sending seas sweeping over the decks. In such conditions the hatches had to be battened firmly down, and the men, women and children below had to endure appalling conditions trapped in the darkness, 'lying together in a state of the most dreadful sickness, groaning in concert, and calling for a drop of water to cool their parched tongues.'[27] An additional danger was when barrels or other stores broke loose and rolled about putting everyone in imminent danger. In August 1813, the 73rd found itself ordered to the island of Rügen to take part in the little-known campaign in north Germany. They embarked at Harwich and sailed in weather so rough that they had to ride it out at sea before putting back to Yarmouth. 'The waves ran so high that they were compelled to close the hatchways,' remembered Sergeant Morris of the 73rd, 'leaving the men, women and children below, in utter darkness, and who therefore fancied the danger greater than it really was.'[28]

The dangers could in fact be very real. William Surtees, a quartermaster of the 95th, recalled a terrible storm on the return voyage from the campaign in Denmark in 1807. As they neared Yarmouth, anchors were cast out in an effort to control the transport he was in, but they failed to hold. The wind was such that a sailor was blown off the foreyard, and the movement was so violent that a woman, the wife of one of the corporals, fell down a hatchway into the hold, and broke her back. She did later recover, Surtees remembered, but she never regained her upright posture.[29] William Thornton Keep of the 28th wrote to his brother describing a storm they were caught in off Cornwall, en route for Spain, which was so violent that as he put it 'what had been the floor turned into a side of the cabin.' He was thrown violently against a table and bruised his ribs badly, but what was worse he could hear the screams of the men and women battened down below 'tumbled together, half drowned and stifled.'[30]

Storms were not only a danger in themselves; they were frequently the cause of out-of-control ships posing a hazard to other vessels. Benjamin Miller, a gunner in the Royal Artillery and bound for Egypt in 1800, was on board a large troopship carrying a force of 1,200 men. Near the Straits of Gibraltar, the fleet was overtaken by a storm which drove several vessels onto the Rock. Miller's ship was running 14 knots under staysails when she was struck by another vessel. Luckily, they lost only some of the rigging and had the stern damaged. But as he said 'It was shocking to hear the cries of the women and men all in confusion.' So severe was the gale that the surviving ships were driven out into the Atlantic where they had to ride it out for a fortnight before being able to resume their course into the

---

27 John Shipp, *Memoirs of the Extraordinary Military Career of John Shipp, late Lieutenant in His Majesty's 87th Regiment* (London: Hurst, Chance, 1829), vol.1, p.7.
28 Morris, *Recollections*, p.10.
29 Surtees, *Twenty-Five Years*, p.72.
30 Fletcher (ed.), *In the Service*, p.109.

Mediterranean. Later in the voyage, near Minorca, the same ship which had struck them ran foul of a brig and sank her, drowning eight artillerymen, a boy, a woman and a child.[31]

James Hale, a sergeant in the 9th Foot had a similar experience. He was ill with a fever, and had been sent back from Coimbra to Mondego Bay for recovery, but his ship was struck by a storm which blew them out to sea. Sailing back again past Lisbon a transport brig ran into them in the darkness. Everyone ran on deck, thinking they had struck a rock 'and hearing some women that were on board squeak and squall in such a manner, we were all in great confusion for several minutes.'[32] The two ships' rigging became entangled but no serious damage was sustained, and as Hale's ship was the larger of the two, they were able to go on their way. Something very similar happened in March 1808 to the 200 ton transport *Royal Yeoman*, bound for Nova Scotia with part of the 23rd on board. They ran foul of the *Ocean*, another transport, and again the rigging was entangled. They too thought they had struck a rock. As Lieutenant Browne noted in his diary, the officers, who were having dinner 'instantly ran on deck, where a great scene of confusion prevailed, ordered down all the women who were screaming and at their wits end, and many of the men also, and thus succeeded in restoring order.'[33]

Sometimes the people on one vessel were aware of the distress of another but were quite unable to help. In February 1808 a fleet of transports sailing from Falmouth to Gibraltar ran into rough weather in the Bay of Biscay. Lieutenant Leslie of the 29th heard a ship firing distress guns, but conditions were so bad that no boat could be launched to go the vessel's assistance. Towards dawn the weather did moderate, and the ship's company were rescued before she sank. 'A heroic action deserves to be recorded' wrote Leslie, 'two ladies, officer's wives, on board the distressed vessel sat on deck during the whole night, cutting up flannel petticoats, and made them into cartridge bags.'[34] It could be a lot worse. In October 1814 Captain Joseph Anderson of the York Chasseurs was ordered to Barbados. A substantial convoy set out from the Cove of Cork, but was driven by a terrific storm to seek shelter in Bantry Bay, which has a narrow entrance. As Anderson's ship drove past the entrance he saw another of the transports, the *Baring*, which was carrying part of the 40th Foot get too far inshore and strike the rocks. The cries of the people on board could be heard, but there was nothing anyone could do until they reached calmer water and boats could be launched. All the soldiers and crew were lost on the rocks except about 15 wretched men, women and children. The sight which haunted Anderson was 'that of an officer's wife standing and screaming on the poop, her infant in her arms, and with no covering beyond her nightdress; I heard afterwards that the child fell out of her arms and was drowned, but she herself was saved.'[35] The survivors camped on the beach until help came.

Heavy weather could on occasions produce ludicrous situations as Sir Richard Henegan recorded with evident delight. The weather got up, and the *Cora* began to roll and pitch violently. The ladies were chatting with the General and Colonel Coghlan, when a sudden

---

31   Benjamin Miller, *The Adventures of Sergeant Benjamin Miller Whilst Serving in the 4th Battalion of the Royal Regiment of Artillery 1796 to 1815* (Uckfield: Naval & Military, nd.), p.14.
32   Hale, *Journal*, p.69.
33   Buckley (ed.), *Napoleonic War Journal*, p.76.
34   Leslie, *Military Journal*, p.11.
35   J. Anderson, *Recollections of a Peninsular Veteran* (London: Arnold, 1913), p.80.

violent lurch of the ship sent them reeling across the deck, catching at anything within their grasp.

> The same plunge that sent poor Mrs Hay in a *pas de glissade* towards the opposite side, where Captain Lancaster was vainly endeavouring to preserve a footing, brought at the next moment that worthy gent most innocently and unintentionally into her embrace. They stood in mute dismay, clasped in each other's arms. It was an opportunity not to be lost. 'Dear lady,' gasped the hero, 'I had the happiness, as a military man, of proposing your health this day in a bumper.' 'General Hay – General Hay!' screamed out the offended lady, still clinging to the object of her horror, who with no less fervour clung to her, as another and another roll of the vessel made the disentanglement less and less practicable.[36]

Hay attempted to extricate his wife, but could not keep his balance, and at last the ship's captain managed to rescue the outraged lady and conduct her to the cabin below.

Worse was to follow. By the time they had reached the open Atlantic, the gale was at its height. Not a stitch of canvas could be set beyond a storm stay-sail. The seas ran high as hills and swept the decks, carrying away the long-boat and one of the crew. The passengers were desperately sick. This went on for days, and Captain Lancaster, unable to move, swung in his cot against the frail canvas partition which separated the ladies. At last there was a lull, and the captain made an attempt to change his shirt. But as he did so there was a roll of such violence that he was catapulted out of his cot, through the canvas screen in his state of undress, landing head first on the bunk occupied by Miss Hay. The Scotch maid grabbed him by the legs and hauled him off, while someone threw a covering over him. He was then hustled back to his cot, half stunned, and the screen nailed back up again. The general's wife was so outraged that she demanded that Lancaster be turned out of the ship, 'and it was only when her husband good humouredly assured her that there was no place but the open sea to put him in, with the improbable chance of a Jonah's escape, that she consented to allow him to remain on board.'[37] Eventually, the *Cora*, her fore-top-mast gone and most of the sails missing, limped into the Tagus to deposit a much-relieved consignment of passengers onto dry land.

If storms were an all-too-common experience, another terrible danger was fire. In January 1808 two companies of the 23rd Foot were ordered to Halifax, Nova Scotia. Sergeant Richard Roberts was aboard the *Harriet* transport, which on the second night out lost contact with the rest of the fleet. The passage took five tedious months during which they experienced calms, storms, a broken rudder, and worst of all, a fire, far from land and alone on the ocean. It had broken out below, possibly in the galley, and spread rapidly. 'The smoke burst through the hatches. In a moment all was disorder and consternation. The women and children screaming; the crew distracted – shouting cursing, bawling; none to direct and none to obey.'[38] The captain was drunk, and Roberts was near to jumping overboard when the fire was got under control by the mate just before the flames reached the magazine.

---

36 Henegan, *Seven Years*, vol.1, p.141.
37 Henegan, *Seven Years*, p.141.
38 J. Crook (ed.), *Incidents in the Life of an Old Fusilier. The Recollections of Sergeant Richard Roberts of the 23rd Foot* (Huntingdon: Trotman, 2011), p.6.

Dr James McGrigor, who later rose to become the Director General of the Medical Department, endured a very similar experience while sailing as regimental surgeon to the 88th Foot, from Jersey to Ostend to take part in the 1799 Helder expedition. Fire was reported on board near the powder magazine, and there was near panic. 'We all jumped up from table, and ran upon deck, where everything was in confusion. About 150 soldiers who were on board with their wives and children ran upon deck, the latter all screaming.'[39] The situation seemed hopeless, and some of the soldiers began to climb the rigging, while those who could swim began to get their clothes off. But the mate, as in the case of Roberts' ship a brave and decisive man, went below and managed to put the blaze out, and the officers restored order amongst the troops and their families.

Fire could indeed be a mortal danger. On 1 January 1811, the 1/28th Foot sailed for the Peninsula from Plymouth aboard a man-of-war, and the entire battalion was on board – 1,200 men, and about 100 women. Fourteen days out, near disaster struck. On the morning of the 14th the rum ration was being issued as usual, when one of the men walked up with a lighted pipe in his mouth, and a burning fragment fell into the cask, which erupted into flames. The deck was quickly flooded, but the flames leaped up the rigging. They were in the end extinguished with wet blankets, but it was narrow escape. 'Never do I remember anything that thrilled to the depths of my soul like that cry of fire, on the wild waste of the waters, where, unless it could be subdued, scarcely a hope remained for the safety of those twelve hundred human beings, confined in the ship's narrow space.'[40] wrote Charles O'Neil. It was an appalling prospect: death by fire or drowning, or possibly for some, a slow death from starvation in open boats. Small wonder the women screamed.

All too often ships were lost at sea or wrecked on the coast, frequently with grievous loss of life. The King's German Legion suffered badly in this way on their return from the Copenhagen expedition in 1807. Terrible storms were encountered in the North Sea, and several transports foundered. The ship carrying the 7th Line Battalion vanished with eight officers, 172 non-commissioned officers and men, and the chaplain with his wife and children. The 2nd Line Battalion lost nine officers, 212 men, 30 women and five children.[41] In January 1816, the 82nd Foot was returning from being part of the allied army of occupation in France. Having landed at Dover, the regiment was re-shipped for Ireland on board the *Boadicea* transport. The ship was wrecked on Garretstown Strand near Kinsale on the night of 30 January and 102 of the 289 people on board were saved, but amongst the drowned were the wife of the regimental surgeon, Henry Scott, and 13 other women and children.[42]

In the age of sail there was nothing very unusual about such losses, which could occur close to home. One dark night in February 1811, a transport was run down by a frigate just off Falmouth, a tragedy in which 197 officers and men, six seamen, 15 women and six

---

39 J. McGrigor, *The Autobiography and Services of Sir Jas. McGrigor, Bart., Late Director General of the Medical Department* (London: Longman, 1861,) p.21.
40 O'Neil, *Military Adventures*, p.38.
41 L. Ompteda, *In the King's German Legion. Memoirs of Baron Ompteda, Colonel in the King's German Legion During the Napoleonic Wars* (London: Grevel, 1894), p.213.
42 J. & D. Bromley, *Wellington's Men Remembered. A Register of Memorials to Soldiers who Fought in the Peninsular War and at Waterloo* (Barnsley: Pen & Sword, 2011), vol.1, p.1938.

children were drowned.⁴³ Falmouth was the scene of another tragedy in January 1814. The *Queen* transport, bringing sick men back from the Peninsula, anchored at Falmouth with 466 men, women and children on board. In the darkness, a gale sprang up and the *Queen* failed to ride it out. Driven onto the rocks near the shore, she broke up, and people were seen buffeted by the waves and battered by pieces of wreckage. Altogether, 363 people perished, but that stark fact conceals several intense personal tragedies. There was an artillery sergeant on board with his family, and an eyewitness saw the sergeant's servant and child washed overboard as the vessel broke to pieces. Then the sergeant and his wife were swept into the maelstrom and perished within sight of the shore.⁴⁴ Also on board was Lieutenant Robert Daniel of the 30th Foot, with his entire family. A headstone in the churchyard at Mylor tells the tale:

> In memory of Catherine, wife of Lieut. Robert Daniel, 30th Regt. Also their children viz Margaret, Eleanor, William, Robert and Edward Alexander, who unhappily perished in the wreck of the Queen transport on the awful morning of the 14th Jan 1814. Leaving an unfortunate husband and father to lament their loss to the end of his existence.⁴⁵

Daniel himself continued to serve, and was present at Quatre Bras and Waterloo. He died in 1852 at the age of 81, and so lived a long time to nurse his grief.

James McGrigor, who had so nearly perished from an onboard fire in 1799, also had the distinction of being shipwrecked twice. In 1809 he was sent to take charge of the medical department amidst the disastrous expedition to Walcheren, and sailed from Deal aboard the *Venerable,* a warship. The pilot made an error near the Dutch coast and the ship struck a sandbank in heavy weather and began to break up. Signal guns were fired and guns and other heavy gear were thrown overboard in an effort to float the ship off the bank. On board were two ladies, the wife of Captain Codrington, and her companion, and about 80 soldiers' wives, most of whom were Irish. As the distress guns fired, McGrigor thought that the Irish wives 'were very troublesome,' running about all over the place, while the two ladies, as befitted their station, remained calm and showed great fortitude. At last, a small brig came to their assistance and took the women off, and the rest of the company were rescued by boats from Flushing.⁴⁶

Dr McGrigor's other experience of shipwreck occurred when he was on passage from Barbados to Grenada with part of the 25th Foot. The ship struck a reef some six miles off the coast. The troops began firing their muskets as a sign of distress, and boats began to come out from the shore to their rescue. The only boat on board was launched, and McGrigor managed to get in it. He saw a woman clinging to the ship's side, begging to be rescued, but the boat was dangerously overcrowded, and the woman was beaten back and abandoned to

---

43 Roger Knight, *Britain Against Napoleon. The Organization of Victory 1793–1815* (London: Penguin, 2014), p.187.
44 Anon., *Memoirs of a Sergeant of the 5th Regt. of Foot, Containing an account of his services in Hanover, South America and the Peninsula* (Ashford: Elliott, 1842), p.120.
45 J. & D. Bromley, *Wellington's Men*, vol.1, p.1933.
46 McGrigor, *Autobiography*, p.233.

her fate. The doctor had lost everything, including his portmanteau. But at breakfast the next morning while he was recounting his experience, a sergeant appeared with the portmanteau. 'It had been taken ashore by his wife, the identical woman whom with others we cut at, to prevent their coming into the boat. The honesty of this couple was great, for in my small trunk I had between one and two hundred dollars, which from their weight must have betrayed part of the contents of the portmanteau.'[47] The woman had been rescued by one of the boats which came out from the shore. How the good doctor felt about the fact that his property had been retrieved by a brave woman who had been abandoned he did not record; nor did he mention her name. But it is to be hoped that she was well rewarded.

There was also the danger posed by enemy ships, including capture by French privateers in the case of a ship becoming separated from the convoy. In 1797, the transport *Three Sisters* was taken by a French privateer off Land's End. On board was Mrs Maguire, wife of the surgeon of the 4th Foot, a real daughter of the regiment, having been born during the American War of Independence as the Battle of Bunker's Hill was in progress. Knowing the sacred importance of the regimental colours, she had the presence of mind to wrap them round her flat-irons and throw them into the sea. She was taken prisoner and confined with her young son in a prisoner of war camp at Brest, where she gave birth to a daughter, before being released in an exchange.[48]

On occasions, it looked as though transports were about to run into an enemy squadron. Sergeant Benjamin Miller was en route for Gibraltar in April 1796 with his artillery battery. His ship, the *Grand* had been becalmed for a fortnight, and then the weather broke and turned into a gale. Some British frigates warned them that the enemy fleet was at sea, and they soon spotted nine men-of-war. 'The women began to sound their trumpets' as he put it, 'for we expected we should all be taken prisoners.'[49] However it turned out to be a British squadron. Sometime after his battery had joined the garrison at Gibraltar, Miller witnessed a minor naval battle from the safety of the shore. In the darkness the frigate *Andromache* was attacked in the bay by a swarm of Spanish gun-boats, and to add to the noise and confusion, one of the frigate's guns burst, killing some of her men. In the midst of this action was Lady Trigge, wife of the Governor of Gibraltar. She was on board the frigate, having just arrived from England, and experienced a warmer reception than she had bargained for.[50]

Inevitably there were occasions when regimental women, like the troops and sailors, were taken ill and died at sea. When the 1/42nd embarked in a transport at Gibraltar, sailing to reinforce Sir John Moore's army in Portugal, Private James Gunn recalled that one of their men, and his wife, were both dying of a fever. He also recalled the fact that the ship was followed by a shark. It was the old superstition which sailors like to impress on landsmen.[51] Samuel Wray of the 61st, who was delayed so long at Spithead, witnessed another such incident. The 61st had a much longer voyage to the Cape, and an old salt told the troops that if anyone on board became ill, the ship would be followed by a shark. When they had been out of sight of land for eight weeks one of the regiment's wives did fall sick, and sure enough a

---

47   McGrigor, *Autobiography*, p.55.
48   Haythornthwaite, *The Armies*, p.130.
49   Miller, *The Adventures*, p.5.
50   Miller, *The Adventures*, p.5.
51   Roy, 'Memoirs', p.90.

shark appeared. 'After we passed St Helena, the woman that I mentioned died. She was the first that I saw committed to the deep. She was sewed up in a blanket with a sand bag tied to her feet. Prayers were read and her body was cast into the sea.'[52] A lonely death.

Inevitably there was sometimes the hazard of child-birth just as there was for women marching with the troops on land. In July 1801 the 25th Foot was on its way from Malta to Alexandria to reinforce Abercromby's army in Egypt. The commanding officer, William Dyott, whom we have already met trying to ensure the cleanliness of his men on board ship, recorded one such incident in his journal:

> I forgot to insert at the time the circumstance of one of the women of the regiment being brought to bed on board. Poor soul, nothing could equal the wretchedness of her situation from the excessive heat, noise, and constant crowd of the between-decks where she lay in. And as the young soldier was literally brought into the world under a 24-pounder cannon and on board the Agincourt, I thought him deserving the name of that memorable battle, and therefore I requested he might be called Agincourt.[53]

Dyott was not called on to actually christen a baby, which was what happened to Lieutenant Browne in April 1809. The 23rd Foot had been campaigning in Martinique and was on their way back to Halifax in Canada. Browne was aboard a hospital ship, having been wounded in the arm. Conditions on board were difficult. Some of the sick were suffering from fever, and as the ship headed north the weather set in bitterly cold, with a stiff northeaster. Some of the men, their bodies emaciated with fever from a tropical climate, suffered severely, and in 11 days eight of them succumbed. Browne himself was ill and sleepless with the pain of his wounded arm, but notwithstanding his condition, when one of the regimental women gave birth, and he was called on to baptize it. 'Under pressing circumstances an Officer is permitted to act as a chaplain.'[54] The woman probably feared the baby would die from illness or the bitter weather and wanted it baptized at once.

At least neither Browne nor Dyott actually had to supervise a delivery, which is what happened to Lieutenant Charles Crowe of the 27th Foot. Crowe had been placed on half-pay at the end of the war, and in March 1817 was sailing from Ireland to Liverpool. It was a rough crossing, and at about six in the morning the mate came below shouting for a doctor. Crowe asked what the problem was. 'Och, sure, a poor creature of a woman, a soldier's wife, in the hold is taken in labour; and the divil a doctor among you to help her!!' It so happened that while waiting in Dublin, Crowe had been induced by a medical friend to attend a lecture on 'rabbit catching', which turned out to mean midwifery. 'I bethought, my lecture in Dublin, on "rabbit catching" may here, in want of better skill, be of service!' wrote Crowe. 'So I quickly huddled on what clothes I had taken off, and repaired to the hold. I found the woman lying within half a yard of the heels of three fine horses. I ordered all men, skulking below with sea-sickness on deck ... There were four soldier's wives: all mothers but not one of them knew what was necessary to be done.' Crowe placed the woman about to give birth

---

52 Glover (ed.), *The Military Adventures*, p.6.
53 Jeffery (ed.), *Diary*, vol.1, p.153.
54 Buckley (ed.), *Napoleonic War Journal*, p.111.

in a suitable position, told the others what to do and left them to it. He had scarcely finished his breakfast when a cry went up for the 'doctor'. 'On my return to my patient she pulled me down and giving me a hearty kiss, declared that I was "A jewel of a doctor!!" A fine boy was born; and everything right. When on deck Captain W. came with his wife's thanks "to the doctor" for his kindness to the woman.'[55] With the captain's assistance, Crowe managed to raise a subscription amongst the passengers to enable the woman, her new-born baby and her husband, who belonged to a recruiting party of the 49th, to travel from Liverpool by coach to Birmingham, instead of having to march.

It is not surprising that child-birth in the brutal conditions on board a ship could sometimes end in tragedy. A young midshipman aboard a troop-carrying East Indiaman later recalled one. During a violent storm one of the women gave birth, but the child only survived a day or two. The ship's carpenter made a tiny coffin, and the little body was committed to the sea with due ceremony, slid from under the union flag. But despite the weights placed inside, the coffin sank and then floated to the surface, before finally disappearing, to the great distress of the mother, who herself died shortly afterwards.[56] On 21 October 1813 a contingent of the 68th embarked at Portsmouth bound for Ireland, amongst them the severely wounded Private Green. The ship was crowded with about 200 troops and 30 or so women, with as many children. Having deposited some men at Cork, the vessel sailed north towards Carlingford and was hit by a violent storm. On the second night of the storm a small boy belonging to one of the women of Green's regiment told someone that his mother 'had got a baby during the night.' This was strange since nobody knew she was pregnant, and she had not seen her husband for the best part of four years. Some of the other wives went to investigate, and found that the woman had indeed managed to give birth in the night, but that she had stifled the baby. Green thought her intention was to throw the little body into the sea, so that her husband, who was expected to join the regiment in Belfast in a few days, would never know. This provoked a storm of indignation on board. Some people, perhaps remembering the story of Jonah, wanted to throw her overboard, to calm the storm. 'I verily believe the captain himself did not know what to do with the poor wretched woman' thought Green, but 'in a few days, however, she died, and was buried in the deep.'[57] The baby was presumably buried with her, but Private Green did not say.

Sometimes voyages could have a lighter and more humane side. Occasionally it seems, women were allowed to transfer from ship to ship in mid-ocean. In April 1813, the same Private Green was returning wounded from the Peninsula, and saw such an incident. The Bay of Biscay was for once relatively calm and the weather clear and serene. There was a woman on board Green's ship whose husband was on one of the other vessels in the convoy, which lay-to in order to take her aboard. 'The woman descended into the boat, and was rowed over the mighty swells of the Bay of Biscay to her husband's vessel. I don't know indeed that there was any particular danger in this, but it was terrifying to see a little boat

---

55 Glover (ed.), *Eloquent Soldier*, p.317.
56 'Flexible Grummet', 'Leaves', p.487. He gives no date for this incident, but it must have been between 1799 and 1804 because he says that Bonaparte was First Consul.
57 Green, *The Vicissitudes of a Soldier's Life*, p.213.

tossed on the mighty surges of this bay.'[58] The woman was not an officer's lady, and one wonders at this act of kindness involving two naval vessels.

There was also sometimes music and dancing. Private Gunn of the 42nd recalled the men and women of the regiment dancing reels on deck in calm weather on passage from Gibraltar to Portugal presumably to the sound of the pipes.[59] This must have had great social and physical benefits to men and women crammed on board a ship for prolonged periods. Henry Browne's diary twice records soldiers and their wives dancing on board in mid ocean. Soon after the collision recorded above, the transports carrying the 23rd were becalmed off the Azores. Browne and some other officers rowed over to the *Lord Collingwood* which was the headquarters ship, carrying the regimental band. The other vessels in company got as close as they could, 'when the band began to play country dances, and the soldiers with such women as were embarked, danced till past midnight.' This was in March 1808. When the wind picked up the ships had to separate, but this little scene was repeated whenever the opportunity arose. An interesting sight it was, thought Browne, to see 'British soldiers dancing to their native tunes, on the bosom of the deep, in such latitudes.'[60] Interestingly enough it was also on a long passage to Halifax that Sir Edward Packenham, commanding the 64th, was enabled to enjoy a little musical entertainment. One of the officers had his wife and sister on board the *Coverdale* transport, and one of these ladies liked to 'open the day by a tune on the lute, which stole on our waking senses through the chinks in the little cabin I stowed them in.'[61] *Nobody coming to marry me* was a favourite, and it helped to pass the long and tedious voyage, with limited company and very little space, no end. Browne's regiment, having made Nova Scotia, was ordered south, to Martinique, and on Christmas Day 1808, Browne, who was something of a musician himself, recorded another rare and pleasant moment of relaxation:

> We passed our Christmas day with cabin windows open, and only one sheet for a covering at night, finding the heat so oppressively great. The weather was beautifully clear, and the Sea a fine calm. In the evening we assembled the men, and such few of their wives as were on board on deck, we played Flutes for them, and they danced and sang till late at night.[62]

Rare moments of peace and calm, these, for men and women alike before landfall, and the realities of warfare which lay ahead.

---

58 Green, *The Vicissitudes of a Soldier's Life*, p.203.
59 Roy, 'Memoirs', p.93.
60 Buckley (ed.), *Napoleonic War Journal*, p.74.
61 Longford (ed.), *Packenham*, p.13.
62 Buckley (ed.), *Napoleonic War Journal*, p.74.

4

On the March

Spent with want, fatigue and anguish,
On th' ungrateful land of Spain,
See a British mother languish!
See her perish on the plain![1]

On the morning of 28 August 1808, August Schaumann, a young and newly appointed commissary, was aboard one of a fleet of transports which had dropped anchor off Maceira Bay on the Portuguese coast. He was nervous, as well he might have been; this was going to be a beach landing. Troops, guns, cavalry horses, stores, everything, was about to be loaded into ships' boats and run in through the Atlantic breakers, and the surf was getting higher all the time. The men were crammed into the boats with their muskets and packs with little room to move, as were their wives. As the boats neared the beach they were picked up by the breakers, and where the sailors failed to keep them head-on, many turned broadside and capsized, spilling men and women into the water. Other sailors, many of them quite naked, were engaged in dashing into the waves to haul these unfortunates onto dry land. At least 60 men were drowned, and possibly some of the women; their skirts would have made struggling in the water almost impossible. Almost everyone must have been soaked. The scene on the beach was chaotic, with guns, waggons, piles of barrels of rum, ship's biscuit, and meat piling up, and out-of-control horses galloping all over the place. But 'Soon a number of fires flared, and various groups formed round them, all pressing towards the flames to warm themselves. There were soldiers, sailors and women amongst them.'[2] No doubt they too had removed much of their wet clothing. There were already Portuguese peasants, turning up with all manner of provisions for sale. Another eye-witness to the scene was Sir Richard Henegan, the commissary we met on the voyage out. He too noticed the women: 'Here and there groups of soldier's wives, with canteens and haversacks slung across their shoulders some wrangling about the payment for the articles they had purchased; others indulging in copious libations of wine, to celebrate their recent escape from the water.'[3] At least they had

---

[1] *On a late noble action* by 'An Orphan', in *The Gentleman's Magazine,* March 1810, p.255
[2] August Schaumann, *On the Road with Wellington. The Diary of a war commissary in the Peninsular Campaigns* (London: Heinemann, 1824), p.1.
[3] Henegan, *Seven Years*, vol.1, p.16.

The landing of the British Army at Figueria da Foz in early August 1808. A number of women and children can be seen amongst the troops. Engraving after Henri Leveque, 1812. (Anne S.K. Brown Military Collection, Brown University)

not had to land in the face of enemy fire, which was what had happened in Egypt in March 1801, when Abercromby's force struggled ashore in Aboukir Bay.

This was very early on in the Peninsular War. Later most British ships deposited their loads in the wide mouth of the Tagus, where Lisbon rose from the water in a wide amphitheatre of white buildings and exotic greenery under the southern sun. It was a spectacle which enchanted most eyewitnesses, but which was soon belied by the insanitary squalor of the streets. Here personnel and equipment could be discharged in less stressful conditions, either at a quayside or by ferry. Not that a harbour always made things straight forward. Near the end of the war, when Captain Mercer of G Troop, Royal Horse Artillery arrived at Ostend at the start of the Waterloo campaign, his transport ran onto the sand next to a quay on a falling tide, so that the ship grounded. A Royal Navy captain and a group of sailors at once swarmed on board and began unloading horses, saddlery and everything else straight overboard, despite protests. Wellington's orders brooked no delay they said; ships were to be unloaded instantly and sent back again. There was chaos on the sand with horses galloping about, dragoons and horse-artillery men trying to catch them, while others struggled to drag equipment and personal possessions up the beach to drier sand. In the midst of all this, disconsolate-looking groups of women and children were to be seen sitting about here and there, or roaming about in search of their husbands and fathers. Things were not much better the following day, and Mercer noted the local boatmen, lounging about with little to do 'amusing themselves with the bustling anxiety of a score of soldiers' wives, who, loaded with children or bundles, their ample grey or faded red cloaks flying out loosely behind them, struggled through all impediments opposed to their progress with an activity, perseverance, and volubility which seemed highly diverting to the mariners.[4]

However the women arrived at the seat of war, and whatever discomforts they may have endured in the process, one thing was certain: the life they now faced would involve the hardships of an immense amount of marching, especially in Spain and Portugal. What with great advances and long retreats and manoeuvres of every sort, the army covered literally thousands of miles. And for almost everyone except the cavalry and the horse artillery, that meant walking. The infantrymen were loaded down with muskets and bayonets, packs, ammunition and personal equipment. The women, until they were able to acquire a donkey or a mule, tramped along bearing their few worldly goods, and in some cases, their children. Across great plains, through mountains, over bridgeless rivers, in the blazing heats of summer, in torrential rain and the snow and ice of winter, the long columns endlessly trudged.

The army had official procedures governing the movements of battalions, brigades or divisions, designed to ensure regularity and order, and to make the movement of large bodies of troops as efficient as possible. The Quartermaster General would issue the Commander-in-Chief's orders to the generals commanding divisions, and then through the Assistant Quartermaster Generals to the generals commanding brigades, and then by way of the brigade majors to the individual battalions or regiments. At the specified time, usually well before dawn, the troops would be roused by the drums and bugles. The men, normally already in uniform, would roll their blankets, stow their personal kit, put on their packs and accoutrements, collect their firelocks, and parade by companies in a very short time. Once the battalion was assembled, it would march to the regimental alarm-post, and thence, formed in close columns, to the brigade assembly point, baggage packed and loaded. The artillery units would parade their guns, the commissariat mules would be drawn up with reserves of biscuit, together with the mules or bullocks carrying the reserve ammunition. If necessary, guides would be allocated to each division by the Assistant Quartermaster General. Once the brigade majors had reported to the Assistant Adjutant General that all their battalions were present and correct, the advanced guard, consisting of a single company directed by the senior brigade major would be ordered 'By section of threes, march', and battalion by battalion, brigade by brigade, the division would move off, arms sloped. Once the long column was properly in motion, the order would be given to 'March at ease.'[5]

Although it was certainly the case that women sometimes marched with the men, often helping with their loads or carrying their muskets, the proper place for the women and children was in the rear of the column, with the baggage. Behind them marched the Assistant Provost Marshal and his guard, a sort of military police force, and finally the rear guard under the command of an officer whose responsibility it was to take up men who had straggled from the column and return them to their units. After about half an hour the first halt would be called, and thereafter the column would halt once an hour. The men would pile

---

4   Mercer, *Journal*, pp.8–15.
5   C. Oman, *Wellington's Army* (London: Arnold, 1913), p.257.

arms and if there was time remove their packs and lay down, though this might depend on the weather and the urgency of the advance. These breaks also allowed men who had fallen out time to rejoin their companies, and perhaps to eat a piece of bread or meat set aside for the march. Then packs would be hoisted back on, canteens and all the rest of the infantryman's load adjusted for as much comfort as possible. The bugles and drums would sound, the ranks would fall in, and the column, women and children included, would slog on its way as before, sometimes to a tune from the regimental band.[6] Fifteen miles a day was probably a fair average in normal conditions; much more and it would have been difficult for the commissariat to keep up with supplies.

It seems unlikely that marches were always conducted exactly this way. For a start, there was a great deal of it. In October 1808, before Sir John Moore's army advanced into Spain, every effort was made to dissuade the women from accompanying it. It was pointed out that they were faced with a march of 600 miles, and that there would be no baggage carts to carry any of their possessions. In any case, even for officers equipped with local maps, it was difficult to estimate distances travelled with any accuracy, and very few seem to have tried. One who did was Captain Bowles of the Coldstream Guards. Writing to Lord Fitzharris in England from Portugal in December 1812, he estimated that during the campaigning of that year he had marched 1,700 miles, and that he had lost six mules in the process, all but one actually dropping dead.[7] Lieutenant John Carss of the 2/53rd, writing from Talavera in July 1809, told his family that the column had just covered upwards of 800 miles, during which time he had not slept under a roof.[8] The women and their children had to keep up. Henry Mackinnon, another Guards officer, sometimes attempted to compute the daily distance covered in this campaign. 'I calculate the distance at 10 miles' Another day he thought it was 27 miles. But he soon lapsed in the easier routine of noting the time spent on the march. '12 hours' march … 11 hours, bad road … pursue the French for 12 hours.' It was not always like this of course. Sometimes the day's route took only four or five hours; it all depended on the tactical situation.[9] In December 1812, Private Wheeler, who must have been keeping a diary, gave a detailed break-down of his movements in a letter home. Since the opening of the year's manoeuvrings in January, he reckoned he had walked the length of Portugal three times, advanced as far into Spain as Madrid and had taken part in the great retreat from there and Salamanca. 'The number of miles marched over this time, if averaged at eight miles per diem, 2328. This is not overrating it.'[10] The regimental women would no doubt have agreed, had they been keeping a record. After the Battle of Vitoria, and by the time the army had made the great final advance from Portugal to the Pyrenees in 1813, George Woodberry sat down to calculate the distance the 18th Hussars had covered since leaving Lisbon. 'I find it as follows' he

---

6 Anon., *Twelve Years' Military Adventures in Three Quarters of the Globe, or, Memoirs of an Officer* (London: Colburn, 1829), vol.2, p.176.
7 Malmesbury (ed.), *Letters*, vol.2, p.332.
8 S. Johnson, 'The Letters of Lieutenant John Carss 2/53rd', *Journal of the Society for Army Historical Research*, vol.26, 1948, pp.2–17.
9 H. Mackinnon, *A Journal of the Campaign in Portugal and Spain from the year 1809 to 1812* (Bath: Duffield, 1812), p.15.
10 Liddell Hart (ed.), *Letters*, p.103.

Cartoon by Thomas Rowlandson, 1798. A detachment of troops have commandeered several carriages. One woman is riding on a waggon, another is running after a cart. Aquatint by Ackermann.
(Anne S.K. Brown Military Collection, Brown University)

noted in his diary on 7 July, 'marched fifty-six days, two hundred and twenty-two leagues; in English miles, about nine hundred.'[11] As a cavalryman, he had of course ridden. The women, like the infantry, had marched.

Even in Britain marches could be a punishing experience. In December 1803, the 53rd Foot were based in the barracks at Sunderland. At midnight on the 23rd an order arrived directing the regiment to march to Carlisle on the way to embark for Ireland. Two companies were to move at 8:00 a.m. the following day, the remainder to march on Christmas morning. Captain Sherwood's company was to start on the 26th. At 8:00 a.m. the Monday morning, Mrs Sherwood, newly married, began her first journey with the regiment, but as an officer's wife she was not obliged to march on foot. With some of their furniture piled on a cart, Mrs Sherwood and the surgeon's wife rode ahead in a post chaise. This was lucky. For Sherwood's men it was a miserable business. They had to slog through half-melted snow and fog, followed by heavy rain. The regiment had recently returned from the West Indies, and the men were not acclimatised to an English winter. Nor was their march discipline up to scratch. Mrs Sherwood noted in her diary that by the next day, almost the whole route was covered with scattered parties of the 53rd, and this included both the regimental wives and

---

11   Glover and York (eds), *With Wellington's Hussars*, p.143.

officers' ladies stranded in various public and private carriages.[12] Even in decent weather movements within the country could be trying. In 1811, George Bell, as a newly-joined ensign in the 34th, had to march with a party from Beverly in Yorkshire to Portsmouth to embark for the Peninsula. It took them 22 days. 'The marches were long at times' wrote Bell, who was not yet the hardened campaigner he became, 'and many a day I almost dropped footsore and weary.'[13] It was the same for the women of course.

Sometimes, when no great exertions were called for, conditions could seem quite pleasant. 'Our Marches have hither to been very comfortable' wrote Lieutenant Le Mesurier optimistically in September 1811. 'We start at about 5 o'clock in the Morning after having taken a light Breakfast. We get into our Quarters about 9 or 10 and have the whole day before us.' Since he had to get up at about 3:00 a.m., he added that he usually took a nap in the afternoon to compensate. Marching in the early hours was a normal practice during the summer in order to avoid the heat of the day. By the following June however, he had changed his tune: '…we arrived on the 15th almost knocked up. We left an immense number of Men behind… We marched at a rate of 5 leagues a day. We started at Day Break and did not once get in till sun Set.'[14] No doubt many of the women were also straggling.

The normal, or at least planned, routine of marching was sometimes interrupted by emergencies which required an unexpected night march, always a difficult business. Major Frazer, commanding the Royal Horse Artillery described one such in May 1813 during the advance from Salamanca to Toro. Everyone who could do so had settled down for the night when Colonel Ponsonby of the 12th Light Dragoons galloped into the camp with orders to march immediately. Frazer described the chaotic scenes as thousands of men moved about in the darkness as the battalions assembled. It was, he said, a scene more easily imagined than described, but being Augustus Frazer, he especially noted the distress of many frightened children, and their mothers, many of them with babies too young to walk.[15]

The tactical situation sometimes also called for the troops to make forced marches, and on some occasions women were left behind. In September 1810, the French having taken Ciudad Rodrigo and Almeida, and with *Maréchal* Massena reported to be advancing in strength, the 29th Foot were ordered to march to join Wellington as a matter of urgency. 'In order that there might be no hindrance on the road, all the sick, and even the weakly men, with the women and children were ordered to remain behind' wrote Lieutenant Leslie. An officer was to be appointed to take charge of them and conduct them to a depot at Thomar. This task fell to Leslie himself as he was himself in poor health, with fits of fever and ague. Having assembled his company, Leslie found that it amounted to 150 of all ranks, 'the sick, the lame, the lazy, besides 50 women and 40 children.'[16] He managed to commandeer some mules the carry the worst cases and the equipment of those who could barely walk, and got

---

12 Kelly (ed.), *Life*, p.251.
13 B. Stuart (ed.), *Soldier's Glory being Rough Notes of an Old Soldier by Major-General Sir George Bell* (London: Bell, 1956), p.3.
14 Greenwood (ed.), *Letters*, p.76.
15 S. Sabine (ed.), *Letters of Sir Augustus Frazer, KCB., Commanding the Royal Horse Artillery under Wellington, Written during the Peninsular and Waterloo Campaigns* (London: Longmans, 1859), p.130.
16 Leslie, *Military Journal*, p.206.

his raggle-taggle column to the depot. The men were given empty houses, and the women and children were accommodated in with the nuns in one wing of their convent.

Marching conditions were made much more arduous by extremes of weather. In summer, heat was the problem. It was by no means unknown for men to die from heat exhaustion. Captain Leach remembered three men of the 52nd dying from heat stroke and thirst on the march from Santarem to Castelo Branco in the summer of 1809.[17] Under such conditions, remembered an anonymous British officer attached to one of the Portuguese battalions, the role of a company officer could be like that of a slave-driver. Heavily burdened men would collapse in the heat or were pronounced unable to go on by the surgeon. On the advance to Vitoria in 1813 he sometimes had to dismount and load his horse with the packs or muskets of men who were unable to stand the pace.[18] The women were not carrying the loads born by the infantrymen, but heatstroke was a danger for them as well. Winter weather could pose different but equally arduous conditions. Major General Mackinnon recorded the frightful conditions in January 1812 when he marched his brigade (45th, 74th and 88th) from Aldea de Ponte in Portugal to Robledo in Spain to take part in the final siege of Ciudad Rodrigo, in which he was blown up, his diary coming to an abrupt end. The distance was 26 miles, a particularly long march, through forests of oak. The snow in many places was knee-deep, and continued to fall during the day. The brigade left at 9:00 a.m. and the head of the column did not struggle into Robledo until after dark; the rear-guard got in at midnight. Between 300–400 stragglers had been left behind. Two soldiers died on the march and several later of fatigue. What happened to the women and children, Mackinnon did not say, though it is not difficult to imagine.[19]

Stragglers often included the women, and sometimes it was necessary to detail an officer and a party of men to collect them up. As the army advanced through the broken country of the Pyrenees in the closing phase of the war, an anonymous officer was detached to perform this unwanted task. He and his party were left behind all night in a forest to collect up any baggage and stragglers who had lost touch with the main column. At daylight, he found a group of women who had become benighted in the forest and who were frightened of trying to advance along the edge of steep drops. This was no idle fear; it was not unknown even for mules, sure-footed as they were, to slip over the edge and be killed far below, and their loads lost. They were making a lot of noise, to keep up their spirits perhaps, and with their weather-beaten clothes and faces they presented what the officer thought was an amusing scene 'as they drove along their lazy *borricas* with a thick stick; and when the terrific blows laid on ceased to produce the desired effect, they squalled with sheer vexation lest they might be overtaken by the enemy's light horse.'[20]

It was quite frequently the case that marching involved not advancing, but retreating. This was the case in the Low Countries during the unhappy campaign in 1795. In January that year, the army was falling back in arctic conditions likely to cause as many casualties as a battle. 'The frost was so intense, that the water which came from our eyes, freezing as it fell, hung in icicles to our eyelashes, and our breath freezing as soon as emitted, lodged in heaps

---

17 J. Leach, *Rough Notes of the Life of an Old Soldier* (London: Longman, 1831), p.78.
18 Anon., *Twelve Year's*, vol.2, p.185.
19 Mackinnon, *A Journal*, p.98.
20 Maxwell, *Peninsular Sketches*, vol.2, p.88.

about our faces' wrote one surviving officer. Men and women began to straggle, unable to keep up, but once the column vanished into the darkness and snow, they lost touch. Anyone who did so was liable to sink into exhausted sleep, never to wake up. Soon the route was littered with the bodies of men, women and children, all frozen to death. When the column managed to reach a halting place, waggons were sent back to search for stragglers. 'In one place seven men, one woman, and a child were found dead; in another, a man, a woman, and two children; in another, a man, a woman, and one child, and an unhappy woman being taken in labour, she, with her husband and infant were all lifeless.'[21] An officer of the Guards brigade described in stark detail a sight he witnessed on 17 January:

> Near a cart … we perceived a stout looking man and a hearty young woman, with an infant about seven months old at the breast, all three frozen and dead. The mother had most certainly expired in the act of suckling her child, as with one breast exposed, she lay upon the drifted snow, the milk, to all appearance, in a stream drawn from the nipple by the babe, and instantly congealed, the infant seemed as if its lips had but just then been disengaged, and it reposed its little head upon the mother's bosom, with an overflow of milk frozen as it trickled from the mouth; their countenances were perfectly composed and fresh, resembling those of persons in a sound and tranquil slumber.[22]

During the war in the Peninsula retreats were often forced on the British army through a combination of circumstances. Sir John Moore's campaign to assist the Spanish in the autumn of 1808 with a force of some 30,000 men ground to a halt because of the defeats the Spanish had suffered, and the fact that Napoleon himself arrived in the country with four times the number of troops. Moore was forced to retreat towards Corunna in terrible winter conditions, with dreadful results for the army including the women and children. After Wellington returned to command the army, he too was forced to retreat on several occasions. The problem essentially was one of numbers. In 1810 for instance, two years after the war had begun, the French had approximately 325,000 men in Spain divided into different armies under various *maréchaux*. What Wellington had to do with about 25,000 British troops and roughly the same number of Portuguese, was to defeat these French generals in detail, while manoeuvring in such a way as to prevent the French from managing to combine and crush him between them. Just such an occasion occurred in the autumn of 1812. Wellington had advanced to occupy Madrid, and leaving Lieutenant General Hill in command, had pushed further north to besiege Burgos. He was confronted by overwhelming numbers of the French, advancing from two directions under King Joseph and three of Napoleon's *maréchaux*, and forced into a difficult retreat from both Madrid and Burgos on Salamanca and then Ciudad Rodrigo. Conditions were appalling. It was bitterly cold. Heavy rain fell and the icy streams became swollen, so that men and women had to ford them and then live in sodden clothes. The ground turned to mud, so that the wheels

---

21 R. Browne, *An Impartial Journal of a Detachment From the Brigade of Foot Guards commencing 25th February, 1793, and ending 9th May 1795* (London: Stockdale, 1795), p.220.
22 L. Jones, *An Historical Journal of the British Campaign on the Continent in the Year 1794 with the Retreat Through Holland* (London: Swinney & Hawkins, 1797), p.174.

of waggons and gun carriages sank up to the naves. 'The men were so worn out, with long marches, lack of rest, sleep and adequate food' recalled Captain Ross-Lewin. 'Some sinking under the weight of their accoutrements, actually sank into the mud, and were smothered.'[23] At one place he saw the wife of one of the Portuguese soldiers lying dead with a baby at her breast, vainly trying to suckle a little milk. Men and women who had not the strength to keep up were in danger of being overtaken by the French, who were in close pursuit. Many were taken prisoner. Captain Thomas Dyneley, commanding E Troop of the Royal Horse Artillery later wrote to his sister describing the scene after the retreat was over: '…the enemy were pushing us hard the whole way and … I saw some hundreds of men, women and children stuck in the mud, and unable to move from hunger and sickness.'[24] The wounded especially, begged to be allowed to ride on the gun carriages, but Dyneley was obliged to refuse their pleas; the battery horses were badly underfed and in poor condition, and could barely drag the guns, which were themselves often deep in the mud.

It was next to impossible to kindle a fire, either to dry out or to cook, and in any case the commissariat had broken down and many of the troops had little or no food to cook. At one point in an oak forest there was a plentiful supply of acorns, and many men were reduced to eating these. 'Providence, by affording us a supply of acorns, had not altogether abandoned us to despair' as the assistant surgeon of the 1st (Royal) Dragoons put it, and the horses ate them as well.[25] There was nowhere dry to snatch a little sleep. One expedient, since to lie down in the rain and mud was impossible, was to place a round canteen on the ground and a knapsack on top of that, and to try to doze in a sitting position. Women in long skirts would have been in an even worse state than the troops.

Relatively few officers took their wives to the wars, but there were those who did. Augustus Frazer, writing to his own wife at home in May 1813, while the army was advancing towards Vitoria, bemoaned the fact that two officers of the artillery were accompanied by their wives. 'What will these ladies do?' he wondered. 'I cannot conceive a situation more uncomfortable than that of women following an army. I fear they will find neither the reality nor even the appearance of civility from anyone: all are occupied with their own business and their own comforts.'[26] Frazer was always observant of the condition of the women, but although he was certainly right about the hardships officers' wives might have to endure, there were in fact soldiers who were prepared to do more than give an 'appearance of civility.' An officer of the Staff Corps Cavalry named Buckham, writing, like Thomas Dyneley, after the retreat was over, described how one night a soldier came to him to report that a lady had arrived and wished to speak to him. The rain was coming down in torrents and in the darkness Buckham found a lady on horseback, with another on a mule with a baby in her arms, and a bat-man leading a baggage mule. The lady, apologising, said that she was the wife of one of the staff surgeons. Her little party had been travelling since daybreak, expecting her husband to overtake them, and they were now quite lost. They were all wet through and had eaten nothing but a biscuit all day. Buckham got then into his billet, and his servant managed to

---

23 Wardell (ed.), *With the Thirty Second*, p.207.
24 F.A. Whinyates (ed.), *Letters Written by Lieutenant-General Thomas Dyneley C.B., R.A., while on Active Service Between the Years 1806 and 1815* (London: Royal Artillery Institution, 1896), p.57.
25 G. Burroughs, *A Narrative of the Retreat of the British Army from Burgos* (Bristol: Egerton, 1814), p.62.
26 Sabine (ed.), *Letters*, p.106.

get a fire going – no mean feat – and gave them some food. They also found some goat's milk and bread for the baby. Buckham then persuaded a corporal and four men who were on duty to give the ladies the shelter and fire they had managed to secure, in exchange for a canteen of rum 'to assist them in wearing away the night in an adjoining shed.'[27]

The situation of those women who could not keep up became desperate as the rear-guard tried to hold off the French, who were hard on their tail and picking off any men who fell out and other stragglers. 'We had not moved thus two miles, until the French advance guard came down upon us,' wrote an anonymous soldier of the 71st. 'picking up every individual who fell out. The cries of the women and children were dreadful, as we left them. We were retiring in square, playing a howitzer from the centre to keep their cavalry back.'[28] It seems likely that some of the women and children and other stragglers were hit by the howitzer fire as well as the French horsemen. At least this was an impersonal experience, which was not the case with Edward Costello of the 1/95th. His company of riflemen were ordered to cover the retreat, and they were hotly engaged in skirmishing. Costello was about to take cover behind a tree when he saw a woman fallen at the foot of it. She was unable to keep up with her regiment, and had collapsed, exhausted. The woman seized Costello's hand, and begged him to help her. But the enemy's balls were striking the tree, which only partially screened them. Then the 'assembly' sounded, and he was forced to leave her to her fate.[29]

At the end of the retreat, when the army reached Ciudad Rodrigo, some waggons were sent back to pick up stragglers. One officer charged with this duty was Thomas Browne of the 23rd, ordered to do so by Wellington himself. Browne made his way back along the route towards Salamanca and reached a village called Spirito Santo.

> As the sun broke out, I never can forget the sight of horrors that was exposed to my view. Groupes of women and children and drum boys lay perishing with cold – some had already died in a sort of rolled up posture – others were not yet dead, but convulsed with a sort of hysterical laugh which sometimes precedes death.[30]

They were laying about in the bushes at the side of the road, together with soldiers, brave men, thought Browne, who would have faced any danger, but who had perished from hunger and fatigue. Browne's men collected many of them up, placed them in the waggons and administered what food and drink they could in an effort to revive them.

Sometimes wives seem to have been able to march with the men, often sharing the infantryman's load, and there were instances, when the route was known in advance, of parties of women managing to get ahead of the column despite the best efforts of the provost marshals. As we have seen, the appointed place was in the rear, with the baggage. To begin with they had to walk, like the infantry, but as the war went on, most managed to acquire a donkey or occasionally a mule which could either be ridden or used to carry their personal possessions. They must often have traded for a donkey with the Spanish, but the aftermath of a

---

27 E. Buckham, *Personal Narrative of Adventures in the Peninsula During the War in 1812–1813* (London: Murray, 1827), p.77.
28 C. Hibbert (ed.), *A Soldier of the Seventy First* (London: Leo Cooper, 1975), p.78.
29 Edward Costello, *The Adventures of a Soldier* (London: Colburn, 1841), p.159.
30 Buckley (ed.), *Napoleonic War Journal*, p.197.

battle was a good time to acquire an animal from the baggage-train of the defeated French. After the Battle of Salamanca for instance, there were many horses, mules and donkeys, not to mention bullocks, sheep and goats wandering about, abandoned by the retreating French, '…so our women, who were not provided with beasts to carry their lumber, were furnished now, if they had address enough to catch the horses and mules.'[31] Not that possessing an animal was trouble-free. There were a lot of them, and together with the commissariat mules frequently set up such a noise at night as to disturb the entire encampment. They also led to disputes, and as one soldier put it, 'dangerous rows took place between the belligerent parties to the no small amusement of our wearied frames.'[32]

These animals became prized possessions, and the loss of an animal was a major catastrophe, especially when it was carrying a woman's spare clothing, cooking equipment or food. This was well illustrated by a minor incident in the Pyrenees in 1814, when the French had fallen back near Bayonne. A corporal in the band of the 94th came across a woman belonging to the 88th, the Connaught Rangers, trying to drag her donkey, which was carrying 'her necessaries' out of a hole it had fallen into. It was getting dark, the baggage had passed, and the woman begged for help. They managed to get the animal out, but found themselves in the dark and unable to find their regiments. There were fires in the hills, but were they British or French? The donkey kept collapsing with fatigue, and the corporal was swearing that he would never stop to help a woman again. The woman, however, was made of stern stuff, and volunteered to creep up the hill towards the nearest fires and to listen to see what language was being spoken. She was in luck. There were Portuguese, and they came to assist her to get her baggage, and the donkey, which was now almost dead with exhaustion, into their camp.[33]

Cavalry wives seem sometimes to have managed to mount themselves on spare troop horses. In the chaos following the Battle of Vitoria, William Surtees of the 95th was 'accosted by five or six soldiers' wives, belonging to one of our light cavalry regiments, who wished to accompany me, in order that they might find their husbands … and as they were all mounted, away we posted'[34] Presumably they were all riding astride, in cavalry saddles.

Occasionally women managed to ride on the baggage waggons, perched high on top of the pile. This was not without its dangers when they were overloaded, even in the apparent safety of England. In June 1801 for instance, one of the waggons belonging to the Royal Horse Guards overturned on a hill near Wellingborough, killing one of the women riding on top and injuring two others.[35] Looking at the contemporary prints such as William Pyne's 1803 series of *Camp Scenes* depicting just such situations, it is not hard to see why. Women riding on baggage waggons could slow the progress of a column, and became the subject of army orders. In July 1810, in Spain, when some divisions seem to have ordered their women to leave, the Adjutant General issued an order stating that while the Commander-in-Chief

---

31 Anon., *Personal Narrative of a Private Soldier who served in the Forty-Second Highlanders for Twelve Years, during the Late Wars* (London: Allman, 1821), p.136.
32 S. Monick (ed.), *Douglas's Tale of the Peninsula and Waterloo by John Douglas, former Sergeant, 1st Royal Scots* (London: Leo Cooper, 1997), p.19.
33 Donaldson, *Recollections*, p.218.
34 Surtees, *Twenty Five Years*, p.210.
35 Haythornthwaite, *The Armies*, p.122.

Watercolour by Thomas Rowlandson, 1800. Cavalry troops escort a baggage waggon with a woman perched on top. Not always a safe ride. (Anne S.K. Brown Military Collection, Brown University)

had no objection either to the women choosing to go to the rear or remaining with their regiments, 'it must be clearly explained to them that they will not be allowed to go in cars [waggons] if they stay with their regiments, but they must keep with the baggage of their several corps if they remain with them.'[36]

After Waterloo, Wellington became concerned about 'the greatest irregularity among the baggage and women … put upon the carts destined to carry tents and hospital stores.' This was holding them up, and General Order No. 6 was issued on 25 June prohibiting it. For good measure officers were informed that if they put private baggage onto these carts and waggons, it would be burnt and the officer concerned brought before a court martial. And just to make sure that this was clearly understood, General Order No. 7 was issued shortly after stating simply: 'The women must not be allowed to get upon the public carts.'[37] This was also to apply to the forge waggons of the cavalry regiments, many of which had broken down. Nothing was to be carried on them except the appropriate tools and equipment. But as the advance on Paris began, there was a problem for Lieutenant George Blathwayt of the 23rd Light Dragoons. He was in charge of the baggage guard, and a sergeant came to him to report that one of the farrier's wives had just gone into labour. What should be done about it? It was a very serious matter indeed to ignore one of Wellington's orders, but Blathwayt decided he had to. 'I said we must risk it, make her a bed with some straw on the forge

---

36   2nd Duke of Wellington (ed.), *Field Marshal Arthur Duke of Wellington Supplementary Despatches, Correspondence and Memoranda* (London: Murray, 1858–1872), vol.XII, p.428.

37   Cheshire Archive and Local Studies: DTM 72: Tomkinson Family of Willington Hall papers, 16th Light Dragoons Regimental Order Book April – August 1815.

wagon and cover the woman and child with some blankets.' Someone got wind of this, and Blathwayt was soon sent for by Lord Hill, commanding II Corps. Had the lieutenant read the General Orders? Blathwayt said he had, but explained the situation. The general, to his eternal credit, replied 'Sir I think you have done quite right although I cannot tell you so.' He then pulled out a handful of silver and said 'Will you have the goodness to take charge of this for the poor woman and if you are stopped again say Lord Hill has passed you.'[38] From then on, Hill's name overcame all obstacles, and the woman and her child were able to ride in the waggon for many days. It was human touches like this which caused the troops called him 'Daddy Hill.'

The baggage-train of a brigade was quite a sight to see, and that of a division even more so, probably occupying a line of at least a mile. Regimental order books contain frequent references to the officer appointed for a day's baggage guard; it must have been an unpopular duty. One officer wrote to his wife that the sight reminded him of Abraham and Lot, there being 'much people and much cattle.'[39] And indeed there probably was something Biblical about such a spectacle. There were the muleteers with long strings of commissariat mules loaded with bags of biscuit, barrels of rum, and the reserve ammunition, and in the later stages of the war, company tents; there were the Spanish ox carts with their solid axles squealing in protest every step of the painful way; herds of bullocks to provide beef on the hoof; occasionally an officer's milk goat, and sutlers and purveyors of all sorts of goods. Swarms of Spanish and Portuguese women had attached themselves to the troops as camp followers and there were local boys who were acting as officers' servants. Some of the British soldiers' wives also picked up boys to assist them, orphans of the war perhaps.[40]

It was important for women to stick with the baggage. To get left behind when the column moved on could involve all sorts of difficulties and dangers. This could happen to quite senior figures. Francis Larpent, Wellington's Judge Advocate General, had struck up a friendship with Colonel and Mrs Scovell at the headquarters at Frenada over the winter of 1812–1813. He met them again during the confused fighting around Maya in the Pyrenees in August 1813, when the three of them ascended a hill in order to view the besieged town of Pamplona. At 5:00 a.m. on the 28th, Larpent began to load his mule ready to move on with Hill's division. But there was a mix-up of some kind, and Larpent found himself alone with Mrs Scovell, the division having disappeared. Larpent and Mrs Scovell therefore set off over the mountains hoping to catch up. At first, they were on the right track, but they got into a wood, took the wrong path and found themselves in the wrong valley. Somehow, they became separated from their baggage, and managed to reach headquarters without it, very late and embarrassed by the fact that the baggage had arrived before them.[41] Mrs Scovell was lucky to have been in company with a British officer.

---

38 George Blathwayt, 'Account of Lieutenant George Blathwayt 23rd Light Dragoons', in Glover (ed.), *Waterloo Archive*, vol.3, p.74.
39 C. Atkinson, 'Letters of Major-General Sir F.P. Robinson', *Journal of the Society for Army Historical Research*, vol.34, 1956, p.153.
40 William Tomkinson, *The Diary of a Cavalry Officer* (London: Macmillan 1894), p.77.
41 G. Larpent (ed.), *The Private Journal of Judge Advocate Larpent attached to the Head-Quarters of Lord Wellington during the Peninsular War from 1812 to its close* (London: Bentley, 1854), p.206.

This was not the only occasion when Larpent experienced difficulties with the baggage train. Writing at the headquarters at St Fé on 12 November 1813, he described how an order had been issued the previous morning for the baggage to assemble prior to the advance which was to take the army to the river Nive. The weather was appalling, wet, and not much above freezing. Forage had been in short supply, with the result that 'So starved and weak were many of the animals, and so clayey and deep the road, that the scene had almost the appearance of a retreat.' This was made more so as they passed through the old French positions where the wounded still lay and the dead had been stripped. Many of the commissariat oxen were so weak that they collapsed. 'Then there were ten or fifteen poor women belonging to the baggage of the division lamenting over their dying donkeys and mules, whilst others were brutally beating some to death, because they would go no further.'[42] Baggage was falling off in all directions, and as these animals carried the women's worldly goods and possessions, their desperation was understandable.

Very often when on the march the troops would not be quartered in a town or village, but have to bivouac in the open. In theory, a camping ground would be selected with reference to its suitability with regard to the line of communications, the position of flanks and rear, the availability of wood and water and the general healthiness of the ground. The Assistant Quartermaster General would direct the officers, usually the quartermasters, riding in advance of their units to different parts of the ground, and as the column arrived each battalion would be directed to its position, and pickets and sentries posted. As soon as the column halted and the men had piled arms and taken off their equipment, fatigue parties were told off to collect bread, meat, wine or spirits, usually consisting of two or three men and a corporal. Other men would be dispatched with canteens and camp kettles to fetch water, while some might pile stones to make a rough fireplace. These were tasks which the women could help with. The company guard would be set, consisting of another corporal and four men. The rest of the company would commence building huts or shelters with whatever materials came to hand. Bill-hooks were used to lop branches off trees, which were dragged to the company lines, and erected to give the best shelter available from the weather, be it sun, rain, wind or snow. Having found enough suitable wood for fuel, the men and women, could then cook their food.

This like the official order of marching, was the ideal to be aimed at. The reality was usually a great deal less tidy and comfortable. As one officer wrote in July 1809, having marched more than 800 miles, he had not once slept in a bed, and the few branches they could usually cut to make primitive shelters could do very little to screen them either from the heat of the sun or the heavy dews which fell at night. Then 'we roll ourselves up in boat cloaks and lie down on the ground amongst thousands of snakes, scorpions and other venomous animals.' Taking off one's clothes had gone quite out of fashion, and perhaps the greatest discomfort of all, 'I have not sat in a chair these two months.'[43] These discomforts applied to all ranks, and the wives were not exempt. There was indeed a lack of chairs – and tables as well; they were not convenient things to carry on campaign. But if the column was to bivouac in one place long enough, and the ground permitted, there was a method of

---

42 Larpent (ed.), *Private Journal*, p.298.
43 Johnston, 'Letters of Lieutenant John Carss 2/53rd', p.14.

overcoming this problem. Two parallel trenches were dug about four feet apart. It was then possible for several people to sit with their feet in the trench using the space between as a make-shift table. With a bayonet stuck in the ground with a candle in its socket, this was a reasonable way of eating.[44]

That sounds quite convenient, even relatively comfortable. The truth was that conditions were often the reverse. Nobody, perhaps, captured the discomforts of bivouacking in bad conditions better than young Thomas Wedgewood, an ensign in the 2/3rd Guards when he wrote to his mother on 24 June 1815 describing the conditions in the immediate lead-up to the Battle of Waterloo:

> We were five days without any baggage tents or anything else, and you have no idea of what we underwent during that time, sleeping in the field without even a hedge to cover us, generally raining the whole night and the ground ankle deep in mud. I was 48 hours without eating anything, even a bit of biscuit, and having very often to send over a mile for water …

The difficulties of the regimental women, especially those with children, are hard to imagine, and this was a situation replicated time and again.[45]

There are many references to making huts, but they were seldom quite what they sound. They could only be constructed in places where there were sufficient of the right sort of trees. The great plains of central Spain were often tree-less, and in any case it was forbidden to cut down olive trees in areas where they grew. Pines were a better bet. Lieutenant Leslie of the 29th wrote how the regiment had made neat rows of huts from pine branches on the long march to Vitoria in the summer of 1813, the men's laid out in front and the officers' behind. Sometimes, when there was little time, they resembled wigwams he said, but if the halt was of a longer duration, they could be more substantial. In this case they might be more like a tent, with two forked uprights supporting a ridge-pole, with other pieces laid across the ridge to provide a frame-work for the roof. This was crudely thatched, using whatever came to hand: straw, heather or pine branches. During the operations against Copenhagen in 1807, the troops made their wigwams of tree branches and were able to thatch them with sheaves of corn.[46] The advantage of such huts was that they were cool on hot weather, but they were not wind or water proof, and rain storms tended to drench the inhabitants. They were probably more of a psychological shelter than an effective physical one, and this was probably especially true for the women and children.[47] It is difficult to believe that such shelters often provided a refreshing night's rest for exhausted men and women; fitful dozing seems more likely. They must however have been regarded as a suitable form of shelter, because they were used in Paris at the end of the war when the army camped in the Bois de Boulogne after Waterloo. 'The single men were in the tents, but the married people

---

44 Leslie, *Military Journal*, p.83.
45 Thomas Wedgewood, 'Letter of Thomas Wedgewood to his mother', in Glover (ed.), *Waterloo Archive*, vol.1, p.148.
46 Wardell (ed.), *With the Thirty Second*, p.71.
47 Leslie, *Military Journal*, p.55.

had huts, in a line parallel with the tents' remembered Thomas Morris of the 73rd, 'and when the boughs of which they were formed were fresh, they had a very rural, gipsy-like appearance.'[48] One night however, one of them caught fire, and the flames quickly spread to the others, and they were all destroyed.

This sort of life could try the toughest constitution, but Mrs Dalbiac, wife of the commanding officer of the 4th Dragoons, was equal to any trial. 'Your nice little friend Mrs Dalbiac is always by the side of her husband, whether lying under the canopy of heaven or enjoying the blessings and shelter of a roof.' So wrote Brigadier General Long to his sister, Elizabeth Howard. 'I am surprised how she has been able to stand the trial without injury to her health, but really, of the two, she is the stoutest.' Long was commanding the cavalry brigade, and went on 'I wished to do almost more than is in my power to lighten the burden her affection has imposed upon her, but no, she is inexorable, and rejects prayer, petition or remonstrance.'[49] All he could do was to wish them well. That was in April 1811. In July the following year, Mrs Dalbiac had an adventure which seems to have been widely known. The night before the Battle of Salamanca there was an exceptionally violent storm of thunder and lightning which panicked many of the cavalry horses. Some broke their picket ropes, and were stampeding about in the dark. The weather was unusually cold for the time of year, but like everyone else, the Dalbiacs were sleeping in the open on the ground and were in great danger of being trampled. A number of soldiers were in fact injured and unable to take their place in the battle the following day. Colonel Dalbiac had the presence of mind to drag his wife under a gun, between the wheels, which probably saved her from becoming a casualty too.

Sometimes, for some people at least, it seems that bivouacking could be relatively comfortable when the weather was kind, and in retrospect at least it could be made to sound like a pleasant camping expedition. 'Seated on the green turf in the shade of an ilex' thought one English officer in a Portuguese battalion, was pleasant. 'And at night…I wrapped myself up in my cloak, and lay down on a bear skin mattress stuffed with fern, I slept as soundly as I could have done in a bed of down.'[50] The other ranks and their hard-pressed wives would certainly have been envious of the bearskin. He was not the only one who found it all a bit of adventure. Young Moyle Sherer of the 34th was especially enthusiastic about it all. 'How often, under some spreading cork-tree, which offered shade, shelter, and fuel,' he remembered, 'have I taken up my lodgings for the night; and here, or by some gurgling stream, my bosom fanned by whatever air was stirring, made my careless toilet … and sat down to a coarse, but wholesome meal…'[51] An officer of the 1/92nd recalled how, during the fighting in the Pyrenees, they would make little bedsteads from tree branches, about nine inches off the ground, and cover these with straw or grass or fern, 'in which we reposed as comfortably as ever we did on the best down bed in England.' Not that this comfort lasted long. Shortly afterwards, near the pass of Roncevalles, there was such a severe snow storm

---

48   J. Selby (ed.), *Recollections of Military Service in 1813, 1814, and 1815* (London: Longmans, 1967), p.92.
49   T. McGuffie (ed.), *Peninsular Cavalry General (1811–13) The Correspondence of Lieutenant-Colonel Robert Ballard Long* (London: Harrap, 1951), p.93.
50   Anon, *Twelve Years*, vol.2, p.178.
51   Moyle Sherer, *Recollections of the Peninsula* (Staplehurst: Spellmount, 1996), p.96.

that some of the pickets were buried and had to be dug out in a pitiable state, having lost the use of their limbs.[52] And even Moyle Sherer, for all his enthusiasm for the outdoor life, had to concede that in bad weather it could be grim. He later mentions being in a bivouac for eight days, during three of which it rained incessantly. The officers sat shivering in their wet tents with nothing to do but wait for the next meal, while the other ranks, 'with their forage caps drawn over their ears, huddle together under banks or walls, or crowd round cheerless, smoky fires, cursing their commissaries, the rain and the French.'[53] And no doubt their women did too.

Troops would make use of any shelter they could find. After the Battle of the Nive, the 42nd bivouacked as usual, their fires soon lighting the night against the wintery weather. There were a few houses about, which were occupied by staff officers, with the guard posted beneath a nearby chestnut tree. The sergeant of the guard had his wife with him, and he managed to find a small pigsty for her to sleep in. This was luxury. It was private, near the guard, and would keep out the worst of the weather. However, the adjutant's clerk, a man who never had occasion to place himself in a position of danger, had been turned out of one of the houses by the staff officers, and decided to invade the pigsty. The sergeant's wife remonstrated with him, but to no avail. She might remain in the sty if she wished, but the clerk was resolved to stay put. This story was recounted by James Anton another soldier in the 42nd who also had his wife with him, and his comment is instructive: 'It is doubtful whether we had a woman in the regiment so regardless of her character as to have taken a night's shelter in the absence of her husband, otherwise than with the crowd, where no advantage could be taken of her situation or weakness.'[54] Indeed, thought Anton, many of the other regimental women would have driven the clerk off, but this woman had not the sternness of character, perhaps because she and her husband had only been with the regiment three months. So she joined her husband under the chestnut tree, and covered with a blanket spent the rest of the night there. It rained hard till about midnight when snow set in, and by morning the countryside was blanketed. The soldiers expressed their disgust at the clerk, for behaving in such a manner to a woman; whether he enjoyed his night in the pigsty is not recorded.

It was of course a way of life in which there was virtually no privacy, either for husbands and wives or anyone else. George Hennell of the 43rd described the scene around the campfire just after the Battle of Vitoria. One man making dough-boys, another cooking a piece of mutton; some smoking pipes, one tending blistered feet; one man treads on another and gets in the way of the fire, and in the midst of it all, 'A woman who is undressing by his side (perhaps the wife of one of the party) raises her shrill voice and blasts him for not being quick.'[55]

Not all women were of the sort to inspire feelings of compassion. One such seems to have been Mrs Morris of the 18th Hussars. Shortly before the Battle of Orthez, in the same kind of weather described by Anton, George Woodberry had offered to take her child and carry

---

52 Anon., *Military Memoirs*, p.350.
53 Sherer, *Recollections*, p.97.
54 Anton, *Retrospect*, p.91.
55 M. Glover (ed.), *A Gentleman Volunteer. The Letters of George Hennell From the Peninsular War 1812 – 1813* (London: Heinemann, 1979), p.93.

it on his horse to save her the burden, but 'she refused with an expletive, cursing everyone and the Regiment in particular.' So when, after a march of 15 miles or so, over bad tracks and in the winter weather, Woodberry had managed to find himself a reasonable house to spend the night in, he was not inclined to gallantry: 'This horrible Mrs Morris, the wife of the Lieutenant, has followed the Regiment here on foot. I could not bring myself to have pity on her, because she is a real bitch.'[56] This was not quite the last Woodberry saw of the odious Mrs Morris. After the army had entered France, and the 18th Hussars were advancing on Bordeaux, she turned up again in the town of Mont de Marsan, this time mounted on a pretty grey pony with beautiful saddlery. 'She has finally persuaded her husband to buy her everything' wrote Woodberry rather sourly. 'There has surely never been a regiment more compromised by an officer, than the 18th, by the position of Mrs M.'[57]

Tents were not made available to the army at large until late in the long French war. Troops did have them during the campaign in Flanders in 1793–1795, possibly on account of the severe weather.[58] Abercromby's force were equipped with tents for the Egyptian campaign of 1800 in recognition of the extreme climate.[59] There are references to some officers enjoying the luxury of tents quite early on in the Peninsular War. Peter Le Mesurier of the 9th Foot, writing to his father in November 1808, mentioned that he and three other officers had been quite comfortable in a tent until in the early hours a storm had blown up and flattened it.[60] In the following year, while the army was following up the French after the Douro crossing, the officers of the 29th were recorded as having a tent for each company, which they shared.[61]

These however must have been unofficial private property, organized by the officers in question, since tents were not issued to the army at large until the start of the great push to Vitoria in 1813, by which time it had been recognized that bivouacking was not conducive to the health of the troops, and that the numbers of sick could be reduced by getting the men under canvas. These were bell tents, the brainchild of an enterprising contractor, John Trotter, and were described in *The Bombardier, and Pocket Gunner* as 'Bell tents, now used for infantry or cavalry; weight, completed with poles, 43 lbs, length of pole, 9 feet, contains 12 men each, requires 40 pegs.'[62] One officer recorded that as far as his regiment were concerned there were three tents per company which implies that not everyone would have been undercover, or that at the least it would have been a squash.[63] Whatever the actual number, tents certainly meant a great improvement was made in conditions on the march. The troops themselves were not required to move their tents. As Peter Le Mesurier told his sister in March 'Orders have been given out for the issue of Tents for the Men, which Tents are to be carried on Mules formerly appropriated for the carriage of Camp Kettles but now

---

56 Glover & York (eds), *With Wellington's Hussars*, p.230.
57 Glover & York (eds), *With Wellington's Hussars*, p.240.
58 P. Harrington (ed.), *With the Guards in Flanders. The Diary of Captain Roger Morris 1793–1795* (Warwick: Helion, 2018), p.20.
59 Daniel Nicol, 'The Unpublished Diary of Sergeant Daniel Nicol', in M. MacBride (ed.), *With Napoleon at Waterloo* (London: Griffiths, 1911), p.53.
60 Greenwood (ed.), *Through Spain with Wellington*, p.14.
61 Leslie, *Military Journal*, p.122.
62 R. Adye, *The Bombardier, and Pocket Gunner* (Boston: Larkin, 1804), p.262.
63 Maxwell, *Peninsular Sketches*, vol.2, p.29.

done away with, a Thin camp Kettle substituted, which the men are to carry and which I think will be highly beneficial to the health of the Men.'[64] Wellington issued orders that if at all possible, tents were to be pitched out of sight of the French so that they could not use them to estimate numbers. The cavalry regiments were not provided with tents; it was assumed that the troopers and their horses would usually be quartered in villages.[65]

Tents were an immense improvement on sleeping in the open, but they were hardly luxurious, and from the point of view of a woman totally lacking in privacy, as James Anton and his wife discovered during the fighting in the Pyrenees. '…the tent was far from comfortable for a poor, wearied, young woman; I shall not mention delicacy, for that would be out of place; we must submit to circumstances.' There were 18 men allocated to the tent including Anton himself, although only 11 of them were actually present, and his wife, Mary, had to bed down amongst them. Half the blankets were placed on the ground, and the men lay like spokes of a wheel with their feet by the pole and their heads to the outside. Knapsacks were used as pillows, and every man slept fully dressed, weapons at his side. The rest of the blankets were arranged on top, so that they were in effect in a communal bed, and Mary's apron was used as a door-flap, with a couple of pins to hold it in place, though it was later destroyed in a storm. Many of the men were suffering from the 'itch', and all were filthy. 'Often did my poor wife look up to the thin canvas that screened her face from night-dew, and wish for the approaching morn.'[66] The couple later contrived to build a crude shelter with branches from trees and bushes, though it was not waterproof.

Faced with the brutal realities of active service, it is to be wondered whether some of the women who had been successful in the ballot back in England still regarded themselves as the lucky ones; or whether, perhaps, they may have come to regard the wives who had been left behind on the quayside as more fortunate. But they were indomitable characters, these regimental women, and the next chapter will describe some of the ways in which they coped with the business of surviving life on campaign.

---

64 Greenwood (ed.), *Through Spain with Wellington*, p.155,
65 Tomkinson, *The Diary*, p.235.
66 Anton, *Retrospect*, p.60.

5

The Bare Necessities

> *The misery one sees shows war in its true light.*
> *In the field one expects to see the fate of the soldiers,*
> *but the distress of women and children sinks deeper in one's mind.*[1]

Unlike the French, who lived off the countryside by systematic plunder, the British Army had its rations supplied by the Commissariat Department and paid for whatever supplies had to be requisitioned locally. There was an official scale of provision, and this was laid down clearly at the very start of the war in the Peninsula by a General Order issued at Mondego Bay on 31 July 1808:

> Until further orders the troops will receive rations from the Commissary. The rations will consist for each day of 1 lb of bread or biscuit, and 1 lb of meat, salt or fresh. If the soldiers should have fresh meat, they are not entitled to spirits or wine; if they should have salt meat, and upon all occasions when it can be got for them, they shall have each one quarter of a pint of spirits, or a pint of wine … The women, that is to say, six for each company of 100 men, will receive half a ration *per diem* and the children a quarter; but no spirits or wine will be issued to women or children.[2]

This was not the whole story, however. In due course, the standard daily ration for British troops came to consist of 1½ lbs of bread or 1 lb ship's biscuit, 1 lb of beef or ½ lb of pork, (which naturally included the bone), ¼ pint of dried peas, 1 oz cheese or butter, and 1oz of rice.[3] Fresh fruit and vegetables did not figure as part of the official diet. There was also a ration of five pints of small beer or one pint of wine, or half a pint of spirits. Women were not issued with alcohol. All this was rather theoretical. There are few accounts of men receiving any cheese or butter for example, and beer, in countries producing large quantities of wine, became a distant memory. There were great variations in what was actually available for issue at any particular time and place. The commissariat might have got hold of some sugar, or issue some oil instead of butter. Oatmeal could be issued, or extra rice substituted for

---

1 Sabine, (ed.), *Letters of Sir Augustus Frazer*, p.154.
2 Wellington (ed.), *Supplementary Despatches*, vol.6, p.92.
3 Haythornthwaite, *Wellington's Army*, p.61.

cheese. On one or two occasions when things were desperate, the commissariat managed to issue Indian corn (maize) but of course, the men and women had no means of grinding it into something they could cook except by using large stones, making the bivouac ring with the noise of the pounding.[4] Catherine Exley remembered that after some fighting near Salamanca, before the retreat began, her regiment, the 34th, 'received no refreshment but a pint of wheat to each person.'[5] What people were to do with this, the commissariat did not explain. She had managed to obtain half a loaf from someone, and was at once besieged by hungry men wanting to know where it had come from. An officer offered her a large sum of money for it, but as she said, gold was of no use as food. In the end she was persuaded to part with a few slices.

The reality was that on many occasions the troops and their wives were lucky to get even the basic allowance. William Dent, surgeon to the 9th Foot, said in a letter he wrote on 11 March 1814, when the fighting was taking place in the Pyrenees, that the men were actually receiving each day 1 lb biscuit, 1 lb meat, 2 oz rice and ⅓ pint of spirits.[6] Moreover, the quality of the food reaching the regiments often left much to be desired. This was especially true of the beef, which arrived on the hoof. Herds of bullocks were driven behind the army, and slaughtered as required. The animals were of course lean and tough in the extreme. Peter Le Mesurier of the 9th Foot, writing to his mother in January 1812, told her that the ration of beef had just arrived from the place of slaughter in the very carts which they had used to bury the dead, and that it was so tough that it required at least six hours of boiling before it was edible.[7] It was nearly impossible to find the fuel or time for such prolonged cooking, and meat was sometimes roasted on the end of a sword or bayonet. Ross-Lewin was reminded of Pharaoh's lean kine, and thought that the cattle were more likely to cause a famine than prevent one.[8] Another problem was that the bullocks were slaughtered wherever the columns halted, and butchered on the ground. Hygiene was impossible; the bloody meat would get sand and dirt in it which made for gritty eating. When provisions were scanty, one popular expedient was to collect the blood of the slaughtered bullocks. Crowds of men and women would gather at the place of slaughter, jostling and sometimes fighting to get some of the blood. This could be cooked in several ways. Sometimes it was boiled, and then eaten cold, when it was apparently of a cheese-like consistency. Or if a little fat or oil could be obtained, it was fried like pancakes, sometimes flavoured with garlic. 'It was not the place, was not a retreat bivouac, to turn up one's nose at the blood of a bullock.'[9]

The basic food rations were slightly modified in November 1811 when Horse Guards issued fresh orders. For units in the field, the number of women remained at six per 100 men. But it was also stated that 'No women or children, except the wives of non-commissioned officers and men, shall be entitled to rations.' In other words, it seems to have been

---

4   Sherer, *Recollections*, p.221.
5   Probert (ed.), *Exley Diary*, p.30.
6   L. Woodford (ed.), *A Young Surgeon in Wellington's Army. The Letters of William Dent* (Old Woking: Unwin, 1976), p.45.
7   Greenwood (ed.), *Through Spain with Wellington*, p.93.
8   Wardell (ed.), *With the Thirty Second*, p.150.
9   Anon., *Narrative of a Private Soldier who served in the Forty-Second Highlanders for Twelve Years during the Late Wars* (London: Allman, 1821), p.160.

assumed that officers would not have their wives in the field with them, but that if they did, they would have to make their own arrangements about food. And there was another slight change. While the rations for women were to remain at half a man's ration, in an unusual act of generosity that for children was increased to one-third of a full ration.[10]

These rations were not really adequate for men living a strenuous life on campaign, and it is difficult to imagine how women, whose exertions were often equally demanding, managed on half-rations. They must often have been badly undernourished. The situation was partially saved by the fact that people formed themselves into messes, small groups in which the cooking was communal activity, the meat and vegetables available being usually boiled in the large camp-kettles. This was a situation in which the women could easily take charge, and ensure an equitable share-out. In the Spanish army, things were managed differently. Spanish troops cooked in messes like the British, and like the British, allowed women half and children a quarter of a man's ration. But the distribution was done differently: '… they all form a circle round the cauldron, each furnished with a tin pot and spoon. At the first signal the men advance, and take out a spoonful. At the second, the men and women advance together. At the third, the men only. At the fourth, men, women and children; and they go on in this order until the whole is eaten up.'[11]

Soldier's wives were also frequently employed by officers, or officers' messes, to act as cooks. At Mafra, in the Lines of Torres Vedras, August Schaumann, commissary to the 14th and 20th Light Dragoons, was busy with letters, book-keeping, arranging stores and distributing supplies. 'The first thing I did was to engage the wife of a hussar, who, I afterwards discovered, knew very little about cooking.' But perhaps he was not too disappointed, because she turned out to be 'as the saying is, a better bed companion than cook'[12] Schaumann's account of his exploits in this direction may need to be taken with a pinch of salt.

The officers of E Troop Royal Horse Artillery did rather better with the artillery soldier's wife they hired. She must have been a remarkably skilful and resourceful woman, because even after the retreat from Salamanca, in December 1812, she managed to provide some elaborate dinners with sauces, ragoûts, hashes and boiled and roast meat. 'I do not think I am a glutton,' wrote Lieutenant William Swabey in his diary, 'but there is a pleasure in entertaining one's friends *comme il faut*'.[13] A remarkable statement in view of what the army had just come through. Acting as mess cook for a group of officers must have represented a valuable opportunity to earn some money in a situation in which there was no normal occupation available, though it could have its drawbacks. The officers of the 47th Foot had intended to employ Mrs Cowell, the wife of one of their sergeants' but she was pregnant. Not to be deterred, Mrs Cowell had followed the regiment from Cadiz, despite being repeatedly advised to stay behind on account of her condition. The result was that she reached the regiment at Madrid, just before the great retreat began, and on the very night of her arrival gave birth to twins. The officers of the 47th presumably had to make other arrangements, while Mrs Cowell had to endure all the hardships of the retreat in appalling weather and little food, her babies in her arms. She was a tough woman however, survived the retreat, got

---

10 Gurwood (ed.), *General Orders*, p.333.
11 Buckham, *Personal Narrative*, p.85.
12 Schaumann, *On the Road*, p.267.
13 Whinyates (ed.), *Diary of a Campaign*, p.169.

Somewhere on campaign a group of redcoats are cooking under a tree, while two women do the laundry in the stream and another hangs it up to dry. Aquatint after Thomas Rowlandson, 1 April 1798. (Anne S.K. Brown Military Collection, Brown University)

safely to Ciudad Rodrigo, then to Lisbon, and finally took passage to England with her children. But her husband, Sergeant Cowell, was killed later at the storming of St Sebastian.[14]

Cooking itself often presented difficulties, since it required two basic things: water and fuel. In selecting a halting place when on the march, staff officers did their best to find places where there was a supply of clean water within reasonable distance, although this was not always possible, especially when summer heat had dried up streams and rivers. The army needed large amounts of water for the thousands of horses and mules as well as men and women, and supplies were often scarce and muddy. Sometimes there were only stagnant pools, and people were so tired and thirsty that they could not be prevented from drinking this 'execrable beverage' despite the filthy state of the water. Francis Larpent, the Judge Advocate General attached to headquarters, personally experienced bad water on the march to Vitoria, and recalled that during the previous year he had seen people 'obliged to hold their noses when they drank.'[15] Illness was all too likely to follow.

---

14 Harley, *The Veteran*, vol.2, p.65.
15 Larpent (ed.), *The Private Journal*, p.123.

Wellington's original orders at the start of the war in Portugal had optimistically envisaged that each man would have 3 lbs of wood a day for cooking purposes, but this was a wild over-estimate.[16] Shortage of fuel was a constant problem. In June 1813, on the great advance to Vitoria, William Webber's battery was camped on a treeless plain with no shelter and no firewood available. People had to go two miles to an old vineyard to collect stubble before they could cook their rations.[17] Sometimes straw or dried grass was the only thing available. In the vicinity of villages, the troops hunted about for any bits of wood they could find, which often included pieces of fences and buildings, much to the annoyance of the inhabitants. Sometimes there were efforts to stop this sort of thing. In 1811, when the 32nd Foot joined the 6th Division at Nave d'Aver, beyond Castello Branco, the brigadier, Colonel Burne of the 36th, issued positive orders that no soldiers or officers were to use any parts of buildings for firewood. The day after issuing this order, Burne saw some men busy taking the roof timbers off a house. Outraged, he sent an officer to take the party prisoner. The officer soon returned however, to say that he had arrested the men concerned, but that they were removing the timber for cooking fuel in the colonel's own quarters.[18] Sometimes it was found necessary actually to allocate houses for firewood, which did little to improve relations with the local inhabitants, who probably regarded the British as being little better than the French. There were also, of course, occasions on which the weather was simply too bad to get decent fire going, and people were obliged to toast bits of raw meat as best they could on the end of a stick, or sword, or bayonet, and eat it half raw without the aid of knife or fork.[19]

It was traditionally said of Spain that it was a country in which small armies were defeated and large armies starved, but the fact was that it was a country in which it was difficult to feed an army of any size. The vast problem of supplying the army with food lay in the hands of the Commissariat Department, the peacetime establishment of which was tiny. By the time the war in the Peninsula opened in 1808, Britain had been at war for almost 15 years. Most operations, such as the campaign on the Low Countries, had taken place within reach of the sea, so provisioning had been greatly simplified. The whole business of supplying an army far inland and constantly on the move had to be organized from scratch by inexperienced officers. It is not surprising that they sometimes failed. Sometimes indeed, there seems to have been no system of supply at all. During the campaign in north Germany in the autumn of 1813, in which a French force under *Maréchal* Davout was defeated, the 2/73rd had no commissariat at all, and since supplies could not be bought with ready money, the battalion had to subsist on whatever potatoes and fruit they could gather on the march – which was exactly what the French armies did.[20] In any case, the task of supplying any considerable force was enormous. At the start of the 1813 campaign for instance, Wellington commanded a combined British and Portuguese force of a little over 80,000 men. This required some 12,000 commissariat mules to bring forward each day 100,000 lbs of biscuit and twice that

---

16   Wellington (ed.), *Supplementary Despatches*, vol.VI, p.92.
17   R. Wollocombe (ed.), *With the Guns in the Peninsula. The Peninsular War Journal of 2nd Captain William Webber, Royal Artillery* (London: Greenhill, 1991), p.154.
18   Wardell (ed.), *With the Thirty Second*, p.149.
19   Sherer, *Recollections*, p.219.
20   Harrington (ed.), *Recollections*, p.16.

amount of forage for the many thousands of horses. Or take the 3rd Division as an example. The Assistant Commissary General to the division had to provide 10,500 lbs of bread or 7,000 lbs of biscuit, 7,000 lbs of meat and 7,000 pints of wine every day. This required 600 mules. In addition to this, he had to keep an eye on the herd of 500 slaughter cattle and the Portuguese herdsman.[21]

The difficulties of this task would probably not have been understood by the men and women of the marching columns, for whom shortages of food were all too common, and near starvation not unknown. This sort of situation sometimes arose because the commissariat had broken down under the stress of a retreat, as happened during the retreat from Salamanca. In June 1809, in the days following the Battle of Talavera, when the British were forced to retire towards Portugal, William Green and his comrades of the 95th were very hungry indeed. They had meat from the cattle driven with the army, but went a week without bread, and were reduced to eating acorns. The Spanish oaks produced larger acorns than found in Britain, and it was discovered that when boiled in camp kettles and with the husks peeled away, they tasted not unlike small potatoes. They also cut standing wheat, which they carried in bundles on their rifles. When they halted, they would cut the ears off, put them in a haversack and beat them with a ramrod or pound them between stones. They then winnowed the grains with their breath, and boiled them into a kind of crude porridge. As another rifleman put it 'Our living here became truly savage.'[22] At one point they were issued with four ounces of flour each, the only way of cooking which was to mix it with a little water, roll it into balls and cook them like small dumplings. Another expedient was to make little cakes and put them on a thin stone in the fire until they were roughly done, or use the lid of a camp kettle. The 95th christened this bivouac 'Dough-boy Hill.'[23] It was just the same for the women and children. It was also during the retreat following Talavera that August Schaumann wrote the, 'The soldier's wives, who as a rule went about decently clad, and were most faithful to their husbands, now rode hungrily in rags on starved donkeys, and gave themselves to anyone who wanted them in exchange for half a loaf of bread.'[24] If Schaumann's interest in the regimental women was distinctly libidinous, that of Joseph Donaldson of the 94th was strictly moralistic, though he told much the same tale. 'Was it to be wondered at, then, if many of them were led astray, particularly when it is considered that their starving condition was often taken advantage of by those who had it in their power to supply them, but who were villains enough to make their chastity the price?'[25]

This was by no means the only occasion when soldiers and their wives were reduced to eating acorns. The siege of Ciudad Rodrigo began in January 1812 in appalling weather conditions, and food supplies failed to arrive. William Bentinck of the 23rd Foot said the men called this 'Starvation Camp', and they were forced to forage in the woods for acorns. Each day half a dozen men were sent out to collect them. They also took their bayonets and killed some of the pigs which were also eating the acorns, and this enabled them to cook

---

21 Michael Glover, *Wellington's Army in the Peninsula 1808–1814* (Newton Abbot: David & Charles, 1977), p.104.
22 Costello, *The Adventures*, p.35.
23 J. & D. Teague (eds), *Where Duty Calls*, p.22.
24 Schaumann, *On the Road*, p.205.
25 Donaldson, *Recollections*, p.219.

the acorns in pork fat. We can be sure the women would have assisted. This was of course strictly contrary to orders, but the officers, who were just as famished, wisely looked the other way and were only too pleased to accept a piece of the meat.[26] Pigs were again slaughtered during the retreat from Salamanca, despite all orders to the contrary, and acorns are mentioned by a number of the survivors. Apparently, they did not taste too bad, and these Spanish acorns had considerable food value. William Webber of the artillery, who recorded that some men and women fell into the hands of the French simply because lack of food left them too weak to go on, wrote 'Our men and officers subsisted on acorns, which are not unpleasant when no rations were to be had.'[27] The assistant surgeon of the 1st Dragoons, G. F. Burroughs, put it more elegantly: 'Providence, by affording us a supply of acorns, had not altogether abandoned us to despair, and in alighting to fill the haversack with those that had fallen from the trees, our horses were now and then enabled to pick up a little grass.'[28]

A dearth of rations could also occur when the troops advanced faster than the lumbering commissariat could keep up; the Spanish bullock carts could hardly manage more than about 12 miles a day. In the bitter weather of early 1811, when the army was following Massena's army as it retreated from in front of the Lines of Torres Vedras, the 1st Foot, drenched through and in the midst of a snow storm, reached a village where they halted to allow the commissariat to catch up. This took some time, and when the supplies did arrive, there was a cry of 'Turn out for bread, beef, rum and rice.' Everyone expected a decent meal, but all the commissariat could come up with amounted to 4 oz of biscuit, ½ lb of beef, 2 oz of rice and half a glass of rum. 'On getting this fine allowance, the Col, addressing the men, says, "Now men be careful of your bread and God knows when we shall have any more."'[29] Hunger over-ruled this good advice, and with half an hour all was eaten.

The most vivid example of the difficulties occurred during the great advance from Portugal to the Pyrenees during May and June 1813. Wellington's Anglo-Portuguese army, numbering 67,000 infantry, 8,000 cavalry and 102 guns, advanced in three great columns, accompanied by another column of Spanish troops. The French were hustled out of every position and driven relentlessly back towards France. The advance went on at unexpected speed, and the columns quickly outstripped their supplies. A soldier of the 42nd Foot recalled that the commissariat was finding it difficult to keep up with the advance after only eight days, and rations began to be scarce. There was a period of 12 days when they had little except beef, the animals being driven with the columns. Sometimes they got half a pound of bread, sometimes a quarter pound of biscuit in lieu. He reckoned that they only received full rations five days in 12, and this for men and women marching all day long. Sometimes their rations would come in at night, and this disturbed their desperately needed rest.

> Language cannot paint the fatigue and hunger we endured. I have seen my comrades and myself going to the fields of wheat, pulling the ears of the wheat, rubbing them between our hands, and then took two stones and ground the grain, till we got it as

---

26 J. Crook, (ed.), *The Very Thing. The Memoirs of Drummer Richard Bentinck Royal Welch Fusiliers 1807–1823* (London: Frontline, 2011), p.66.
27 Wollocombe (ed.), *With the Guns*, p.119.
28 Burroughs, *A Narrative*, p.62.
29 Monick (ed.), *Douglas's Tale of the Peninsula and Waterloo*, p.29.

small as possible. Then we made it into a sort of pottage, and supped it without salt or anything else, and thought it very delicious.[30]

'Hunger is a sharp thorn' however, and in such situations people had no option but to emulate the French, and try to live off the land – or in other words, to plunder. Sometimes it was a case of stealing from the local peasants, who were themselves hungry. Sometimes it was more organized. A British officer in one of the Portuguese battalions of the Light Division described how they camped in a bean field. Supplies of bread having totally failed, the men naturally began to help themselves. This was against standing orders but fortunately it was possible to purchase the crop, and fatigue parties were sent out to gather the beans.[31] Not all the regiments were as particular. The 45th Foot, like the rest of the army, practically starving, and they too raided the bean fields, tearing the plants up by the armful. Not that this was quite what it seemed. The crop was nowhere near maturity, only partly grown in fact, so 'the hulls, leaves, and tender tops of the straw, were boiled and devoured with the greatest avidity.'[32]

All this naturally effected the regimental women as much as the men, and some of them were certainly in a desperate state. John Green, a private in the 68th, remembered one such situation well:

> At this time a poor woman belonging to the army came by, and in a most affecting manner begged for a morsel of bread, saying, she had not eaten any for three days: but such was the scarcity of that valuable article, that we could not spare her one morsel, not knowing when we should get another supply. Some may think it strange that we did not relieve this poor woman's necessity; but it will not appear so when it is considered that the loaf weighed only three pounds, and there were six hungry men to partake of it; besides, there were hundreds on the same road in her condition; indeed, at this crisis, it was every man for himself, as it invariably is in time of famine.[33]

Wellington's orders against plundering were draconian, and the rules were especially rigorously enforced after the army broke into France. Wellington knew that if his men behaved as the French had in Spain, the inhabitants would quickly turn against the British. The death penalty was enforced. Drummer Bentinck saw a soldier who had been hanged for plunder near Toulouse, with his jacket turned inside out as a sign of disgrace. Another was flogged for stealing apples, but as he said, these brutal measures could not stop hungry people pilfering food – they just became more careful. And there were certainly plenty of instances where the officers, who should have enforced the orders, were so hungry themselves that they were prepared to turn a blind eye and get a bit of the plunder for themselves. They had no option. Bentinck described how one night near Toulouse he managed to kill a sheep with his pocket knife. He took the meat into camp, and deposited one leg at the captain's tent and another

---

30   Anon., *Narrative of a Private Soldier*, p.184.
31   Woodford (ed.), *Young Surgeon*, p.34.
32   S. Brown (ed.), *The Autobiography, or Narrative of a Soldier* (Solihull: Helion, 2017), p.122.
33   Green, *The Vicissitudes of a Soldier's Life*, p.159.

at the lieutenant's. Some men went so far as to bring carcasses into camp and butcher them there, and the colonel merely told them to clear up the mess.[34]

The British army had no equivalent of the French *vivandières*, the women who accompanied the troops selling small comforts and luxuries, but there were a few exceptionally enterprising women who managed to set themselves up as unofficial sutlers. One such was Mrs O'Neil, wife of the sergeant major of the 88th Foot. Mrs O'Neil 'a fine, fat, well-looking woman' was the sister of Mrs Carsons, wife of Dan Carsons, soldier-servant to William Grattan – it was perhaps unusual to have two sisters in the same regiment. Mrs O'Neil had kept close to the regiment from the time they landed in the Peninsula, and she had somehow or other managed to acquire a stock-in-trade of food and drink and two mules to carry it all. As such, she had proved invaluable to the officers of the 88th, supplying them with wine, bread, and various small comforts. Quite how she managed to do this was a mystery, but as Grattan said, she was an exceptional forager even by the standards of the Connaught Rangers. During the Salamanca retreat, in which Mrs Cowell was struggling with her newborn babies, Mrs O'Neil lost her mules and their precious cargo. This was a serious matter; William Grattan thought she may have had at least 300 dollars' worth of goods. She had already been ill with fever, and weakened by the appalling conditions of the retreat, she became sick and then lapsed into delirium, crying out to Dan Carsons about her mules.[35]

Most of the troops were in no position to buy extra supplies from sutlers as their meagre pay was often months in arrears, and the same applied to many of the regimental officers. Some sutlers however managed to attach themselves to Wellington's headquarters, where they seem to have plied a better trade. Captain Thomas Browne of the 23rd Foot was attached to the headquarters staff of the Adjutant General's department, so was in a good position to know what was going on. A good deal of the sutlers' stock was of poor quality and exorbitantly priced, hard Dutch cheese and butter for instance. But they also had tea, sugar and tobacco, and cigars especially were in great demand among the officers. One of the sutlers was a woman named Antonia:

> She was a stout lusty person of rather a jolly countenance, dirty enough, but one who in the midst of her filth, always wore a massy gold necklace, to which a cross of the same metal was attached & a pair of long pendant ear-rings. This Antonia was the greatest cheat of the whole set, & amassed a considerable fortune by her attendance on Head-Quarters.

With each succeeding campaign her goods became worse and her prices ever higher, but she made a considerable fortune by her enterprise. 'There were several candidates for her hand amongst the Gentlemen Suttlers but she steadily declined the honour of any alliance with them.'[36]

The commissariat system often worked according to plan, and food was plentiful. When the Peninsular War entered its final stages in the Pyrenees, the army was able to shorten its supply lines dramatically. Instead of having to haul every pound of food

---

34 Crook (ed.), *The Very Thing*, p.118.
35 William Grattan, *Adventures with the Connaught Rangers 1809–1814* (London: Arnold, 1902), p.312.
36 Buckley (ed.), *Napoleonic War Journal*, p.200.

from Portuguese ports and across the breadth of Spain, it was now possible to use the harbours on the Franco-Spanish frontier. As soon as the port of Passages was secured, ordnance stores and ammunition and supplies of all sorts began to pour in from Britain. For the officers at least, these included warm clothing and other comforts sent by their wives. English merchants made the most of the opportunity, and soon there were plentiful supplies of tea, sugar, butter, hams, fresh beef and vegetables and much else. The army became much better fed, but most of the troops, officers included, were in no position to buy any of these tantalizing extras, as the army was habitually months in arrears with pay. Most of the wives of course had no income at all. Once the French frontier was crossed, St Jean de Luz began to resemble a fashionable watering place, according to Sir Richard Henegan, as 'many fair ladies, wives and maidens, some of whom had taken compassion on the state of celibacy to which the sons of Mars were doomed, had arrived from England to solace them by their presence.'[37] They probably sailed back to England once the fighting resumed again.

Although great hardships could be involved with bivouacking when columns were on the march, this was not always the case. If the army was not near the enemy, and if the halting place at the end of the day's march was to be in a town, it was necessary to arrange for quarters. When it was practical to do so, an officer of the Quartermaster General's department rode on 24 hours in advance in order to make arrangements with the local magistrates. This involved dividing the town into areas, each to be parcelled out between the arriving brigades. Arrangements were also made for the quarters of the commanding general, which was naturally in the best house available, the staff, orderly rooms and guardroom. Each battalion also sent a quartermaster on ahead with a detachment of orderlies, to be informed as to which area their people were to be directed to, and the orderlies would chalk up on doors the number of the company to occupy the accommodation. The quartermaster and the orderlies would then direct the companies of their respective battalions to the part of the town allocated to them, and the women would seek out their husbands. The Assistant Quartermaster General of the division would if possible resolve any disputes and problems of overcrowding. In the case of cavalry regiments or horse artillery batteries, it was also necessary to find shelter for the horses.

Naturally enough, this careful system sometimes failed to work. After Massena had retreated from before the Lines of Torres Vedras, and Wellington's army was in pursuit, the 34th marched into a town called Caregada to find the place completely full – every house and stable was occupied. So, Lieutenant Moyle Sherer and his men, who were also without any rations, spent a comfortless night in the streets. They made fires of whatever wood they could find, but as Sherer discovered, your feet tended to get scorched while your back was chilled by the autumn rains.[38] On the other hand, things could be quite pleasant. In September 1812, on the advance towards Aranjuez, William Webber was with a 9-pounder brigade of the Royal Artillery. Headquarters were established at a village called Campillo de Llerena, where the staff occupied all the houses, but Webber's brigade was able to get all its men into quarters in the surrounding area, while the horses were picketed in a garden.

---

37   Henegan, *Seven Years*, vol.2, p.81.
38   Sherer, *Recollections*, p.128.

It was an area in which there was a good supply of clean water, always a vital consideration, and plenty of forage.[39] Sometimes officers found themselves in villas with their men and women in the outbuildings in the gardens.

In the Low Countries there were many good barns which could be used for accommodation for both horses and men, but there was no equivalent in the Peninsula, and convents, either of monks or nuns, were frequently used where villages were not large enough to get all the troops under cover. There were many of them in Spain and Portugal, and they are frequently mentioned in letters and diaries. Sometimes the officers would be in billets and the men and their women in the convent buildings, or the officers in the convent itself, perhaps with a cell apiece. To quote William Webber's diary again, on 19 September, near Almaraz, he noted 'We moved on and were provided with quarters and good stables. The Brigade horses were in the chapel of a convent having bare walls and roof only and the men were in the cloisters'.[40] Churches were sometimes an alternative. During the time the army was occupying the Lines of Torres Vedras, Moyle Sherer's company of the 34th, together with another, was quartered in a church – some 200 men in all. The senior officer took the sacristy, the next most senior a little room behind the high alter, while the rest of the officers made themselves as comfortable as possible in the organ loft. It was an odd scene that Sherer looked down on. Here, a grenadier sergeant was writing his reports on the communion table; a fifer was ensconced in the pulpit, and the rest of the men and women were cutting up their ration beef on the marble tombs.[41]

When houses were available, they were not often very comfortable. During the winter of 1810 when the 29th Foot was in garrison at Portalegre, Lieutenant Leslie for one found them ill adapted to winter conditions; the only warm place was the kitchen.[42] Billets were frequently without doors or windows (they had probably been burned). Lieutenant Le Mesurier, in a letter dated 12 January 1812, shortly before the assault on Ciudad Rodrigo, informed his father that they had been trying to improve the huts they were living in by building chimneys, which were unknown in the Peninsula, and by patching the holes in the shutters with pieces of oiled paper, which let in a little light and kept out some of the weather.[43]

Whenever there was a pause in operations and the army found itself in one place for more than a few days, all manner of entertainments were indulged in. Hare coursing was popular with all ranks, there being some excellent greyhounds available. Wellington himself maintained a pack of fox hounds which were used to hunt jackals and foxes. Horse racing was popular. When a substantial number of troops were in cantonments at Portalegre in the spring of 1810 a small jockey club was instituted and a course laid out on the plain, all under the patronage of Lieutenant General Hill, who had a fine stud of horses. Sometimes it seems that wives were actually allowed to participate in the racing. In April 1806, many races were held by the Gibraltar garrison. In one of them, Mrs Short, wife of an officer in the 10th Foot, rode against Captain Francis Smith of the Royal Artillery. It was a tightly contested

---

39 Wollocombe (ed.), *With the Guns*, p.45.
40 Wollocombe (ed.), *With the Guns*, p.62.
41 Sherer, *Recollections*, p.123.
42 Leslie, *Military Journal*, p.190.
43 Greenwood (ed.), *Through Spain with Wellington*, p.89.

race, and Mrs Short won by a length.[44] The soldiers and their wives held great celebrations in March, on St Patrick's Day, there being large numbers of Irish in the ranks. The regimental bands played Irish tunes, and there was a good deal of singing, and a great deal of drinking. In April, the English, not to be outdone, organized St George's Day celebrations, when buildings were adorned with flags and greenery.[45]

No opportunity seems to have been lost to organize dances to which very often the local families were invited. In the autumn of 1810, when the army had retired behind the Lines of Torres Vedras, Major General Sir Lowry Cole, commanding the 4th Division at Azembiza on the River Tagus, held a ball. His soldier-servant mentioned this in a letter home. 'The General gave a grand ball and many ladies, the wives and daughters of officers then in Lisbon, were invited. They all came up in boats, mostly men-of-war boats.'[46] It is a wonderful image: boatloads of British wives and daughters being rowed across the broad reach of the Tagus by warships' crews on their way to a dance. Or there might be dinners. Colonel Grey, commanding the 30th Foot, had brought his wife out to the Peninsula with him, and in December 1811 John Carter, one of the ensigns, recalled being asked to dine with the Greys. It was very agreeable, and Mrs Grey was evidently a charming lady. On Christmas Eve, Carter and the regimental doctor rode out from the village where they were quartered specially to gather oranges for her.[47] When the army was stationary for any length of time, officers' wives could take the opportunity to organize genteel social occasions, just as they might at home. Mrs Currie for instance, the wife of Captain Currie who was on Lieutenant General Hill's staff, had also accompanied her husband to the seat of war. She used to make tea for Hill and the 2nd Division staff, and whenever the division settled down in billets for a few days she held little receptions.[48]

Young Robert Blakeney, a lieutenant in the 1/28th Foot knew all about this, and seems to have enjoyed her civilizing influence. When he came to write his memoirs, having described the shooting and hunting (Hill, like Wellington, kept a pack of hounds) and the general conviviality of Hill's headquarters mess, he added 'As his aide-de-camp, Captain Curry was married, the amiable Mrs Curry always dined at the general's table, so that we neither forgot the deference due to beauty nor the polished manners of the drawing room.'[49] That was in late 1811, but Mrs Currie seems to have remained with her husband throughout the following year, when she gave birth to a son. While the army was in cantonments in the winter of 1812, prior to the great advance to Vitoria, George Bell of the 34th also seems to have come under her spell. 'There was one fair and beautiful Englishwoman always present,' he remembered years later, 'joyous and happy, a charming representative of those bright stars of Albion, whose presence was always cheering amongst so many red-coats.'[50]

---

44 Landmann, *Recollections*, vol.1, p.45.
45 Leslie, *Military Journal*, p.191.
46 M. Lowry Cole and S. Gurgan (eds), *Memoirs of Sir Lowry Cole* (London: Macmillan, 1934), p.67.
47 G. Glover (ed.), *Ensign Carter's Journal 1812. The Peninsular Diary of Ensign John V. Carter 30th (Cambridgeshire) Regiment of Foot* (Huntingdon: Trotman, 2006), p.7.
48 McGuffie (ed.), *Peninsular Cavalry General*, p.137.
49 Robert Blakeney, *A Boy in the Peninsular War* (London: Murray, 1899), p.214.
50 Stuart (ed.), *Soldier's Glory*, p.63.

Following the failure of Wellington's moves against Madrid and Burgos, and the arduous retirement from Salamanca in November 1812, there was a six months pause in operations. Wellington's headquarters were established at Freinada, just west of Fuentes de Oñoro, and the army was cantoned across a wide area of northern Portugal. There were no active operations between the end of November and the opening of the great advance to Vitoria which began in late May the following year. Six months were spent recovering from the fatigues of the retreat and allowing the sick to recover. Food supplies returned to normal, and the troops were well housed – even quite comfortable. New clothing and shoes were issued. Reinforcements arrived. There was a good deal of drilling. For the first time there was a general issue of tents, and the old, heavy iron camp kettles were replaced with lighter ones of sheet metal; both improvements which were to improve the welfare of the army. All ranks took the opportunity of the winter rest to enjoy themselves as best they could. There seems to have been only one woman at Wellington's headquarters, Mrs Scovell. She was the wife of Major George Scovell, who was on the staff and who was responsible for cracking the codes the French used in their correspondence. Francis Larpent, the Judge Advocate General, who was also attached to headquarters, was charmed by 'Mrs S', and particularly enjoyed her dinner parties. 'I now dine out three or four times in the week, generally once or twice at head-quarters – and occasionally with Major and Mrs Scobell who give very pleasant little dinners, and tender meat, and a loo [a card game] party afterwards.'[51] It all sounds rather cosy.

By the first week of February 1813, the officers of the Connaught Rangers had established an evening club in lieu of a regular mess, which had proved impractical. Mrs O'Neil, wife of the sergeant major presided over this comfortable institution, where officers could meet after the day's duties, play whist and have a few drinks.[52] Rather more surprisingly perhaps, there was a taste for amateur dramatics, and a theatre was established in an old convent building. The place was well fitted up with good scenery and the performances gave much satisfaction. The local shops, 'offered nothing which answered for the dresses, and such things as could not be collected among the officers of the Division and their wives (the few who were with them) were sent for from Lisbon.' Captain William Webber of the Royal Artillery recorded in his diary going to a number of plays. On 13 February it was *The Poor Gentleman*; on 21 April *The Honeymoon*; and the 27th he enjoyed *The Road to Ruin* and *The Bee Hive*.[53] The performances were always crowded, with many private soldiers and their wives amongst the audiences. There were dances and balls, to which the local senoritas were naturally invited, and dinners on the part of the officers. For the other ranks there was great deal of drinking and music and songs such as *The Downfall of Paris, or Britons Strike Home*.[54] In May the anniversary of the Battle of Albuera was celebrated with great festivities. 'The army has been so well paid [a very unusual event] lately that every man has plenty of money, and wine and music were the order of the day.'[55] The other

---

51 Larpent (ed.), *Private Journal*, p.46.
52 Grattan, *Adventures*, p.316.
53 Wollocombe (ed.), *With the Guns*, pp.135–144
54 Anon., *Journal of an Officer in the Commissariat Department of the Army* (London: Porter and King, 1820), p.189.
55 Wollocombe (ed.), *With the Guns*, p.145.

ranks decorated the streets with green boughs, and the officers gave a grand dinner for the local dignitaries.

It was often a very ragged army. Vegetable dyes were not fast, and colours faded rapidly. No clothing made of natural fibres could withstand for long the rigours of campaigning. Men and women alike lived in the open air for weeks on end, exposed to the extremities of the weather, sleeping rough and often not having the opportunity of changing their clothes for long periods. As Lieutenant Simmons of the 95th told his parents in a letter in February 1810, 'The lying out at night in the fields for months together soon puts your raiment in disorder. I am nearly in rags.'[56] The women's raiment was certainly in a similar state of disorder. Parade-ground smartness quickly became a thing of the past from the very earliest phase of the long French war. In November 1794, in Flanders, Captain Morris of the Coldstream Guards was dismayed by the appearance of an officer and some men of the 89th Foot who had arrived to relieve him of picket duty: 'A Ragamuffin crew, whose appearance beggared description' was how he put it. They were without shoes or stockings, 'and the whole picquet, from their rags and filth, had more the appearance of a jail delivery, than anything else.'[57] It was much the same years later, in 1811, when a draft of men sent home from Spain arrived at the 9th Foot depot in Canterbury. 'You may suppose what kind of a Coat that must be a Man wears constantly for two years' wrote Lieutenant Le Mesurier in a letter home, 'not only in the day but often obliged to sleep in it. Such is the state of the 1st Batt at present … for naked they are absolutely are.'[58]

Men and women were often obliged to plunder the casualties for items of clothing. After the Battle of Talavera, William Green of the 95th was in such straits for a new shirt that while helping to tend the wounded he also ransacked the dead. He opened the knapsack of one of the 31st Foot hoping to find what he needed, but instead discovered a bundle of letters from the man's wife in Ireland. Green read one of them, and learned that the couple had three children. He kept the letter, and when 'a short time after an order was issued through the camp, for letters to England to be ready on the next day. I felt it my duty to answer the poor woman's letter, to let her know the fate of her husband, and did so.'[59]

Wellington, who usually eschewed uniform and favoured a blue civilian frock coat, cared little about uniform. As William Grattan of the Connaught Rangers wrote in a well-known passage, 'Provided we brought our men into the field well appointed, and with sixty rounds of good ammunition each, he [Wellington] never looked to see whether their trousers were black, blue, or grey; and as to ourselves, we might be rigged out in all the colours of the rainbow if we fancied it.'[60] Letters, diaries, and memoirs contain many references to the appalling state of clothing. Men mended their scarlet jackets with bits of grey trouser material or cloth of every possible colour, some looted from the dead French, till their uniforms became things of shreds and patches. It was often a case, literally, of 'the old red rag'. Trousers, sometimes short of what mere decency required, were improvised out of blankets.

---

56   W. Verner, (ed.), *A British Rifleman. Journals and Correspondence during the Peninsular War and the Campaign of Waterloo* (London: Black, 1899), p.51.
57   Harrington (ed.), *With the Guards*, p.123.
58   Greenwood (ed.), *Letters*, p.56.
59   J. & D. Teague (eds), *Where Duty Calls*, p.22.
60   Grattan, *Adventures*, p.50.

By the time the army had fought its way as far as the frontier of France, Harry Ross-Lewin of the 32nd thought that uniforms were in such a state of patched and multi-coloured wretchedness, that anybody who had never seen British troops would have been able to recognize them as such. Indeed, he said, 'we must have born an undesirable resemblance to Falstaff's ragged regiment.'[61] This was despite the fact that officially, men were to be issued with new clothing at the end of each year. Ensign Edward Macready of the 2/30th said it all in a letter to his father he wrote from Paris in July 1815 describing the aftermath of the Battle of Waterloo. 'Having lost my baggage, my dress is rather ludicrous; a pair of shoes belonging to a French Grenadier, a pair of blue trowsers taken off a dead officer, shirt taken out of a portmanteau on the field …'[62] In other words, all these items were looted. The rest of his kit was satisfactory, but black with blood and powder.

But what of the women and their clothing? What was true of the men must have applied every bit as much to their wives, if not more so. The women may not have been in uniform, but if anything their clothing was even more vulnerable to the wear and tear of active service. In 1803 William Henry Pyne published a series of illustrations entitled *Camp Scenes* which depicted soldiers and their women both on the march and engaged in various activities in camp. He followed this two years later with *The Costume of Great Britain*, which contained 60 paintings of working-class men and women in scenes of everyday life. Both were successful, and both are an invaluable source of information as to the kind of clothing army wives were likely to be wearing. The illustrations of J.A. Atkinson and cartoons of Thomas Rowlandson are also rich in depictions of contemporary costume.

Empire-line dresses in white muslin or Manchester cotton prints may have been popular with officers' wives, but they were probably not suitable for most working women, who are usually shown wearing one of two types of dress. One was known rather misleadingly as a bedgown. This was a loose thigh-length garment with long sleeves, worn over the petticoat and held together with an apron or a tie. The other popular option was the open robe or gown, which had a fitted bodice, elbow-length sleeves and a split skirt which could be worn down or hitched up using buttons or loops. These garments may have started life in floral patterns, checks or stripes, or just plain colours, and women at home in Britain who could change their clothes, undress at night, and wash and repair clothes easily, may have been able to maintain them in decent condition. When campaigning for months on end however, they would very quickly have become faded, dirty and torn, and even ragged. So far as hats were concerned, the famous mob-cap was probably not much in evidence: it would have given little protection either from sun or rain. Straw shepherdess hats were popular, and more suitable for hot weather, and more easily replaced locally with Spanish or Portuguese versions. These would have given women much better protection from the sun than military caps, but like the men, they no doubt suffered from painfully burnt lips. One solution to this was to place a leaf in the mouth the protect the bottom lip. Contemporary drawings also show working women wearing a round-topped felt hat with a brim, not unlike a bowler. When the weather got cold, a good option was a woollen shawl crossed over the shoulders and tucked into the apron or waistband. Best of all was a full-length hooded

---

61 Wardell (ed.), *With the Thirty Second*, p.235.
62 Edward Macready, 'Letter of Ensign Edward Neville Macready to his father', in G. Glover (ed.), *The Waterloo Archive*, vol.1, p.163.

cloak. These came in a variety of colours, and there are various references to them, usually in a very tattered and faded state. Most critically of all in a marching army, there were either flat shoes or black leather ankle boots, which are sometimes depicted as being worn with short gaiters.[63] When these gave out, a pair of old soldier's shoes would do, or perhaps a pair looted from a dead Frenchman. When one officer, detailed to sweep up any baggage or stragglers during the battles in the Pyrenees, saw a noisy group of wives emerging from a forest track 'many dressed in soldiers' jackets, battered bonnets, and faded ribbons, with dishevelled locks hanging over their weather-beaten features,'[64] he was certainly witnessing a common scene. The jackets might well have been French: absolutely anything could be pressed into service.

There must have been occasions when British women were able to acquire new items of clothing, or material to turn into garments from the Portuguese of Spanish, but it seems very likely that a desperate shortage of clothing accounted for at least some of the after-action looting which took place. As the 45th reached Leiria, as the army fell back on the Lines of Torres Vedras, William Brown saw a group of soldiers set about looting a grocer's shop. That was for food, but when he went upstairs, Brown 'found two women, belonging to our army, deliberately folding up the bed-cloths, which they had appropriated to themselves.'[65] Very useful they would have been to make new dresses from. After the storming of Badajoz many eyewitnesses described the frenzied looting of goods of all sorts, including bizarre items of dress. Vast piles of plunder were dragged out of the city, and heaped up under the guard of soldiers' wives. 'The plunder with which our camp was now filled was so considerable, and of so varied a description, that numerous as were the purchasers and different their wants, they all had, nevertheless, an opportunity of suiting themselves to their taste.'[66] The ragged state of clothing, and the difficulty of replacing worn-out items meant that any garment or material that could be obtained was a real wind-fall. It was much the same when the French baggage was captured shortly after the Battle of Vitoria. On 18 June 1813 the Light Division and the 1st German Hussars were engaged in an action at St Millan in which the French lost all their baggage, much of it looted. On the 20th there was a day's halt to allow the army to concentrate, and the French horses, mules and other loot to be auctioned off. 'Portmanteaus and trunks were consequently forced open, and various articles exposed for sale; amongst others, a large assortment of female dresses. Silks, satins, muslins, cambrics, gauzes, lace, flounces, bobbinets, tabbinets, poplins, and all sorts of finery, were put under the hammer.'[67] It was typical of the French to be laden with such loot, and it provided the British women with a vast and welcome array of new clothing, and they were seen all over the place with all sorts of extravagant outfits. They enjoyed a second windfall after the battle the following day. It was probably the first chance they had had in months to get decently dressed

A memorable event occurred to Catherine Exley in June 1814, when 'two ladies from the 39th … sent myself and child a present of some linen. I had occasionally washed for them.'

---

63   K. Hazzard, 'Working Women's Clothes, 1810 – 1820', 95th Rifles, <http://www.95th-rifles.co.uk/civilian-clothing/working-women-clothes-1810 –1820/>, accessed 3 February 2019.
64   Maxwell, *Peninsular Sketches*, vol.2, p.88.
65   Brown (ed.), *The Autobiography*, p.54.
66   Grattan, *Adventures*, p.211.
67   Leach, *Rough Sketches*, p.314.

A watercolour by Edward Eyre c.1780 showing a camp in in Green Park, London. The women are busy with the laundry, using a wheelbarrow to move the tub. (Anne S.K. Brown Military Collection, Brown University)

The ladies were presumably officers' wives, and this small act of generosity was memorable. Catherine believed that her husband had been killed in action (actually he was a prisoner), and just before returning to England, she recalled 'I had some time before bought a coarse cloth sheet of one of the inhabitants, with the intention of reserving it for my husband's corpse, but which I now converted into articles of dress.'[68] This of course required needles and thread, and no doubt many of the women had provided themselves with these essentials before leaving Britain, but they would not have lasted indefinitely, and were not easy to come by in the field. Charles Paget of the 52nd thought it worthwhile to mention his purchase of soap, needles and thread at Torres Vedras in August 1808, very early on in the war in the Peninsula. Four years later, in the spring of 1812, Private Green of the 68th noted that the army was greatly in need of many items, needles and thread included.[69] This would have made the task of women either repairing old and worn-out clothes, or making new garments, especially difficult.

The regimental women were expected to be responsible for washing clothes, and in some cases this was placed on a formal footing: the washing and repair of clothing was usually kept within the regiment, and distinctions of rank were to be observed. Thus, when the

---

68 Probert (ed.), *Exley Diary*, p.41.
69 C. Esdaile and M. Reed (eds), *With Moore to Corunna, The Diary of Ensign Charles Paget, Fifty Second Foot* (Barnsley: Pen & Sword, 2018), p.69, and Green, *Vicissitudes*, p.85.

regulations for the conduct of the newly raised 95th Rifles were drawn up, the role of the regimental wives was not overlooked: 'To help the married women all regimental needlework and washing was to be done by them. The Colonel requests that the officers will never give their linen to wash out of the regiment, and also that they will distribute it nearly equally among the sergeants' wives.' Women of the other ranks were evidently not to be allowed to wash officers' clothing. The regulations went on to lay down that 'The washing of all soldiers to be distributed in equal proportion among the other women of the companies.' The women were expected to wash two shirts and pairs of socks per soldier per week, 'and at least two turnovers.' Turnovers were a linen band tied around the neck and turned down. For this each laundress was to paid 5d by the pay sergeant, so it was a means of earning a little extra income. Hence the insistence on a fair distribution of the work. Rules for sewing were much the same – at least as far as the 95th were concerned. The work was to be 'in house' and was to be seen as a way in which the regimental women might earn a little more money: 'The Quartermaster will never give any needlework out of the regiment which can be done in it, and officers are requested to do the same; the women are also to be recommended to look for needlework in the neighbourhood of wherever the regiment may be, and the officers to give them any aid in their power to procure the same.'[70] This too was intended to give the women some limited earning power. Whether washing and sewing was always done 'in house' under the conditions of actual campaigning seems doubtful. The distinction of rank in respect to laundry was reflected in much the same way in the Cavalry Regulations of 1795, where it was stated that 'No Non-commissioned Officer's wife is to wash for a Farrier, Trumpeter, or Private Man, if such a thing is detected, he [the husband] will be reduced.'[71]

Catherine Exley's mention of washing for officers' wives is an uncommon reference to a women actually performing this service. Another example concerned Captain Dyneley of E Troop Royal Horse Artillery, and illustrated what a disaster it could be when washing got lost. Dyneley was captured along with several others in a skirmish at Majalahonda. The worst of it was they lost their baggage, and with it every stitch of spare clothing. Dyneley escaped, but as he wrote to his mother on 21 August 1812, the woman who did their washing lost all her kit, and with it four of his shirts – a serious matter. What happened to the captured woman he did not relate.[72] Officers did not expect to do their own washing, and seem to have been at a loss if no washerwomen were available. Kincaid, in his well-known *Adventures*, remarked that at the beginning of 1811 that the 95th had no women with them, and therefore no washing. So 'the ceremony of washing a shirt amounted to my servant's taking it by the collar, and giving it a couple of shakes in the water, and then hanging it up to dry.'[73] It was much the same in the closing days of the war. In June 1815, as the army approached Paris in the days after Waterloo, Sir George Scovell's civilian servant recorded that three troopers of the 1st Dragoon Guards had been attached to Scovell's staff 'for letter duties.' One of these men had his wife with him, 'which was a very good job as we were

---

70 Fuller, *Sir John Moore's*, p.159
71 Anon., *Rules and Regulations for the Cavalry*, p.26.
72 Whinyates (ed.), *Letters*, p.53.
73 John Kincaid, *Adventures in the Rifle Brigade and Radom Shots from a Rifleman* (London: Maclaren, 1911), p.18.

beginning to want a washerwoman.'[74] Sir George, who was on Wellington's staff, took care to keep the married dragoon and his invaluable wife with him in his own billet.

When women did do the washing, the materials and methods at their disposal must have been primitive, and would have done nothing to prolong the life of any garment. Soap was usually in short supply. The difficulty was often how to pay them given the fact that the whole army was frequently months in arrears with pay. After the failure of siege of Burgos the 34th Foot received orders to march at short notice. George Bell's washer woman was the well-known Mrs Skiddy, and she came to him with two of his shirts. 'No money yet, Mrs Skiddy. I owe you a long washing bill' he said. But Mrs Skiddy was well aware of the consideration Bell showed her husband Dan. 'Och, never mind that, jewil, if you never paid me. Sure, you're always mindful of Dan on the march, and carry his firelock sometimes a bit when the crather's goin' to drap wid all the leather straps on his back, and nearly choked wid that stock round his thrapple.'[75] Not all women were as reliable as Mrs Skiddy apparently.

By the time Sir John Moore's army had reached Salamanca in December 1808, Charles Paget of the 52nd was not satisfied with the service he was receiving. 'Turned off my washing woman, Mrs Gurwood, and got Mother Sutcliffe' he noted laconically in his diary.[76] Paget's diary suggests that soldier's wives sometime performed other duties for officers. He was very keen on making and colouring sketches of the country which was of course an important military skill, but in October, before the advance began, he noted that 'All my sketches lost by Mrs Walker.' This rather suggests that she had been 'doing' for him, perhaps in place of a soldier-servant. He must have regarded her as trustworthy however, because when she was sent home in October, he entrusted her with a letter.[77]

The importance of women to act as laundresses is shown by the fact that Wellington's headquarters had three women attached to it. The list of the his personal domestic staff included footmen, grooms, orderlies, huntsmen, a goatboy, a butler and a valet, muleteers, farriers and three women. Since there were also three cooks and three assistants, the function of the women must have been to keep Wellington his usual immaculate self. They were presumably soldiers' wives, but their names are not recorded.[78]

Whoever they were, they needed to be tough and resourceful. The 92nd Foot had one such, 'who used to tell with pride how, when a sudden order to march came while the linen of the men she washed for was in the tub she took advantage of the fact that she was billeted on a wood merchant to make a roaring fire, and succeeded in giving every man his shirt as he stood on parade emerging … undefeated by the difficulties of the situation.'[79] This redoubtable old woman also gave brandy to the wounded after actions, made her husband's breakfast before a fight, and lived to be the respectable hostess of an hotel in Argyllshire.

---

74 D. Chandler, 'The Journal of Edward Heeley, servant to Lieutenant Colonel Sir George Scovell, KCB., Assistant Quartermaster General to the British Army in the Campaign of 1815,' *Journal of the Society for Army Historical Research*, vol.64, 1986, pp.94–117
75 Stuart (ed.), *Soldier's Glory*, p.49.
76 Esdaile & Reed (eds), *With Moore*, p.110.
77 Esdaile & Reed (eds), *With Moore*, p.86.
78 S.P.G. Ward, *Wellington's Headquarters. The Command and Administration of the British Army during the Peninsular War* (Oxford: Oxford University Press, 1957), p.194.
79 Gardyne, *The Life*, vol.1, p.298.

Occasionally there was a real wind-fall of fabrics. Just before the Battle of Toulouse opened, the 23rd Foot captured a French vessel on the river. It was carrying a cargo of cloth. This was a godsend to the men, many of whom were wearing trousers they had contrived out of blankets. The women were in a similar state. The colonel distributed the cloth to each company, with orders that every man who could cut or sew was to be put to work making new trousers. One wonders how well they fitted, but the effect was certainly surprising. 'As the cloth embraced every colour of the rainbow, blue, green, red and even yellow, the effect was laughable in the extreme, but the poor fellows had so long been near to breechless that they wore then with pure joy.'[80] The women must have appeared every bit as colourful. This may have been the same incident involving the 18th Hussars. As were driving in the enemy picquets, they captured a herd of bullocks and a quantity of food. But better still, as Arthur Kennedy wrote to his mother, 'A quantity of shirts, cloth etc for their troops also fell into our claws, the former not at all out of the way to some of our *sans chemise* gentry [the British troopers] who were considerably put to their shifts in that useful article.'[81] He might well have remarked that many of the women were also *sans chemise*, and both the shirts and the cloth would have been a god-send.

It not only very often a ragged army, but frequently a very badly shod one. The men were entitled to two pairs of shoes a year – if they were lucky, but this did not apply to the women. Leather footwear wore out very rapidly with the incessant marching over bad roads in all weathers. Fresh supplies from Britain were not often forthcoming, and the parlous state of their shoes is frequently lamented in the diaries and letters of the time. It became a case of making do with whatever came to hand, and some women certainly used soldiers' shoes when they could. As Catherine Exley explained, during the Salamanca retreat: 'I was putting on a pair of regimental shoes belonging to my husband, having previously thrown aside a pair of worn-out boots, which had never been taken off since the first day of wearing, about three months before.'[82] Which gives some idea of the life of a pair of boots or shoes in campaigning conditions.

One way of getting a new pair of shoes was of course to plunder the dead – British or French, it made no matter. Drummer Bentinck described how they were involved in an action near a village called Aldea de Ponte shortly after Wellington had to give up the first attempt on Ciudad Rodrigo. The fight had been close and fierce. Bentinck was grazed by a ball which took off his cap, and the man in front of him, Private Finch, fell back shot through the head. Bentinck had a good pair of shoes on his own feet, but, still under fire, had no hesitation in removing his dead comrade's shoes to give to another man who was nearly barefoot. But this man too was killed, and Bentinck kept them for himself.[83] It was the same after the Battle of Salamanca. The men, ill clad and hungry, would go through the haversacks of the casualties to see if they could find anything edible, anything to wear, or a pair of useable shoes. There was no hesitation about this; it was matter of survival. As Catherine Exley put it after the Battle of Vitoria, 'We stripped the French of everything they

---

80   Crook (ed.), *The Very Thing*, p.121.
81   Eric Hunt (ed.), *Charging against Napoleon. Diaries and Letters of Three Hussars 1808–1815* (London: Leo Cooper, 2001), p.205.
82   Probert (ed.), *Exley Diary*, p.32.
83   Crook (ed.), *The Very Thing*, p.64

had – baggage, ammunition, boots, money, etc. Many enriched themselves by plundering the dead, but I did not take a single crown, for I had other objects of greater interest to engage my attention.'[84]

It was recognized that shoes would be a problem while campaigning, and at the start of the war in the Peninsula at least, there seems to have been an effort to overcome the difficulty, at least at battalion level. Rifleman Harris of the 95th, who had been brought up to be a shepherd on the Dorset downs, had another skill as a shoemaker, and in his famous *Recollections* he describes, how in addition to the usual mountain of kit and ammunition, he was obliged to carry a haversack full of leather, a hammer and other tools for repairing the company's shoes: 'the lapstone I took the liberty of flinging to the devil'. While the opening manoeuvres of the Battle of Vimeiro were taking place, Harris lay down to get some much needed rest. But he was soon disturbed by a sergeant poking him with a rifle, telling to get up and see about repairing shoes, including those of the captain. Some idea of the importance attached to this can be gained from the fact that as the battle developed, and Harris's company was ordered to storm a windmill in the hands of the French, Captain Leach ordered him to fall out: 'We want you here, my man … what shall we do without our head shoemaker to repair our shoes?'[85]

From time to time there were issues of new shoes. After the Battle of Vitoria and the fighting in the Pyrenees which followed, much of it in severe winter weather, a free pair of shoes were issued to troops who had been present between certain specified dates. This act of governmental generosity was considered to be significant enough as to require a General Order, but the soldiers' wives would not have been entitled to any, and would have had to make do with whatever they could buy locally, loot or improvise.

Whether regimental shoe-makers were usual or not, the fact remained that the men and women were sometimes reduced to marching bare-foot. This was the case during the fighting in the mountains in 1813. Major General Robinson, writing to his wife in July, told her that 'Many of my poor fellows have traversed the Pyrenees without either shoe or stocking to their feet.'[86] There was a desperate remedy for this sort of situation. Several diarists and letter writers mention the men, and sometimes the officers as well, using the hides of the slaughtered commissariat bullocks as raw leather to bind their feet as improvised coverings. Young Drummer Bentinck refers to this practice twice. The siege of Badajoz began on 17 March 1812 in cold, wet and muddy conditions which rapidly destroyed their footwear. 'I went many a time and waited until the butchers had killed the cattle and brought the hides for the men to make shoes of as we had no supply from England.'[87] The same thing happened during the Salamanca retreat, when many men were barefoot and bleeding. 'The suffering soldiers tore the warm hides from the beasts as the butchers killed them, and wrapped them round their wounded feet in lieu of shoes.'[88] The women must often have followed suit out of sheer necessity. During the retreat after

---

84 Probert (ed.), *Exley Diary*, p.38.
85 Hibbert (ed.), *Recollections*, p.25.
86 C.T. Atkinson (ed.), 'Letters of Major-General Sir F P Robinson', *Journal of the Society for Army Historical Research*, vol.34 (1956), p.161
87 Crook (ed.), *The very Thing*, p.70.
88 Crook (ed.), *The Very Thing*, p.89.

Talavera, under the usual conditions of bad weather, rough terrain and shortage of rations, an officer of the King's German Legion noted 'The wives of the English soldiers, who were in general so neat and cleanly, were now completely barefooted, and with scarce a whole garment…'[89] They looked altogether forlorn, but they did at least have donkeys to ride, which was more than the infantry had.

---

89 J. Hering, *Journal of an Officer of the King's German Legion* (London: Colburn, 1827), p.177.

6

Hazards

> *I to follow the camp wheresoever the fortune of war,*
> *or rather Divine Providence, might call me.*[1]

The hardships and difficulties with which regimental women had to contend, arduous marches, sleeping rough in all weathers, ragged clothing and frequent hunger were all to be expected on campaign. There were other hazards to be faced, though, one of which was the danger of illness and disease. In almost every campaign and in every theatre of war, deaths by sickness and injury far outnumbered battle casualties. In Spain and Portugal, this was the case by almost three to one. This presented the regimental women with a double challenge. On the one hand, they must have suffered death and sickness in proportion to their numbers, although it was not considered important to keep records, while on the other being frequently called on to help nurse the sick.

Some postings were considerably worse than others, and the West Indies were a particularly unhealthy place to be. On 12 July 1796 the sad remains of the 25th Foot marched from their barracks at Richmond Hill in Grenada to embark on the *Atlantic* transport to return to England. In 15 months, the regiment had lost through sickness, 11 officers, 30 sergeants, 15 drummers, and upward of 500 rank and file. 'We embarked at a most fortunate time' wrote the commanding officer with remarkable understatement, 'as sickness was becoming extremely alarming.'[2] He did not mention the losses amongst the women, but they were certainly considerable. It was much the same when the 70th Foot was posted to Antigua in the autumn of 1803. In the following June yellow fever struck, and the regiment was decimated. Men were dying at the rate of eight to 10 a day, and between June and October 1804 they buried two-thirds of the officers. One of the survivors was Lieutenant Leach, who later transferred to the 95th, whose memoirs record that, 'The ravages occasioned by this infernal pestilence amongst the soldiers, their wives and children, bore a full proportion to that of the officers.'[3] Yellow fever, also known at the time as 'black vomit fever' or 'putrid fever', was by no means the only killer. There was also intermittent fever (malaria) and the flux (dysentery), not to mention the effects of contaminated water, a poor diet, unsuitable clothing in conditions of heat and humidity, and the effects of alcohol, especially raw cane rum. A

---

1 Kelly (ed.), *The Life*, p.242.
2 Jeffery (ed.), *Diary*, vol.1, p.123.
3 Leach, *Rough Sketches*, p.13.

posting to the West Indies was indeed considered to be akin to a death sentence, and it was not unknown for officers to exchange into another regiment or even resign their commissions rather than go there. This is not to be wondered at when the fate of some regiments is considered. In 1784, for example, the 23rd Foot had 315 dead in June, July and August, or 48% of its strength. In March 1796 the 66th was 1,105 strong; by July it had lost 479 men dead, or 43% of its strength.[4] If the regimental wives were in the usual proportion, they may well have comprised 6% of the casualties. Most were probably laid to rest in unmarked graves – perhaps communal graves. One exception was Elizabeth White, wife of Sergeant William White, who died on St Kitts in 1810. Her grave is marked with a tombstone at Brimstone Hill, where she lies with four of her children.[5]

The West Indies were by no means the only dangerously unhealthy place to be posted. The troops sent to Egypt in 1801 were exposed to all manner of diseases, made worse by the appalling heat and dust. The plague made an appearance, and victims were buried without much ceremony in hastily dug holes. A corporal of the 92nd was in charge of a burial detail which threw seven bodies into one hole, and the body of one of the regimental surgeons together with two women in another.[6] In the autumn of 1804, despite the better climate, the garrison at Gibraltar was badly affected with what was described as 'inflammatory fever'. The 54th Foot alone had 456 fever cases and more than 100 deaths out of a strength of 747 all ranks, and the epidemic continued for four months. By the time it was over, the garrison as a whole had lost 54 officers, 864 men and 164 soldiers' wives and children.[7] This appears to be the same devastating outbreak of illness that Bombardier Benjamin Miller of the 4th Battalion Royal Artillery described as plague. Every day, he recorded, parties of soldiers were ordered on grave-digging duty, and frequently many of them would be buried the following day in the very hole they had helped dig. There was little ceremony to it.

> One of the artillery was ordered on this duty; he had left his wife in bed well and hearty in the morning, but in the course of the day, as he was helping to bury a cart load of dead, he threw his own wife into the hole not taking notice till after she was thrown in, when he thought he knew her stockings, which were blue. He stood for a time quite struck, but recovering from his stupor he jumped into the hole to ascertain the truth, for the faces of those who died suddenly in the plague were much disfigured, and very bloody. He examined her hand and her two gold rings, which he took off. She left a large family.[8]

India was another unhealthy posting, not least because a battalion was left there for a prolonged period; short periods of rotation were simply not practical in an era when the voyage out would take several months. The 2/1st Royal Scots for instance had landed at Madras in September 1807 and remained there seven years, not sailing for home till January

---

4   D. Geggus, 'Yellow Fever in the 1790s: The British Army in Occupied Saint Domingue', *Medical History*, 1979, 23, pp.38–58.
5   Howard, *Death Before Glory*, p.174.
6   Anon., *Narrative 92nd*, p.101.
7   Anon., *Records of the 54th West Norfolk Regiment* (Rookee: Civil Engineering Press, 1881), p.32.
8   Miller, *The Adventures*, p.31.

1814, taking with them a number of sick including Sergeant Butler and his wife. Before they left, Butler was sufficiently curious to find out the losses the battalion had sustained. In 1807 there had been 1,006 of all ranks, and during the years in India drafts of a further 941 men had arrived at different times, making a grand total of 1,947. Out of that number, 845 had died or been invalided home as unfit for further service – 43% of the total. Unusually, Butler was also able to ascertain the figures for the regimental wives which were not usually recorded; 62 had been with the battalion on arrival, and a further 20 had come out subsequently with the drafts, or 82 altogether. Of these, 32, or 39% had died. Fifty-seven children had also succumbed to climate and disease. There were also eight women who had left their husbands in favour of officers in other regiments. If they had expected to better their conditions by doing so, they were certainly disappointed. Three of them had died in miserable poverty, and four had become common prostitutes in Madras.[9] Casualties were principally caused by tropical diseases, but as with the West Indies, excessive consumption of raw alcohol added to the problem, in this case arrack rather than rum. In Ceylon, there was 'a still more pernicious drink called Toddy' as William Harness, trying hard to maintain the health of the 80th Foot, told his wife in August 1797. Toddy was made from the fermented sap of coconuts, and was totally forbidden. But it was a losing battle. 'It is utterly impossible to keep the soldiers from it. The women bring it into the Fort under their clothes.'[10]

The worst medical disaster to befall British forces, however, was much nearer to home: the Walcheren expedition of 1809. It was decided to seal the mouth of the Scheldt in order to prevent Antwerp being used for offensive French operations, to destroy the French fleet believed to be at Flushing, and to open a new front in order to assist the Austrians. In July, some 40,000 men sailed in a vast fleet across the North Sea. The force seized the island of Walcheren at the mouth of the Scheldt and captured Flushing after a fierce bombardment. The French quickly poured in reinforcements, and it became clear that Antwerp was not going to be captured. The real problem however was not the French, but the outbreak of Walcheren fever which rapidly began to decimate the British regiments. By 24 September for instance, the 6th Foot, which had arrived 1,000 men strong had lost 100 men dead and had 700 in hospital. Walcheren fever is now believed to have been a lethal cocktail of malaria, typhoid, typhus and dysentery. At the time little of this was understood, and in any case medical facilities proved utterly inadequate. Within a month of landing the British had more than 8,000 cases, with men dying so fast that it was difficult to keep up with the burials.[11] Harry Ross-Lewin, an officer in the 32nd, recorded that by the start of October, the 23rd, 81st and 91st had been struck off duty because they had no men fit. 'An order to bury the dead at night was issued, with a view of concealing the frightful extent of the daily ravages of the fever in our ranks. All the carpenters in Middleburg were fully employed in making coffins for the British.'[12] Casualties from fighting were less than 100. The expedition was defeated by sickness, and called off in September. By October, over 4,000 men had died, and 12,000 were still sick by the following February. Many of the survivors had their health and strength permanently impaired, and Wellington was later to ask that no Walcheren survivors be sent

---

9   Butler, *Narrative*, p.185.
10 Duncan-Jones (ed.), *Letters*, p.114.
11 Wardell (ed.), *With the Thirty Second*, p.136.
12 Wardell (ed.), *With the Thirty Second*, p.136.

to Spain and Portugal; their health would not stand it.[13] Fortunately, the women had been ordered to remain in Britain and not accompany the troops or their fatalities would have surely been in proportion to the deaths amongst the troops.

No particular provision seems to have been made for sick women. The regulations of the 95th Foot stated that 'Whenever a soldier's wife requires some pecuniary aid for illness, her husband will apply to the surgeon, who will represent it to the Commanding Officer, when such assistance as the Charity Fund can afford will be given her.'[14] This was all very well in peacetime. On campaign it was another matter. Catherine Exley certainly had a hard time of it when ill, and was reliant on private charity for survival. After her daughter was born in 1809 (her little son had died previously) she was destitute. Luckily, she was recognized by a corporal who had known her at home in Wakefield, and he and his comrades made room for her in their billet and provided her with food and blankets. She then had an attack of dysentery, and was found collapsed on the floor with her child in her arms, but was saved from this condition by the corporal's wife who made her a fire and supplied her with food. She also recorded being taken ill with a fever sometime before the Battle of Albuera, and being taken to a hospital in Lisbon. She thought that this was reserved for women, but no other sources confirm that was the case.[15]

At the time of the Napoleonic Wars, medical provision was as basic as medical knowledge was limited. The British Army did not employ nurses in its ranks. What nursing there was had to be carried out by untrained soldiers, some of whom may have been sick or wounded themselves, under the supervision of the regimental medical officer. Female nurses are never mentioned in the surviving letters or diaries of army doctors or hospital assistants. William Ferguson, who became Inspector General of military hospitals deplored the use of soldiers as medical orderlies, describing them as 'a collection of incorrigible and incapable villains' who were hopelessly prone to drunkenness. Even if they were not, 'it cannot be supposed that any class of males will make the best nurses for patients confined to a sick ward.' Ferguson's solution was to employ women, since 'the worst woman will make a better [nurse] as being more handy and compassionate than an awkward clumsy man'[16] He appreciated that it would be difficult to find enough women to act as nurses on active service, so their attendance on the sick and wounded should be made a condition of being allowed to accompany the army. In practice, this would have been very difficult. The wives selected 'to go' were certainly expected to make themselves useful, and this included nursing the sick when necessary. But they were not nurses in any formal sense, and since the women who went with the army were there to accompany their husbands, and were part of the marching regiments, they could hardly have been left behind in the general hospitals, though no doubt they may have assisted their regimental surgeon in the regimental hospital.

Some women certainly did possess useful medical skills. On 10 June 1796 Lieutenant Colonel Graham of the 42nd was badly wounded in an attack on a French redoubt on the island of St Vincent. A ball entered his side and came out of his chest, and he was unconscious.

---
13   M.R. Howard, 'Walcheren 1809: a medical catastrophe', *British Medical Journal*, <https://doi.org/.1136/bmj.319.7225.1624>, accessed 2 February 2019.
14   Fuller, *Sir John Moore's*, p.159.
15   Probert (ed.), *Exley Diary*, p.25.
16   William Fergusson, *Notes and Recollections of a Professional Life* (London: Longman, 1846), p.63.

No assistance could be got but that of a soldier's wife, who had been long in the service, and was in the habit of attending the sick and wounded soldiers. She washed his wounds and bound them up in such a manner that when the surgeon came and saw the way in which the operation had been performed, he said could not have done it better, and would not unbind the dressing.[17]

Graham lived to tell the tale after a long convalescence in Britain, and almost certainly owed his life to the expert ministrations of this anonymous soldier's wife.

Some women did find employment in hospitals. One woman who did was Elizabeth Law of the 2/95th. During the Waterloo campaign she remained behind in Brussels, and acted as a nurse at the Jesuits' hospital where she cared for 18 wounded soldiers, and was herself ill with fever. Her husband William was wounded in the battle, and by chance brought to the same hospital, where she found him conscious and sitting in bed.[18] It seems to have been more the case that if wives found themselves in hospitals they were there to nurse sick or wounded husbands, and were then employed to look after other men as well. Catherine Exley's husband Joshua was a corporal in the 34th, and being sick himself was sent in charge of a party of sick men to a hospital in Lisbon. The colonel appointed him ward-master, and gave Catherine the task of looking after other sick men and taking charge of the provisions. Later, near Aranjuez, when the adjutant's wife was struck down with fever, Catherine's hospital nursing experience came in useful, when the officer 'wished me to attend upon his wife during her indisposition.'[19] Hospital work was not without its own risks. Private Wheeler had been wounded at the Battle of the Nivelle, and was sent to the hospital at Fontarabia in June 1814. One of the men in the ward was an acquaintance, a sergeant in the 82nd. His wife was acting nurse to the ward when she pricked her finger with a pin left in one of the bandages. 'She caught the infection, her finger was first amputated, then her hand, the stuff appeared in the stump, she refused to undergo another operation, the consequence was she soon died.'[20]

There were other examples of sick or wounded men being looked after by British women who happened to be on the spot. William Green of the 95th was wounded at the storming of Badajoz, and was sent to a hospital in a convent at Elvas, in Portugal. Here he encountered two English women who were presumably soldiers' wives. He was in great pain and begged the surgeons to amputate his arm. One of the women dressed his arm, but the pain was so bad that he asked her to loosen the bandages. She did so, and as she rubbed the wound with a piece of lint a large piece of bone fell away and onto the floor. 'It was that which pained me' he remembered saying. It was decided in the end to evacuate him to England. One of the Englishwomen took a shirt of his to wash but said it needed darning. There were two shot holes in the left sleeve. 'I told her that was not mine as there were no shot holes in the one I gave her to wash, mine was almost a new one. "Well" said the woman, "Let me see your jacket?" She took it off the bed, and on examination we found two shot holes in the

---

17 David Stewart, *Sketches of the Character, Manners and Present State of the Highlanders of Scotland with details of the Military Service of the Highland Regiments* (Edinburgh: Constable, 1822), vol.1, p.447.
18 Personal communication from Philip Martin, based on family research.
19 Probert (ed.), *Exley Diary*, p.29.
20 Liddell Hart, *Letters*, p.39.

sleeve, although on my person no marks of this kind had been discovered.'[21] The woman had discovered that he had had a narrow escape without being aware of it.

Lieutenant Leslie of the 29th also found an English woman to minister to him when he was dangerously ill with typhus in September 1808, shortly after the French had been driven from Portugal. He was taken to a gentleman's house near Lisbon which was being used as a temporary hospital. 'During my long convalescence, which lasted for several weeks, I was much indebted to the hospital surgeon's wife, Mrs Gundley, who had been our housekeeper during our long abode on board the transport ship during the previous winter. She used to make me light chicken-broth and sago nicely prepared.'[22] Mrs Gundley seems to have been something of a permanent presence in the hospital. Leslie was not so lucky the following year, when he was shot in the leg at Talavera. In great pain, he managed to get as far a house a couple of miles from the battlefield. 'The batman of the company and some women of the regiment got me some straw, and a blanket being spread upon it, I was laid down.' His pain became intense, but there was nothing for it, as he put it, but to grin and bear it, The women themselves were in great distress about their husbands. 'All came in to visit me, and made anxious enquiries about the fate of their husbands …They most kindly made some tea for me.'[23] After that, Leslie had a nightmare journey in search of proper medical help.

Other soldiers managed to acquire better assistance. Ensign Bakewell of the 3/27th was taken very ill with what he called cholera morbus, now known as gastroenteritis, caused by contaminated food and water. He also had the ague (malarial fever), and between the two he could barely stand. He needed to get to a hospital in Lisbon, and fortunately the regiment's transport waggons became available. 'Meanwhile, a young woman belonging to the 97th Regiment offered her services, I agreed to take her with me, thinking she might serve as nurse.'[24] They got to Abrantes in two days, during which he was too ill to take much notice, and then proceeded down to Lisbon by river which was a much more comfortable way of travel. Unfortunately, Bakewell failed to mention what happened to the girl. Did she go to Lisbon with him, and how did he reward her? He does not say.

There were instances of soldiers only surviving through the devoted ministrations of a wife. When the 1st Foot, the Royal Scots, were posted to India in 1807, Sergeant Robert Butler had been instrumental in persuading the colonel to allow the wife of another man, whose name was Allen, to sail with the regiment as a supernumerary. Things turned out unexpectedly. Allen died in India, and Butler married his widow. 'I had then very little knowledge that I was taking out a wife for myself' as he put it, 'and one too, that was to be the means in the hand of Divine Providence of prolonging my days, for had it not been for her nursing care, I must, in all probability, have gone the way of hundreds of the regiment … I was in a very poor state of health when married to her.'[25] The devoted Mrs Butler marched with the regiment on campaign, nursed him when he was ill, and they came safe home at the end of it all.

---

21   J. & D. Teague (eds), *Where Duty Calls*, p.40.
22   Leslie, *Military Journal*, p.72.
23   Leslie, *Military Journal*, p.155.
24   Robertson (ed.), *Exploits*, p.111.
25   Butler, *Narrative*, p.83.

Even in Britain, the ministrations of a good woman could save a life. Joseph Mayett had enlisted in the Buckinghamshire Militia in 1803, and in the August of that year fell ill with smallpox at the Harwich camp. He and another man were in a bad way, but neglected by the regimental doctor. He was saved by the barrack sergeant's wife, who made them mint tea and provided a remedy of her own and looked after them until they were at last admitted to hospital. 'I went to bed in my tent that night and on thursday morning I was quite Blind with them [the pox marks] and helpless in this state I lay till Sunday the Surgeon never Came near me neither had I any assistance only from the Barrack Sergeants wife…' The other man died. '… however the Barrack sergeants wife and some other good natured women whom the Lord had put it into their heads to attend me which they did gratis' were his means of salvation, and nursed him back to health.[26]

Occasionally, there were times when a wounded man got himself into a rather bizarre situation with a woman who might have been expected to assist him. Many years later, when William Grattan came to write his *Adventures in the Connaught Rangers,* the memory of what happened to him when he was wounded in the chest by a musket ball at the storming of Badajoz was still fresh. Grattan was an amusing descriptive writer, and a powerful one too, with a good ear for the brogue of his Irish soldiers. Two of his men got him to his tent, only to find that Nelly Carsons, the wife of his batman, Dan, 'had taken to drinking divers potations of rum to such an excess that she lay down in my bed, thinking, perhaps, that I was not likely again to be its occupant; or, more probably, not giving it a thought at all.' One of the soldiers, Macgowan, tried to wake her, but she was unconscious. 'Why then, sir,' said he, 'sure the bed's big enough for yees both, and she'll keep you nate and warm, for, be the powers, you're kilt with cold and loss ov blood.' Grattan was in not state to argue, and allowed himself to be laid down next to Nelly Carsons. Weak from loss of blood, he fell asleep, and might have remained so had Nelly not woken up. But she came to with a loud grunt, and putting her hand on his leg exclaimed 'Arrah! Dan, jewel, what makes you so stiff this morning?'[27] She was quickly undeceived, and managed to get up and make her officer some tea and chocolate.

Shortly afterwards Dan Carsons himself arrived, bearing a pig-skin of wine which he insisted on putting under Grattan's head as a pillow – one with a handy spigot to suck the wine from. But it leaked, the red wine spilling out over the blanket. 'Oh, Jasus!' was Nelly's reaction, 'he's kilt out and out; see, Dan, how the blood is in strames about the blankets.' Laughing too much can be a dangerous thing thought Grattan, 'and Dan Carsons and his wife made me laugh so immoderately, that a violent discharge of blood from my wound nearly put an end to my career in this world.'[28] It was only the timely arrival of Dr Grant, the divisional staff surgeon which saved the situation.

The sight of columns of troops marching to confront the enemy accompanied by women may seem incongruous enough to the modern imagination; how much more so the presence of children, who represented another hazard for women to deal with. Even at the time there were those who deplored the gaggles of children who seemed to be everywhere. On 8

---

26   A. Kussmaul (ed.), *The Autobiography of Joseph Mayett of Quainton 1787–1839* (Buckingham: Buckingham Record Society, 1986), p.27.
27   Grattan, *Adventures,* p.213.
28   Grattan, *Adventures,* p.214.

'To pack up her tatters and follow the drum.' A satirical cartoon by Thomas Rowlandson, published April 1811, in which the women are depicted carrying the men across a stream. (Anne S.K. Brown Military Collection, Brown University)

June 1813 Major Augustus Frazer, officer commanding the Royal Horse Artillery, noticed a string of mules pass by, one of which was carrying an unusually neat pair of panniers. On closer inspection, Frazer discovered that one of the baskets was lined with scarlet cloth, and inside was a small child, fast asleep. The 'little treasure' as he put it, belonged the mess sergeant's wife of the 23rd, 'and the mother, a respectable-looking young woman, who was riding just by, told me she had carried the little one so far more than a year very safely. The rain was just coming on, and Frazer feared that it was going to be a comfortless night for them. A week later, he was watching the 1st Division, part of Graham's corps, trudge past. He had not seen this division for a while, and the troops looked well. 'The curious figures of the lady and other followers, of all divisions' was however 'beyond description.' Frazer was a compassionate man and a close observer of the plight of the women and children, and he noted on this occasion 'that the only smiling face which passed was that of a little girl of three or four years old; the child was tied on an ass with a string' and was amusing herself with the end of it.[29]

Many of these children had come out with their parents aboard the transports; others were born aboard ship. A very particular hazard faced by many women, however, was giving

---

29   Sabine (ed.), *Letters*, p.150.

birth in the field. In the spring of 1809, when the British army was near Abrantes in Portugal after the taking of Oporto, the weather had turned very hot, and the troops had taken to beginning the day's march before daylight, to avoid the worst of the heat. One day's march had taken the columns through a large pine forest, where they halted and made camp. During the night the wife of one of the 7th Fusiliers gave birth. Next morning however, 'she was placed on a horse and marched with the column,' presumably with the baby in her arms.[30] There was nothing very unusual about the incident, except perhaps that someone had found her a horse – a sympathetic officer with a spare animal perhaps. Childbirth on the march was a common enough occurrence, and it frequently took place in far worse conditions. William Grattan remembered the morning of 4 January 1812, when the 3rd Division began its march to take part in the siege of Ciudad Rodrigo. It was a bitter morning, and they had over 20 miles to go to their resting place for the night:

> At half past six the brigade was in motion, and I scarcely remember a more disagreeable day; the rain which had fallen in the morning was succeeded by snow and sleet, and some soldiers, who sunk from cold and fatigue, fell down exhausted, soon became insensible, and perished; yet strange to say, an Irishwoman of my regiment was delivered of a child on the road, and continued to march with the child in her arms.[31]

The hardihood of many of these regimental women was extraordinary. Captain John Harley of the 47th took part in the harrowing retreat from Burgos. He was acquainted with three brothers serving in the 87th, one of whom was wounded and another stricken with dysentery. Both were placed in a hospital waggon by another friend, together with the wife of an assistant surgeon who had gone into labour. The two lads died the following morning, though the woman apparently survived. Another incident which made an impression on him during the retreat also involved a woman, Mrs Cowell in his own battalion, already encountered as cook to the officers' mess, and the wife of one of the sergeants. She had been advised to stay behind because she was pregnant, but she had refused to listen to advice and marched with the men in the direction of Madrid. No sooner had she reached the camp than she went into labour and gave birth to twins. There were no tents at that stage of the war, and she had to lie under a tree. Some of the soldiers took off their coats to cover her and the babies. Two days later the retreat began, and Mrs Cowell was obliged to march, with her infants, through incessant rain and hail. Several times she had to ford rivers up to her knees, sometimes with enemy shot and shell falling round. Her shoes wore out. Conditions of this retreat were especially dreadful, with thick mud, very little food and no dry bivouacs. Yet despite all this, she managed to struggle on to the safety of Ciudad Rodrigo, from where she was able to get to Lisbon and procure a passage back to England.[32]

Mrs Cowell's experience may have had a happy outcome, but this was not always the case. Joseph Donaldson, a sergeant in the 94th, remembered a harrowing incident on this same retreat. It concerned the wife of a young soldier who to begin with had managed to

---

30 Cooper, *Rough Notes*, p.17.
31 Grattan, *Adventures*, p.134.
32 Harley, *The Veteran*, vol.2, p.64.

keep up with the army as it retreated from Salamanca, until the point came when she could go no further. Her husband was given permission to fall out in order to find her a place in one of the spring waggons, but when they appeared, they were full to capacity, and already numbers of men and women were being abandoned at the side of the road – such as it was. The French cavalry were close behind. The man was now in the most terrible dilemma. If he remained with his wife he would be unable, alone, to defend her, and they would both be captured. He would also be guilty of desertion. This is how Donaldson put it:

> In despairing accents she begged him not to leave her, and one time he had taken the resolution to remain; but the fear of being considered as a deserter urged him to proceed, and with feelings easier imagined than described, he left her to her fate, and never saw her again; but many a time afterwards did he deprecate his conduct on that occasion, and the recollection of it imbittered his life.[33]

Women were not always obliged to give birth in the open, by the wayside, though conditions were always utterly basic. In March 1814, the night after the forcing of the river Adour, the weather was bitter and everyone wet through from the storms of rain and wind. Lieutenant Charles Crowe and two companies of the 3/27th were sent to seek shelter in a scatter of farm houses, where they found seven women of the 6th Division already sheltering. Crowe got his men under cover in some stables where there was plenty of straw, and the officers occupied the house, which proved much less comfortable. The internal walls were merely wattle and daub, and while they were eating what food they had, one of the women in the next room went into labour. During the night, which was marked with rain, hail, thunder, lightning and snow, one of the others also gave birth. Crowe remembered that somewhere in his baggage he had a cake of chocolate which he had brought the whole way from Lisbon, and before they marched on, he generously had his soldier servant make it into 'two good messes for the lying-in women, for which they were very thankful.'[34] When the battalion did march the next day, the two women marched with it, their new-born infants wrapped in soldiers' fatigue jackets.

There was nothing very unusual about such an incident, nor, perhaps about a similar one recounted by an officer named John Stevenson from an unidentified unit which occurred near Santarem during Wellington's advance in pursuit of Massena after the French had withdrawn from in front of the Lines of Torres Vedras. What does make it interesting is the slightly Biblical overtones which he gave to his recollections:

> During these two or three days we went into the nearest villages for the night, as it was cold weather and short days, and the first night I entertained a great stranger. I had taken a small house with winepress and outhouses as lodgings for my company, when one of the men said to me, 'There are some women of some other regiment coming into the yard.' It being then nearly dark, and they unable to find their quarters I went to the door to see who was coming, and one of them, seeming to have

---

33   Donaldson, *Recollections*, p.182.
34   Glover (ed.), *Eloquent Soldier*, p.236.

a child in her arms, I asked to come in, the others passed on to the out houses and got in among the men where they could, for every place was occupied and all were much fatigued and lying down for the night, clothed and accoutred. I saw this woman looked poorly and tired, and I gave her a little of the tea and sugar that I happened to have…and she was with the women of our company all night. In the course of the evening one of our women asked me how old I thought the child was? Of course I replied, 'I do not know.' 'Not twenty-four hours!' said she. The fact was the women had been on the march all the day before, and after dark could not find their regiment, as was often the case with the women that followed the army. So they got into some shed or stable near the road side, and this child was born during the night, and then was carried about during the next day, and the night after I entertained it. The poor woman and her infant were out of doors all the next night.[35]

Stevenson happened to see the woman the day after when she told him that she feared that she and her baby would die. However, she did survive and months later her husband managed to identify him, and came to thank him for his kindness, and to say that all was well.

One wonders how many of these children of war were ever baptised. The answer seems to be very few indeed, if for no other reason than the fact that army chaplains were few and far between. There is a rare entry in the Macduff baptism register for 1808: 'Adam lawful son of Thos Urquhart private in the 10th Regt. of Foot & Margaret Fraser his wife was born and baptized July 3rd in the Isle of Sicily by the Chaplain to the Brigade before witnesses.'[36] The 10th had been based in several locations in Sicily, and Adam's birthplace in censuses is sometimes given as simply Sicily, and sometimes as Messina. It is interesting that the Urquharts did not have the child baptized till they returned to Scotland. It may simply have been that in a Roman Catholic country they could not find a Protestant minister.

It must have been the case that while spared the pains of childbirth, the fathers of these children were presented with a terrible problem, and not just in terms of their military efficiency. As one soldier in the 92nd Highlanders put it, on coming back from picket duty to find that his wife had been delivered of twins, and overwhelmed by this new responsibility, 'Gude preserve me, Betty Watt, what can I do wi' them?'[37] This dilemma was especially acute in cases where the mother died leaving the soldier to cope with the situation as best he could. Judith Hoy for instance, died of fever at Gibraltar in 1813, leaving her husband James with three young children. The situation was more than he could cope with, and he became 'subject to acts of derangements.' The wife of private Michael Corrigan of the 8th Foot also died at Gibraltar, and left six children aged between two and 12.[38] What happened to such children probably depended on the willingness of other regimental women to take them on,

---

35   John Stevenson, *A Soldier in Time of War; or the Military Life of Mr John Stevenson* (London: publisher unknown, 1841), p.128.
36   Personal communication from Graham Robertson.
37   Gardyne, *The Life*, vol.1, p.299.
38   P. Lin, 'Caring for the Nation's Families: British Soldier's and Sailor's Families and the State 1793–1815' in A. Forrest, K. Hagemann and J. Rendall (eds), *Soldiers, Citizens and Civilians: Experiences and Perceptions of the French Wars 1790–1820* (London: Palgrave Macmillan, 2009), p.111.

though some soldiers did try to cope. Joseph Donaldson remembered a man in his brigade whose wife had died leaving him with a baby only a few months old. He might have got some of the other women to take the child, but preferred to look after it himself. Day after day he would march with the child perched on top of his pack. In the end he too became sick and was sent to a hospital somewhere in the rear. What became of them Donaldson never knew.[39] Sometimes, the death of a wife was more than a man could withstand. Benjamin Miller knew of one such case when he was in Gibraltar in 1802. A sergeant who had just lost his wife went to the burying-ground, and blew out his brains with a pistol.[40]

In the case of a soldier who also had his family with the regiment being wounded or disabled, the problems were multiplied. Augustus Frazer had been attending a court martial in Coimbra in March 1813, when, as he explained in a letter to his wife, he met with a military family in a sad state. The soldier concerned belonged to the 88th, and was 25 years old. He had been blinded in action. He was accompanied by 'a decent-looking wife' who was carrying a five-week-old baby in her arms, with a little girl of about two and a half running at her side. Frazer went on 'I was struck with the children, and stopped the poor fellow to hear his story. He was going to Lisbon to be invalided, was quite cheerful, and seemed only to feel for the little girl whom he was obliged to carry on the march, and who was both frightened and hurt when he stumbled or fell down for want of sight. They had possessed a donkey, he said, but it had been stolen from them. I never saw more cheerfulness, or more resignation.'[41] Frazer used his rank to persuade the local commandant to get the family a passage down to river to Lisbon by boat. He was always observant of the women and children, and ready to do something to assist them. In June that same year he saw a very similar sight on the wharf at Passages near the Pyrenees. He met a poor woman, leading a stubborn donkey, with two ragged children, one at the breast, making her slow and painful way to the point of embarkation. Her wounded husband was coming in a boat, and they were to be put aboard a transport. 'It was impossible not to compare our relative situations' Frazer wrote to his wife, 'yet the poor soul made no complaints.' And then he added thoughtfully, 'These accidental meetings do me good.'[42]

Conditions on campaign were such that many children were lost in one way or another. Malnutrition or near starvation accounted for some, while others succumbed to exposure or neglect. A few perhaps were silently disposed of by women unable to succour them in the circumstances they found themselves in. Edmund Wheatley was serving as an ensign in the 5th battalion of the King's German Legion. He had been wounded in the fighting around St Jean de Luz and carried to a barn where the family consisted of some French peasants and an Irish woman belonging to an English regiment. The Irish woman begged him for charity, 'but I saw her pour brandy down the throat of her little suckling one morning probably with the intent to kill it,' so he gave her only a little tea and sugar.[43] One wonders how many desperate women did likewise. Many were prey to illness. In July 1809 for instance Catherine Exley and her husband arrived at Lisbon with the 34th. When the men marched

---

39 Donaldson, *Recollections*, p.225.
40 Miller, *Adventures*, p.30.
41 Sabine (ed.), *Letters*, p.86.
42 Sabine (ed.), *Letters*, p.212.
43 C. Hibbert (ed.), *The Wheatley Diary* (London: Longmans, 1964), p.18.

up to the front, the women on this occasion were left behind in a camp at Alcantara. Six weeks after the troops had left, Catherine's little son died of measles. She had no money and only a change of clothing, the rest having somehow been taken back to England on board the transport they had come out on. Her accommodation was wretchedly bad – she was sleeping on the bare ground – but she managed to sew some material together and stuff it with straw on which to lay the child's body. One of the officers advanced her a little money against her husband's pay, with which she managed to obtain a little coffin, and reserved half a crown for the clergyman who performed the burial. She was fortunate to be able to find one. Catherine was by this time pregnant with another child and shortly gave birth to a little girl. But the child lived only about a year and died the following October.[44]

In the midst of an army at war in a foreign country, one hazard the British women faced was the possibility of sexual violence. British soldiers were certainly guilty of raping Spanish women in situations of particular bloodshed and stress. Contemporary accounts hint darkly at widespread atrocities committed at the storming of Badajoz for example. They are however silent so far as British women are concerned, and it seems unlikely that regimental wives would have been assaulted by their own men, who were after all their husbands' comrades. This is not to say that some British soldiers were unwilling to take advantage of women in some circumstances. In the previous chapter it was seen that Commissary Schaumann described women so hungry at the time of a particularly acute shortage of rations that they offered to sell themselves in return for food, and how Sergeant Donaldson of the 94th expressed his disgust at the men who would exploit a woman's distress in this way. It is difficult to assess to what extent British women may have been the victims of sexual assault because clear evidence is lacking. The primary sources of evidence are the letters and diaries which soldiers wrote at the time, and the memoirs written later, some of them in the era of Victorian propriety. These either make no mention whatever of the problem, or if they do, skirt around it with a variety of circumlocutions. The real danger faced by British wives was during the aftermath of battles, when there was the possibility of being captured by the French. In such cases, as will be seen in the following chapters, the risk of rape was a very real danger.

If the evidence for sexual assault is rare, there was another hazard, especially for the women, for which the testimony is plentiful: the business of crossing rivers. Sometimes there were convenient bridges, and in the later stages of the war in the Peninsula there were also pontoon bridges erected by the pontoon train which made its laborious way in the wake of the advancing troops. More often than not however, rivers were obstacles across the path of the advance which had to be crossed by means of a ford if one could be identified, and if not, by wading. Troops would link arms and march right in, sometimes up to their armpits. This was often a hazardous undertaking, and for women in long skirts, an especial nightmare.

In the autumn of 1810, when the French under Massena were withdrawing from Wellington's position in the Lines of Torres Vedras, the pursuing British came up to the river Mondego, 50 yards wide and three feet deep, and with a strong and dangerous current.

---

44   Probert (ed.), *Exley Diary*, p.25.

The allied army crossing the Mondego river, 21 September 1810 by Thomas St Clair. The troops marched into the ford, here narrow and shallow. However, deep and fast flowing crossings were a great hazard for the women especially. (Anne S.K. Brown Military Collection, Brown University)

The cavalry rode across, the infantry waded in columns so that the men could support each other. As one observer noted:

> Many of our women were obliged to wade through the river, which I was heartily sorry to see; but it was not in my power, nor any other man's to give them assistance. But, however, all got safe over, except two or three neddy-asses [donkeys] which, in consequence of being so heavily loaded, were carried away with the force of the current.[45]

This was disastrous; the women involved would have lost all their worldly possessions.

Walter Henry, a surgeon attached to the 66th Foot, witnessed something similar when the Douro at Toro had to be crossed early in the Vitoria advance. The bridge had been destroyed by the French, but repaired sufficiently for the infantry to use it, but the cavalry and the artillery had to ford the river. The water was too deep and the current too swift for some of the donkeys belonging to the women, and a number were swept away. As Henry watched, one of the soldier's wives 'mounted on a good stout ass, swam her animal gallantly a quarter

---

45 Hale, *Journal*, p.62.

of a mile down the river, directing its course to a shelving bank on the proper side, which she reached in safety, assisted by a volley of cheers from the Division. I chanced to be near this gallant person when she first got afloat, and observed that she encouraged her animal in Spanish as volubly as she could.'[46] She was very lucky.

It was sometimes the case that cavalry would ride into the river and help those on foot across by forming a barrier to break the current, or allow foot-soldiers to cling on to the stirrups. This is what happened to Catherine Exley during the Salamanca retreat. She managed to cross a river by hanging onto the bridle of one of the King's German Legion cavalry with one hand, while holding her child aloft with the other.[47] This was not always successful however. The crossing of the Esla in northern Spain on the way to Vitoria was especially dangerous as the river was swollen with rain and snow-melt. Initially it seems to have been almost impossible. William Dent, the surgeon of the 9th Foot, wrote to his cousin describing how Lieutenant General Picton directed the 3rd and 5th Divisions to cross on the evening of 27 May, but it simply was not fordable and they had to return to their camping ground. Some of the cavalry managed to get across lower down, but several men and horses were swept away and drowned.[48] Several men of the 51st Foot were also carried away and drowned in the attempt. It was not surprising that, as at the crossing of the Toro, some of the women lost their donkeys, as they were swept off their feet and taken down stream.[49] The pontoon train finally came up and a temporary bridge was thrown across, and this allowed most of the infantry and the baggage to get across safely, but as one eyewitness put it: 'Here was a scene of jolly confusion, the cavalry forded the river and the commissariat bullocks swimming over by their side. I got over on one of the pontoons very lucky. The German infantry floated further up but many unfortunately lost their lives in the attempt.'[50] What chance the women and their children?

Things were rather easier when it came to the crossing of the Nivelle during the campaign in the Pyrenees on 11 November 1813. It had been raining torrents, but the infantry descended from the surrounding heights in files, then formed orderly columns on the bank. The ford was wide enough to allow the troops to march into the stream in platoons, and although the water was deep, they reached the far bank in high spirits if rather muddy. Captain Batty of the 1st Guards watched as the regimental women made the crossing: 'Many of the soldiers' wives were seen wading through the river and dragging themselves through the muddy banks and swampy ground on the opposite shore by the side of the companies to which their husbands belonged.'[51]

When it came to the crossing of the river Nive the following month, the order for which was issued during the night, the women of the 34th were all up and busy with their fires before first light, to prepare a little hot tea for their men before they had to plunge across the

---

46 Walter Henry, *Events of a Military Life* (London: Pickering, 1843), vol.1, p.144.
47 Probert (ed.), *Exley Diary*, p.32.
48 Woodford (ed.), *Young Surgeon*, p.33.
49 Crook (ed.), *The Very Thing*, p.91.
50 W. Graham, *Travels through Portugal and Spain during the Peninsular War* (London: Phillips, 1820), p.19.
51 R. Batty, *Campaign of the Left Wing of the Allied Army in the Western Pyrenees and South of France in the Years 1813–14* (London: Murray, 1823), p.57.

icy river. For some reason a positive general order had been issued that the women were not to cross with the troops, which caused great consternation. More than half a century later, when George Bell was writing his memoirs of these stirring times, he could recall the scene clearly, especially the person of Mrs Skiddy, wife of one of his company, whose formidable personality and Irish talk clearly had given him so much amusement:

> The ladies assembled round a big fire on a dark winter's night to discuss this point; Mother Skiddy, Brigadier-general of the Amazons, so called, addressed the meeting. 'I have the weeest donkey of you all, an' I'll take the *wather* if I'm to swim for it, and let me see who's to stop me, Bridget Skiddy, who *thravelled* from Lisbon here into France; if Dan falls, who's to bury him? God save us! divil a vulture will ever dig a claw into him while there's life in Biddy, his *laful* wife. Now, girls, you may go or stay'; and she began to saddle her ass.[52]

The Adjutant General, one suspects, was no match at all for women like Biddy Skiddy.

There were some narrow escapes in these river crossings. When the army had invaded France itself and the wide river Adour was reached, some of the women decided not to wait for the bridge to be repaired. One of them, with two greyhounds on a leash, stepped into deep water and was immediately carried downstream, and was only saved by the dogs swimming ashore.[53] Others were not so lucky. When the 3rd Division crossed the river on 1 March several of their women and children were drowned.[54] A particularly tragic incident on the same day was recorded by James Anton, in the 42nd Foot. The ford by which the Highlanders were to cross was about three feet deep, and the bottom very stony and uneven. The men got through by supporting each other, but the wife of one of the sergeants, who had a child in her arms, attempted to get through the river on her donkey with the column of troops. The animal slipped and the child fell from her arms into the water. The woman screamed and leaped into the water to save the child, and both were swept away. The husband then plunged in to rescue them, but they were gone forever, and it was only with difficulty that the man was rescued by some of his comrades.[55] After that, the women waited until the engineers had repaired the bridge. At the place where the 6th Division crossed, the water was almost five feet deep, and of course bitterly cold. Cavalrymen rode into the water to assist, but in fact it was necessary to throw ropes across the river, fastened to gun-carriages on either side, so that the troops could hang on to them as they waded.[56] For women in voluminous skirts, trying to hold onto a child or a bundle of possessions, it must have presented the likely prospect of death by drowning or hypothermia. As Mother Skiddy put it when she managed to catch up with her regiment during the closing phase of the Battle of the Nive, 'I'd been up two days ago, only I was drowned *crassin' that bit ov a sthrame,* an' sure I've niver been dry since.'[57]

---

52 Bell, *Rough Notes*, vol.1, p.133.
53 Cooper, *Rough Notes*, p.108.
54 Anon., *Journal*, p.292.
55 Anton, *Retrospect*, p.116.
56 Wardell (ed.), *With the Thirty Second*, p.232.
57 Bell, *Rough Notes*, vol.1, p.143.

The British lines before Alexandria, June 1801. An aquatint after Captain Walker, 3rd Guards. Soldiers and their wives can be seen sheltering from the Egyptian sun in the middle tent. (Anne S.K. Brown Military Collection, Brown University)

Hazards like these were of an obvious nature, but the military life exposed women to all sorts quite unexpected dangers and accidents their stay-at-home sisters were unlikely to encounter. Rather improbably, in South Africa, while in barracks near the Cape of Good Hope, the wives of the 22nd Foot had to contend with aggressive baboons. This was a problem with the washing. Blankets washed and hung out to dry were liable to be stolen by the baboons, never to be recovered. This was serious matter when every item had to be accounted for and the loss of equipment was a military crime.[58] Or there was the case of a woman with the force sailing to Egypt in January 1801 who was eaten by wolves. The fleet had put in to Marmorice Bay to collect wood, water and some extra horses. There were wolves about, and it was necessary at night to keep fires alight near the tents where the sick lay. 'Two men and one woman were devoured by the wild beasts through straggling too far into the woods. Their clothes and part of their bones were afterwards found.'[59] Then there were accidents. Once in Egypt, the force had to establish a hospital at Rosetta. There was an ammunition store not far enough away, and there was an explosion caused by a spark from a pipe. The store was destroyed, the hospital shaken and several people, including a sergeant's wife, were killed.[60]

There were also occasions when officers' wives in particular got more excitement than they had perhaps bargained for. The 12th Light Dragoons had an excellent commissary who managed to travel with more comforts than most of the officers – a wife included.

---

58   Shipp, *Memoirs*, vol.1 p.80.
59   Miller, *The Adventures*, p.17.
60   Anon., *Narrative of a Private Soldier*, p.116.

Lieutenant Hay and other officers had been invited by the commissary to a dinner shortly after the French had been routed at Vitoria. As they were enjoying their cigars one of the wives rushed into the room followed by some of the servants to announce that French dragoons were in the street cutting down anyone within reach. It was in fact a false alarm, some of the muleteers having mistaken a group of Spanish guerrillas for the enemy. There were a few moments of confusion while patrols were sent out to investigate. When it was established that the alarm was indeed a false one, it was discovered that the commissary's wife, a Portuguese servant named Jose and the regimental money chest had all vanished. Fearing the worse, the colonel sent out more patrols to overtake and arrest them, as they were supposed to be on the way back to Portugal. The search seemed hopeless, till one of the muleteers was heard to remark that now they knew the French were not coming, somebody had better go and tell Jose the panic was over. What had happened was that the servant, thinking that the treasure and the commissary's wife were both in danger of capture, had with great presence of mind quickly placed the money chests on a mule, Mrs M. on another, and hurried off into the forest. Here he helped the lady up into a tree, got up another one himself, hauled the chests up and lashed them to the branches. Here indeed they were found, 'more dead than alive from fright' at the prospect of falling into the hands of the French.[61]

It was also unsafe for women to travel alone as one officer's wife found when, having reached Burgos from Lisbon, she was prevailed on to return, a journey of some 300 miles. She lost her purse which made it difficult to find accommodation and food. Then the Portuguese boy she had with her decamped with her horse as well as his own mule, taking her spare clothing. It was more by luck than judgement that she was able to reach Lisbon at

---

61 S. Wood (ed.), *Reminiscences 1808–1815 Under Wellington* (London: Simkin, 1901), pp.119–123.

all.⁶² Another officer's wife, this time trying to reach her husband's regiment from Lisbon on a different occasion, had a bad experience of a different kind. She was, according to Ross-Lewin who told the tale, 'a person of rather masculine appearance', who chose to wear men's riding clothes, a wide black hat and ride astride her mule. Not being with a body of troops or a baggage train, the local peasants thought she might be a man in disguise, and accordingly must be a spy. Despite her threats and entreaties, she was arrested and confined, and then unceremoniously marched back to Lisbon a prisoner. Luckily for her, the assistant surgeon of her husband's regiment chanced to be in the city, and was able to identify her.⁶³ Then there were officers' wives who decided to make the voyage out to join their husbands quite independently, risking both the dangers of the sea and the disapproval of their husbands, like 'Mrs H', wife of a quartermaster, whose husband 'did not wish her to run the dangerous chances of war,' but 'whose natural affection led her to make this voyage to join him.'⁶⁴ Or take the example of Mrs Tonyn, wife of Captain Charles Tonyn of the 48th Foot. In his diary for 2 September 1811, William Swabey of E Troop Royal Horse Artillery noted that he had dined with Captain Macdonald, 'who was endeavouring to procure quarters for Mrs Tonyn, who had come from England to find her husband.'⁶⁵ This was certainly a plucky thing to do, but created difficulties. How was suitable accommodation for an officer's lady to be found at short notice, and how was she to join her husband's regiment, wherever it was in the Peninsula?

These were some of the hardships and dangers faced by women who had been lucky enough to win a place in the ballot to accompany their husband's regiment on active service, or in the case of officers' ladies who chose to go. Arduous marches, sleeping rough, accidents, sickness, childbirth, sexual violence, hunger and thirst, ragged shoes and clothing, all endured in bitter cold or blazing heat; these were the realities of their daily lives. There was however one event in particular when all these factors conspired together to produce unparalleled misery: Sir John Moore's retreat to Corunna in the winter of 1808–1809.

---

62   Harley, *The Veteran*, vol.2, p.67.
63   Wardell (ed.), *With the Thirty Second*, p.163.
64   Graham, *Travels*, p.5.
65   Whinyates (ed.), *Diary*, p.24.

7

Corunna

> *The horrors of this retreat have been again and again, described in terms calculated to freeze the blood of such as read them; but I have no hesitation in saying that the most harrowing accounts which have yet been laid before the public, fall short of the reality.*[1]

After the signing of the controversial Convention of Cintra on 30 August 1808, and the consequent recall to England of Lieutenant Generals Wellesley, Burrard and Dalrymple, the British forces in the Peninsula were left under the command of Lieutenant General Sir John Moore. Moore's army was the only army Britain had in the field at that time, a fact of which Moore was acutely aware, and the government was anxious to make full use of it in cooperation with the Spanish armies in expelling the French from Spain. In order to do this, Moore was to leave a garrison in Portugal, in the area of Lisbon, and to advance into northern Spain with 22,000 men. A further force of 8,000 infantry and additional cavalry were to be sent out to Corunna under Lieutenant General Sir David Baird, with orders to advance into Spain to form a junction with Moore's men advancing from the south. Moore would then command a force of more than 30,000 men, which was much the largest British force to be deployed in the war so far. His intention was to threaten French communications and to operate against any additional French troops entering Spain, giving the Spanish the opportunity to strike a blow further to the south.

From the start, there was concern about the large number of women and children who seemed determined to accompany the troops. Brigadier General Charles Stewart, commanding the hussar brigade, thought too many women had been allowed to come out 'by a strange neglect, or in the indulgence of mistaken humanity.'[2]. However it had happened, Moore was worried about their presence, which he foresaw was likely to cause difficulties for the army and suffering for the women. The *Regulations of the Rifle Corps* stated that the usual proportion of women 'should never be exceeded on any pretext whatever, because doing so is humanity of the falsest kind.'[3] Prescient words indeed. Moore issued a General

---

1   W.V. Londonderry, 3rd Marquess of (Charles Stewart), *Story of the Peninsular War* (London: Colburn,1848), p.128.
2   Londonderry, *Story of the Peninsular War*, p.128.
3   Fuller, *Sir John Moore's*, p.159.

Order designed to discourage as many women as possible from marching with the troops, and offering a generous and humane alternative:

> As in the course of the long march which the army is about to undertake and where no carts will be allowed, the women would unavoidably be exposed to the greatest hardship and distress, commanding officers are, therefore, desired to use their endeavours to prevent as many as possible, particularly those having young children, or such as are not stout, or equal to fatigue, from following the army. Those who remain will be left with the heavy luggage of the regiments. An officer will be charged to draw their rations, and they will be sent to England by the first good opportunity; and when landed, they will receive the same allowance which they would have been entitled to, if they had not embarked, to enable them to reach their homes.[4]

Very few of the women were ready to accept the offer of repatriation even on these generous terms. The Irish wives especially were concerned that they would be shipped to England with no means of returning to Ireland except at their own cost. Most refused to leave their men and prepared to face whatever hardships the coming campaign presented.

Moore's leading regiments began their advance from the camp near Lisbon on 11 October, perilously late in the year. Moving in four columns, the troops had some 300 miles to cover to reach the rendezvous point with Baird's force at Salamanca. From the start there were problems. The Portuguese military maps proved misleading, and the advice from the Portuguese engineer officers regarding the state of the roads was unhelpful. The commissariat department was inexperienced, and there were insufficient carts and waggons to move the army's supplies and equipment. The Treasury had failed to provide sufficient bullion, and the Portuguese suppliers were reluctant to accept anything other than ready cash. In fact, Moore's military chest contained only £25,000, which was not even sufficient to cover the cost of hiring the transport which could be found. Moore informed the government that he intended to rely on the commissariat only for the supply of bread, wine and forage, and to allow the advancing troops (and their wives) to find their own meat – but that this would require a sufficient amount of ready cash.[5]

The difficulties of supply were exacerbated by the number of women who had declined to accept the offer Moore had made of generous repatriation terms, and who insisted in sticking with their husbands. Almost as soon as the advance began, commanding officers were repeating the advice to the women not to stay with their regiments. Only three days after the long march got underway, Charles Paget, an ensign in the 52nd, was conscientiously noting down the gist of what sounds like a reiteration of Moore's original General Order. 'The commanding officer cannot permit any woman with child, (that is pregnant) that hath a child or is not stout and equal to the fatigue in the long march which is about to take place' to go forward. They were urged to return to England, and the names of those willing to do so were to be sent in by tattoo that evening. This appeal had little effect. On 18

---

4   Christopher Hibbert, *Corunna* (London: Pan, 1967), p.38.
5   Hibbert, *Corunna*, p.37.

CORUNNA 125

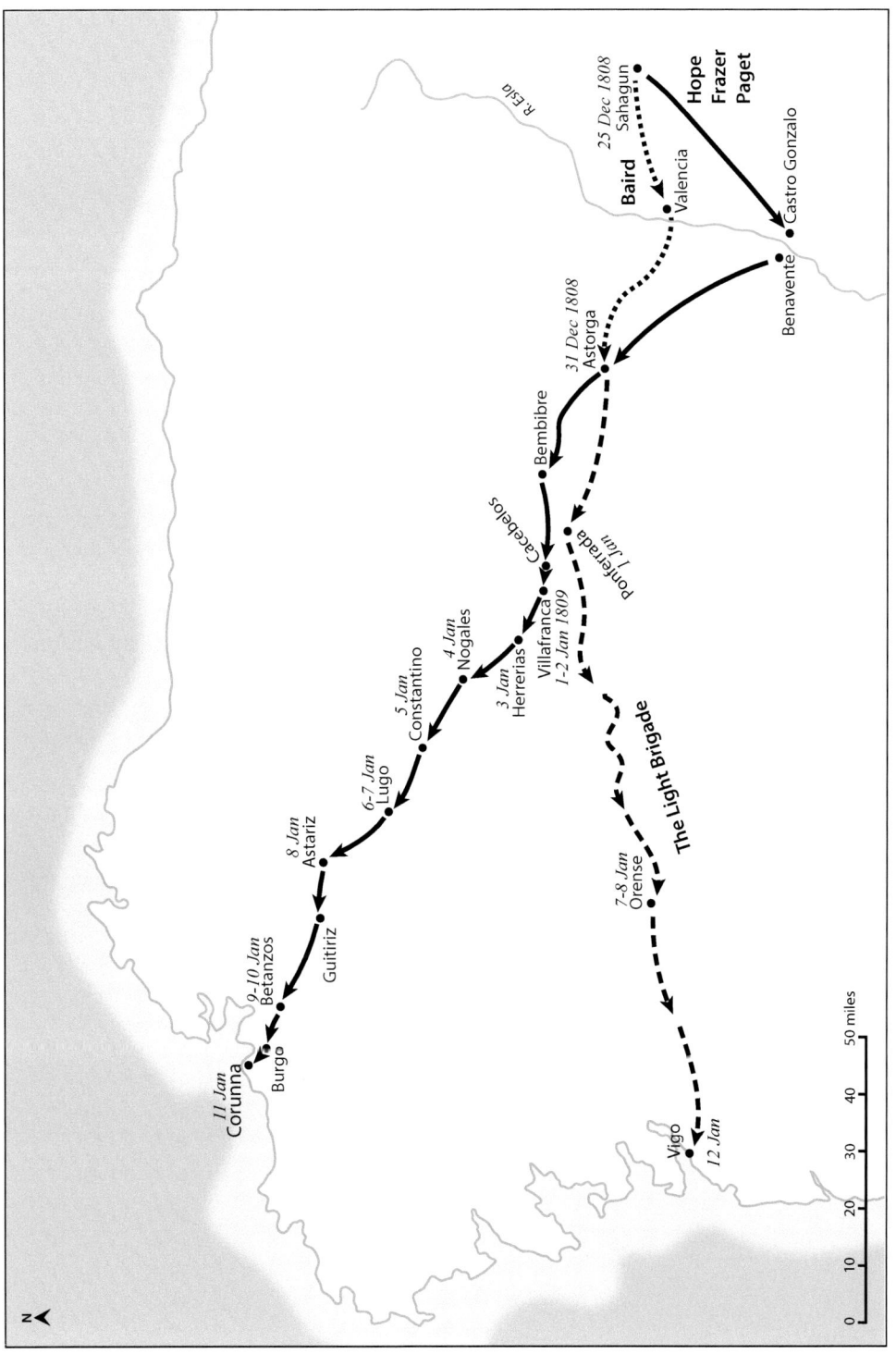

The retreat to Corunna.

October, young Paget's diary returned to the subject. Women were again urged to remain behind with the heavy baggage, and this time, pressure was to be put on their husbands: '… commanding officers are particularly recommended to impress in the minds of married soldiers that the divisions in this part of Portugal are particularly liable to pass through places where the women will be exposed to the greatest hardships at this advanced season of the year.'[6] But whatever lay ahead, soldiers were reluctant to part with their wives, and wives were not prepared to abandon their husbands, and the advice was largely ignored.

At first all went reasonably well, but as they moved north towards the mountains, conditions began to deteriorate. Rain began to fall in torrents, and the rutted tracks became quagmires. Charles Paget was on baggage guard in these conditions and found himself lost and without either food or a guide. 'I was in a dreadful pickle here' he wrote in his diary, 'having given away all my rum to keep the wet from a soldier's wife.'[7] Later, he heard a crash as a cart carrying a sick man and woman went over a precipice. Sometimes the men could sleep in the draughty corridors of convents, and sometimes the women and children were housed with the nuns, who found these foreign women objects of great curiosity. However, all too often they had to bivouac in the open, and the weather was turning bitter. As they approached Salamanca, one soldier of the 71st Highlanders recorded:

> It was one of the severest nights of cold I ever endured in my life. At that time we wore long hair, formed into a club at the back of our heads. Mine was frozen to the ground in the morning and when I attempted to rise my limbs refused to support me for some time. I felt the most excruciating pains over all my body, before the blood began to circulate.[8]

It was the same for everyone including the women and children, and matters did not improve as the army crossed the frontier into Spain.

Moore reached Salamanca on 13 November, where he was assailed by serious news. Napoleon himself was in Spain, having reached Vitoria on 7 November, and was driving the Spanish before him like chaff. Despite their confidence, the Spanish armies of Estremadura, and of Galicia, the very forces he was supposed to be assisting, had been destroyed piecemeal by the French in a series of encounters. Burgos was in French hands, and their cavalry were already at Valladolid, only three marches from Salamanca. Baird's force was still on the way down from Corunna in the northwest, and Lieutenant General John Hope, with the cavalry and most of the guns had yet to arrive. Moore had fewer than 17,000 troops with him, and a single battery of light artillery. He was in a dangerously exposed position, and with no cooperation to be expected from the Spanish, he was already considering that it might be necessary to retire from Salamanca as soon as Hope's column joined him. The matter was decided by the arrival of a dispatch from the British representative with the Supreme Junta at Aranjuez. The only undefeated Spanish army had been destroyed at Tudela on the river Ebro on 23 November. There were now no Spanish forces between Moore's small army and Napoleon's swiftly advancing force which was estimated to be at least 80,000 strong, but

---

6 Esdaile & Reed (eds), *With Moore*, p.85.
7 Esdaile & Reed (eds), *With Moore*, p.101.
8 Hibbert (ed.), *A Soldier of the Seventy-First*, p.22.

which were in fact considerably stronger. There seemed no option but to retreat. Moore was assured that the inhabitants of Madrid were determined to defend their city to the bitter end, but the advanced cavalry of the Imperial Guard were in Madrid by the last day of November, and Napoleon entered the city on 4 December. Despite the fact that Moore believed he could not rely on Spanish promises of cooperation, he was under such intense pressure not to abandon them that he countermanded the order to retreat and instead ordered an advance on Valladolid, which the French had evacuated. He knew that he could not risk a full-scale battle, but calculated that he might be able to get across the French lines of communication and draw off their forces, and so give the Spanish the opportunity the take the offensive again. He was well aware that he might have to run for it in the end.

The advance from Salamanca began well. Rumours of a retreat had dampened the troops' spirits; now they were buoyed up with the prospect of action. Sir Robert Kerr Porter, an artist who had served as historical painter to the Czar of Russia, and who had somehow attached himself to Moore's army, found the beginning of the advance colourful and animating to his painterly eye. The ammunition waggons, the guns and limbers, thousands of bayonets glittering in the rays of the rising sun, the motion of the cavalry, the bat-men and servants leading spare horses, 'and groups of women and children mounted on asses; with hordes of followers of all descriptions, driving heavily laden mules hung with bags, trunks, and portmanteaus; formed, altogether, a scene of animation and of military array that enchanted the soul.'[9] For all his martial enthusiasm however, Porter was well aware of the sufferings attending the army's women, as he described in a letter to a friend written from Sahagun:

> On the day we left Salamanca, I saw a poor creature bearing her infant in her arms, and following her husband, who was attached to one of the regiments then on its march: she had only three days before brought this misery-doomed babe into life; and, pale and faint, she now dragged her enfeebled limbs along, clasping the little sufferer to her breast. To lend her any assistance was totally out of my power; and with a pain at heart … I saw her pass on. Whether she has reached thus far, I am ignorant; but I hardly think her strength would hold out even through the first day's march.[10]

Sights such as these had in fact rapidly convinced Porter that government should take steps 'to prevent these accumulations of the feebler sex following the army'[11] and especially women with children. In many cases they occupied the few waggons and carts intended to convey the wounded, and they consumed already short rations. Porter stated in a letter written at Corunna, at the end of the campaign: 'She almost made it to safety, but died of fatigue, exertion and misery, as the columns were entering Betanzos.' Presumably her baby perished with her.[12]

The 18th Hussars had a small but encouraging engagement with French cavalry at Rueda, from which it became clear that the French had been unaware of the British presence. The

---

9   Robert Porter, *Letters from Portugal and Spain written during the March of the British Troops under Sir John Moore* (London: Longman, 1809), p.200.
10 Porter, *Letters from Portugal*, p.211-212.
11 Porter, *Letters from Portugal*, p.211.
12 Porter, *Letters from Portugal*, p.281.

infantry meanwhile had pushed on via Villapando to Valderas. This was quite a large town but by no means large enough to accommodate the number of troops pouring in. By the time Porter and his party arrived, they found the place filled with cavalry, infantry and all the artillery 'and droves of asses laden with women and children, like gangs of gypsies, crowding the streets.'[13] Then there was a stroke of luck. A French dispatch from *Maréchal* Berthier in Madrid to *Maréchal* Soult at Saldaña on the river Carrion was captured, from which it was apparent that the British army was believed to be in retreat towards Lisbon, while Soult was in an isolated position 100 miles to the north with some 18,000 men. If Moore could attack Soult while he was unsupported, a useful victory might be won. The army pushed on in heavy snow, and at Sahagun Brigadier General Paget led the 15th Hussars in a small but decisive engagement against the French cavalry. Porter inspected the battlefield and discovered that it was not only the British army which was marching with some of its women. Ten or a dozen French cavalrymen lay about, already half-covered with snow, their bodies having already been stripped of their uniforms by the local peasantry. Amongst them, he was surprised to find the body of a woman. Perhaps 'she was some love-impelled damsel, and followed her soldier to the field; or that being enamoured like many an Amazon of war for its own sake, she became an appendage of the camp; and here, by some accidental shot, was deprived at once of life and her military ardour.'[14]

Soult's army was now only some 20 miles away, and he would certainly by now be aware of the British approach. Moore had been receiving messages which indicated that French troops were marching from Madrid to Soult's support, but at first he thought there would be time to attack Soult on Christmas Day and still have time to retire. However, fresh dispatches revealed that the French reinforcements were very much closer than had been realized, – their cavalry patrols had been seen only 100 miles away – and Napoleon himself was believed to be close behind with large numbers of men. This was all too true. Napoleon had learned on 19 December that far from retreating to Portugal, the British were actually advancing. By the 21st he had a clearer picture, and at once gave orders for the concentration of all available French forces which he would lead in person. He would fall on the tiny British army with 80,000 men and destroy it. 'If only these 20,000 were 100,000' he wrote, 'if only more English mothers could feel the horror of war.'[15]

Retreat towards Corunna on the coast was now the only option, but it would be touch and go. Moore was all too well aware of the difficulties. Winter was upon them. The countryside was barren and unlikely to provide fuel, which would make bivouacking almost impossible. The few towns and villages were small and would be unable to provide much food or shelter. The commissariat, already inadequate, would almost certainly be unable to provide enough rations in the frozen landscape. There were far too many women and children and they would have over 200 miles to cover.

The immediate objective was for the army to reach Astorga, beyond the river Esla, and Moore hoped he might be able to steal two marches on the French. The divisions commanded by Hope and Frazer marched out on Christmas Eve in driving rain, taking a southerly route to cross the Esla at Castro Gonzalo and reach Benevente. Baird's troops took the more

---

13   Porter, *Letters from Portugal*, p.210.
14   Porter, *Letters from Portugal*, pp.210–229.
15   Hibbert, *Corunna*, p.90.

northerly road, crossing the Esla at Valencia de Don Juan on 26 December. Napoleon had rested his main force on Christmas Day at Tordesillias, 50 miles to the south, but Soult's cavalry were already snapping at the heels of Baird's column. Paget's cavalry skilfully held them at bay, but there were some casualties. As a sergeant of the 43rd remembered, his regiment being in the rear, the French cavalry pressed forward with great impetuosity, and were frequently in sight, 'and unable perhaps to do more, captured some women and baggage.'[16] What happened to them was not known, but they were perhaps spared the horrors of the retreat. The last of Hope's division crossed the Esla at Castro Gonzalo late on 28 December, and while the 95th Rifles, which had only joined the main force at Sahagun, acted as rearguard, the engineers blew the bridge.

The troops were already in a mutinous mood because they were being forced to retreat, and in some regiments discipline had already begun to break down on the march into Spain. As many units reached Benavente, the men broke ranks and went in search of alcohol, and their officers were in many cases losing control. Extensive wine vaults were discovered under the main square, and hundreds of barrels were rolled up onto the paving above. Muskets were fired into them, the wine gushing out in all directions. Men gulped it up, sometimes on their knees. In the large convent and in the castle in which several regiments and three artillery brigades were quartered, casks of sacramental wine were broached, window shutters were torn off and furniture smashed and used for fuel in every room. August Schaumann, a German assistant commissary-general observed the great fireplaces blazing, well supplied with smashed furniture, much of it antique, he thought. 'On these fireplaces stood a number of camp kettles. The soldiers' wives were washing their things and hanging them just where they chose.'[17] They were no doubt grateful to have some shelter and warmth. The army did not linger long in Benavente. The French were soon on the outskirts of the town, and the scenes as the troops began to march out were chaotic. The alarm began to sound, cavalry galloped about, and the men of the infantry not quite drunk got under arms. 'Meanwhile,' as Schaumann remembered, 'the women and children remaining in the town filled the streets with their wailing and tore their hair with fright.'[18] Some were left behind.

Sergeant Anthony Hamilton of the 43rd Foot remembered that his regiment had been in the convent when the bugles sounded and the regiment fell in. 'A soldier of our company left his wife stupid with intoxication in third storey of the Convent. Hardly had we evacuated the place, when it was occupied by the enemy, and the woman, by some of the soldiers, was thrown from the window and most horribly mangled.'[19] Benavente had been a commissariat depot, and heaps of clothing and food now lay in confusion at the side of the road. There was no time to distribute any of this in an organized fashion; the troops were told to take whatever they wanted and could carry. The rest, heaps of biscuit, salt meat, blankets and uniforms, casks of rum, which would have saved the lives of many in the days to come, was thrown onto great bonfires, while the Spaniards helped themselves. As the last of the infantry marched out of the town, Paget's cavalry surprised the leading elements of

---

16 Anon., *Memoirs of a Sergeant late of the 43rd Light Infantry* (Stroud: Nonsuch, 2005), p.46.
17 Schaumann, *On the Road*, p.93.
18 Schaumann, *On the Road*, p.93.
19 Anthony Hamilton, *Hamilton's Campaign with Moore and Wellington during the Peninsular War* (Staplehurst: Spellmount, 1998), p.45.

the French horse, some chasseurs of the Imperial Guard, and scored a small but brilliant victory, capturing a French general into the bargain.

While Soult's force struggling south from Sahagun, and Napoleon himself was advancing towards Benavente, still hoping to catch Moore's army in a pincer movement, the British were well on the way to Astorga. Things in the army were going from bad to worse. Unable to understand why they were running away from the enemy they would rather fight, some regiments were verging on the mutinous, and not even the prospect of being caught by the French and almost certainly killed, could persuade some men to keep up with the columns. Snow was falling again, and the cold was becoming more intense. Some of the mules and bullocks were beginning to collapse and soldiers' wives had to take their children off the baggage carts and trudge with them on foot. Some of the weaker men were starting to fall by the wayside, to perish in the cold. In the dying hours of 1808, the last of the infantry staggered into Astorga.

The situation here was every bit as bad as at Benavente, and made worse by the presence of the ragged, starving and typhus-ridden remnants of the Spanish army under Romana. Every barrack, convent, church and other building was crammed full of men. The men broke open the wine stores, staved in the casks and drank the flowing wine from the gutters. It was the only thing in plentiful supply. Some of the draught bullocks were shot and butchered, but it was not enough. The nearest substantial food supply was 50 miles further to the west, at Villafranca, and quite apart from the danger of being out-flanked, Moore knew he had to drive his disintegrating army on to reach it. The bulk of the cavalry had already been sent ahead; they could be of little use in the mountainous country which lay ahead. Since the commissariat was already collapsing, Moore also decided to split his force, and send the 3,500 men of the Light Brigade on the road to Vigo, on the coast, where they could be taken off by ship. This would at least do something to ease the passage of rest of the army in the frozen and barren wilderness they now faced on the route to Corunna. As the new year dawned, they were on their way.

As the Light Brigade, commanded by Brigadier General Robert Craufurd (1/43rd, 2/52nd, 2/95th), made its way down the Vigo road the snow was falling fast, as was the temperature. As the track wound up into the mountains, the way became icy, and men slipped and fell. Some were unable to rise again. Rifleman Harris heard Lieutenant Hill say to another officer, 'This is New Year's Day; and I think if we live to see another we shall not easily forget it.'[20] The other officer collapsed and died soon afterwards, and the march now indeed became a matter of survival. 'It was everyone for himself, and God for us all!'[21] Harris, by his own admission, now began to lose track of time, but even in his own distress, marching day and night and virtually starving, he was still able to notice the plight of other members of the regiment, including the women. Towards the evening of what may have been New Year's Day, he told Curling:

> I remember passing a man and woman lying clasped in each other's arms, and dying in the snow. I knew them both; but it was impossible to help them. They belonged to the Rifles, and were man and wife. The man's name was Joseph Sitdown. During

---

20   Hibbert (ed.), *Recollections*, p.82.
21   Hibbert (ed.), *Recollections*, p.82.

this retreat, as he had not been in good health previously, himself and wife had been allowed to get on in the best way they could in the front. They had, however, now given in, and the last we ever saw of poor Sitdown and his wife was on that night lying perishing in each other's arms in the snow.[22]

The conditions of the retreat were such that Harris later reflected that incidents that in other circumstances he would have entirely forgotten became seared into his memory. One such concerned an Irish woman named M'Guire, who was struggling forward in the ranks, in the last stages of pregnancy. When she could walk no further, she stepped aside and lay herself down in the snow, her husband with her. To leave the column in such arctic conditions, and the enemy behind, seemed certain death, and as the riflemen slogged on, they were forgotten. Sometime later, however, the rearguard troops were surprised to see M'Guire, and his wife with a baby in her arms, hurrying after the column. Mrs M'Guire was a hardy soul said Harris, 'and lucky it was for herself and babe that she was so, as that night of cold and sleet was in itself sufficient to try the constitution of most females.'[23] Or anyone else indeed.

Not everyone was so lucky, or tough. When Captain Charles Steevens of the 20th Foot came to write his reminiscences, he particularly remembered the plight of the women during the retreat, especially one whom he described as 'particularly well-conducted' and who had been with the regiment 11 years. Despite this, she lacked the iron constitution require to come through the ordeal: 'She was missed during the retreat; it appeared that her daughter – quite a young girl – lost her mother in the dark one night, and never heard of her again.'[24] Whether the girl survived or not, Steevens did not record; perhaps he never knew.

As the Light Brigade regiments made their painful way towards the port of Vigo, Napoleon had reached Benavente, where, realizing that Moore's army was already into the mountains ahead he decided to leave the pursuit to Soult, while he returned to Paris. A considerable part of the forces under his command were dispersed to other duties, but Soult would still have over 30,000 men, with another 16,000 under Ney in support. This seemed more than enough to drive the disintegrating British army of barely more than 20,000 men into the sea. The safety of the coast was where Moore was heading, and the main force was now trudging on in the direction of Villafranca, where there was a substantial depot of supplies, and where Moore hoped to find a position in which to make a stand.

By New Year's Day, the main part of the army had reached the crumbling little town of Bembibre, where once again fearful scenes of disorder prevailed. Houses were broken into, shops pillaged, and whatever supplies the famished troops could find were seized in the streets – waggon-loads of biscuit, salt meat, clothing, ammunition. 'There was,' wrote one soldier, 'an heterogeneous mass of marauders, drunkards, muleteers, women, children.'[25] Neither the commissariat nor the regimental officers could control the situation, despite the fact that Moore ordered summary executions in the main square. Drunkenness prevailed. Lieutenant Blakeney of the 1/28th remembered rivers of wine running in the streets where

---

22 Hibbert (ed.), *Recollections*, p.83.
23 Hibbert (ed.), *Recollections*, p.85.
24 Steevens, *Reminiscences*, p.71.
25 Anon., *Memoirs of a Sergeant of the 5th*, p.52.

hogs-heads had been staved in, 'where lay fantastic groups of soldiers (many of them with their firelocks broken), women, children, runaway Spaniards and muleteers, all apparently inanimate except here and there a leg or arm was seen to move, while the wine oozing from their lips and nostrils seemed the effect of gunshot wounds.'[26]

These drunkards paid a terrible price. As the French dragoons approached the town, every effort was made to get them on the march, but the rearguard was compelled to abandon them leaving only a small party of cavalry to rescue anyone they could. 'But the enemy came on in force, and the French dragoons, charging onward, through a crowd of men, women and children, slashed to the right and left with their sabres, sparing neither age nor sex.'[27] Lieutenant Blakeney also described the scene: 'Frantic women held forth their babies, suing for mercy by the cries of defenceless innocence; but all to no purpose. The dragoons of the polite and civilized nation advanced, and cut right and left, regardless of intoxication, age or sex. Drunkards, women and children were indiscriminately hewn down.'[28]

At Cacabelos the rearguard fought a spirited holding action, inflicting heavy casualties on the French, which lifted morale and did much to restore discipline. The columns pushed on to Villafranca amidst scenes which by now had become normal. Sir Robert Porter was still managing to write to his friend: 'the road leading to the town whence I now address you was covered with these unhappy fugitives, both male and female of every age.'[29] Here again there were chaotic scenes, though one at least did provide a rare moment of amusement. Schaumann was with another commissary named Moore, who had presumably been stationed at Villafranca with his wife, and was attempting to stow his possessions into the gig which he still possessed, but such was the crush, he was unable to do so, and had lost his temper:

> His wife, a fat woman, who was looking out of the window implored him to be more patient, and urged him above all to keep his presence of mind. But she was nicely rewarded for her pains; for never in my life shall I again hear such a flow of choice invective as this fellow Moore poured forth against her.[30]

She, however, retaliated in kind, with a volley of pots, pans and cups to the delight of the wounded men who were standing nearby.

These were not the only people having difficulties with their private transport. The Paymaster General was one of the small number of officers who had brought his wife on campaign, and was probably now regretting it. Remarkably, he had managed to convey her as far as Villafranca in a four-wheeled carriage drawn by a pair of fine English horses. As Sergeant Robertson of the 92nd remarked, this meant that the troops often had to get out of the way to let the carriage through, 'not a pleasant matter for poor fellows worn out with the want of food and clothing.'[31] Just beyond Villafranca, the carriage became so stuck that

---

26 Blakeney, *A Boy*, p.49.
27 Hamilton, *Campaign*, p.45.
28 Blakeney, *A Boy*, p.51.
29 Porter, *Letters from Portugal*, p.256.
30 Schaumann, *On the Road*, p.116.
31 Robertson, *Journal of Sergeant Robertson*, p.56.

Regimental baggage on the march in mountainous country. Two women can be seen, one with a child on her back, the other on a mule. Aquatint by Thomas St Clair, 1812. (Anne S.K. Brown Military Collection, Brown University)

it could not be extricated, and the Paymaster and his lady were obliged to continue on foot, no doubt to the satisfaction of the struggling infantry.

As the columns struggled into the increasingly mountainous country beyond Villafranca, increasing numbers of the weaker men and women fell out to die of hunger, cold and exhaustion in the bitter weather. John Patterson, a captain in the 50th, never forgot the sights he saw:

> It was a pitiable sight at this period, to behold the forlorn condition of the women and children. Those who could not get upon baggage waggons, trudged along with painful steps, scarcely able to bear up to the weight by which they were encumbered. Many sank during the bitter night famished, way-worn, and in the snow with infants at their breasts, or in their arms, and in this situation were found lifeless and frozen on the following morning. Others took refuge from the storm in the dismantled ammunition carts, that lay about the road, and trying to shelter there, perished with their children in this frail tenement as they crouched in groups together.[32]

---

32 Patterson, *The Adventures*, p.93.

By now the road, such as it was, was strewn with dead horses which had collapsed and been shot, and the snow was stained with blood. There were dead mules and donkeys, broken carts, discarded ammunition and impedimenta of all sorts, spiked guns and starved and frozen soldiers, women and children. It was somewhere on this part of the journey that a soldier of the 42nd remembered these stragglers begging for aid, and 'in the bitterness of their soul, cursed their hard fate, or laying dying beside the dead, and in their last moments seldom breathed a prayer of forgiveness.'[33] This was near Herrerias, where young Blakeney of the 28th came across a group of figures frozen to death.

> Through exhaustion, depravity, or a mixture of both, three men, a woman and a child all lay dead, forming a kind of circle, their heads inwards. In the centre were still the remains of a pool of rum, made by the breaking of a cask of that spirit. The unfortunate people must have sucked more of the liquor than their constitutions could support. Intoxication was followed by sleep, from which they awoke no more; they were frozen to death.[34]

Altogether, remembered one officer, these scenes of suffering 'furnished pictures of human distress and misery which it would be difficult for the imagination to colour too highly.'[35]

Beyond Herrerias the route ascended still further towards Nogales, and on the ascent Captain Charles Cadell of the 28th saw something very similar. Two Spanish waggons had been overturned, and beneath them he saw the bodies of two men, and a woman with a baby at her breast, all frozen to death.[36] On the same stretch of road Captain Gordon of the 15th Hussars saw yet more figures strewn in the deepening snow. Perhaps they had drunk themselves into oblivion as a release. But there was worse to come, for many of the women with the column were pregnant:

> The women who followed the army displayed astonishing energy, but the sufferings they endured beggar all description. This night [probably 3 January] proved fatal to many of these unfortunate creatures. One of them, who had been delivered of twins only three days before, and another with an infant at her breast, were amongst the victims. The children in both these instances were alive when discovered, and owed their preservation to the humanity of some infantry soldiers.[37]

One wonders whether they did in fact survive.

As the retreating army approached Lugo, the next town on the route, the French were snapping at the rearguard's heels, and some of the women were having difficulty staying ahead of them. Some did not, including the wife of the pay sergeant of the 42nd. She gave birth to

---

33 Anon., *Personal Narrative*, p.65.
34 Blakeney, *A Boy*, p.67.
35 T. Sorell, *Notes on the Campaign of 1808–1809 in the North of Spain* (London: Murray, 1828), p.47.
36 Charles Cadell, *Narrative of the Campaigns of the Twenty Eighth Regiment since their return from Egypt in 1802* (London: Whittaker, 1835), p.54.
37 Wylly (ed.), *A Cavalry Officer*, p.172.

a daughter by the wayside, and fell into the hands of the enemy, though she 'was as kindly treated as the circumstances would allow, and suffered to join her husband in Corunna.'[38]

Nobody by now can have been keeping a very accurate record of either times or places, and it is difficult to know whether there were a number of similar incidents, or whether the same incidents were being witnessed by a succession of passing officers and men. Porter, for example, writing to his correspondent in England from Lugo, said that if he described what he had seen 'I should unman your heart, and send my reader weeping from the tale.'[39] He did however tell of a place where the road, skirting the edge of a precipice, turned at an angle, where there lay the body of a woman, while the two babies to which she had just given birth struggled in the snow. Someone found a blanket from somewhere, and a woman who came up in one of the few bullock carts with animals left to pull them took charge of the babies. It may have been this incident, or something very like it that was seen by Adam Neale. Somewhere after Villa France he remembered, though by this time things were getting confused, he noticed women and children frozen to death on the baggage waggons which had been abandoned for want of draught animals to pull them, and he went on:

> …some died of fatigue and cold while their infants were seen vainly sucking at their clay-cold breasts. One woman was taken in labour on the mountain; she lay down at an angle, rather more sheltered than the rest of the way from the drifting sleet and ice – and there she was found dead, and two babies, which she had brought forth, struggling in the snow. A blanket was thrown over her corpse; and the infants were given in charge to another woman, who came up in one of the bullock-carts, to take their chance of surviving through such a journey.[40]

Their chances must have been slim indeed. How could another woman, struggling to survive herself, have contrived to have fed them and kept them warm? Surely, they must have died in that near-arctic wilderness.

It was almost certainly the same scene witnessed by Schaumann, who thought it happened on about 6 January, though he believed the babies were a day or two old. He described the soldier's wife as lying by an overturned cart, with two dead mules laying nearby. Like Porter, he too saw a blanket produced, and the babies handed to a woman in a bullock cart, though he adds that some officers offered the woman a substantial reward for taking care of them.[41] The woman may have been the same seen by Sergeant Robertson, because he remembered that 'she had not gone far when the waggon she was in broke down, and she was left in the middle of the road up to the waist in mud and melted snow.'[42]

Most of these unfortunate women were unknown to the passers-by, but occasionally one was recognized. Sergeant Morley of the 5th Foot was moved by the sight of Mrs Ashton, the wife of one of the regiment's bandsmen, who, 'in that cold and cheerless night, with

---

38 Roy, 'Memoirs', p.98.
39 Porter, *Letters from Portugal*, p.299.
40 Adam Neale, 'The Spanish Campaign of 1808', in Anon. (ed.), *Memorials of the Late War* (Edinburgh: Constable, 1831), vol.1, p.191.
41 Schaumann, *On the Road*, p.121.
42 Robertson, *Journal of Sergeant Robertson*, p.57.

no covering but her tattered clothes, and no shelter during nature's greatest struggles, gave birth to a son.[43] Whether Mrs Ashton and her child survived, he did not mention. Anthony Hamilton also saw a woman he knew – Mrs Thomas, the wife of his pay-sergeant, whom he describes as one of the unfortunate women taken in labour on the march, 'and amid the storms of sleet and snow, gave birth to infants, which, with their mothers, perished as soon as they had seen the light.' But some he described as toiling on 'in the unconquerable energy of maternal love' with their child or children on their backs, only to discover that the little ones had frozen to death.[44] Hamilton was one of those who believed that women had no place on active service, and he was appalled by the curses and imprecations on the lips of women, often intoxicated, laying themselves down to die.

Along the same stretch of road Schaumann seems to have seen another, similar incident. Again, there was a cart, this time with its Portuguese driver dead beside it together with the fallen bullocks, and a woman frozen to death beneath it, '… and the tragic part of it was that her child, who was still alive, was whimpering and trying to find nourishment at her frozen breasts!' This time one of the officers had the child taken from her, and wrapping it up, carried it away with him.[45] This seems to be the same incident described by the anonymous soldier of the 71st, who was by his own account pretty far gone himself. He thought the child was perhaps six or seven months old, and he too describes the harrowing scene, with nobody quite knowing what to do as the child tried to suckle. Then an officer whom he describes as one of Moore's staff came up, and asked that the child be given to him. He rolled it in his cloak 'amidst the blessings of every spectator. Never shall I efface the benevolence of his look from my heart, when he said "Unfortunate infant, you will be my future care."'[46]

There were other instances of men who in their extremity found the strength to show compassion. There were the men of the 43rd who had found shelter from the icy night in a wayside hovel, where they had managed to kindle a fire, who heard a knocking at the door, and found the wife of one of the regiment begging for shelter. As she approached the fire they realized that she had a new-born baby. She had gone into labour the previous day, utterly alone on the mountainside, and was trying to catch up with her husband. The men did what they could, giving some of their own ragged linen to wrap the child in. The following day they told the woman's story to one of their officers, who 'with kindness which none but a great and gallant heart possesses, he alighted from his horse and tramped with us in favour of the poor woman and child.'[47] Some men of the 20th came across a little abandoned boy and supposed that his parents had perished on the road. Colonel Ross took the child up on his saddle, and the orphan was somehow cared for by the men of the regiment and brought safely back to England. Captain Steevens recalled that 'one of the soldiers (an armourer I recollect he was, but I forget his name) adopted him, and treated him as his own child.'[48] The boy grew up in the barracks and was well taken care of, but to the great sadness of the soldier who had adopted him, he later became ill and died.

---

43   Anon., *Memoirs of a Sergeant of the 5th*, p.62.
44   Hamilton, *Campaign*, p.47.
45   Schaumann, *On the Road*, p.121.
46   Hibbert (ed.), *A Soldier of the Seventy-First*, p.30.
47   Anon., *Memoirs of a Sergeant of the 43rd*, p.64.
48   Steevens, *Reminiscences*, p.73.

Surgeon Griffith, of one of the cavalry regiments, who while riding fast to escape the French dragoons who were close behind, came across the body of a woman stretched in the snow with a baby still alive and attempting to suckle. Griffith dismounted and picked up the infant, and as a result was overtaken and captured by the enemy cavalry, baby and all. This story was also related by the anonymous sergeant of the 43rd, according to whom the story had a surprising ending. Griffith ended as a prisoner in France, but had somehow kept the baby with him. He was later paroled and returned to England, where the child was placed in the Military Asylum at Chelsea. Several years later, a soldier turned up and recognized the likeness of the child to a surviving son, and claimed him as the baby he had lost in Spain when his wife died. The sergeant's memoirs are heavily religious in tone, and he told this story to demonstrate the working of divine providence to which he attributed his own survival.[49] It would be heart-warming to think the story is true. The difficulty is that the soldier was able to identify the lad as his son by a scar on one leg, which is difficult to square with the idea that the child had just been born by the wayside.

The point had now been reached where there were insufficient draught animals to drag anything other than the guns, which were to be saved at all costs. The Paymaster General had been forced to abandon the carts carrying the military chest when the bullocks collapsed under the strain. At one point a soldier had been left at the side of the road desperately guarding barrels containing more than £20,000 worth of silver dollars, imploring every passing officer to relieve him of his duty. The Paymaster could find no replacement animals, and with the sound of fighting close in the rear, and the fear of the money falling into the hands of the French, the order was given to Lieutenant Bennet of the 28th to have the barrels thrown over a cliff into the abyss below, and to shoot any man who attempted to seize any of the money. Brigadier General Stewart thought this 'an unwise, and also useless measure.'[50] Far better, he thought, to have distributed it amongst the men, who would somehow have contrived to carry some of the coins; it might even have been an incentive for survival. As the barrels fell and hit the rocks below, a shower of silver coins cascaded over the snow. The sight of more money than they could dream of was too much for some of the women despite their situation, and some of them managed to clamber down the gorge and pick up some of the dollars, including the wife of Corporal Riley of the 42nd, and Mrs Maloney, wife of the master-tailor of the 52nd, both of whom struggled on with a fortune in silver dollars concealed in their clothing. Mrs Maloney, according to the regimental records, was 'a merry one, and often beguiled a weary march to the men with her tales.'[51] Some of this was witnessed by Captain Steevens, of the 20th Foot. 'Many of the soldiers' wives went down into the valley and loaded themselves with dollars, and several were, in consequence, taken prisoners; and the French ... sent them back into our lines in double quick, *but without the money.*'[52]

---

49 Anon., *Memoirs of a Sergeant of the 43rd*, p.65. There is no Surgeon Griffith in any of the cavalry regiments in the 1809 Army List, the closest match is Assistant Surgeon John Griffith of the 23rd Fusiliers, noted as being 'on the staff in Portugal'.
50 Londonderry, *Story*, p.129.
51 William Leeke, *The History of Lord Seaton's Regiment (the 52nd Light Infantry) at the Battle of Waterloo* (London: Hatchard, 1866), vol.2, p.310 and Hibbert, *Corunna*, p.132.
52 Steevens, *Reminiscences*, p.70.

Many of the men, and many of the women too, were by now in tatters, barefoot, leaving bloody footprints in the snow, and some of them dressed in a strange collection of Spanish clothing which they plundered from carts found abandoned by the wayside: blue trousers, white breeches, odd shoes, even blankets with holes cut in them, worn like a shepherd's cloak. And it was the same for the officers. 'I have seen officers of the Guards, and others, worth thousands, with pieces of old blankets wrapt round their feet and legs' remembered a private soldier, 'the men pointing at them, with a malicious satisfaction, saying "There goes three thousand a year."'[53] It was at about this time that one officer, Captain Diggle of the 52nd was assisted by one of the soldier's wives. 'Well do I remember' he recalled, 'the kind act of a worthy woman, Sally Macan, the wife of a gallant soldier of my company, who, observing me to be falling to the rear from illness and fatigue, whipped off her garters, and secured the soles of my boots, which were separating from the upper-leathers, and set me on my feet again.' Diggle was by now in a dangerously weak state, and would have been captured had not a brother officer given him his horse. Wonderful to relate, Diggle had the opportunity of repaying Sally Macan's kindness when the regiment was sent back to Spain: 'A year or so after this I had the opportunity of requiting the kindness of poor Sally Macan, by giving her a lift on my horse the morning after she had given birth to a child in the bivouac.'[54]

More demoralizing even than these conditions was the constant retreating. The men could not understand why they were running away from an enemy they had not fought and who they were confident of beating. The French tended to fall back every time they had a brush with the ragged rearguard. Both officers and men had lost confidence in their general, and Moore seems not to have appreciated that the army's morale and discipline would have quickly returned if a stand had been made. It looked as though there was to be such an action at the village of Constantino, where the ground afforded a good defensive position, and its strength was demonstrated at once when the French were driven back from it several times. However, after dark the position was abandoned and the retreat, some were calling it a flight, went on. Moore had in fact decided to fight at Lugo, which he reached on 6 January. Here there were supplies of both food and ammunition, and the ground was strong. Perhaps this would pull the army together. Orders were even issued for the men to smarten themselves up. When Soult began to probe the British position on the morning of the 7th, he received a decisive check. British discipline and morale had returned, and the fighting power of Moore's troops, ragged and hungry though they were, was clearly displayed. As Captain Gordon passed Moore and his staff, he was surprised to see that 'they were accompanied by a lady mounted on a white charger who I understood to be the wife of Colonel MacKenzie of the 5th Regiment. She betrayed no signs of uneasiness, although the enemy sent a few balls at the party.'[55] MacKenzie was killed on 15 January during the battle at Corunna, so his wife, with or without her white horse, must have been left to return alone to England. Moore, however, was concerned that the French might contrive to outflank him, and Soult indeed ordered Ney to try to do precisely that, and intercept the British via Orense, on Moore's right. The food supplied at Lugo was rapidly consumed, and the retreat was ordered to continue.

---

53   Hibbert, *Soldier*, p.33.
54   Leeke, *History of Lord Seaton's*, vol.2, p.311.
55   Wylly (ed.), *A Cavalry Officer*, p.180.

Remarkably, Sir David Baird, who was still in possession of his carriage, also had his cook. At a village called Guitiriz some of the remaining cavalry found some shelter for their horses in the stable of a large posada and some of the troopers crowded into the rest of the building to attempt to dry their clothes and warm themselves, Captain Gordon of the 15th Hussars amongst them. They found a fire, 'but were soon disturbed by Sir David Baird's cook, who insisted upon having the fire entirely to herself, that she might boil his tea kettle. She was so violently outraged at our non-compliance with this reasonable demand that, after scolding herself out of breath, she retired in great dudgeon.' An aide-de-camp then appeared and ordered everyone out of the house, but they remained where they were.[56]

This must have occurred on 8 or 9 January, at about the same time another small personal tragedy was acted out on the road as the column neared Betanzos. Sergeant Charles M'Gregor of the 92nd had his wife and three little sons with him. Mrs M'Gregor had a donkey for carrying the children, but somehow they fell out of the line and disappeared. Whether the donkey had become too knocked up to move on, or whether Mrs M'Gregor had collapsed, nobody in the regiment could say but they were never seen again. The Quarter Master General ordered M'Gregor to be reduced to the ranks for falling behind to look for his family, perhaps in a desperate effort to maintain discipline. M'Gregor himself was later killed at Maya in the Pyrenees in 1813.

Precisely the same sort of scenes were being witnessed further to the south of the main army, as the Light Brigade made its way towards Vigo. At one point, Rifleman Harris, barefoot and starving, had collapsed and fallen out. He recovered and made his way after the retreating brigade. 'After progressing some miles, I came up with a cluster of poor devils who were alive, but apparently, both men and women, unable to proceed. They were sitting huddled together in the road, their heads dropping forward, and apparently patiently awaiting their end.'[57] The road was littered with dead and dying people and animals, and ahead of him Harris could see the tail-end of the column staggering onwards, women huddled together in the rear, mixed up with the sick soldiery. 'Some of these poor wretches cut a ludicrous figure, having men's great-coats buttoned over their heads, whilst their clothing being extremely ragged and scanty, their naked legs were very conspicuous. They looked like a tribe of travelling beggars.'[58]

Craufurd was determined to bring his brigade through this nightmare and reach Vigo with as many men as possible, and to this end enforced the most ruthless discipline. 'The Rifles liked him, but they also feared him; for he could be terrible when insubordination showed itself in the ranks' recalled Benjamin Harris. During the early part of the retreat, two men were found straying from the main body. Craufurd halted the brigade, convened a drum-head court martial, and sentenced the men to a flogging. While this was going on, Craufurd heard a rifleman named Howans cursing at this proceeding. Howans was immediately tried, and sentenced to 300 lashes despite the fact that the French were close behind. Since the sergeants of the rifles carried no halberds, there was nothing to which to tie Howans, but he was a tough character, and folding his arms, took his flogging without a sound. 'His wife, who was present with us, I remember, was a strong, hardy Irishwoman.

---

56   Wylly (ed.), *A Cavalry Officer*, p.188.
57   Hibbert (ed.), *Recollections*, p.101.
58   Hibbert (ed.), *Recollections*, p.99.

When it was over, she stepped up and covered Howans with his great-coat. The general then gave the word to move on … Howan's wife carrying the jacket, knapsack, and pouch, which the lacerated state of the man's back would not permit him to bear.'[59] Brutal though this was, Harris for one admired Craufurd. Nobody else, he considered, could have saved the brigade, 'and if he flogged two, he saved hundreds from death by his management.'[60] And save them he did. Near the end of the second week of the retreat the column crested a hill, and below them could see the masts of British ships anchored in Vigo harbour. The men had long and ragged beards, and their weapons were rusty. Uniforms and clothing were in shreds, their heads wrapped in bits of cloth, and many were barefoot. Some, through exhaustion, exposure and near starvation, had gone blind.

As the leading troops of the main column approached Betanzos, they too were nearing the end of their *via dolorosa,* but dreadful scenes continued to assail the sight of men who still had the ability to notice. Schaumann noted that there were few women left. Most had fallen by the way somewhere between Villa Franca and Lugo. Somewhere before Betanzos, at a village called Quitterez, he saw a woman fall into a bog and sink up to her waist, 'whereupon, the mud and slime preventing her from rising, she fell, and the whole column marched over her.'[61] From the hills around Betanzos the sea was visible, and officers with telescopes could see the colours of the Royal Navy flying from the shipping in the harbour at Corunna. As the troops descended to the coastal plain, the bitter weather was replaced with gentle sunshine. There was grass and flowers and growing crops. It was like a different world, and in Betanzos, there was food.

Before entering the town the regiments sorted themselves into some sort of order, and it became apparent how many men had been lost to enemy action, the cold and hunger. The 9th Foot could initially muster only some 60 men; between 300–400 were missing, though some stragglers were slowly rejoining. According to Sergeant James Hale, the entire brigade of which they were a part, consisting of the 9th, 23rd, 43rd and 52nd regiments, could only muster 250 men.[62] Stragglers were dribbling in, however, and William Green of the 95th, whose company was the outlying picket of the rearguard, was surprised to see a redcoat approaching accompanied by a woman. He belonged to the 91st, and explained that the previous night his wife had been taken in labour in a hovel by the wayside. The regimental surgeon had attended to her and had told the man to stay with his wife, and if necessary be taken prisoner. Before daylight the next morning, the woman had decided this was not a good idea. '"I don't like the thoughts of *your* going to a *French prison*; and I don't know how ill the French may use *me*"' she said, and declared that she would get up and walk. 'She had no shoes or stockings, and the babe was wrapped in an apron, or shawl. She was almost famished.'[63] The men of the picket had plenty of food, gave her some bread and pork, and told the two to make their way towards Corunna. Green often wondered whether the woman and her baby reached safety, or died on the road, but he was never able to learn what happened.

---

59 Hibbert (ed.), *Recollections*, p.90.
60 Hibbert (ed.), *Recollections*, p.92.
61 Schaumann, *On the Road*, p.130.
62 Hale, *Journal*, p.32.
63 J. & D. Teague (eds), *Where Duty Calls*, p.17.

The engineers blew up the bridge at Burgo across the river Mero, just short of Betanzos, leaving the French cavalry patrols stranded on the other side, and affording Moore's army some respite. By the morning of the 12th French infantry had appeared, and for two days they and the British rearguard, now plentifully supplied with ammunition, exchanged fire as the rest of the army retired to Corunna, where the destruction of all unwanted stores began. Since it had been decided that it would not be possible to get the remaining cavalry horses on board ships, they had to be shot on the beach, to the great distress of many of the troopers who had brought their mounts thus far. One animal did survive, however, greatly to the surprise of Captain Cadell: 'All our animals were left on the beach at Corunna. I recollect but one exception. The wife of Sergeant Monday, the orderly-room clerk, actually carried a lap-dog in a basket over her arm, throughout the whole of this dreadful retreat, and brought it home to England with her.'[64] How she had managed to feed it was a mystery. On the evening of 14 January, the fleet of transports which had been at Vigo sailed into Corunna harbour, and the embarkation of the now redundant cavalry troopers began, while the infantry and artillery were placed around the town to fight a defensive battle. With his army's morale and discipline restored, their hunger appeased and with plentiful supplies of ammunition, Moore was confident of the result.

It had not taken Soult's engineers long to repair the bridge at Burgo, and by 15 January the French were making probing attacks on the British positions. By first light the following morning, they were ready to attack. However, before the Battle of Corunna began there was a pause, and the men of the 50th Foot saw a woman coming directly towards them, carrying a baby:

> She was an Irishwoman, the wife of a soldier of the light company of the 50th regiment, [who] had lain-in on the march, was kindly attended by the doctors of the French army, supported at the expense of Marshal Soult, arrived with his baggage, and was this morning sent over with Soult's compliments, that he would soon visit the 50th regiment.[65]

The fighting started almost as soon as the woman was within the British lines, and the picket of the 50th was driven in as the French artillery opened fire. The regiment, together with the rest of Lord William Bentinck's brigade, the 4th and 42nd, were ordered to fall in. Major Charles Napier, commanding the regiment, ordered the ensigns to unfurl the colours so that Soult would know where to find them.

The Battle of Corunna raged all day, and the British were hard pressed. By evening the French attacks had been brought to a stand-still. Unfortunately, Moore was dead, killed by a cannon ball which had torn his chest to pieces, exposing the internal organs and leaving one arm hanging by a thread. He was hurriedly buried on the high ground near the ramparts of the citadel.

As evening came on the French attacks began to peter out and the bulk of the army was withdrawn to the harbour to commence embarkation in the squadron of ships which

---

64 Cadell, *Narrative*, p.73.
65 J. MacCarthy, *Recollections of the Storming of the Castle of Badajoz. To Which is added Memoirs of the Battle of Corunna* (London: Clowes, 1836), p.199.

had providentially just arrived. To disguise this movement, the rearguard piled fuel on the fires which had been lit and moved about between them to give the impression of a strong force. The troops had to be taken out to the waiting ships in boats, and it was a slow business. One of the vessels which had arrived in the harbour on the morning of the 15th, while the fighting was still in full swing, was HMS *Endymion* (44). Her crew spent most of the night in the ship's boats embarking what one of the officers, Basil Hall, referred to as 'the encumbrances of the army', by which he meant the wounded, some of the horses and guns, and the baggage, what there was left of it. 'In this curious assembly I observed several women, who, strange to say, had gone through the whole campaign, unbroken in spirit, and apparently not much fatigued. They even talked as if they had done no great things.'[66] Some feared they were to be abandoned. Benjamin Miller was with an artillery brigade, and as his ship drifted down the harbour 'we saw hundreds of our soldiers [who] had been doing duty in the garrison, sitting on the rocks by the water's side at the back of the town, waving their hats and calling for boats to take them off and many women and children among them.' When the ships were out of range of the French guns, boats were in fact sent back to bring off the remaining artillery companies, by which time 'The people that were on the rocks what with cold, hunger and fright at being left behind, were almost dead.'[67] Not everyone was so lucky. Mrs Maloney, one of the women who had loaded herself with silver dollars when the military chest was thrown away in the mountains, had managed to get thus far, but as she attempted to scramble out of the boat which had taken her off and up the side of the transport, 'her foot slipped and down she went, like a shot, and owing to the weight of the dollars secured about her person, she never rose again.'[68]

The voyage home was unpleasant. The weather in the Bay of Biscay lived up to its reputation, and in the storm-lashed seas the fleet became widely separated. The transports were desperately overcrowded and jammed with seasick men and women, the wounded, guns, baggage and the few horses it had been possible to save. Two ships were wrecked on the Cornish coast with the loss of 273 souls. In the last days of January, the battered ships began putting in at ports all along the south coast of England, and the survivors of Moore's army limped ashore, their clothing torn and lice-ridden, and scarcely recognizable as uniforms. The troops were bearded, very often barefoot, smeared with dirt. Many were ill or wounded and most were emaciated. The local people, and then the country as a whole, were horrified. The appearance of the surviving women was equally shocking. In Plymouth many of the local people did what they could, as one anonymous soldier of the 42nd described gratefully in rather Biblical terms, he himself felt that he had been saved from perishing by their generosity in raising a subscription: '…you gave the poor destitute widows that had survived, and the poor fatherless children, flannel, and clothes, and comforts; you covered the naked and fed the hungry; for you may well recollect how naked, and bare, and famished, and squalid, the poor women and children were…'[69]

---

66   Basil Hall, *Fragments of Voyages and Travels* (Edinburgh: Cadell, 1831), vol.2, p.326.
67   Miller, *The Adventures*, p.37.
68   Leeke, *History of Lord Seaton's*, vol.2, p.310.
69   Anon., *Narrative of a Private Soldier*, p.94.

One of the 71st Highlanders had come back in a ship in which men from 17 different regiments were mixed up in a state of total disorder:

> Among the women who were put ashore on our arrival at Portsmouth, there was one belonging to our regiment who had rather the appearance of a bundle of rags than a human being. Upon some of the men calling out to her not to expose the regiment, by telling the good English people that such a scarecrow belonged to it, she answered, that she would soon have more prize-money than any of us. This eventually turned out to be the truth; not long afterwards she joined us again, finely dressed, and having 30L in her pocket: she had procured all this by begging:– her lamentable story had taken well; but, I dare say, she got the money more readily on account of having a beautiful child in her arms.[70]

There was a strange post-script to the Corunna retreat, as Benjamin Harris told Henry Curling, his amanuensis, years later. A rifleman named Richard Pullen had his wife with him, and their two children: Charles, 12 years old, and his 14-year-old sister, Susan, who had already lived through the Copenhagen campaign of 1807. Pullen began to weaken almost at once, and his wife and children, were also beginning to fall behind. By the third or fourth day of the retreat, Pullen, who was about ready to drop, had lost his family, and had no idea of their whereabouts. Harris saw no more of them, and when the survivors landed at Plymouth, he was surprised to see Pullen; many better and stronger soldiers had died. The man knew nothing of the fate of his wife and children. Miraculously, they then saw Mrs Pullen making her way up the beach from one of the transports. Of the children, there was no sign. Pullen had hoped they were with his wife; she, that he had charge of them. None of the other riflemen had any information. After a fortnight, Pullen and his wife advertised in the newspapers, and to the surprise of the other 95th survivors, men of one of the artillery brigades, also back in Plymouth, said they had found an English girl in the mountains, lost and crying, whom they had cared for as best they could, and brought back to England. It was Susan, and she was sent on to the regimental depot at Hythe. There was no news of their son, however.

To add to her problems, Mrs Pullen was pregnant when she got back to England. Harris did not know whether her husband was aware of this. The 95th was sent on the disastrous Walcheren expedition the following year, and he died there. She did tell her husband's comrades that 'the child she had given birth to after the retreat, she had every reason to believe, was a Frenchman by his father's side.'[71] She and other women had been raped in a barn where they had taken shelter, by some of the pursuing French. Or as Harris put it, they 'were overtaken by the French in the night, and treated by those gentlemen in a very unceremonious manner.'[72] After the death of her husband, Mrs Pullen was sent back to her home parish in Warwickshire, with Susan and presumably her baby. Sometime after this, a letter arrived at the battalion from her son Charles, who had miraculously survived. He had been rescued by some French troops who had taken care of him, and he was now a prisoner

---

70   Anon., *Vicissitudes*, p.83.
71   Hibbert (ed.), *Recollections*, p.64.
72   Hibbert (ed.), *Recollections*, p.64.

in France. The bugle-major had opened the letter, and Harris was the only man left in the battalion who had known the parents. The old captain of Pullen's company was dead, Harris himself seriously ill, and nobody, as far as he knew, ever replied to the boy's letter. Nor did he know whether Mrs Pullen ever saw her son again, or even knew of his survival.

8

Under Fire

Lightly ye rose that dawning day,
From your cold couch of swamp and clay,
To fill, before the sun was low,
The bed that morning cannot know[1]

Sir John Moore believed that the safety of his army lay in retreat to Corunna rather than in giving battle. Wellington himself, almost always outnumbered, was very careful only to fight on advantageous terms. Throughout the Napoleonic Wars the experience of battle was the exception rather than the rule in the lives of the men and women of the army. It was in any case never the intention that the wives who accompanied the troops on campaign should become involved in actual fighting. When the order 'women and baggage to the rear' was given, they were supposed to do just that, and leave the men to face the enemy.

This was a moment for the taking of what, in all too many cases, was a final farewell. Accounts of these bitter moments differ. Lieutenant John Malcolm of the 42nd, the Black Watch, remembered the occasion of the storming of the Bidassoa during the campaign in the Pyrenees. Awakened at midnight by the roll of drums, he found the camp in motion, the troops forming up in the darkness. As the order to march off was given, he could hear the sound of weeping, and saw one of the soldier's wives 'locked in the farewell embrace of her husband, from who she was parting, as they do who have no hopes ever to meet again.'[2] This was a common sight. It was the same in June 1815, in Brussels, when the order came for the troops to march towards Waterloo. The city was at once full of marching men. One young lady who saw these departures was Charlotte Eaton, who had gone over to Belgium with her brother and sister on 10 June. She had been at the Duchess of Richmond's ball, but was woken from her sleep by the commotion as the regiments assembled and were despatched southwards. She watched the troops from her window.

> Numbers were taking leave of their wives and children, perhaps for the last time, and many a veteran's rough cheek was wet with tears of sorrow. One poor fellow, immediately under our windows, turned back again and again to bid his wife

---

1 Sir Walter Scott, *The Field of Waterloo*.
2 J. Malcolm, 'Reminiscences of a Campaign in the Pyrenees and the South of France in 1814', in *Memorials of the Late War* (Edinburgh: Constable, 1828), p.257.

farewell, and take his baby once more in his arms; and I saw him hastily brush away a tear with the sleeve of his coat, as he gave her back the child for the last time, wrung her hand and ran off to join his company which was drawn up on the other side of the Place Royale.[3]

She also noted that many of the soldiers' wives marched out with their husbands, and saw one young English lady on horseback, an officer's wife, riding along with his regiment towards what was to be the battlefield.

The regiments arriving at Quatre-Bras were thrown straight into the effort to check the advancing French. The 3rd Guards, having marched from Enghien in the very early morning of the 16th, had reached a point near Nivelles, where they expected to halt. Knapsacks were dumped and watering parties were sent out. The sound of cannon fire could be heard in the distance however, and the battalion was ordered to push on with all speed. Before they did so, the women were ordered to be left where they were, and Private Matthew Clay painted a vivid picture of the heart-rending moments of separation whenever the order 'women and baggage to the rear' was given:

> The men whose wives had followed us to the halting ground were permitted to take farewell of them; they being ordered to the rear, and going a short distance apart from the throng; in the open field were joined by others, who delivered to them for security their watches, with various other small articles they held in esteem, also others whose families were absent desired that their expressions of affection might be communicated to their absent wives and families; now the parting embrace although short was sincere and affectionate and expressed with deep emotions of grief as though a state of widowhood had suddenly come upon them, while the loud thunder of the destructive cannon was sounding in their ears.[4]

On the other hand, George Gleig, then a lieutenant in the 85th, and a close and sympathetic observer, could remember a very similar situation in November 1813 when his regiment was assembling, also in the dark, for an attack on Urrugne, when the reaction of the wives seems to have been very different. This was of course very near the end of the war in Spain. 'On these occasions, I have always been struck with the great coolness of the women', he wrote. 'You seldom hear an expression of alarm escape them; indeed, they become, probably from habit, and from the example of others, to the full as indifferent to danger as their husbands.' Gleig thought that the kind of life they led with the army 'sadly unsexes them (if I may be permitted to coin such a word for their benefit).'[5] He could, he thought, recall only one instance of real sorrow being expressed in this situation. Ensign Edward Macready of the 2/30th Foot took much the same jaundiced view. 'Some of our regimental women came up, blessed us, and kissed their husbands, many for the last time', he wrote of the moments

---

3   Charlotte Eaton, *Narrative of a Residence in Belgium during the Campaign of 1815 and of a Visit to the Field of Waterloo* (London: Murray, 1817), p.42.
4   G. Glover (ed.), *A Narrative of the Battle of Quatre-Bras and Waterloo; With the Defence of Hougoumont* (Huntingdon: Trotman, 2006), p.7.
5   Gleig, *The Subaltern*, p.12.

before the battle at Quatre Bras. 'Some memories agitate the hearts of even soldiers' wives, the most callous and insensible creatures in existence.'[6]

The fact was, however, that from the earliest stages of the long war against revolutionary and Napoleonic France, women very frequently managed to flout orders and get into the thick of the action. The desire of women to be with their husbands sprang from the very natural urge to be on the spot if a man became a casualty. The army seems to have been unable to prevent this. Officers, faced with the task of leading troops into the noise, smoke and confusion of action, had other things on their minds than the uncontrollable urge of many of the regimental women to stay close to their husbands in time of danger, and bowed to the inevitable. In 1799 for instance, William Surtees, at that time in the 56th Foot, but who later rose to the rank of Quartermaster in the 95th Foot, was involved in the fierce fighting around Egmont during the campaign in Holland. In the midst of the action, he noticed a girl who had followed one of the grenadier company of his regiment, a man who had volunteered out of the Militia. This girl 'accompanied her protector during the whole of this day's operations, and shared with him every danger and fatigue to which he was exposed.' The hazards were indeed great, with the British troops being in danger of being overwhelmed, and the musket balls flying thick and fast. However, 'no argument could prevail upon her to leave him till the whole business was over, and till the battalion to which her sweetheart belonged was sent to the rear at night.'[7] John Cooper of the 7th Fusiliers noted a very similar scene on 12 March 1811 at the actions at Redinha. This was a vicious firefight, with the air thick with missiles. 'In this rough skirmish I noticed a German woman belonging to the Brunswick rifles, trudging boldly close behind her husband, with a heavy load on her back, in the midst of the battle.'[8]

It seems to have been the case that on some occasions women were actually requested to stay with the regiment. As the 2/34th marched towards the French positions at Vitoria, the colonel called a halt and ordered the men to load their muskets and fix bayonets. 'As usual, I marched with the regiment' remembered Catherine Exley. 'As I was loosing down my husband's ammunition, the colonel, in passing by, asked me to remain with the men all day.'[9] It is not quite clear how this would have worked. Infantry tactics were governed by the need to volley-fire the musket, and to be able to form square if attacked by cavalry. The movements of men were in lines or columns, usually in close order, with light troops skirmishing ahead. So, it is difficult to understand what the women in such situations were actually doing. They could not have marched in the ranks, so perhaps they moved behind, keeping as close as possible to the unit they were attached to. They may perhaps have remained close to the action with the baggage guard, or in company with the regimental staff – the quartermaster, the paymaster and the surgeon. Possibly they watched out for the regimental colours to guide them, though there are no descriptions of this, nor of women present in the squares.

More usually, it was a question of women being reluctant to go the rear when ordered to do so. One such was Mrs Ross, the wife of the quartermaster of the 3/14th Foot. On the

---

6   Edward Macready, 'Letter to his father' in Glover (ed.), *The Waterloo Archive*, vol.6, p.162.
7   Surtees, *Twenty Five Years*, p.28.
8   Cooper, *Rough Notes*, p.52.
9   Probert (ed.), *Exley Diary*, p.36.

morning of the Battle of Waterloo, the battalion, 640 men strong and under the command of Major Tidy, was drawn up on the forward slope of the right wing of the Allied position about 500 metres behind the chateau of Hougoumont. George Kepple, who had just joined the battalion as an ensign, fresh from school and little more than a boy, noted with some awe that Mrs Ross was no stranger to the battlefield: she had been badly wounded in 1807 during Lieutenant General Whitelock's ill-managed action at Buenos Ayres, when her husband had been a sergeant in the 95th Rifles. Mrs Ross stubbornly remained with the battalion after the French assault on Hougoumont had begun and the situation became serious.

> She was loath to quit the field, 'accidents might arise' she told us, 'that would render her services useful.' At last it was suggested to her that what was right and proper in a sergeant's wife, was not so becoming in an officer's lady. Upon this hint she withdrew and passed the rest of Sunday in a neighbouring church, not in the aisle, in attendance upon divine service, but in the belfry, where she enjoyed a better view of the battle than could have been obtained by the Commander of either army.[10]

Young Kepple, who enjoyed the dangerous privilege of carrying one of the battalion's colours, lived to tell the tale, and to become in due course the 6th Earl of Albemarle. Mrs Ross's belief that situations might arise in which she could be of service was exactly the idea which motivated other women, though, in the case of some soldiers, it was too late. At the Battle of Toulouse for instance, John Cooper saw a comrade badly wounded, his leg hanging by a bit of flesh. His wife had been killed at Salamanca some years earlier while giving a drink to another wounded man, and there was nobody to give him succour.[11] It was also at Toulouse that one of the assistant commissary-generals witnessed a sight of a woman going forward under fire to find and rescue the body of her husband, an occasion he never forgot:

> I was induced particularly to observe this woman's proceedings, her object in view being evident from the beginning, and the moment she arrived at the spot where the corpse among several of the dead lay, put in immediate execution. Seating herself on the ground and raising the body to a sitting posture, back to back, she drew the arms one on each side of her neck across her shoulders, raised herself on her feet, and thus performing the pious office, in a stooping position, regained a place of safety.[12]

Something similar happened at the Battle of Vitoria. An unidentified woman had been living with one of the captains of the 94th Foot, the Scotch Brigade, as his wife. 'She accompanied him through the campaign, exposed to all the dangers and privations attending on such a life, with the devotedness that no legally married woman could have surpassed.'[13] During the battle she was left with the baggage, but as some of the wounded made their way to the rear, she heard that her lover was wounded. She mounted her pony and rode into the

---

10   George Thomas Kepple, 6th Earl of Albemarle, *Fifty Years of My Life* (London: Macmillan, 1876), p.24.
11   Cooper, *Rough Notes*, p.17.
12   George Head, *Memoirs of an Assistant Commissary-General* (London: Murray, 1837), p.343.
13   Donaldson, *Recollections*, p.360.

action, regardless of danger, to find him. Unfortunately, she was too late, and the only thing she could do was to remain with his body until it was buried. Sergeant Donaldson, who recorded this incident, went on to say that this woman received no support or help, and was left friendless in a strange country. Perhaps the other officers disapproved of an irregular liaison. She lost her pony and everything else that the captain had provided for her, and the last Donaldson saw of her, she was struggling to keep up with the line of march, the shoes torn off her feet by the mud. What became of her, he never knew.

Many women performed remarkable acts of courage and mercy. At Waterloo, a private of the 27th named McMullen was severely wounded, and his wife, though heavily pregnant, carried him off the battlefield, and in the process was herself badly wounded by a shell. The pair of them were lucky enough to be cared for in a hospital in Antwerp. The man lost both his arms, but the woman recovered and gave birth to a daughter. It was said that Frederick, Duke of York, impressed by this tale of heroic endurance, stood godfather to the child, who was named Frederica McMullen Waterloo.[14] When Charlotte Eaton visited the field a month later, one eyewitness told her how the wife of a wounded sergeant of the 28th was helping him to the rear when she was herself hit and wounded in two places by shell fragments. This story so impressed Miss Eaton that on her return to England she made enquiries, and wrote that she believed that woman had been allowed a pension from Chelsea Hospital. Nor was this all.

> I heard of several similar instances of heroic conjugal affection; and I myself saw one poor woman, the wife of a private in the 27th, whose leg was dreadfully fractured by a musket-ball in rescuing her husband. When struck by the ball she fell to the ground with her husband, who was supposed to be mortally wounded, but she still refused to leave him, and they were removed together to the rear and afterwards sent to Antwerp. The poor man survived the amputation, and is still alive. The woman, who was then in a state of pregnancy, has, since her return to this country, given birth to a son.[15]

Captain Landmann of the Royal Engineers recorded a remarkable encounter he had with a lady (presumably an officer's wife) during the Battle of Roliça in 1808, the second action of the newly landed British army in the war in the Peninsula. The order had been given 'women and baggage to the rear' but Landmann overtook a lady, 'dressed in a nankeen riding-habit, parasol, and straw bonnet, and carrying a rather large rush hand-basket.'[16] He was nonplussed by the sight of this apparition, as the enemy musketry was making the dust fly up all over the road. What was worse, several dead men, and others fatally wounded, lay scattered about the road, all of them already stripped naked by the local scavengers, and the lady was obliged to step over some of them. Landmann thought she must have got there by accident, or perhaps was so confused by the noise of battle that she did not realize where she was, and so he told her that she was going in the direction of the enemy. 'Upon this, she drew herself up, and with a very haughty air, and, seemingly, a perfect contempt of the danger

---

14   W. Trimble, *The Historical Records of the 27th Inniskilling Regiment* (London: Clowes, 1876), p.72.
15   Eaton, *Narrative*, p.317.
16   Landmann, *Recollections*, vol.2, p.145.

The Battle of Vimeiro. As the troops advance a woman and child can be seen hurriedly seeking a place of safety. Engraving after Henri Leveque, 1812. (Anne S.K. Brown Military Collection, Brown University)

of her situation, evidently proceeding from extreme agitation, she replied "Mind your own affairs, Sir, – I have a husband before me."'[17] Landmann thought he had better obey, and she continued on her way. When the battle was over, this mysterious lady appeared again. Landmann was riding with Major General Hill and his staff when the lady, now hurrying towards the advance guard, passed close by. 'General Hill inquired who she was, but no one knew her, though several of the staff-officers, forming the group, had seen her, as well as myself, during the morning, exposed to the severest fire which we had that day experienced.' Who the lady was, and whether she found her husband, they never discovered.[18]

There were other ladies prepared to get into the thick of it. A few days later at the Battle of Vimeiro, the word ran through the ranks that the colonel of the 5th Foot had been shot. This turned out to be a false alarm, but 'his lady hearing this rushed through every restraint down the hill, which was an excuse for many of our men to follow in protection.'[19] This was most gallant of them but probably just an excuse to get into action. Then there was Mrs Grey, 'equally lovely in form and amiable in disposition' who had accompanied her husband, Lieutenant Colonel George Grey, commanding officer of the 30th Foot to Spain. She was not to be put off. '… neither toils nor privations, much less the entreaty of friends, could disuade her from accompanying her husband in all his campaigns, and almost sharing with him the

---

17 Landmann, *Recollections*, vol.2, p.146.
18 Landmann, *Recollections*, vol.2, p.157.
19 Anon., *Memoirs of a Sergeant of the 5th*, p.49.

dangers of the field.'[20] Wherever he was, she was never far away. With wifely care, she also ensured that whenever he went into action he carried a tourniquet. But on 6 April 1812, at the storming of Badajoz, he forgot it. He was mortally wounded, and his last words were for his beloved Eliza.

Another lady, whose exploits were more widely known was Susanna Dalbiac, wife the commanding officer of the 4th Dragoons, whom young George Bell of the 34th described as 'beautiful and delicate'.[21] Beautiful she may have been, but she seems also to have been as tough as any of the soldiers' wives. Her narrow escape during the night-time stampede during the storm which preceded the Battle of Salamanca has already been mentioned. Sleeping on the ground however was not unusual as far as Susanna Dalbiac was concerned. 'She always sleeps in her colonel's tent when the regiment is in bivouac.' wrote Captain Tomkinson of the 16th Light Dragoons, and ended his diary entry on a note of awe: 'In 1811, she lay out a couple of nights on the Gaudiana, in incessant rain, with nothing but a blanket to cover her.'[22] Undaunted by these sort of experiences, she rode onto the battlefield of Salamanca searching for her husband after his regiment had charged into action. Such was her reputation that William Napier, who no doubt knew her, paid her this tribute in his monumental history of the Peninsular War:

> The wife of Colonel Dalbiac, an English lady of gentle disposition and possessing a very delicate frame, had braved the dangers and endured the privations of two campaigns with that patient fortitude which belongs only to her sex. In this battle, forgetful of everything but the strong affection which had so long supported her, she rode deep amidst the enemy's fire, trembling, yet irresistibly impelled forward by feelings more imperious than horror, more piercing than the fear of death.[23]

Years later George Bell, writing his memoirs, recalled the incident vividly. 'In this Battle of Salamanca' he wrote, 'forgetful of herself, supported by strong affection for her gallant knight, irresistibly impelled forward, trembling at the fear of death, she rode amidst the enemy's fire, exposing herself to imminent peril.' This, thought Bell, did wonders for the morale of the troops: 'There was no man present that day fighting the battles of his country that did not fight with more than double enthusiasm seeing that fair lady in such danger on the battlefield.'[24] Her dashing courage was certainly widely known in the army.

Mrs Dalbiac was not the only officer's lady to encourage the troops at Salamanca. Harry Smith of the 95th proudly recorded the popularity of his young Spanish wife, Juana, amongst the ranks, though he was certainly a very partial witness. Still, he described in his autobiography how on the morning of the battle Juana had caracoled her horse, Tiny, amongst the men, to their great delight, because she was always ready to talk and laugh with them. 'Blackguards as many of the poor gallant fellows were,' wrote Smith, 'there was not a man

---

20 Harley, *The Veteran*, vol.1, p.142.
21 Stuart (ed.), *Soldier's Glory*, p.46.
22 Tomkinson, *Diary*, p.185.
23 William Napier, *History of the War in the Peninsula and in the South of France* (London: Boone, 1832–40), vol.4, p.276.
24 Stuart, *Soldier's Glory*, p.47.

who would not have laid down his life to defend her.' After the action began, Smith's groom, a soldier named West, led Juana to the rear, where she had to listen and wait in a state of great anxiety. 'She and West slept on the field of battle, he having made a bed for her with the green wheat he had cut in full ear.'[25] There she slept, holding her horse, which slowly ate her bed of wheat, before she and Harry were reunited the next day.

Relatively few officers took their wives with them to war. The Dalbiacs were a couple exceptionally well equipped, mentally and physically, to withstand the hardships and stresses of life on active service. This was not always the case. At the start of what became the Waterloo campaign, many officers brought their wives out to Belgium, but most of them had been wise enough to leave them in the safety of Brussels, awaiting the outcome of the fighting. A few foolishly allowed their wives to get to the front. One such was Ensign Thomas Deacon of the 73rd. It was unusual for so very a junior officer to be married, and perhaps his inexperience accounted for the fact that Mrs Deacon and her three children were with the baggage train, uncomfortably close to the fighting at Quatre Bras. Deacon was standing next to a soldier named Thomas Morris when a musket ball went through his arm, taking part of the sleeve with it (a dangerous source of infection). 'You are wounded, Sir' said Morris. 'God bless me! so I am,' replied the ensign, dropping his sword, and going to the rear to get the wound dressed.[26] What followed illustrated the difficulties and distress inherent in such situations, no doubt replicated many times over. By the time Deacon had had his wound dressed it was dark, and he spent the night attempting to find his wife and children who should have been with the baggage train. Unable to do so, he at last collapsed from the effects of his wound and had to be conveyed towards Brussels with the baggage. Mrs Deacon, meanwhile, having heard that her husband had been wounded, had spent the night searching for him. When she, at last, heard that he had been sent back to Brussels, her problem was how to get there herself, with the children.

> Conveyances, there were none to be had; and she was in the last stage of pregnancy; but, encouraged by the hope of finding her husband, she made the best of her way on foot, with her children, exposed to the violence of the terrific storm of thunder, lightning, and rain, which continued unabated, for about 10 hours. Faint, exhausted, and wet to the skin, having no other clothes than a black silk dress, and light shawl, yet, she happily surmounted all these difficulties; reached Brussels on the morning of the 18th, and found her husband in very comfortable quarters, where she also was accommodated; and the next day gave birth to a fine girl, which was afterwards christened 'Waterloo Deacon.'[27]

Mrs Deacon was lucky to reach Brussels unmolested. There were reports of wives being plundered by some of the Belgian troops who had fled the battlefield and were infesting the road. Nor did she have to give birth on the field of battle itself, which is what happened to Eliza Tolmie.

---

25 Harry Smith, *The Autobiography of Lieutenant-General Sir Harry Smith* (London: Murray, 1901), vol.1, p.77.
26 Selby (ed.), *Recollections*, p.69.
27 Morris, *Recollections*, p.69.

Eliza was a real daughter of the regiment. Her father was Corporal Wood of the 2nd Dragoons, the Scots Greys, and she had married one of the troopers, Adam Tolmie. Although heavily pregnant, she had managed to follow the regiment to Belgium. It was reported that both her husband and her father had been killed during the Battle of Waterloo, and she spent the night searching amongst the horrors of the area where the regiment had been in action with the assistance of a wounded drummer-boy. Corporal Wood had indeed been killed, but she managed to find her husband, Adam, still alive though badly wounded. With the help of some other women, Eliza got him back to Mont St Jean, where she was able to clean and dress his wounds. The stress of these events caused her to go into labour, and she gave birth to a daughter, Margaret.[28] Another battlefield birth took place at Vitoria. The 1851 census for Bethnal Green records the place of birth of John Gardiner, a 37-year-old linen draper, as 'Spain, Vitoria battlefield'.[29]

It was not surprising that Ensign Deacon was unable to locate his family behind the lines as the troops began to fall back from Quatre Bras towards the Waterloo position. Contemporary descriptions make the rear areas sound more chaotic than the actual scene of the fighting. Edward Costello, a rifleman in the 1/95th, was wounded in the arm at Quatre Bras, and as he made his way to the rear he noticed the contrast between the order and discipline of the regiments drawn up in battle order and the uproar and confusion which existed in the rear. 'This however is generally to be imputed to the soldiers' wives and camp followers of all descriptions, who crowd in great numbers, making enquiries after their husbands, friends, etc, and for whom they generally are prepared with liquors, and other refreshments.'[30] Costello was not a married man himself, and he was amused by the antics of another unmarried rifleman, Josh Hetherington. Too badly wounded to walk, he was being carried back in a cart. In the darkness he could hear the voices of women he knew looking for their husbands, and he had the uncanny knack of being able to imitate their husbands' voices so well that he managed to dupe them into handing him the flasks of liquor – much to their fury when the trick was discovered, and the merriment of other wounded men.

As the army fell back on 17 June, amidst the heaviest rain anyone could remember, there were disconsolate women to be seen everywhere. Lieutenant Jackson came across a group of people clustered around a 12-pounder gun 'upon which sat or clung a dozen or more wounded men, bloody and dirty, with head or limb bound up, and among them two or three females' who may also have been wounded.[31] Ensign William Leeke, (later the Reverend Leeke) newly appointed to the 52nd Light Infantry, saw the same sort of sights as the retreat to the Waterloo position continued. Somewhere between Nivelles and Hougoumont he recorded that 'Each side of the road was now *lined* with soldiers of different regiments, and with some women and drummer boys who had fallen out from fatigue.'[32] In conditions like these, it was all too easy for a soldier and his wife to lose touch with each other. This had always been the case. Earlier in the war Sergeant Robertson of the 92nd had his wife and

---

28 Joanne Major, 'Margaret Tolmie – another "Waterloo Child"', Georgian Era, <https://georgianera.wordpress.com/2015/06/18/margaret-tolmie-another-waterloo-child>, accessed 3 July 2019.
29 Information from Ian Cameron's genealogical research.
30 Costello, *The Adventures*, p.213.
31 B. Jackson, *Notes and Reminiscences of a Staff Officer* (London: Murray, 1903), p.19.
32 Leeke, *The History of Lord Seaton's*, vol.2, p.13.

children with him during the fighting around the pass of Maya in the Pyrenees. His wife became separated from the troops and managed to lose everything belonging to herself and the children. 'I did not see her for seven days after the affair. She thought I was killed, and I was afraid she was carried off.'[33] It is difficult to imagine the stress of such a situation.

At least these women did not have to undergo the ordeal of losing a child on the battlefield, which was a very real danger for those women who ventured too close. Just after the Battle of Orthez, when Wellington's troops were still driving the French back, a corporal of the 94th and one of the bandsmen of the 83rd discovered a child under rather strange circumstances. They were attracted by the cries of a wounded French officer laying in a ditch. They gave him some wine to drink, and noticed a movement beneath his cloak. It was a small boy, about four years old, dressed in English clothes. The Frenchman said that as he had lain wounded, he saw the child coming down the road, obviously lost, in the midst of a fierce exchange of fire between the French and British troops. He had called the child out of the way and sheltered it under his cloak. The corporal and the bandsman took the child to the British camp, and notices were sent out to the various divisions in an effort to trace the mother. After a few days, a woman, who was unhurt, turned up to claim her lost child. 'Her feelings on finding her child, may be better imagined than described.'[34] What became of the French officer who had saved the child was not related.

It could be even worse. During the retreat after Burgos, some of the women had their children in panniers carried by donkeys, and in chaos became separated from them, and they were caught by the pursuing French. 'One Irishwoman, in particular, I remember seeing,' wrote rifleman Costello, 'whose grief seemed inconsolable for the loss she had sustained.' The French, unsurprisingly, were unable to cope with small British children, and sent them back under a flag of truce. 'This was followed by a most interesting scene, as the different mothers rushed forward to clasp their darlings in their arms.'[35]

Sometimes the regimental women found themselves involved in fighting in the rear. During the Battle of Albuera in May 1811 for instance, the women were left helping to defend the baggage, which they did while the ground around them was ploughed up with cannon shot.[36] At the storming of Ciudad Rodrigo on 19 January 1812, some troops had been left in the camp as baggage-guard. When the first shots of the assault rang out, many of the baggage-guard were unable to withstand the temptation to leave their post and join in the attack, leaving too few men behind to defend the camp. This was a serious matter, because locals who infested the camp on the lookout for what they could steal, began to plunder the baggage. 'But the women, with a bravery that would not have disgraced those of ancient Rome, defended the post with such valour that the miscreants were obliged to desist, and our baggage saved in consequence.'[37] The fighting apparently was fierce.

The fighting at Quatre Bras in 1815 was equally ferocious, and some women, despite remaining with the baggage in the rear, were actually mixed up in it. The light company of the 2/3rd Foot Guards were heavily in action defending part of the wood of Bossu, and

---

33 Robertson, *Journal of Sergeant Robertson*, p.110.
34 Donaldson, *Recollections*, p.224.
35 Costello, *The Adventures*, p.159.
36 Probert (ed.), *Exley Diary*, p.28.
37 Grattan, *Adventures*, p.165.

Private Matthew Clay and his comrades 'were led to admire the wife of a soldier of the Coldstream light company, she having fearlessly passed over the slain bringing a supply of provisions for her husband and companions in defence of the wood.'[38] Unfortunately, Clay did not record the name of this devoted woman. Another such was a woman who had 'gallantly follow'd the camp through the war' and who was near an ammunition wagon when it exploded 'and by which her countenance was rendered a blue, shapeless, noseless, mass.' Indeed, as Edward Costello remembered it, 'she actually had no face, or, at all events, was so defaced, it amounted to the same thing.' Despite this frightful disfigurement, shortly after Waterloo, she was married to one of Costello's comrades in the 95th, the redoubtable Tom Plunket. Her service on the battlefield was eventually rewarded with a pension of a shilling a day, so that Plunket was given to saying facetiously 'It was an ill blowing up of powder that blew nobody good.'[39] Plunket was one of the great characters of the 95th. Promoted, reduced to the ranks for drunkenness, flogged and wholly irrepressible, he was celebrated as a marksman for having shot dead a French general during the Corunna retreat. Tom and his new wife no doubt made a famous pair, and it is sad to record that they ended their lives in poverty, Tom keeping body and soul together by selling matches.

There were other occasions when women took an active part in the fighting. The same un-named soldier's wife who had rendered first aid to Lieutenant Colonel Graham of the 42nd Highlanders at the attack on the French redoubt on Vizie mountain on St Vincent in June 1796 was as bold and fearless in the field as she was useful as a nurse. Lieutenant Colonel Stewart had ordered the woman's husband to remain behind as a baggage guard, to look after the knapsacks which the men were directed to discard for the assault. His wife however did not consider this order applied to her, and pushed forward with the troops.

> When the enemy had been driven from the third redoubt, I was standing giving some directions to the men, and preparing to push on to the fourth and last redoubt, when I found myself tapped on the shoulder, and turning round, I saw my Amazonian friend standing with her clothes tucked up to her knees, and seizing my hand, she exclaimed, 'see how the Brigands scamper like so many deer!' – 'Come' added she, 'lets drive them from yonder hill.'[40]

When Stewart enquired later, he discovered that the woman had been in the hottest fire, cheering and animating the men. If only he had thought to record the name of this gallant woman.

Sergeant Douglas of the 1st Foot called to mind something similar which he witnessed at the siege of Flushing during the Walcheren expedition of 1809, when on 13 August the French were driven into the town.

> One of the grenadier's wives got smuggled on board, and I believe was the only woman on the expedition. Her name was Ross, a smart little woman. In the hurry of driving the enemy into the town, a good number got shut out, as the bridges were

---

38 Glover (ed.), *Narrative*, p.7.
39 Costello, *The Adventures*, p.28.
40 Stewart, *Sketches*, vol.1, p.448.

drawn up before all were in, and of course were made prisoners. I saw the same woman with an entrenching shovel take charge of 6 prisoners and march them safe to the rear.[41]

In late January 1810, the Spanish Central Junta, which had been based in Seville, moved to Cadiz, where they were besieged by *Maréchal* Victor with an army of 19,000 men. The Spanish accepted the offer of a contingent of British troops to strengthen the garrison, some of whom were posted in Fort Matagorda, which occupied an isolated position on the landward side of the Bay of Cadiz. The contingent included a number of women, one of whom was Mrs Retson, wife of a sergeant in the 94th.

The fort, which was hardly more than a hundred yards square, came under intense bombardment from a French battery of 13 guns. There was insufficient space for the whole garrison in the casemates, and some had to shelter in the huts which had been built on the gun-platform, Mrs Retson and her four-year-old son amongst them. A 24-pound round shot struck the fascine which she was sheltering by, so she took her child down to one of the bomb-proofs, where she began assisting the surgeon with dressing the wounded, whose numbers were fast increasing. Bandages were running short, so Mrs Retson tore up some of her own linen and that of her husband. Water was also needed for the wounded men, and the surgeon ordered one of the drummer boys to go to the well to fetch some. The drummer, a young lad, hesitated, as well he might given the ferocity of the bombardment. Mrs Retson took the bucket from him and ran out into the courtyard to the well. The enemy fire was so fierce that the bucket rope was severed by a shell fragment, but she managed to retrieve it, filled it, and carried it back to the casemate to give the wounded men some relief. Nor was this all. Despite the fact that some of the other women had been reduced to hysterics, Mrs Retson continued to take an active part in the defence. She carried sandbags to repair the battery, handed out ammunition, and supplied the men at the guns with water and wine. Napier was one of several writers to record Mrs Retson's courage, and found it 'difficult to say whether it were most feminine or heroic.'[42] He might well have said it was both.

Fort Matagorda finally became untenable, and the survivors, their ammunition expended, were evacuated across the bay to the isthmus on the other side by boats from the fleet. Mrs Retson, still undaunted, made three journeys back across to the battery to collect her possessions and those of her husband, and finally to collect her child, who was still safe in one of the bomb-proofs. 'I think I see her yet, while the shot and shell were flying thick around her, bending her body over it to shield it from danger by the exposure of her own person', remembered John Donaldson, one of the sergeants in the same regiment.[43] At the time Donaldson was writing, 1817, Mrs Retson was living in Glasgow with her husband, who had been discharged from the army. She had never received any recognition for her heroic conduct, and she had been induced by some of the regiment's officers to apply to the Commander-in-Chief for some small reward. He recommended her case to the Secretary at War, but was told that no funds were available. Sergeant Retson had his pension, but was

---

41 Douglas, *Tales*, p.9.
42 Napier, *History of the War*, vol.2, p.338.
43 Donaldson, *Recollections*, p.359. The incident is also recorded in Anon., *Memoirs of a Sergeant*, p.76.

unable to work, so he and his wife were subsisting on one shilling and ten pence a day. Not, thought Donaldson, the mark of a generous nation.

Not all women survived these encounters. Towards the end of 1812, as the army retreated towards the Agueda following the retirement from Burgos and Madrid, conditions became very difficult indeed. The French pursued so closely that the 28th Foot lost the mule carrying the regimental books and documents. Then, just as the regiment was bivouacking in a wood, some Polish lancers got in amongst them, and cut down some of the women who were lagging behind.[44]

Women were not often killed at such close quarters: more often they seem to have been the victims of a cannon ball. During the same retreat for example, Major Samuel Rice of the 51st Light Infantry recorded in a letter that while they had been holding the enemy back near the bridge at Tordesillias, they had taken very few casualties, but 'a poor woman, singularly enough, was killed by the first cannon ball fired' and an officer lost an arm.[45]

One woman at least was found dead on the field of Waterloo. The 1895 regimental journal of the Royal Scots, (1st Foot), *The Thistle,* carried an account by an old soldier calling himself 'An Old Milestone' of picking up a small child in the midst of the fighting. The mother was dead, and the infant trying to nestle into her bosom. The soldier picked him up and put him on top of his knapsack, and resumed his place in the line. The real identity of the child was never known, but he was brought up as a child of the regiment, and named Donald Crawford, possible after the soldier who rescued him.[46]

The sometimes-random nature of artillery fire probably accounted for the fact that women seem sometimes to have been killed on the very periphery of an action. While the British and French armies marched parallel to each other, about a mile apart before the Battle of Salamanca, as Wellington sought for the appropriate moment to strike, 'every now and again the enemy unlimbered their guns, and fired on the British lines; but no execution was done, with the exception of one poor woman, who was killed by a cannon-shot.'[47] In a letter dated November 1812, after Wellington's failure to capture the fortress at Burgos, Private Wheeler of the 51st described a similar incident during a skirmish near Almos:

> On the morning of the 28th October the enemy brought some guns and fired into the camp. The first round they fired killed Sergeant Maibee's wife, her husband had just gone to the bridge [on the retreat to Valladolid] on duty and left her to prepare his breakfast, she was in the act of taking some chocolate off the fire when the shot carried away her right arm and breast.[48]

---

44 Cadell, *Narrative*, p.142.
45 A. Mockler-Ferryman (ed.), *The Life of a Regimental Officer During the Great War 1793–1815 Compiled from the Correspondence of Col. Samuel Rice, 51st Light Infantry* (London: Blackwood, 1913), Letter dated 5 November 1812, p.218.
46 The Army Children's Archive, <tacadrum.blogspot.com/2015/06/waterloo-veterans-army-children-of.html>, accessed 2 July 2019.
47 Green, *The Vicissitudes of a Soldier's*, p.96.
48 Liddell Hart (ed.), *Letters*, p.99.

There was another fatality at much the same time, also near Burgos. After the army had crossed the bridge at Valladolid, troops were left to guard it while the engineers made preparations to blow it up. The French opened fire, but some of the men had discovered a field of potatoes, and despite being under artillery fire, persisted in foraging. It was too good an opportunity to miss. 'The only person killed at this place was a woman of the 51st regiment, who had heedlessly approached too near the bridge.'[49]

It will probably never be known how many women were killed, as nobody ever thought to include them in the regimental returns of killed, wounded or missing. There were certainly some amazing escapes. In the concluding phase of the Battle of Orthez, Walter Henry, the surgeon of the 66th Foot, watched as a cannon ball struck the ground, ricocheted upwards and knocked over the wife of one of the soldiers, who, as he said, usually managed to keep up with the regiment. Fearing the worst, Henry ran to her, but to his amazement found only a graze and a contusion to her shoulder. The woman was frightened, thinking she was badly injured, and was so pleased to be told that she was alright, 'that she pulled a fowl out of one enormous pouch by her side, and half a yard of black pudding, of large diameter, out of the other, of which she begged my acceptance.'[50] The woman had obviously been plundering, and Henry declined. Something similar happened at the Battle of Toulouse on 10 April 1814. As the 7th Fusiliers moved forward to storm a French position, one of their wives, contrary to orders, went with them with her fully loaded donkey. As she did so a shell burst close behind her, but miraculously neither the woman or the donkey was injured.[51]

With army wives in such close attendance on the troops, and often actually on the field of battle, it was inevitable that some of them sometimes fell into enemy hands. An early example occurred during the Duke of York's campaign in Flanders in the bitter weather of 1794–1795. During the British retreat to Deventer the 6th Infantry Brigade with some cavalry, acted as rearguard. There were frequent skirmishes with the enemy, and the rearguard was so closely pressed that at the beginning of March the greater part of the baggage, and the women and the sick fell into enemy hands.[52]

In April 1811, after the action at Campo Maior, and while Beresford's force was moving against Badajoz, a squadron of the 13th Light Dragoons suffered a serious mishap. One squadron had crossed the Jerumenha river and bivouacked in what they took to be a safe position. They had in fact been observed by French hussars, who attacked the unwary squadron in the small hours of the 6th. It was a minor but humiliating disaster. With the exception of two cornets who managed to escape, one in his nightcap and the other by hiding in a riverbed, the whole squadron, 52 officers and men, one wife and 65 horses, were captured, leaving three men wounded on the ground.[53] This woman was apparently actually riding with the troopers, but her name is now unknown.

A captured woman whose name was recorded was Mrs Howley, the wife of the black cymbal-player in the band of the 88th, the Connaught Rangers. At the Battle of El Bodon in September 1811, the 88th found itself dangerously isolated and facing overwhelming

---

49 Green, *The Vicissitudes of a Soldier's*, pp.122–123.
50 Henry, *Events*, vol.1, p.195.
51 Cooper, *Rough Notes*, p.118.
52 Trimble, *The Historical Records*, p.72.
53 McGuffie (ed.), *Peninsular Cavalry*, p.82.

enemy numbers. The fighting was so severe that even some of Wellington's staff officers found themselves personally engaged with enemy cavalry troopers. Lieutenant King of the 11th Light Dragoons lost his arm to a sabre-cut, and an officer named Prior had all his front teeth knocked out by a musket ball. In the midst of this was Mrs Howley, who was captured by a French lancer. 'The fate of the officers I have mentioned was deplored' wrote William Grattan in his memoirs, 'but the loss of Mrs Howley was a source of grief to the entire division. The officers so maimed might be replaced by others, but perhaps in the entire army such another woman, take her for all and all, as Mrs Howley could not be found.'[54] Unfortunately, Grattan failed to explain what were this amazing woman's qualities, and did not think to say whether she ever came back to her regiment.

What happened to British women who did fall into enemy hands seems to have been a matter of luck. Although they were usually sent back to the British lines, the French being unwilling to feed them, there were some occasions when they were kept prisoner. In July 1812, just before the Battle of Salamanca, Ensign Mills of the 1st Coldstream Guards noted that a squadron of enemy cavalry captured most of the baggage belonging to the hussars of the King's German Legion, and with it, several of their women. Most of these were returned, except four, whom they kept.[55] Perhaps they were willing to go over to the French side, or possibly they were the most desirable. A similar incident took place in November of the same year, during the siege of Ciudad Rodrigo. Lieutenant Hennell of the 43rd described in a letter to his brother an incident in which he was almost captured while out collecting stores. 'Had I found bread on the road I must inevitably have been a prisoner for the women and sick belonging to our regiment, who were a short distance behind, were taken. The women they took some of (the handsome ones) and let others go.'[56]

During the retreat from Burgos which has already been mentioned, conditions for the women were especially difficult, when a combination of appalling weather, thick mud, exposure and hunger prevented many of them from keeping up with the columns. The French cavalry were pressing hard, and many eyewitness accounts speak of them being captured. 'The rain had increased to such a degree that the water was up to our knees.' remembered an anonymous soldier of the 71st. '…in the midst of this interesting scene, a number of soldiers' wives and children, mounted on asses, finding it impossible to keep up with us, began a concert of cries and tears; but as no assistance could be afforded, they fell into the enemy's hands.'[57] The French were themselves enduring the same conditions, and needed no extra mouths to feed, and were quite prepared to send the women back. It does however seem that a considerable number of women had been captured, so much so that according to the diary of Ensign Mills for 27 October, 'About eleven o' clock Lord Wellington sent in a flag of truce to request that some women who had been taken on the 24th might be returned.' The French took the chance offered by the flag of truce to bring up some horse artillery and

---

54 Grattan, *Adventures*, p.115.
55 I. Fletcher, (ed.), *For King and Country. The Letters and Diaries of John Mills, Coldstream Guards, 1811–14* (Staplehurst: Spellmount, 1995), p.147.
56 Glover (ed.), *Gentleman Volunteer*, p.61.
57 Anon., *Vicissitudes*, p.237.

open fire. 'But General Souham sent sixteen women in with a message for Lord Wellington' apologising for the gun fire, which he claimed not to have authorized.'[58]

The French were not always so generous, and there were certainly cases of British women being raped. This is not an easy matter to disentangle because of the reluctance of the eyewitness accounts to address the issue. The same thing applies to their descriptions of atrocities committed by British troops on some occasions, notably the capture of Badajoz. So perhaps it is necessary to read between the lines. During the Corunna campaign for instance, when conditions for both pursued and pursuer were appalling, several British women were captured, and sent back after being given food, but not until a price had been exacted. Some of the men were unable to march any further, and sat by the wayside in a state of complete exhaustion. 'We had seven or eight women belonging to the regiment' remembered William Green. There were no baggage wagons left for them to ride on by this stage in the retreat, 'and some of them fell into the hands of the enemy; and after using them as they pleased, they gave them some food, and sent them to us!'[59]

Another such incident occurred at the Battle of Vimeiro, the third action of the Peninsular War in August 1808. Shortly before the action began, Captain Landmann, of the Royal Engineers, heard a great disturbance coming from a group of 30 or 40 soldiers' wives who had been washing in a stream. Landmann went to enquire the cause of their outrage. His account of the incident was written almost half a century later, in 1854, and his memoirs show him to have been something of a humourist. Nevertheless, the incident, with its recollected dialogue, is a vivid, if stereotyped, image of the Irish women who made up such a large proportion of the army's wives:

> 'Fait, and I tink we have had enough to make us cry murder; warn't we all washing, down dare in de river, as safe, we taught, as if we had been on de banks of dear Channon, when we was all pounced upon by a party of French dragoons. The villans was not satisfied with taking the biggest liberties with us, but had the impudence afterwards to rob us of our shoes which plaise your honour,' she continued, 'was a dirty, unmanly, mean, vile, cowardly, blackguard, ungentlemanly trick, to pass off on us poor harmless creatures, who had never once given dem an ugly word.' On my making some remark on the first part of their grievance, she repeated, louder than before, 'Ough de dirty villans! to take away our shoes was worse than anything!'[60]

From which it would seem that these particular women regarded having their shoes stolen (a serious matter in a marching army) was worse than being sexually assaulted.

By and large however, the French appear to have behaved with considerable kindness, not to say gallantry, towards female prisoners. The fact that the French army had its own women, especially the *vivandieres,* probably had a lot to do with this. Another important fact was that the ferocious hatred which existed between the French and the Spanish during the Peninsular campaigns did not apply to the British. The British and French troops often behaved towards each other with a level of chivalry which now seems extraordinary. It

---

58 Mills, *For King and Country*, p.250.
59 J. & D. Teague (eds), *Where Duty Calls*, p.13.
60 Landmann, *Recollections*, vol.2, p.199.

was also the case that the French, existing as they did by foraging, and without a regular commissariat, would have found British women and children a severe encumbrance.

An example of French humanity occurred very early on in the war, during the Flanders campaign of 1793. On 18 May a group of British wives were captured by the French and taken into Lille. A few days later, they were returned to the British lines, and when they arrived back, the women had nothing but good to say about their captors: 'They are loud in praise of the French, whom they extol to the skies for their civility and kindness to them … they say they were loaded with wine and other provisions, and accompanied to the gates of Lille with a band of music, and from thence conducted to the advanced posts'.[61] So said Corporal Brown of the Coldstream Guards, reporting a particularly generous episode.

When Lord William Bentinck was operating near Tarragona in southern Spain, he made the mistake of sanctioning the advance of the mules, waggons, and the women and children before it was safe to do so, and they were captured by the French. The women, however, were treated well, 'not only with delicacy, but with kindness.' Tents were pitched for them, guards were posted to ensure they were not molested, 'and rations of bread and meat, and wine, were served out as regularly to them and their little ones as to the troops.' After three days they were all sent back under escort, each woman with provisions for herself and her child, 'and all vying with one another in the praises which they bestowed upon their captors.'[62]

Perhaps it was because of such incidents that the capture of women was occasionally treated with a degree of rough humour. On 25 September 1811 shortly before the investment of Ciudad Rodrigo, there was a brief but hard-fought action at El Bodon, in which a strong force of French cavalry managed to capture a quantity of baggage and stores, and most of the women belonging to the 3rd Division. According to William Brown of the 45th Foot, however, the husbands concerned did not seem to be deeply affected. 'The same night when seated round the fire, an Irishman, who had lost his wife, being condoled with on the occasion, replied, "Faith, boys, I would not have cared a straw about it at all, but Jenny the b—h has got my pipe away with her."' Not long afterwards the women were escorted to the British outposts by a party of French cavalry, and so restored to their husbands. Whereupon 'many a coarse joke and broad surmise were passed regarding the treatment they had experienced during their captivity.'[63]

---

61 Brown, *Impartial Journal*, p.158.
62 G. Gleig (ed.), *The Hussar* (London: Colburn, 1837), vol.2, p.199.
63 Brown (ed.), *The Autobiography*, p.78.

9

The Fatal Field

> *Oh, tell me! is the body found?*
> *And is it pierc'd with many a wound?*
> *And is it left a while to bleed,*
> *Where the slow flighted ravens feed?*[1]

No aspect of women's experience of the war could be worse than the immediate aftermath of a battle, when wives went in search of their husband's bodies. It was a sight which burned itself in to the memories of those who witnessed it. This was a moment when women and children could be seen 'looking for those whom destiny had decreed that they should never again behold, except as lifeless corpses, or as objects more to be shunned than sought after.'[2] One of the consequences of women being with the army, and in close proximity to the field of battle, was that the anxiety they felt took on a dreadful immediacy. 'When the roll was called after the battle' recorded Rifleman Harris, writing of Roliça, the first major encounter of the Peninsular War, 'the females who missed their husbands came along the front line to enquire of the survivors whether they knew anything about them.' It was as brutal as that. One of the names called out was that of Joseph Cochan. He had been firing away very close to Harris, and being thirsty with the heat and action, lifted his canteen to take a drink. 'Here's to you, old boy' he remarked, and as he did so, a ball went through his canteen and into his brain, killing him instantly. Mrs Cochan was now sobbing and calling out, but Harris could not bring himself to tell her what happened until Captain Leach called out 'Does any man know what happened to Cochan? If so, let him speak out at once.'[3] Harris now told what he had seen, and the distraught woman, hopeful of finding her husband still alive, begged him to take her to the body. Leach ordered Harris to take Mrs Cochan to the spot if he was sure he could find it. Harris had noted his position carefully during the firefight, as he had been looking for cover, and thought he could do so. They found the body. Mrs Cochan embraced it, and turning it over, looked for the last time at the now disfigured face of her husband, the tears streaming down her own. Then she produced a prayer book from her pocket, which suggests she was perhaps a woman of more education than many soldiers' wives, and read the service for the burial of the dead. When she had finished she

---

1 'T.M.' *The Widow* in *The Morning Chronicle*, 28 December 1801
2 Maxwell, *Peninsular Sketches*, vol.1, p.357.
3 Hibbert (ed.), *Recollections*, p.21.

seemed much calmer. Harris beckoned to some other men nearby, and they dug a hole and buried the body. He accompanied the widow back to the company, where, as he put it she 'laid herself down upon the heath near us. She lay amongst some other females, who were in the same distressing circumstances with herself, with the sky for her canopy, and a turf for her pillow, for we had no tents with us. Poor woman! I pitied her much; but there was no remedy. If she had been a duchess she must have fared the same.'[4]

Captain Landmann of the engineers also witnessed a tragic scene at the Battle of Roliça. A friend of his, Captain Henry Geary of the Royal Artillery, was fatally wounded and carried into a cottage. Geary had clearly been a popular officer, and his soldier-servant, deeply grieved, was cradling his head when Landmann arrived. The servant's wife, an Irish woman, seemed almost deranged, wringing her hands with wild looks. She took the corpse by the arms, lamenting louder and louder 'Mr Geary! Mr Geary! Mr Geary! will you not spake one word for your dear wife and children!'[5] Geary in fact left a widow with four children. Landmann could not console the servant and his wife, and left them to their grief.

It was exactly the same six years later at the Battle of Toulouse, the final battle of the war in the Peninsula. The baggage camp happened to be very near the field of action, and the women could not be prevented from coming forward to find out what had happened to their men. One particular scene troubled John Edgecombe Daniel, an officer in the 45th. He watched the wife of a dead artilleryman become so frantic that she ran into the enemy fire till she was dragged to the rear by a sergeant. While they were attempting to bury this man another corpse was carried to the spot to be buried also. There were several weeping women there at that moment, one of whom recognized the new body as that of her own husband, 'and she prevailed in her entreaties that it might not be buried until she had wept over it awhile, and had put a clean shirt upon it and some socks.'[6] The last, sad act of wifely care.

Nor were officers' ladies spared the trauma of combing battlefields in search of husbands, or of not knowing whether they were alive or dead. On 22 July 1812, after the Battle of Salamanca, William Tomkinson, a captain in the 16th Light Dragoons, was moved to make an entry in his diary regarding the redoubtable Mrs Dalbiac. As we have seen, she had spent the day of the battle close to the scene of action and had ridden onto the field in search of the husband. She had not found him by the time the light began to fail. 'At nightfall she was anxious to ascertain the fate of her husband, and set out to seek him.' wrote Tomkinson. 'She was accompanied by a dragoon of the 4th, and had the ill-luck to lose him. She wandered some time alone on the hill where the action had taken place, amongst the killed and wounded. I cannot conceive a more unpleasant situation for a woman to be it, particularly at night.'[7] She did however find her husband alive and in one piece.

Not everyone had the Dalbiac's luck at Salamanca. Lieutenant Browne of the 23rd, serving as a deputy assistant adjutant general spoke to a fellow staff officer who had been taking a survey of the battlefield. He had seen a beautiful young woman, her hair loose, running wildly about the battlefield. 'She was looking about with earnest anxiety & a distracted air

---

4 Hibbert (ed.), *Recollections*, p.22.
5 Landmann, *Recollections*, vol.2, p.154.
6 John Daniel, *Journal of an Officer of the Commissariat Department* (London: Porter and King, 1820), p.322.
7 Tomkinson, *Diary*, p.188.

amongst the dead, & those wounded who had not yet been removed. She stopped at every corpse, the greater number of which had already been entirely stripped by the Spaniards or women of the army.'[8] Browne later discovered that her name was Mrs Fitzgerald, and that she had been searching for the body of her husband, who had but recently joined the 88th as a young lieutenant. Whether she found the body, Browne did not know. Mrs Prescott, wife of Captain Prescott of the 7th Foot was engaged in the same task, only her situation was made more harrowing by the fact that when she found her husband shot in the head, she had her two children with her.[9]

The presence of children on battlefields was by no means unusual, and they too were witnesses to the carnage. John Jeffers Wilson, who later became the editor of the *Fifeshire Advertiser* in Kirkcaldy, could remember the experience. His father, John Jeffers, was an artillery driver at Waterloo, and Ann his wife was with the baggage with their seven-year-old son. Wilson later remembered that although he was too young to be 'in harness' as he put it, he and his mother 'not only shared the danger, but were usefully employed, especially among the wounded and the dying.' He added that he had no hesitation in saying that they had been 'under Providence, instrumental in saving life.'[10] Little Barbara Jones had been born in 1811 at Gibraltar, where her father was a rifleman in the 95th. She and her mother were with the battalion at Quatre Bras and in later life she could remember riding in a waggon at Waterloo. Her father died from his wounds on the evening of the battle, his head resting in his wife's lap, so presumably Barbara witnessed his last moments. Barbara later married a man named Moon, lived to a ripe old age and died on 26 September 1903. She is buried in the churchyard of St Mary the Virgin, Rolvenden, Kent. Elizabeth Gale was five when her mother Mary followed her husband's unit – also the 95th – to Belgium at the beginning of the Waterloo campaign. Much later in life, when she had married and become Mrs Watkins, she gave an interview in which she recounted her experiences at the battle. She had, she recalled, 'sat by her mother's side shredding lint and helped some of the women to rudely dress the wounded soldiers. She had a vivid recollection of several men dying in the camp, and was much frightened when her mother lifted a cloth which covered the face of one of them…' Elizabeth died in 1904 aged 95, and is buried in the Brockley and Ladywell cemeteries in Lewisham where her gravestone describes her as a Waterloo veteran.[11]

The immediate aftermath of the storming of Ciudad Rodrigo on 8 Jan 1812 was an example of the sort of horror soldiers' wives might face. Both the defence and the assault had been conducted with the utmost violence, and the state of many of the dead was horrific. Rifleman Costello of the 95th was a lucky survivor of the forlorn hope, and the following morning, hoping as many men did, that he might find some old comrade alive, he went back to inspect the area near the breach where so many of them had been killed. He knew that the 88th, the Connaught Rangers, had suffered dreadful losses at this point, and he watched a number of poor Irish women hopelessly trying to distinguish the horribly burnt

---

8   Buckley (ed.), *Napoleonic War Journal*, p.173.
9   Haythornthwaite, *The Armies*, p.129.
10 Information supplied by Andrew Campbell from his family archive.
11 'Waterloo Veterans: the army children of Waterloo', <tacadrum.blogspot.com/2015/06/waterloo-veterans-army-children-of.html>, accessed 2 July 2019.

and disfigured faces of their husbands.[12] Another witness to the same scene was an anonymous sergeant of the 43rd Light Infantry. He too was in the ditch amongst the dead bodies, and noticed one woman in particular:

> Nothing struck me more forcibly than the conduct of a soldier's wife. Suspecting that her husband had fallen, she traversed this vale of death to seek him. Never shall I forget the anguish of her soul when she discovered the much-loved remains. The brave man had fallen covered with wounds. His countenance was sadly disfigured, and suffused with blood. She fell upon his face, and kissed the faded lips. She then gazed at the lifeless form, repeated her embraces, and gave way to the wild and ungovernable grief which struggled for expression.[13]

The sergeant was a deeply religious man, engaged in a spiritual journey from Catholicism to Methodism, and much concerned with sin and redemption, and could not help adding a Biblical 'Sin! what hast thou done?'

The frightfulness of the assault on Ciudad Rodrigo was however dwarfed by the horrors of the storming of Badajoz and its immediate aftermath in April 1812. British casualties were appalling, especially amongst the Light Division men who entered the breach. James Hale, a sergeant in the 9th Foot recorded that the sight of so many British soldiers lying dead, one across another, 'occasioned many a man to shed tears, in particular when we saw two women lamenting over their dead husbands.'[14] Another witness to this desperate scene of carnage was Sergeant Joseph Donaldson of the 94th. Crossing the moat near the breach, Donaldson saw a woman with a child at her breast and another by her side, examining each dead body in turn with a distracted air. At last, she found her husband's corpse which she raised and released with a scream before collapsing. Donaldson's tastes lay in the field of literature, and his *Recollections* gave plenty of scope to indulge his powers of expression, and if his descriptions now read like a sentimental Victorian novel, complete with imagined dialogue, that is no doubt a reflection of the way in which the sufferings of the woman he describes had burnt itself indelibly into his memory. The eldest child 'now drew himself close to her side, and looking at the bleeding corpse which she sustained, in a piteous tone, inquired "Is that my father? is he asleep? why doesn't he speak to you? I'll waken him for you" – and seizing his hand, he drew it towards him, but suddenly relapsing his hold, he cried, "Oh mother! his hand is cold- cold as ice."' This ghastly scene continued for a while, the woman apostrophising both her child and her dead husband. Donaldson watched helpless, feeling he could not interfere. 'I considered her sorrow too deep and sacred for commonplace consolation.' as he put it.[15] At last, a woman and two soldiers of the same regiment came looking for her, and a burial party joined them in trying to console her. Donaldson made his way back to the lines wondering how many more widows and orphans the action had made, since the British casualties amounted to some 3,000 men.

---

12 Costello, *Adventures*, p.115.
13 Anon., *Memoirs of a Sergeant of the 43rd*, p.133.
14 Hale, *Journal*, p.77.
15 Donaldson, *Recollections*, p.160.

The field of Waterloo after the battle. Several women can be seen searching for the dead or wounded, and one is overcome with horror and emotion. Aquatint after John Heaviside Clark, 1817. (Anne S.K. Brown Military Collection, Brown University)

He was not the only soldier to feel that these moments of intense grief were something which could not be intruded upon, even when the onlooker wished to offer help or consolation. As an ordnance commissary in the field train, Sir Richard Henegan had taken no direct part in the Battle of Vitoria, but he did have to cross the field of battle with all its hideous sights. A young woman 'of a most interesting appearance' caught his attention, sitting by the side of a shallow grave which she had presumably dug herself. 'Stretched close beside her, in the cold sleep of death, lay the form of a British soldier, over whom she leant in all the convulsive writhings of genuine grief ... the grief of the mourner was too sacred for intrusion.'[16]

Private Wheeler of the 51st had survived the Battle of Vitoria, but was badly wounded five months later at Battle of the Nivelle. He was eventually taken to the military hospital at St Jean de Luz, but in the immediate aftermath of the battle had manage to get as far as a place he called 'The Farm'. Here there were many wounded and dying men, and many of their women. It was, thought Wheeler, a scene which require the genius of Hogarth to depict. Many of the wounded had managed to find enough alcohol to get totally drunk and many of the women who had come in search of their husbands had consumed so much that 'they had transformed themselves into something more like fiends than angels of mercy.'[17] Some, who

---

16 Henegan, *Seven Years*, vol.2, p.12.
17 Liddell Hart (ed.), *Letters*, p.140.

had just received the news that their husbands were dead, were running about distracted. Others still were quietly supporting the bodies of dying men, or weeping bitter tears as life slipped away, oblivious of their surroundings.

Sometimes such scenes were particularly poignant when the man and wife were especially well known and liked within a regiment. Some women seem to have inspired widespread respect and liking amongst the ranks by their simple goodness and sweetness of temper. 'It is true' wrote Lieutenant Gleig, remembering one such incident, 'that virtue is respected and a virtuous woman beloved, even by common soldiers.' One such was Nance M'Dermot, the wife of Gleig's company pay-sergeant. There was something lady-like about Nance. She had at least been a lady's maid to a person of rank, and had, Gleig believed, married a common soldier against the wishes of her relations. In the fighting around Bayonne and the Adour in February 1814, M'Dermot was hit by a cannonball which smashed his head, a hideous disfigurement, and the reaction of his comrades was immediate: '"O, who will tell Nance of this?" said another non-commissioned officer, his principal companion, – "Poor Nance!" cried the soldiers, one and all.' Nance was indeed deranged with grief. 'She was removed with gentle violence to the camp, and the body was buried.'[18] Then they planted a young fir tree to mark the grave.

Something similar happened after the Battle of Toulouse amidst the wreckage of the 42nd Foot. A soldier named Cunningham, a corporal in the grenadier company, had been killed and his wife insisted on going to the spot to find his body in spite of the efforts of other men to prevent her seeing the scene of carnage. Many of the men accompanied her around the field, 'for they respected the man and esteemed the woman.'[19] The wounds were in the chest, and Mrs Cunningham cleaned the body, kissing the cold lips, and wept as his comrades wrapped the body in a blanket and lowered it into a hastily dug grave. She was appointed sick-nurse by one of the officers of the company until arrangement were made to enable her to return to England.

Mary Gifford was married to a sergeant in the 28th Foot, and on the evening of the 16 June 1815 was making her way from Brussels, through the Forest of Soignes, towards the battlefield at Quatre-Bras to attempt to find her husband. She was an old campaigner, weather-beaten and wrapped in an old red cloak, which did something at least to keep out the weather. A young lady, whose brother was an officer in the same regiment, and who was on the same ghastly errand, had placed herself under Mary Gifford's protection. As they made their way, they passed waggon after waggon bearing wounded men back to Brussels, which did nothing for their peace of mind. Nor did the news that the 28th had been badly cut up. As day dawned on the 17th, and as the army was falling back towards the position at Waterloo in the midst of the heaviest rain anyone could remember, the two women pressed on against the tide of wounded men towards the cross-roads at Quatre-Bras. Amid the dead and dying, Mrs Gifford left her weaker companion in the care of some other soldiers' wives who were clustered round a brandy-flask, and searched till at last she found her husband. He was lying on a littler of straw and covered with a blanket. Both his legs had been shot off. They just had time to recognized each other before he died. The young lady who had

---

18 Gleig, *The Subaltern*, p.333.
19 Anton, *Retrospect*, p.141.

placed herself under Mary Gifford's protecting wing, and who was identified only as Emma, fared no better. She searched about amongst the bloodied bodies of the 28th in a state of near delirium, till she found what she had come for: the cold and stiffening body of her brother William.[20] When the Scots Greys reached the battlefield after dark, and the fighting was over, Sergeant Archibald Johnston witnessed another tragic sight. They came across a woman who believed she had lost not only her husband but her two sons as well. 'And she in the dead hour of night on her way to range the field amongst the dead in search of them whom she so deeply deplored.'[21]

While some women were engaged on these harrowing tasks, there were others taking the opportunity to loot. Looting on the field of battle as distinct from plundering as a form of foraging, was regarded as quite normal and legitimate. It was at least accepted as inevitable, and was quite beyond the power of anyone to prevent. It occurred from the earliest days of the Peninsula War amongst the women who had landed with the army in Mondego Bay. After the Battle of Vimiero, Landmann, for example, mentioned seeing a party of soldiers' women, accompanied by some of the Portuguese peasants, chasing after loose French dragoon horses, whose riders had been killed. These would have been useful prizes.[22] Sergeant Norbert Landsheit of the 20th Light Dragoons also witnessed women plundering after Vimiero. As his troop moved forward to the edge of the high ground, and looked out over the plain below, they could see it was covered with the dead and wounded. 'There they lay, English and French thrown promiscuously together, while hordes of peasants, together with the women from our own army, were already in full occupation as plunderers.'[23]

The successful storming of Badajoz in April 1812, an event terrible both in its cost in lives and the uncontrollable behaviour of the troops afterwards, witnessed looting on an epic scale, and the women of the army were heavily involved. Indeed, they seem to have looked forward to the prospect. William Green of the 95th was wounded in both the wrist and thigh in the initial assault. As he and an injured comrade were making their painful way back to the lines, they passed a group of women not far from the fighting who demanded to know 'Have our troops got into Badajoz yet?'[24] They knew that the rules of war allowed the place to be sacked. Green told them he thought they never would, but get in they did and the scenes of murderous indiscipline which followed beggared description. Nobody put it more eloquently than William Napier, himself an officer, in his history of the war in the Peninsula: 'Shameless rapacity, brutal intemperance, savage lust, cruelty and murder, shrieks and piteous lamentations, groans, shouts, imprecations, the hissing of fires bursting from the houses, the crashing of doors and windows, and the reports of muskets used in violence resounded for two days and nights in the streets of Badajos!'[25] The women were every bit as involved as the troops. As one eyewitness put it, 'The town now became a scene of plunder and devastation; our soldiers and our women had lost all control over themselves

---

20   Henegan, *Seven Years*, vol.2, pp.159–163.
21   Archibald Johnson, 'The Journal of Sergeant Archibald Johnston of the 2nd Royal North British Dragoons' in Glover (ed.), *The Waterloo Archive*, vol.1, p.45.
22   Landmann, *Recollections*, vol.2, p.232.
23   Gleig, *The Hussar*, vol.1, p.274.
24   J. & D. Teague (eds), *Where Duty Calls*, p.37.
25   Napier, *History of the War*, vol.4, p.122.

... Hundreds of both sexes were lying in the streets in a state of hopeless intoxication, habited in various costume.'[26]

The quantity of loot taken at Badajoz was vast, and for a period of time, the situation was more or less out of control. Occasionally, the situation might be ludicrous. Thomas Henry Browne, serving on the staff as a deputy assistant adjutant general, seems to have had considerable personal contact with the commander of the forces, Wellington. In his journal he recorded an amusing incident that Wellington had described at dinner: The great man had passed a soldier outside the walls of Badajoz hopelessly drunk and so laden with loot that he could scarcely move or speak. Wellington was about to speak to him when a woman appeared, equally drunk and heavily laden. He addressed her, asking what business she had there and threatening her with instant punishment. The woman said nothing, but the soldier, too far gone to realize whom he was speaking to, said 'Now that's what I call right you see that we poor fellows fights hard and gets nothing, and that these here devils comes and carries off all that belongs to us.'[27] The situation was so ludicrous, wrote Browne, and so far past remedy in the general horrors of the sack, that Wellington, who in other circumstances might have had them hanged on the spot, rode on without another word. In their drunken frenzy men and women seized on anything. George Bell of the 34th saw them staggering about with tables and chairs, priests' vestments, looking glasses, sausages, women's clothing of every description, wine-skins and even an old-fashioned eight-day clock.[28] Charles O'Neil of the 28th watched the soldiers' wives guarding piles of plunder which had been carried out of the town, and William Grattan of the Connaught Rangers witnessed exactly the same scene: 'The plunder so captured was deposited in our camp, and placed under a guard chiefly composed of the soldiers' wives.'[29] No doubt, he added, the women were heavily involved in auctioning it off afterwards.

Thomas Browne's position on the staff gave him the opportunity to range further than many regimental officers may have done, and he was both an acute observer and careful recorder of what he witnessed, and was one of those soldiers who particularly noted the doings of the women. After the Battle of Salamanca on 22 July 1812, many of the British wives, who had been ordered to remain in the depots in the rear, managed to get on to the battlefield itself, despite all orders and threats to the contrary. Accompanied by numbers of Spanish women, they set about unrestrained plundering, as Browne vividly described: 'All ideas of conduct or decency had disappeared – plunder and profligacy seemed their sole object, & the very Soldiers their husbands evidently estimated them in proportion to their proficiency in these vices. They covered the field of battle when the action was over, & were seen stripping & plundering friend and foe alike.' Nor was that the end of it. Browne was sure that in some cases the women finished off wounded men in order to make looting easier Major Offley of the 23rd, Browne's own regiment, who lay wounded and unable to move, was believed to have been one of their victims.[30] Browne's suspicions were well founded.

---

26   Anon., 'Table talk of an Old Campaigner', *United Services Journal and Naval and Military Magazine*, 1834, part 3, p.52.
27   Buckley (ed.), *Napoleonic War Journal*, p.154.
28   Stuart (ed.), *Soldier's Glory*, p.28.
29   Grattan, *Adventures*, p.210.
30   Buckley (ed.), *Napoleonic War Journal*, p.174.

After the Battle of Roliça on 17 August 1808, the first major action of the struggle in the Peninsula, Captain Landmann was surveying the ground in order to prepare a map. He had already witnessed local peasants moving about finishing off some of the wounded when he heard an English voice calling for help. Pushing his way through some bushes he found a British soldier, his leg shattered by a musket ball, and 'a woman, one of the British nation too, with a large stone in her hand levelling a finishing blow at a poor fellow of the 9th or 45th Regiment, I do not now recollect to which he belonged.' The woman was behind the man, and he was unable to defend himself. Landmann's reaction was to draw his sword, but as he did so, a German rifleman of the 5/60th Rifles appeared from the undergrowth. Obviously absent from his unit and intent on plunder, the man took the scene in with a glance, sprang at the woman and with the words '"You be no fouman, py Got! You be de tifle!" he put his rifle close to her ear, and before I had had time to form any clear conjecture as to his views, the upper half of her head vanished, and was dispersed into atoms amongst the bushes, and her body in falling almost extended to the wounded soldier.'[31] The rifleman reloaded his weapon, then carefully untied the woman's apron, which was filled with watches, rings and other valuables she had already looted, and disappeared into the bushes. Landmann gave the wounded man some wine from his canteen and arranged for him to be taken to a dressing station.

Not all British women were busy with such activities. Some, like Mrs Dalbiac of the 4th Dragoons were engaged on errands of mercy. She had a cousin in the regiment, the curiously named Lieutenant Norcliffe Norcliffe. He had been wounded by a shot in the head, and after being plundered by French dragoons, and laying out all night bleeding from his wound, he had succeeded in regaining the British lines. Mrs Dalbiac took him under her wing, as she explained in a letter to her uncle, Norcliffe's father, and had the casualty moved into the town. 'I took him, my dear Uncle myself to Salamanca, procured him the best advice, – an excellent House & Bed & every possible comfort – I also bathed his wound – preparatory to the surgeon dressing it, – as I thought my hands would do it more tenderly.' She then got him clean and comfortable, and in the afternoon, after he was asleep, she set out to rejoin the regiment and her husband, the Colonel, who was unwell himself. 'Although I travelled all night on horseback (she did not mention whether she had a trooper with her as escort) I did not reach him till 8 o'clock yesterday.' She had intended, she told her uncle, to return to Salamanca the following morning, but she received good news about Norcliffe from another officer, 'and to say the truth I am so much fatigued that Dalbiac would not allow me to go.'[32] The only surprise perhaps, is the fact that she found the energy to sit and write letters.

Battlefield plundering was not without danger. Sergeant William Clarke of the Scots Greys, surveying the battlefield at Waterloo, noticed several women among the dead, who, he thought, 'in all probability, had been shot by the wounded in their plundering expeditions.'[33] There was also the possibility that army wives would themselves become victims of violent theft. Peter Hawker, who served in the 14th Light Dragoons, recorded that after the Battle of Talavera in July 1809, some of the British women were robbed by fugitive Spanish cavalry

---

31 Landmann, *Recollections*, vol.2, p.174.
32 East Riding Archives: DDHV/73/5: Letter dated 24 July 1812, to her uncle, Thomas Norcliffe.
33 G. Glover (ed.), *A Scots Grey at Waterloo. The Remarkable Story of Sergeant William Clarke* (London: Frontline, 2017), p.221.

troopers. 'One poor wretch (of our regiment) they not only plundered of everything in her possession, but took her very clothes, and an ass, on which, from infirmity, she was obliged to travel.'[34] Catherine Exley was perfectly frank about the looting after the Battle of Vitoria. 'We stripped the French of everything they had – baggage, ammunition, boots, money etc. Many enriched themselves by plundering the dead…'[35] One anonymous British officer serving with a Portuguese battalion in the Light Division who saw this going on described the women as 'jackals' who used their plunder to set themselves up as sutlers. Some were soldiers' wives and others were widows, 'who, on the demise of their lords, had set up for themselves, and, having possessed themselves of a mule, carried on a lucrative, if not very honourable traffic.'[36] Who could blame them? He might have reflected that as widows, these women had to do something to keep body and soul together. Lieutenant Browne also recorded the rapacity of the British women after Vitoria, though on this occasion the loot abandoned by the fleeing French was in such prodigious quantities and richness, that no battlefield barbarity was called for. 'Soldier's wives were seen for weeks after the action in muslins, three or four gowns one over the others, trimmed with fine lace, several pairs of earrings dangling from their ears, reticules, watches and fans as part of their costume' he wrote. 'The contrast of these decorations with their brazen tanned faces and brawny arms was ludicrous enough.'[37]

Battlefield plundering of this kind was to a considerable extent a matter of survival. The clothing of the troops was frequently in tatters, but they at least could look forward, if they were lucky, to occasional replacement uniforms and shoes. Wives received no such help, and their clothing must often have been in tatters. So, the opportunity to acquire decent clothing was too good to be missed. It was the same two months later, after the fall of San Sebastian. 'The town having been taken, the old trade of plunder and drunkenness commenced.' Every house was ransacked, if necessary using 'the soldier's key', that is a musket ball through the lock, until fires were accidentally started and the town was reduced to ashes. The hoard of loot was staggering, and as far as the women were concerned, that included new clothing. 'Even the soldiers' wives scarcely know what to wear, for grandeur. Those who a few days before had scarcely as much on them as would make a respectable mop were now rigged out with silks and satins of the richest dyes.'[38] At Vitoria in particular there were extraordinary amounts of money amongst the French dead and in their baggage train and there was always the chance of getting rich. One woman actually managed this after Waterloo. For days after the battle British women wandered the field looking not for dead husbands, but loot. They were not alone. Many eyewitness accounts speak of the local peasantry stripping the dead and, in some cases, finishing off the wounded in the process. One soldier's wife was spectacularly lucky. Going through the pockets of a dead soldier, she came across two fine diamonds. She took them to a jeweller in Brussels, and asked 40 francs for them, but as Caroline Capel told her mother in a letter, '…the jeweller, with a degree of honesty not very

---

34 Peter Hawker, *Journal of a Regimental Officer during the Recent Campaign in Portugal and Spain under Viscount Wellington with a Correct Plan of the Battle of Talavera* (London: Johnson, 1810), p.99.
35 Probert (ed.), *Exley Diary*, p.38.
36 Anon., *Twelve Years*, vol.2, p.227.
37 Buckley (ed.), *Napoleonic War Journal*, p.219.
38 Monick (ed.), *Tale*, p.84.

often to be found, told her that they [were] worth at least 6000£ being two of the finest stones ever seen and supposed to have belonged to the Queen of Westphalia who had been robbed.' The dead soldier was Prussian, 'who you know are the greatest Plunderers that ever existed' and a great deal more jewellery was discovered by other women.[39] In any case the soldier's wife had her fortune made, as the diamonds, which had roused sufficient interest to be put on public display, were bought by an Englishman.

It was not necessary for women to be anywhere close to the action to feel acute anxiety in the immediate aftermath of a battle. As the long war apparently came to an end with the abdication of Napoleon on 4 April 1814, many Englishmen and their families, for so long shut out of the continent by the hostilities, were quick to seize the opportunity to travel again. Many of them crossed to Belgium. Amongst them was the Honourable John Thomas Capel, the second son of the Earl of Essex, whose wife was Caroline Paget, eldest daughter of the Earl of Uxbridge. Capel was deeply in debt as a consequence of gambling and moved to Belgium as an economy measure. They had settled in Brussels as early as June 1814 and with the renewal of hostilities found themselves in the eye of the storm. Caroline's eldest brother, Lord Uxbridge commanded the Allied cavalry, and the Pagets must have listened to the sound of the battle at Quatre-Bras with growing anxiety. As she told her mother in a letter written on the evening of the 18th 'About 2 o'clock [in the afternoon] of the 16th we first heard the distant Cannonading which approached for some time, and awfull as it was, every breath was hushed to listen the better.'[40] They were right to be anxious; Uxbridge had lost his leg while riding with Wellington. A number of British officers had also taken their wives and children to Belgium at the beginning of the campaign in the belief that they would be in no danger. Colonel Sir Augustus Frazer for instance, commanding the Royal Horse Artillery, mentioned in a letter dated 10 May that he had dined in Antwerp with Colonel Gold and his wife, and that their five children were with them. Whether Mrs Gold and her offspring moved to Brussels before the campaign opened is not known, but as her husband commanded the artillery attached to the 2nd Infantry Division at Waterloo, she must have endured an anxious time.[41] One woman who certainly did was the wife of Colonel Muttlebury, who with her two small daughters were left in Brussels when the army marched out on the news that Napoleon had crossed the frontier and was advancing on Charleroi. When on the 17th the wounded began to trickle back into the city, Mrs Muttlebury saw an officer of her husband's regiment, who told her that her husband was alive and well, and later a pencilled note arrived from the colonel himself. Then, on the 18th, as the Battle of Waterloo itself opened, the gun fire swelled to a new intensity. Deserters from some of the Belgian regiments began to appear in the city, crying that the day was lost and the French were coming. There was widespread panic. Mrs Muttlebury's manservant fled, and she hid herself and the children as best she could. To calm herself, she read the psalms. *He shall defend thee under His wings and thou shalt be safe under His feathers.* In the evening French prisoners began to trickle in, and it began to look as though the battle had not been lost after all. By dawn the next morning, real news of the victory arrived, and while Mrs Muttlebury, torn between dread and hope, was awaiting intelligence

---

39 Marquess of Anglesey (ed.), *The Capel Letters* (London: Cape, 1955), p.124.
40 Anglesey, *Capel Letters*, p.112.
41 Sabine (ed.), *Letters*, p.510.

of her husband, he himself, begrimed with the stains of battle, and exhausted by hunger and fatigue, came into the room. Her feelings are better imagined than described.[42]

As an officer's wife, Mrs Muttlebury was lucky in that she discovered that her husband was alive and well very quickly. Others were not so lucky, and had to endure many hours of suspense. Harry Smith of the 95th had left his wife, Juana, in Antwerp. On the afternoon of the 19th she heard that the great battle had been fought, and ordered that her horses should be ready at three the following morning so that she could set out to find her husband. Accompanied by their old groom, West, and in what she called 'light marching order', Juana reached Brussels by 7:00 a.m. She found some of the 95th, who told her that Brigade Major Smith had been killed. In desperation, she rode on to Waterloo, picking her way through the clutter of smashed or abandoned waggons, dead horses and dead and dying men. In agony she rode around the battlefield with its hideous sights, searching for 'Enrique' as she called Harry, imagining him to have been buried, and not knowing where. At last, she found an officer she knew, Charlie Gore, aide-de-camp to Sir James Kempt, who assured her that Enrique was alive and well, though concerned about her. At first, she refused to believe Gore, because the men had told her that he had been killed. Gore explained that the dead officer was named Charles Smyth, Major General Denis Pack's brigade major, and at last Juana did believe him. Gore said he was on his way to Mons, and she rode on with him. They reached the town at midnight, by which time she had ridden 60 miles, and after having some food, she fell into an exhausted sleep. The following day, the 21st, she pushed on to Bavay, where she and Harry were at last reunited in a storm of emotion.[43]

Other women were less fortunate. The other ranks' wives who had been left in the rear at the start of the battle, or who had been swept back to Brussels on the tide of panicking deserters from the Dutch-Belgian brigade, were stranded in the gathering darkness and had no means of knowing the fate of their husbands. Sergeant William Clarke was with a party of the Scots Greys detailed to escort a group of French prisoners back to the city. The wounded were everywhere, staggering or lying about, many bloody and dying, while riderless horses wandered around and groups of Belgians were rolling drunk on every corner. In the midst of all this, Clarke could see 'soldier's wives hurrying from hospital to hospital and from group to group in hopes of discovering their beloved husbands, even wounded and bleeding among their fellow men … Others ran towards the field of battle, on hearing from some comrade newly arrived from the sad scene, the news of the death of their bosom companions.' This was a risky course of action. As Clarke's men rode back to rejoin the regiment and reached the Forest of Soignes, they found the dead and wounded lying ever more thickly at the roadside and the ditches full of muddy bodies, and Clarke notice there were women and children among them, mixed up with the broken-down carts and waggons, baggage panniers and the wreckage of their contents. It was not clear who they were, but it seemed all too likely that they were British women and children killed by the deserting Belgians.[44] It certainly was not a safe place for women to be. 'To advance through the forest … by night, and on a road they had so lately traced, marked with confusion, blocked with

---

42   Jackson, *Notes and Reminiscences*, p.24.
43   Smith, *Autobiography*, vol.2, p.285.
44   Glover (ed.), *Scots Grey*, p.202.

overturned baggage, helpless wounded soldiers, and, worst of all, by prowling stragglers, would have been madness.' recorded an infantryman who witnessed the same destruction.[45]

One woman who did brave the hazards of the Waterloo road was Lady Magdalene De Lancey. Her husband was Colonel Sir William De Lancey, quartermaster general of the army. He had been riding close by Wellington's side in the thick of the battle when he was struck in the back by a cannonball. He was hideously wounded, the ribs being torn from the spine, and it was astonishing that he was not killed outright. Lady De Lancey had retired to the safety of Antwerp, but with the help of several officers she was able to get to Brussels and then through the stragglers infesting the road to the battlefield. Magdalene found her husband and was able to nurse him as his condition deteriorated. 'I stood near my husband, and he looked up at me and said "Magdalene, my love, the spirits." I stooped down close to him and held the bottle of lavender to him. Then he gave a gulp, as though he had something caught in his throat, and the doctor who was in attendance said "Ah, poor De Lancey! He is gone."'

Perhaps the account which Lady De Lancey wrote, in harrowing detail, acted as a catharsis. It was, she wrote, a time 'when the violence of grief is more like delirium than the sorrow of a Christian', and she tried to find consolation in 'the perfection of my happiness while it lasted.' It had not lasted long. Magdalene De Lancey buried her husband's mutilated body on the 28th, in the cemetery of the Reformed Church just outside Brussels on the Louvain road. 'At eleven o'clock that same day, I set out for England. That day, three months before, I was married.'[46]

---

45 Anton, *Retrospect*, p.217.
46 B. Ward (ed.), *A Week at Waterloo in 1815. Lady De Lancey's Narrative Being an Account of how she nursed her husband, Colonel Sir William De Lancey, Quartermaster-General of the Army, mortally wounded in the great battle* (London: Murray, 1906), p.98.

10

Bad Behaviour

It is well known that in all armies the Women are at least as bad, if not worse, than the men as Plunderers! and exemption of the ladies from punishment would have encouraged Plunder![1]

The regimental women quite frequently posed serious disciplinary problems, especially when they were a lot of them. In barracks, they could be unruly, and on campaign, they frequently ignored orders and verged on the mutinous.

Life in barracks was not conducive to refined behaviour. One officer noted how quickly a newly-wed woman, delighted with her new matrimonial status and given military quarters, was liable soon become 'tamed down into a very languishing, slip-shod house-wife'. This was not surprising given the hardened company she was likely to be keeping. One of the problems was that a barrack room was breeding ground of scandal and gossip. The women 'are for ever sifting and prying into one another's business; and politics run so high at times, that the interference of their lords and masters is resorted to, in order to check the progress of a civil war.'[2] There was little or no privacy; a woman simply lived cheek by jowl with the men. She and her husband, and possibly a child, might have to share a bed whilst other men were sleeping all around them. She might find herself in the sort of Napoleonic barrack room which can be seen reconstructed at Fort George near Inverness. Here there were eight men to the room, two to a bed, (which was certainly an improvement on the communal sleeping platform of earlier days). There was one wife to the room, and married quarters consisted simply of a blanket screening the matrimonial bed.

Some of the older hands amongst the women were only too ready to take advantage of the arrival of an innocent new recruit, his bounty money in his pocket. Joseph Donaldson, a new recruit in the 94th Foot, joined the regiment at Dunbar in January 1809, and soon discovered that all and sundry were anxious to spend his bounty on drink. Alcohol was sent for, the room cleared, and to the deafening sound of the pipes, the men and women of the company began dancing. More drink was consumed, fists, pokers and tongs began to fly, and the officer of the guard had to break it up with some of the troops in the guard house.[3]

---

1 Lady Burghclere, *A Great Man's Friendship. Letters of the Duke of Wellington to Mary, Marchioness of Salisbury* (London: Murray, 1927), p.110.
2 Patterson, *Camp and Quarters*, vol.1, pp.116–120.
3 Donaldson, *Recollections*, p.39.

This was not an unusual state of affairs. Seventeen-year-old George Farmer enlisted in 1808 in the 11th Light Dragoons. He was sent to Maidstone to be attested and given his bounty. Like many a raw youngster, he was soon parted from it. The NCOs of the depot pounced on the new recruits and invited them to their rooms. There they were then introduced to the NCOs wives, 'who made much of us, – praised, favoured, screened, and cajoled us, till our funds began to run low, and then they would have nothing more to do with us.'[4]

Discipline at this depot was clearly lax, and in such an atmosphere respectable regimental wives might find themselves keeping somewhat dubious company. In the summer of 1815, just before the Waterloo campaign, Ensign Bakewell was quartered at Hilsea barracks with the 3/27th. He seems to have had a jolly time of it. He and the surgeon had three rooms between them, where twice a week they were visited by their 'fair friends'. These girls had introduced themselves by passing a note while out promenading but would not reveal their names or addresses. They made themselves useful by keeping Bakewell's linen, handkerchiefs and stockings in good repair, but it is difficult to believe that that was the limit of their services. Indeed, young Bakewell described the barracks as a place 'where indeed a great degree of immorality took place.' But as he said, the girls 'were elegantly dressed in silks, and the only expense to us was feeding them.'[5]

If the punishment book of the 82nd Foot for 1866, (a somewhat later period) is anything to go by, the demon drink was often the cause of undisciplined behaviour in barracks or quarters. We read of women being drunk and abusing NCOs in the execution of their duty; of using language variously described and 'filthy', 'improper' or 'disrespectful'; of being drunk and fighting with other women, or even being drunk while in hospital under medical treatment. The punishments for such misdemeanours were usually being fined, admonished or having allowances stopped. Severe cases, such as trying to stab another woman, could meet with being struck off the strength of the regiment and being turned out of the barracks: a serious matter for a woman with no means of support.[6] When the *Regulations of the Rifle Corps* were drawn up, it was foreseen that there might be problems with some regimental women, and stated that 'all women of immoral or drunken characters, or who refuse to work for the men, are warned that they will not be permitted to remain.' They could not however contemplate simply throwing a woman out, as that would reflect badly on the regiment. Instead, 'their friends will be written to or they must be received into some poorhouse, or situation where they can earn their bread.'[7] It is difficult to believe that writing to a woman's friends would have been very useful.

There were occasions when alcohol brought about situations which were difficult for any officer, especially a junior one, to deal with. Lieutenant Charles Crowe of the 2/27th had to deal with one in 1814, at Condon in France, while the battalion was waiting for a route to Bordeaux, prior to embarking for Ireland. One of the sergeants of the 5th company came to him and asked him to go and deal with Mrs Fisher, the wife of one of the fifers. She was mad drunk and behaving like such a 'frantic demon' that the local inhabitants had shut

---

4   G. Gleig, (ed.), *The Light Dragoon. The Story of Private George Farmer 11th Light Dragoons* (London: Routledge, 1850), p.5.
5   Robertson, *The Exploits*, p.143.
6   Lancashire Infantry Museum: 846/3.1.132: Preston Wives' Punishment Book.
7   Fuller, *Sir John Moore's*, p.159.

A cavalry barrack room. A woman is peddling refreshments, but the other two, one with a child and the other washing, appear to be soldiers' wives. Aquatint by Thomas Rowlandson, 1788. (Anne S.K. Brown Military Collection, Brown University)

themselves in their houses. Crowe ordered the sergeant to place her under arrest, only to be told that she had been placed in the guard room three times already and forced her way out each time. Crowe went to the guard house himself to confront this 'beast of a woman', sent for the husband and told him to get his wife under control. The man however 'declared his incapability for she had knocked him about like a ninepin; and the poor fellows face and clothes confirmed his assertion.' He was frightened to go near her. The lieutenant thought that his rank and authority would subdue her, but she attacked him like a fury and he had to ward off her blows with his sheathed sword. The only solution seemed strength of numbers, and she was overpowered by a group of soldiers who dragged her back into the guard house. By this time Crowe had decided on drastic measures. 'I made the drummer take the sling from his drum and unbraid it' wrote Crowe in his diary. 'I very soon wipt the cord round and secured the woman's legs, carried it up and tied her hands behind her, but could not affix it to her tongue … to stop this nuisance I was obliged to put a drumstick across her mouth and bound it behind her head.' Gradually her noise and struggles subsided, and she went to sleep thus trussed up, when the gag was removed. When finally released, she went back to her quarters quietly. Crowe seems to have earned a lot of kudos by his resolute dealing with this incident. The local French saluted him when he past them in the street, and more importantly, so did the Inniskillings: 'Everyone in the regiment, not even excepting her own husband, was rejoiced at my having abashed the dauntless Mrs Fisher, well known to be as desperate a marauder as ever followed an army.'[8]

Private Fisher was not the only soldier to experience difficulties controlling his wife, and this could have serious consequences. Shortly before the Battle of Orthez in February 1814, the 18th Hussars had to convene a court martial on a trooper accused of having lost his trousers. This was a flogging offence, and Arthur Kennedy, the senior captain noted, 'he will be punished this morning if his wife has not come to swear that it was she that sold them.'[9] Luckily for the man, his wife did come forward to confess that she was to blame. 'I have heard of women who wear the trousers' was George Woodberry's comment, 'but not yet women who sell them!'[10] He may have been amused, but a woman who would knowingly commit an act which was likely to result in her own husband being flogged must have been a hard case.

Not every junior officer had Crowe's determination or self-confidence in dealing with the women. In May 1811, 22-year-old Peter Le Mesurier was acting as adjutant at the depot of the second battalion of the 9th Foot at Canterbury. He found the women frankly intimidating. A number of new officers were expected to join, and some spare rooms in the barracks would be required for them. They had been taken over by some of the wives, and Le Mesurier had to warn them that they would shortly be required to give them up. Since that, 'the Ladies' as he referred to them, had taken a great dislike to him, but as he wrote to his father, 'I have now adopted the plan of sending my Sergt. to them, as I was not received with common civility and I was afraid they would proceed to extremities and scratch my face.'[11] His sergeant was probably a much older man and experienced at dealing with the women. That a junior officer felt he was at risk of assault from the regimental wives is revealing. Any soldier doing so would have faced an immediate court martial and the death sentence.

On the other hand, situations could arise which were ludicrous, or just comical. The 22nd Foot were stationed in India in 1805, taking part in Lord Lake's operations against Bharatpur. One of the soldiers, an Irishman, presented himself before the colonel to complain that another man had accused him of not actually being married to his wife, whom he had accused of being no better than she should be. Could the man produce proof that he was indeed legally married? 'Faith, your Honour,' said the soldier, removing his cap and displaying his cut skull, 'Does your Honour think I'd be after taking that abuse from any body but a wife?' But did he have a marriage certificate? persisted the colonel. 'None, your Honour, except the one on my head. Don't your Honour think I am married?' Wisely, perhaps, the colonel agreed that this was proof positive. On another occasion, a sergeant of the regiment went to the adjutant's office to complain that another NCO had been denigrating his wife's character and calling her abusive names. The adjutant wanted to know what names she had been called. The sergeant replied that he could not repeat them in front of a gentleman, but her parentage and family abstraction had been called into question, and the worst of it was that she had been called a drunken blackguard, and never sober. 'Now, your Honour, my wife never gets so right down drunk but she can always stand upright

---

8   Glover (ed.), *Eloquent Soldier*, p.273.
9   Hunt (ed.), *Charging*, p.180.
10 Glover & York (eds), *With Wellington's Hussars*, p.229.
11 Greenwood (ed.), *Through Spain with Wellington*, p.66.

without tumbling; and when she does take a drop of the cratur, she never says a word to nobody, but lies quiet in her bed till she gets sober again.'[12] The adjutant not unreasonably replied to this that if the woman did get drunk in this manner, she could expect remarks to be made, and advised the sergeant to control his wife's drinking.

There was another source of trouble – of near mutiny in fact – amongst regimental wives in the summer of 1808, which came about from the order of 20 July that the ancient military custom of wearing the hair in a queue was to be abolished, and that the men's hair was to be cut short. In the army at large, the queue was a pigtail, in which the hair at the back of the head was allowed to grow to about seven inches in length, then doubled up, bound with a ribbon and greased with tallow or lard. In the case of the 23rd Foot, the Royal Welch Fusiliers, regimental procedure was more elaborate. The hair was grown a foot long, then clubbed in a single roll gripped by a polished leather strap with a plaited grenade in the centre. The whole was then greased and powdered. This arcane procedure was difficult and time consuming for the men, who had to be properly turned out on parade. So 'the talents of the women were very conspicuous in this head dressing of their respective husbands, and as the Officers of companies were always well pleased when they saw a smartly frizzed pate, the credit of their good humour was naturally given to the wife who had operated so successfully.' The wives concerned naturally enjoyed the credit they received, and held their heads high. Indeed, the estimation in which the women were held by many of the men did not derive from their good conduct or personal charms, so much as their ability to dress the hair. In fact, in the Welch Fusiliers at least, it was reported that 'a woman of first rate talents in this department, was not unfrequently bespoken by one or two candidates for her hand, in case of misfortune to her actual lawful Lord.'[13]

When the order arrived that queues were to be shorn, the regiment being at that time in Halifax, Nova Scotia, it was not greeted, as might be thought, with relief that so useless a custom was to be abandoned, but with great resentment, from the colonel down. The officers, after a few drinks, decided to hack each other's plaits off with a carving knife and make a bonfire of them. With the men and their wives however, there was near mutiny. The soldiers assembled in noisy groups. Their women did likewise, adding to the uproar.

> They swore every oath that a soldier's wife has no difficulty in uttering that the order should not be carried into execution, and that they would murder the first operator who should dare to touch a hair of their husband's head. They felt at once, that should the barbarous decree be carried into execution, they descended more than one step in the scale of female perfection, and that widowhood would inevitably be their lonely portion, in case of that event to which some of them looked forwards with complacency.[14]

In other words, they believed that their skills would be held at nought, and that their chances of remarriage were diminished. The colonel's response was immediate. Each company was ordered on parade and a roll call was taken. Benches were brought out of the barracks

---

12 Shipp, *Memoirs*, vol.2, p.173.
13 Buckley (ed.), *Napoleonic War Journal*, p.114.
14 Buckley (ed.), *Napoleonic War Journal*, p.115.

and the men were ordered to sit down and remove their forage caps. Half a dozen haircutters then were ordered to work, and in short order the clubbed hair was no more. Each company was paraded in the same manner till the whole battalion was shorn. The women watched, muttering and cursing quietly because they knew that anyone whose voice could be recognized would be immediately turned out of the barracks. The men, as it turned out, quickly became reconciled to this improvement and officers were pleased with the increase in general cleanliness. As for the women, they 'soon discovered some other foundation on which to build their hopes of perpetual wifehood', and the question of clubbed hair was quietly forgotten.[15]

Somehow or other more women managed to reach Lisbon, the usual port of entry during most of the Peninsular War, than were authorised to do so. Women like Mrs Clark of the 1st Foot, whom we met cursing the ship when she was ordered back to dry land when the battalion sailed. By some means, she had contrived to raise sufficient funds to get herself smuggled out to Portugal while the army was still in the Lines of Torres Vedras. This must have been about end of 1810. Since these women were not allowed to march with the regiments, they congregated in the city and posed something of a problem, made more serious by the so-called 'Belem Rangers', the officers and men who found life more agreeable in Lisbon than at the front, and who were malingering and claiming to be sick. George Farmer described Lisbon as being in a state of perpetual bustle and confusion, with crowds of women who had been unable to march with their husbands constantly asking newcomers from the front for news. Often there was no news, but when it was bad there was a good deal of shrieking and weeping.[16]

Many of these women were actually waiting to be repatriated, since by 1809, quite early in the Peninsula War, the army had decided that unauthorised wives should be sent home. Crowds of them milled about on the beach, waiting their turn to sail. Not all of them were willing to go, and stern measures had to be adopted. Sometime after the Corunna campaign the 40th Foot's order book contained the following threat: 'It is to be expressly understood and made known to the women of the regiments left in Lisbon to be sent to England that should they fail to embark when ordered that no rations can or will be allowed them after the transports sail.'[17] This was serious; women who failed to comply would be cast adrift in a foreign city without means of support. The problem was that there were thought to be about 800 of these women in Lisbon, and no doubt drawing strength from their numbers, they were in mutinous state. The officer with the bad luck to be in charge of the problem was Major General John Sontag. The women were quartered in a barrack by themselves, under the immediate supervision of a few married sergeants who issued their rations and were responsible for locking the barracks at night. Instructions arrived stating that most of the women were to be sent back to England, and that they would have to draw lots to determine who was to go. On arrival, they would be given a guinea as well as the cost of travelling back to their home parish. Sontag sent an officer to announce these generous arrangements. The women loudly expressed their defiance, and refused to take part in any balloting. The officer said that he would have to report their behaviour to the general, at which the women

---

15 Buckley (ed.), *Napoleonic War Journal*, p.116.
16 Gleig, *Light Dragoon*, p.30.
17 Lancashire Infantry Museum: 846/3.2.13: Preston Regimental Order Books 1804–1814.

'shouted defiance, and all swore that if he ventured to show his nose amongst them again they would tear his wig off and souse him under the pump.'[18]

Many of them also made unauthorised attempts to leave the city and travel to the front. Wellington was concerned about this, and while at Badajoz in October 1809, issued a General Order to stop this happening:

> The Commander of the Forces observes that the women of the regiments have come up from Lisbon along with the clothing, to the great inconvenience of the army and to their own detriment; and as they travel on the carts they delay and render uncertain the arrival of the regimental clothing for the troops, and defeat all the arrangements for bringing it up to the army.
>
> The Commander of the Forces desires that General Peacocke will prevent the women from leaving Lisbon with the clothing and regimental baggage; and the Officers and non-commissioned officers coming up from Lisbon in charge of clothing are desired to prevent the women travelling on the carts.[19]

Peacocke may have been in command at Lisbon, but his position was not an enviable one. Dr McGrigor, head of the army's medical services, noted in 1810 that the general had told him, 'that the ladies were the most insubordinate and troublesome part of his charge.'[20]

The other side of this particular coin was that the wives who were legitimately with their regiments had to be allowed to stay there. In the summer of 1810, it appears that Major General Thomas Picton had decided on his own authority that the women of the 3rd Division were such a nuisance that they should be sent back to Lisbon. This provoked an anxious response from the Adjutant General at headquarters. On 23 July he wrote to Picton that the women and their escorting officer had arrived at Lisbon 'very much dis-satisfied at leaving their regiments.' The officer in charge of them had received no money for their subsistence, and no arrangements had been made for their accommodation in Lisbon. Under these circumstances, 'the Commander of the Forces feels that the women cannot be compelled to proceed to the rear, and such of them as are unwilling to go must return to their regiments, of which you will duly apprise the officers commanding regiments...'[21] This was all very well, but how many of these women actually were there? Nobody really knew, and two months later, Wellington's headquarters had become concerned enough to issue a further order to establish the facts about the situation: 'Regiments and corps will immediately send in to the Adjutant General's office returns of women and children actually in the country.'[22]

It was not only in Lisbon that the regimental women tended to ignore orders. They frequently did so in the field. A vivid example of this occurred during Moore's Corunna campaign. On Christmas Eve 1808, just before the retreat began, the brigade under Major General Beresford was ordered to advance and attack what was believed to be a position occupied by the French troops under *Maréchal* Soult. As the troops fell in that evening, the

---

18 Leslie, *Military Journal*, p.90.
19 Gurwood (ed.), *General Orders*, p.322.
20 McGrigor, *Autobiography*, p.264.
21 Wellington (ed.), *Supplementary Despatches*, vol.XIII, p.424.
22 Gurwood (ed.), *General Orders*, p.322.

women were ordered to remain in the village of Santa Martha. They were so resentful of this order that a guard was placed over them to ensure they stayed where they were. The troops marched off into the snowy darkness with extra supplies of ammunition and a Spanish guide. They reached the supposed enemy position before daylight, to find that the French had slipped away, '…but in place of the enemy we found the women, who had with the perseverance of their sex out-manoeuvred the guard, got a Spanish to guide them by a nearer route, and were quietly awaiting our arrival in the morning at the turning of a cross road.' It was as well that the French were not there, but as 16-year-old Lieutenant Samuel Thorpe of the 24th Foot went on to say rather dryly, 'I believe during the remainder of the campaign no further attempt was made to keep the ladies in the background.'[23]

The indiscipline of some of the wives could have more serious effects. Despite orders that the women were to march with the baggage at the rear of the columns, they frequently ignored this, and starting on their way very early would sometimes get ahead of the troops. This might have been dangerous had they run into the French, but more usually they simply got in the way, blocking up narrow passes with their donkeys and generally impeding progress. Orders were repeatedly issued that donkeys were to follow in the rear of their respective corps, and not impede the progress of the troops, but none of this had much effect. During the retreat from Madrid and Salamanca in 1812, this became a serious problem. The provost marshal decided on drastic action and announced that donkeys going ahead of the columns would be shot. This was a dramatic step since the beasts carried the women's worldly goods and possessions. Despite this, they refused to take the threat seriously. 'I'd like to see the man that would shoot my donkey' said Biddy Flyn of the 34th Foot, 'I'll be too early away for any of 'em to catch me.' Sure enough, she, Betty Wheel, and the other women were away in dawn's early light, cracking jokes about orders, commanding officers and Wellington himself, with Mrs Skiddy leading the way with her celebrated donkey 'Queen of Spain'. However, the provost marshal was there before them with an advance guard, ready loaded with ball. As the ladies came round a narrow turn in the road he gave the order to fire, and several of the donkeys fell dead or wounded. 'There was a wild, fierce, and furious yell struck up at once, with more weeping and lamentation than one generally hears at an Irish funeral', and curses and execrations on the head of the provost marshal, but nothing could be done about it. By the time the column came up, the women whose animals had been shot were gathering up what they could carry, and marched along with the troops, crying and lamenting as they went. Not that this terrible example deterred Mother Skiddy, who was up and away in advance the next day as usual, for, as she said, 'We must risk something to be in before the men, to have the fire an' a dhrop of tay ready for the poor crathers after their load an' their labour.'[24] George Bell, who rose to become a major general and a knight of the realm cherished the memory of Mrs Skiddy and her adventures. Years later indeed, he wrote that any old soldiers of the regiment still alive would remember them vividly. He had an eye for the absurd and the comic, and although he must have invented much of the dialogue, as an Irishman himself, he had an affectionate ear for the talk of his troops and their wives.

---

23 Samuel Thorpe, *Narrative of Incidents in the Early Military Life of the late Major Samuel Thorpe KH* (London: Seeleys, 1854), p.30.
24 Stuart (ed.), *Soldier's Glory*, p.60.

Armies have always looted. The Napoleonic Wars were no exception, and right from its earliest phase the regimental women showed themselves to be amongst the most ruthless in looting after a battle or the storming of an enemy stronghold. These were exceptional events, and a more persistent problem lay with plundering during the general movements and operations of the armies in the field, and the women were amongst the most determined of all. A rare eyewitness account of the unsuccessful Flanders campaign of 1793–1794 was recorded by Robert Brown, a corporal in the Coldstream Guards. His detachment of the Guards was overwhelmed near Tourcoign and forced to withdraw towards Roubaix. This retreat developed into a running fight, beset on all sides by cavalry and infantry. The batthorses, panicked by the gunfire, became uncontrollable. The situation was made even more confusing by the women: 'The women also, who inadvertently had been permitted to follow us, caused no small disorder; some being killed, others wounded, and some loaded with plunder, so as to be unable to keep up with the men.' This was near Lannoy. It was probably this incident which led the Duke of York to issue the following general order:

> Head Quarters, Tournay, 23rd May 1794
> It is His Royal Highness the commander in chief's order, that whenever the troops, or any particular corps, march without their camp equipage, no woman is upon any pretence whatever to be permitted to follow the column. His Royal Highness desires this may be considered as a standing order, and expects the commanding officers of regiments will take care it is most strictly complied with.
>
> It is necessary at the same time to warn the women and followers of the army, that the provost-marshal is hereby directed to inflict on every offender the most exemplary punishment; and if the offence deserves it, even to execute on the spot, any woman or follower of the army, of any description whatever, who by cruelty, plunder or marauding, may bring disgrace on the troops under his Royal Highness's command. This order to be read at this evening's roll call, at the head of every troop or company in the army, on which occasion all women and followers of the army are ordered to attend, that none may plead ignorance of the awful punishment to which they will subject themselves by this crime.[25]

The Duke of York obviously felt the plundering situation was out of hand, and drastic punishments by the 'bloody provost' were indeed carried out. Brown records that on 5 June a general court martial was held at which two followers (he did not identify them) were tried, one for stealing a horse, the other for robbing a soldier. They were each sentenced to 1,000 lashes. An even more drastic punishment was visited on a woman following the Austrian troops. In a fit of revenge for some supposed slight, she had managed to set fire to an entire village. She got no sympathy from Captain Morris of the Coldstream Guards, who noted laconically that he 'was glad to hear that the Prince of Saxe Cobourg had ordered her to be shot thro' the head for her pains.'[26]

---

25 Brown, *An Impartial Journal*, p.144.
26 Harrington (ed.), *With the Guards*, p.24.

There were always thieves amongst the ranks, and two decades later, near the end of the fighting in Spain, shortly after the Battle of Vitoria, while the army was in the Pyrenees, Lord Aylmer's tent was robbed by some soldiers of the 24th Foot on the night of 16 July 1813. They were identified, tried and sentenced to death. The executions were arranged for the 25th, and all available troops were assembled, as was usual, to witness the event. Amongst them was Private Green of the 68th Foot. When his regiment arrived at the place of execution, Green 'saw the two poor wretched culprits at their prayers, surrounded by the whole of the women of that regiment who were bitterly lamenting the sad condition of the unhappy men. The prisoners were dressed in white, and were preparing for death in the midst of their kind-hearted country-women.'[27] Two of them may have been the culprits' wives. This was by no means the only occasion on which punishment was witnessed by a wife or wives. Not long after this incident, when the army had entered France early in 1814, Corporal John Thompson of the 18th Hussars was tried by court martial for drunkenness and hitting a sergeant. He was sentenced to 100 lashes. Lieutenant Woodberry found this a trying experience. 'His poor wife was within hearing of her husband's sufferings' he wrote in his diary, 'and I must say, I was never so much affected, more by her sobs than her husband's cries; I wanted to be one hundred miles away.'[28]

Wellington issued yet more stringent orders against plundering. He was all too well aware that if his troops treated the French peasants as their own army had treated the Spanish, the British would be regarded as hostile invaders rather than as liberators. The provost marshals were accordingly ruthless. 'More than one delinquent we passed, when on the line of march' remembered one old soldier, 'dangling to the limb of a tree by the road-side, as a terrible warning to all evil doers.'[29] That included the regimental women.

Looting goods of one sort or another was one thing. A more widespread problem, especially during the war in Spain, was plundering for food, which given that the army was frequently desperately short of rations, and that women were in any case allowed only half a soldier's ration, is unsurprising. The situation was often made worse because the troops, and therefore their wives, often had no money with which to buy extra provisions locally. In September 1812 for instance, while advancing on Aranjuez, William Webber of the artillery noted in his journal that they were five months in arrears, 'and we of course can get nothing but our rations.'[30] So it seems quite likely that a woman who was adept at foraging – or plundering – would have been regarded as an asset by her husband and his comrades, whatever the general orders to the contrary, and despite the risks.

During the unsuccessful siege of Burgos in September 1812, Ensign Mills of the 1st Battalion Coldstream Guards noted in his diary that no less than 40 soldiers and four women had been tried by court martial for stealing onions, though he did not record the penalty.[31] The threat of the death penalty in the case of women was not idle. After the Battle of Busaco in September in September 1810, as the army fell back towards the Lines of Torres Vedras, Wellington issued strong orders against plundering. Commissary Schaumann, with

---

27 Green, *Vicissitudes of a Soldier's Life*, p.175.
28 Glover & York (eds), *With Wellington's Hussars*, p.49.
29 Chelsea Pensioner, *Jottings*, p.188.
30 Wollocombe (ed.), *With the Guns*, p.49.
31 Fletcher (ed.), *For King and Country*, p.225.

the 14th and 20th Light Dragoons, remembered an incident in which the provost marshal caught a sergeant of the King's German Legion coming out of a shop. The sergeant had in fact gone in to fetch one of the carters under his command who had entered the building to steal sugar. Despite his explanation, and his rank, the sergeant was flogged on the spot for plundering. 'The carter, however, together with an English soldier's wife who had stolen a little flour, were immediately hanged in front of the house.'[32]

Orders against plundering for food were regularly issued from headquarters. For example, a General Order was promulgated from headquarters at Cuellar on 1 August 1812: 'The followers of the army, the Portuguese women in particular, must be prevented by the Provosts from plundering gardens and fields of vegetables: the women must be informed that they must obey orders, or they will be turned out of the army.'[33] As Wellington well knew, this sort of behaviour would alienate the Spanish civilian population. There was also a problem with the women roaming around the countryside (those with any money), buying up bread which was being baked for issue as rations. In a General Order dated Medellin, 23 August 1809, Wellington instructed officers commanding divisions or brigades to take steps to prevent this happening, because the women were disrupting the regular supplies to the regiments, and possibly helping to inflate prices. The order was clear and detailed, and went on:

> The women of the army must be prevented from purchasing bread in the villages within two leagues of the station of any division of the army: when any woman wants to purchase bread, she must ask the Officer of the company to which she belongs for a passport, which must be countersigned by the Commanding Officer of the regiment. Any woman found with bread in her possession, purchased at any place nearer than two leagues, will be deprived of the bread by the Provost or his assistants, as will any woman who goes out of camp to purchase bread without a passport. Women who will have been discovered disobeying this order will not be allowed to receive rations.[34]

A considerable number of women must have been involved in this illegal bread-buying in order to pose a threat to the troops' rations, and the penalty, being denied rations in a foreign land, was suitably drastic.

When regimental women plundered vegetables, or consumed bread to which they were not entitled, or blatantly disregarded orders on the march, how were they dealt with? Since they were on the strength, they were subject to military law. Scattered in the diaries and letters of some of the eye-witnesses to these events are references to women being court martialled, as in the example of theft of onions at Burgos. The few surviving regimental order books are however tantalizingly silent on the subject and it is likely that where women were tried in the field it was simply a drum-head affair and effectively unofficial. In such cases, the regimental clerks would not have considered it necessary to record either the crime or the punishment. If the offence was more serious, a woman would probably have

---

32 Schaumann, *On the Road*, p.259.
33 Wellington (ed.), *Supplementary Despatches*, vol.VII, p.367.
34 Gurwood (ed.), *General Orders*, vol.VI, p.335.

been tried by an official regimental court martial, and given the nature of the offences likely to have been committed, this is most likely what usually happened. These were convened to try soldiers for lesser offences. General regimental courts martial dealt with cases beyond the competence of the ordinary regimental courts martial, and these were obliged to forward details to the Judge Advocate General. However, they required a board of five commissioned officers, which was not easy to assemble in the field, so it is unlikely that women came before them. Beyond this, there were also general courts martial which dealt with commissioned officers and the most serious offences committed by the other ranks.

There was a requirement for six-monthly inspection returns to be sent to the Adjutant General giving a general report on the condition of each regiment, its strength and the names of officers present or absent, and many of these returns contained abstracts of regimental courts martial. A database compiled from more than 10,000 of these returns, covering the whole period of the Napoleonic Wars, indicates that very few women ever came before an official court martial at any level. Only three have been identified. Elizabeth Fay, wife of Private J Fay of the 87th, was tried at Coimbra on 6 March 1813 for 'Absence from Quarters and Theft'. The fact that this was before a general court martial suggests that the theft was of a serious nature, and not merely stealing foodstuffs. She was however acquitted. During the same month, and also at Coimbra, Bridget Dougan, described only as a 'Follower of the Army' also faced a general court martial, and on a very serious charge. She was accused of 'firing into and breaking open a house'. Perhaps she had purloined a musket, and possibly she had been drinking, but she was found not guilty. At Cambrai, in February 1816, during the Allied occupation of France after Waterloo, Jane Richards, wife of Jonathan Richards of the Grenadier Guards, was tried on the somewhat unlikely charge of sacrilege. She too was acquitted, which suggests that on the rare occasions a soldier's wife did appear before a court, justice was administered with some care.[35]

The kind of fines or admonitions which may have been suitable punishments in a British barrack were not adequate for the situation in the field, and the army simply resorted to arbitrary punishment applied on the spot with varying degrees of brutality. 'The powers of the Provost Marshal of an Army are very considerable' as Captain Browne noted in his diary. 'He has life & death in his hands, & in case of his seeing a soldier in the act of plundering, there is no need of Court Martial or evidence, but with his cord ready ... the culprit is suspended from the nearest Tree.'[36] Or the culprit might be flogged or beaten. Such a situation was described in his journal by Charles Leslie of the 29th, in July 1809 during the pursuit of Soult's army after the crossing of the Douro:

> After proceeding about two leagues we were encamped at Zarza Maior ... Here several of the soldier's wives, have[ing] preceded the column, (itself contrary to orders) had taken the liberty of helping themselves to various articles in the shape of vegetables and other eatables. On complaint being made by the injured inhabitants,

---

35 I am grateful to Zack White for sharing this information from his PhD thesis *Plunder, Provost and Punishment. Discipline under Wellington's command, 1808–1818*, University of Southampton, 2022.
36 Buckley (ed.), *Napoleonic War Journal*, p.256.

Lord Hill consigned the delinquents to the provost, *who exercised schoolboy discipline* on a few as an example to the rest.[37]

That sort of circumlocution was not unusual, especially when the writer was remembering his adventures years later during the Victorian period. According the anonymous Chelsea Pensioner, whose *Jottings* were published in 1847, 'a rumour was rife that the active provost-marshal of the division detected some of the tender sex of the hussar brigade violating the path of honesty towards the inhabitants, and that he had, *proh pudor!* ['for shame'] inflicted or threatened to inflict punishment by flagellation upon a nameless part!'[38] This was after the army had entered France, but the result was that the provost in question received a good deal of abuse when passing the hussars on the line of march.

Sergeant John Cooper of the 7th Fusiliers mentioned a similar example, but one which had an unexpected outcome. He was sick with fever in a hospital at Pamplona in July 1813, where he saw a man he knew, a Sergeant Bishop, badly wounded. In Ireland, at Clonmel, Bishop had married a local girl who had previously been married to another soldier. She accompanied Bishop for several years in the Peninsula, until one day she was caught stealing. Justice was swift: '…the provost-marshal flogged her on the breech.'[39] After this, she decided that life in the ranks did not suit her, and she abandoned her wounded husband and went to live with the colonel of another regiment.

In reality, no sanctions, however draconian, were likely to be effective when the cause of the trouble was hunger. Shortly after the Battle of Salamanca, in August 1812, Lieutenant Peter Le Mesurier described the situation with some of the women in a letter home:

> Lord Wellington had been forced to issue very severe orders with regard to Women plundering. I must do them the justice to say that they are ten times worse than the Men. A little wholesome discipline is now administered to them when they are found at it. A few days ago the Provost of the Division desired one of them to walk out of a Field where the Industrious Lady was very busy digging Patatoes else he would punish her. With a tremendous Oath she replied 'You may Flog me every Day for a Meal of Praties.' and went out well loaded.[40]

The food was clearly worth the risk of a thrashing.

Lest this sort of treatment should be seen simply as military brutality, it is worth remembering that the penal code in Britain at the time was every bit as severe, and in many cases more so. There were some 200 offences which carried the death penalty, including for example, the pickpocketing of goods worth more than a shilling. As late as 1789 a woman was burned at Tyburn for coining. The pillory was not abolished (except for perjury) until 1816. And the public whipping of women was not abolished till 1817. Until then, a woman could be whipped, as the expression was, 'at the cart's tail' along the street. The provost marshals never seem to have gone that far.

---

37   Leslie, *Military Journal*, p.123.
38   Chelsea Pensioner, *Jottings*, p.204.
39   Cooper, *Rough Notes*, p.99.
40   Greenwood (ed.), *Through Spain with Wellington*, p.121.

It is difficult to know exactly what was meant by the word 'flogging' when applied to the women. Flogging in the British service meant that a man was stripped to the waist and tied to the triangle, which was a frame made from sergeants' halberds lashed together. The cat o' nine tails was then laid on by one of the drummers. A man often received hundreds of lashes, leaving his back a bloody pulp. There seems to be no evidence that this was ever inflicted on one of the British wives, although there is a reference to the cat being used on Portuguese followers. Writing to his sister in June 1813 Peter Le Mesurier described how, while he was on baggage guard, he was surprised to see troops of Portuguese women rounded up and placed under guard. They had been ruthlessly plundering the Spanish countryside and this was the only means of controlling them, 'for the Cat even could not deter them from Plundering on the March; it has been tried and found not to answer so well.'[41]

The term 'flogging' seems in fact to have been used to describe any sort of beating or whipping administered on the spot with whatever instrument the provost marshal had to hand. But whatever kind of punishment it was that was actually administered, the subject of flogging women was one which came back to haunt the Duke of Wellington in later years. In September 1850, 35 years after the end of the Great French War, Wellington was receiving anonymous letters accusing him of having authorised such punishments. Writing to the Marchioness of Salisbury on the 23rd, he said that 'I should not be surprised if I was attacked for flogging the Women in the Army in the Peninsula! I receive numbers of anonymous letters on the subject, which is the usual fore-runner of these attacks!' Two days later he returned to the subject. He felt that a storm was brewing, 'Whether true or false the Newspapers will comment on calumny', and he thought that he might have to defend himself.[42]

The Marchioness had written to him some days previously, saying that she believed that the rumour had originally been started by Sir Walter Scott. Scott had been an early visitor to the battlefield at Waterloo, and could have picked up some such story from a soldier, but since he had died in 1832, it is strange that the matter should have surfaced so many years later. Wellington replied thanking Lady Mary for the information, and explaining the role of the provost marshals in suppressing plundering. He described how troops would get into wine-cellars, make holes in the casks to fill their canteens, and sometimes be found dead drunk up to their waists in wine. 'Mind, there were always Women in these Cellars as well as men! and it is not improbable that the women were the least capable of running away!' In such cases, the provosts would certainly use their lawful authority to punish the offenders, and the Duke went on: 'As I said there was no order for punishing women! But there was certainly none for exempting Women from punishment! Such an order would have rendered the existence of such an institution (the provost marshal) entirely nugatory!'[43] So, while it was quite possible that women had been flogged on occasion, he could not say for certain whether it had ever actually happened. After the end of September, the correspondence makes no further mention of the subject, and it appears the storm, whoever caused it, quietly subsided.

---

41   Greenwood (ed.), *Through Spain with Wellington*, p.170.
42   Burghclere, *A Great Man's Friendship*, p.113.
43   Burghclere, *A Great Man's Friendship*, p.110.

Given the capacity of some of the regimental women to pose disciplinary problems, it may seem strange that those officers and men who were opposed to their presence with the army were mainly concerned about the hardships they would have to endure rather than the trouble they could cause. Drunkenness being the besetting sin of the rank and file it must have been accepted that some of the women would be no better. Plundering in times of hunger, when the commissariat had failed was inevitable with men and women alike. Women in unauthorized numbers, or delaying transport heading for the front were certainly a great nuisance. What is more surprising is the way in which regimental wives were able in some cases to disobey the clearest of general orders and manage to get away with doing so within a system of the most draconian punishments. They were ordered to stay in camp and promptly marched off. They were ordered not to attempt river crossings and did so anyway. They were ordered to stay with the baggage in the rear of the marching columns and somehow contrived to get ahead of the troops instead. In fact, they often seem to have been one too many for the provost marshals, and it is difficult not to admire their sturdy determination to stick with their men at whatever cost.

11

Marriage à la Mode

> *Prythee why so melancholy?*
> *Sighing cannot give him life:-*
> *Cease, those tears are unavailing,*
> *Oh! thus early widow'd wife!*
> *Poor Mary.*[1]

What with the hazards of battle and the dangers of disease, which throughout the Napoleonic period claimed more lives than fighting ever did, married life in a campaigning army was a precarious business. The prospect of sudden widowhood in the midst of a war in a foreign country was an ever-present possibility, and a bleak prospect it was. A woman who lost her husband lost her official place in the regiment and was not entitled even to continue drawing her rations, although the regiment might pay her passage back to Britain.

The most practical way in which the comrades of a dead man could help a widow was to make an offer marriage, and such an offer constituted about the only way in which a woman so situated could survive and maintain a shred of respectability. These were not so much marriages of convenience as a matter of survival, and were generally regarded as a sensible arrangement, carrying no suggestion of indecent haste or promiscuity. They were certainly commented on as such by men writing home, keeping a diary, or recalling their experiences in later years. James Anton was one of the men of the 42nd whose wife was with him, and might be said to have an informed view of the question:

> I feel free to offer this remark, in justification of many a good woman, who, in few months, perhaps weeks, after her sudden bereavement, becomes the wife of a second husband; and although slightingly spoken of by some of little feeling, in and out of the army, yet this is perhaps the only alternative to save a lone innocent woman's reputation; and the soldier who offers himself may be as little inclined to the connection through any selfish motive, as the woman may be from any desire of his love, but the peculiar situation in which she is placed renders it necessary,

---

1   'W.N.H.', *Poor Mary* in *The Monthly Magazine*, January 1798.

without consulting false feelings, or regarding the idle remarks that may be made, to feel grateful for a protector, and in a soldier, the most binding is the surest.[2]

Richard Bentinck sailed as a drummer with the 1/23rd from England to Portugal in the autumn of 1810. The voyage took a month, and despite good conditions, there were several deaths amongst his comrades. He described one burial at sea, with the body sewn into a hammock and a round-shot at the feet, sliding into the water from a plank. His comment on the bereaved wife was matter of fact: 'His widow proved herself to be worthy of a soldier's wife, for she married another soon after they landed.'[3] At the time of the Battle of Salamanca in July 1812, Thomas Henry Browne wrote a rather amused entry in his journal that, 'They had no hesitation in engaging themselves three or four deep to future Husbands … in case of disaster to her lawful Lord.' One woman was heard to say to a soldier who offered himself as a new husband should her present one be killed, 'Nay, but thou'rt late, as I'm promised to John Edwards first, and to Edward Atkinson next, but when they two be killed off, I'll think of thee.'[4] Which seems a good insurance policy.

Some women even seem to have been proud of their feats in the marriage market. Mrs Sherwood was the wife of a captain in the 53rd, and in 1810 was with a group of other ladies making a passage from Northumberland to Ramsgate prior to foreign service. They had with them the wife of a sergeant, Mrs Strachan. Mrs Sherwood had never met anyone quite like her before, and left a vivid description. Mrs Strachan was a woman of no more than 35, though she might have been anything between 30 and 50. She had carroty hair and a red face, no doubt weather-beaten, with a cast in one eye, was stout and rather clumsy, and the most memorable thing about her clothes was a cap with many bows and an enormous pair of gilt drops hanging from her ears. She nursed the children, waited on the ladies, and entertained them with an inexhaustible fund of stories about her adventures. She had been with the regiment in the West Indies, where she had buried her first husband and married another.

> She gave us a full and detailed account of six offers which she had had before her deceased husband had been laid in the ground. Of course we at first believed that she was inventing these stories, as women will sometimes do, in order to enhance their charms; but I now believe, from further information, that she only told us the truth.[5]

In India, widowhood usually came about as a result of the pestilential climate rather than battle casualties. The sad story of a Scottish girl named Nelly Stevenson was a terrible illustration of the fact. Nelly was the daughter of a Glasgow weaver, and when she was 20 she married a man called M'Dougal, who had volunteered into the 1st Foot, the Royal Scots. The regiment was posted to southern India, and M'Dougal died of the flux (dysentery) at Wallajalibad. She then married a Sergeant Fleming of the light company by whom she had a

---

2 Anton, *Retrospect*, p.142.
3 Crook (ed.), *The Very Thing*, p.36.
4 Buckley (ed.), *Napoleonic War Journal*, p.174.
5 Kelly (ed.), *Life*, p.258.

child, but two years later he too died of the flux. Six weeks later Nelly married Sergeant Lee of the grenadier company, and had a second child. Lee however died of the same complaint as her other husbands while the battalion was at Trichinopoly in 1811. She was now a widow for the third time in six years, and worn out perhaps by grief as much as by the climate, she herself died of dysentery as well. She was 26. Sergeant Robert Butler and his wife took on one of the orphans, and Sergeant and Mrs Brown the other, but Mrs Brown also died, and the Butlers were obliged to adopt the second child as well.[6]

The fact that Butler had a wife at all was itself the result of yet another death. When the wives had drawn lots to see who was to go with the battalion and who had to remain in England, a Mrs Allen had been unlucky. Butler however, who was one of the musicians, persuaded the colonel to bend the rules and allow her to go, because she was the wife of a fellow bandsman. Mrs Allen's husband died another victim of the Indian climate and Butler married her on 8 March 1808. As things turned out, this was providential, because he too was sick with dysentery, and as he put it himself, was more in need of a doctor than a wife. 'But I knew her to be an excellent woman, and as she had no objection to me as a husband, I could have none against her as a wife; but happily for me I found in her both a doctor and a wife.'[7]

However casual such attitudes may now appear, they actually reflected in a practical way the real state of affairs, and many women remarried over and over again. While the wounded were being attended to after the Battle of Salamanca, the baggage and women of the 68th Foot arrived, amongst them the wife of Sergeant Dunn. He had been killed early in the action, and his widow was half frantic with grief. Terrible though her loss at first appeared, 'in less than a week she took up with a sergeant of the same company, whose name was Gilbert Hinds, with whom she has lived ever since. This poor woman was unlucky, for she had lost five husbands.'[8] After the Battle of the Nivelle in November 1813, during the Pyrenees campaign, Private Wheeler of the 51st Light Infantry, who was wounded, and had managed to crawl to a building he referred to as the farm, where he watched the regimental women searching for their husbands. One of them was a Mrs Cousins. Wheeler heard one of the other men say of her 'I think she is devilish lucky in getting husbands, she has had a dozen this campaign.'[9] The man, Wheeler wrote in a letter home, was drunk, but the reality was still tragic. Mrs Cousins had in fact just been widowed for the third time since the Battle of Vitoria, which had been fought on 21 June. In other words, she had already survived three husbands in the space of five months. It is worth considering the point of view of the men. If swift remarriage offered women support and protection far from home, the soldiers were presented with a rare opportunity in a foreign land, of getting a British wife. These men were abroad for years on end with no chance of leave, and although many of them acquired a Spanish or Portuguese camp-follower, or in some cases a wife, the chance of getting hold of a recently made British widow may well have been seen as an opportunity not to be missed. Sometimes an offer of marriage might be refused. Benjamin Harris, the rifleman who had witnessed the death of Joseph Cochan at Roliça, and who had guided his widow to find the

---

6   Butler, *Narrative*, p.174.
7   Butler, *Narrative*, p.82.
8   Green, *Vicissitudes of a Soldier's Life*, p.102.
9   Liddell Hart (ed.), *Letters*, p.141.

body, was evidently touched by Mrs Cochan's plight. And as he put it, '…the circumstances of my having seen her husband fall, and accompanied her to find his body, begot a sort of intimacy between us.' The company to which Harris belonged was now Mrs Cochan's only home. Four days after her husband's death she was with the regiment on the battlefield of Vimeiro, and marched with them to Lisbon, and during this time Harris chivalrously did what he could for her: 'The circumstances of our intimacy were singular, and an attachment grew between us during the short time we remained together. What little attention I could pay her during the hardships of the march I did, and I also offered on the first opportunity to marry her.' However, Mrs Cochan declined this offer, because, as she said, the shock of her husband's death had been so great that she could never wed another soldier, but she thanked Harris for his good feeling towards her, and shortly afterwards managed to secure a passage home.[10]

These re-marriages were sometimes so quick as to lead some officers to take a somewhat cynical attitude to the situation. Lieutenant George Gleig of the 85th thought that since there were only 60 women permitted to a battalion, any one bereaved could have as many new husbands as she chose, and regarded them indeed as 'a highly favoured class of female society.'[11] Not that the women concerned would have agreed with him. He was writing about the fighting in the Pyrenees in November 1813, but Lieutenant William Grattan, describing the preparations for the storming of Ciudad Rodrigo in January 1812, and the way in which husbands and wives of the Connaught Rangers made their farewells before the action began, would have agreed with him. If a man fell in the assault, wrote Grattan, 'his place was sure to be supplied by some one of the company to which he belonged, so that the women of our army had little cause of alarm on this head. The worst that could happen to them was the chance of being in the state of widow-hood for a week.'[12]

It is not easy to know the exact nature of these marriages in the field, or how many of them were officially solemnised by a chaplain. Prior to 1796 few regiments had a chaplain, and most of those were frequently absent. The Army Chaplains Department was established in 1796 in order to regularize the situation, after which chaplains were appointed to brigades and not regiments. This does not initially seem to have helped much. When Major General Fraser landed in Egypt in April 1807 with 6,000 men there was no chaplain present. The situation was the same when Sir Arthur Wellesley sailed for Spain with 9,000 men at the start of the Peninsular War, although Sir John Moore did have a staff chaplain with his troops in 1808. The situation does appear to have improved as the war wore on. The memoirs of the period refer occasionally to services being conducted by brigade chaplains. 'Divine service was performed by the brigade clergyman, before the regiment on parade, this afternoon' noted an officer of the 18th Hussars in March 1813.[13] The Light Division certainly had a padre in the autumn of 1811. His name was Parker, and he distinguished himself by getting himself captured by French dragoons during the marching and counter-marching before the capture of Ciudad Rodrigo.[14]

---

10   Hibbert (ed.), *Recollections*, p.22.
11   Gleig, *The Subaltern*, p.122.
12   Grattan, *Adventures*, p.146.
13   Glover & York (eds), *With Wellington's Hussars*, p.38.
14   Verner (ed.), *British Rifleman*, p.196.

Divine service in the field. The padre has his Bible or sermon laid out on the drums. The soldiers and officers listen attentively as do the four women, three of them with babies. A rather idealised scene by Thomas Rowlandson, 1798. (Anne S.K. Brown Military Collection, Brown University)

Where a chaplain was not available, the War Office's answer to the problem was to authorise officers of the rank of captain and above to perform certain religious offices in lieu of a clergyman.[15] As Lieutenant Browne of the 23rd put it, when his regiment was returning aboard transports from Martinique to Halifax, Nova Scotia in April 1809, when he was called on to baptize a baby born on the ship, 'Under pressing circumstances an Officer is permitted to act as Chaplain'[16] So it seems likely that these marriages in the field may have sometimes have been performed by a man of the cloth and on other occasions by a regimental officer, perhaps the captain of the company, no doubt with the agreement of the colonel. Or that they were simply common-law marriages without any formal religious ceremony, but recognized as valid by both partners and the rest of the unit concerned. Under the circumstances, that was probably quite good enough.

---

15   R. Burley, *An Age of Negligence? British Army Chaplaincy, 1796–1844*, Unpublished M.Phil. thesis. Birmingham University, 2013, pp.19–48.
16   Buckley (ed.), *Napoleonic War Journal*, p.111.

Sometimes the regimental officers would come to the rescue of a recently made widow, especially in cases where the woman was well liked and respected. In April 1807, when the 3rd battalion of the 1st Guards were part of a force occupying Sicily, a detachment was stationed at Taormina where one of the sergeants was shot dead by a private. This was a distressing case, as the man had a wife and children. Colonel Anderson asked a sergeant who acted as clerk in the adjutant general's office what had become of the poor woman. The reply was that the officers of the regiment had raised a subscription and gathered enough money to take care of the woman for the immediate future. One junior officer however, Ensign James Stanhope, had been moved to settle £10 a year on the woman for life – an act of remarkable and surprising generosity, even for a member of the illustrious and influential Stanhope family.[17] Another such example occurred as a result of the fighting at Toulouse in 1814, in the closing phase of the Peninsular War. A soldier named Cunningham of the 42nd was killed, his distraught wife helping to bury him, and there she stood, 'a lonely unprotected being, far from her country or the home of her childhood.' The officer commanding the company, Lieutenant M'Laren, had been badly wounded, and sending for Mrs Cunningham, appointed her his sick-nurse, 'and under his protection [she] was restored in decent respectability to her home.'[18]

Catherine Exley of the 34th was another woman who experienced nothing but kindness and consideration from the officers when her husband Joshua was believed to have been killed in the fighting at Maya in the Pyrenees. 'The colonel and the officers were quite lavish in their kindness, allowed me my husband's rations appointed me to sleep with a sargeant's wife, and assured me of redress if I met with any incivility.' Whether she received any offers of marriage from Joshua's comrade she did not say, but she was advised to stay with the regiment until she could return safely to England. Some officers' ladies belonging another regiment in the same brigade sent her a present of some linen for herself and her child and they gave her washing to do to earn a little money. In due course the colonel gave her £1, and the officers as a whole came up with two dollars apiece, so that Catherine was able to save 12 guineas before embarking for England. Just before she left the camp the two ladies gave her two more dollars each and some change. Catherine was clearly a well-known and respected woman within the regiment.[19]

Catherine was fortunate in being treated generously and allowed to draw rations; this was not always the case. Michael Quinn of the 100th Foot had died in June 1807 in Quebec, and Elinor his widow was in great distress. Unable to work because of her two small children, 'she has no means of support in Consequence of no Rations being allowed her since the death of her Husband.' She was dependent on the humanity of some of the garrison officers. In July 1808 she petitioned Lieutenant General Sir James Craig, the Governor and Commander-in-Chief begging him 'to assist her as she wishes to return home to Ireland, and having not the least means at present to support herself & helpless Orphans unless through the humanity of your Excellency whose assistance Petitioner implores by allowing

---

17 Gareth Glover (ed.), *Eyewitness to the Peninsular War and the Battle of Waterloo* (Barnsley: Pen & Sword, 2010), p.8.
18 Anton, *Retrospect*, p.141.
19 Probert (ed.), *Exley Diary*, p.43.

her Rations until she may be enabled to procure a passage home.'[20] In December that year Sir James Craig received another, very similar petition from Margaret Fraser. Her late husband had served the King for upwards of 31 years, much of it with the 71st in India, but had also died in Quebec while serving with the 10th Royal Veteran Battalion. Like Elinor Quinn, she had had her rations cut off, and was unable to work because of her small baby. So, she wrote that she 'humbly begs you Excellency would pity her distressed situation and be graciously pleased to allow her, One Ration, or any kind assistance that your Excellency may be pleased to think fit until she can procure a Passage to Scotland her native Country.'[21] What it came down to, was that these two women, whose husbands had faithfully served years in the ranks, were at risk of starving.

Sometimes a regiment would rally around a recently widowed woman, as in the case of Nance M'Dermot of the 85th. 'They had been married about a year and a half, during the whole of which time she had borne the most unblemished character, and they were accounted the most virtuous and the happiest couple in the regiment.' So when M'Dermot was killed in the fighting around Bayonne in February 1814, and Nance was almost deranged with grief, there was concern throughout the regiment. She would not listen 'as women in her situation generally listen, to the proposals of some new suitor' and wished only to go home. 'We raised for her a handsome subscription, every officer and man contributing something; and I have reason to believe that she is now respectably settled in Cork, though still a widow.'[22]

Occasionally the other ranks seem to have assumed joint responsibility for a comrade's widow. Sergeant Edward Sargent of the 1/51st developed a bad cold during the Waterloo campaign, which turned into a fever from which he died, in Paris, on 1 September 1815. Private Richard Armstrong wrote to his mother and sisters explaining that the widow 'is in such a state at present grieving after her lost partner that she cannot be spoke to in any reason.' However, the dead man's comrades intended to write to her parents pressing them to think it was 'their duty to look upon her and the poor orphan as sufferers of Waterloo.' When she had settled her affairs in the regiment, they were going to 'prevail upon her to visit her deceased husband's friends.'[23]

Not all regimental women were so virtuous, and there were certainly cases of marital infidelity. 'I knew two women who changed their husbands just as a servant would leave one family and go to another' remembered James Aytoun of the 58th, 'but they certainly mended their conditions by getting better men who kept them comfortable during life.'[24] That was in the West Indies in the 1790s. These changes seem to have been managed peacefully, but the consequences could be tragic. Sometime after the storming of Badajoz in April 1812, when the 95th were cooking their evening meal in a grove of cork trees, a grenadier of another regiment – William Surtees the quartermaster thought it was the 88th, though Rifleman Costello remembered that it was the 61st – came into their bivouac. He had come to find his wife, who had taken up with a Sergeant Battersby. Her name was Nelly, and both

---

20   Buckley (ed.), *Napoleonic War Journal*, Appendix C, p.309.
21   Buckley (ed.), *Napoleonic War Journal*, Appendix C, p.309.
22   Gleig, *The Subaltern*, p.333.
23   Glover (ed.), *The Waterloo Archive*, vol.4, p.159.
24   Howard, *Death Before Glory*, p.173.

eyewitnesses agree that she was a gay and attractive woman. However, it turned out that she had abandoned not only her husband, but their small child as well. According to Costello's account, the soldier asked, while looking hard at Battersby, 'How can you stoop to such a disgraceful, so dishonourable a protection?' To which she replied that she was now with those who treated her better than he had ever done. But, persisted the deserted husband, what about their three year-old child? How did she expect him to be able to look after it? The pair walked off into the wood, where their argument continued. Both accounts agree on what happened next. The grenadier, whose name was Bryen, drew his bayonet and plunged it into his wife's body, killing her almost instantly. He was quickly arrested, according to Costello's somewhat colourful account, contemptuously wiping the blood from his bayonet with his fingers, and waiting calmly for the arrival of the provost. Strange to say, he escaped any serious punishment, possibly because it was thought that the balance of his mind was disturbed. He was killed later in the fighting in the Pyrenees. Sergeant Battersby also fell in action, shot through head at the start of the Battle of Quatre Bras on 16 June 1815. As for Nelly, she was buried near where she fell, the riflemen digging her grave with their bayonets, the only tools they had to hand.[25]

As the war wore on and casualties mounted, the government became aware of the plight of widows and orphans left stranded abroad with no means of getting home. Sometimes there were exceptional circumstances requiring an exceptional response. Towards the end of 1809, the deaths amongst the troops employed in the Walcheren expedition had reached such numbers that something out of the ordinary had to be done for their widows and children. On 15 November Horse Guards issued a general order stating that the King had directed that the women concerned were to receive double the usual allowance to enable them to get home from the barracks where they had been living after their men had embarked and that those who came from Scotland or Ireland would be granted free passage at public expense.[26]

This was a one-off response to a particular situation. By August 1810, however, two years after the Peninsular War had begun, it was realized that provision would have to be made to deal with the wider problem. The War Office wrote to Wellington as follows: 'I have the honour to acquaint your Lordship that His Majesty has been pleased to direct that the same allowances shall be made to the widows and children of soldiers dying abroad, and sent home in consequence thereof, as are granted to the wives and children of soldiers embarking for foreign service.' In order to claim these allowances, the woman concerned would have to have a certificate signed by the officer commanding the unit to which her husband had belonged, and stating that she was indeed on her way home.[27] This did at least provide women who had been widowed with an alternative to quick remarriage. In the meantime of course, they needed to be supported with basic rations, and the predicament of these unhappy women continued to be a concern. On 8 December 1811 Wellington felt it necessary to issue a general order from his headquarters at Frenada reminding those concerned that 'Widows and orphans of Officers and soldiers are to be victualled until they can obtain a passage home.'[28]

---

25 Costello, *Adventures*, p.143, and Surtees, *Twenty-Five Years*, p.158.
26 Gardyne, *The Life*, vol.1, p.218.
27 Gurwood (ed.), *General Orders*, p.322.
28 Gurwood (ed.), *General Orders*, p.333.

By 1812 Britain's war effort had become so extensive that more comprehensive arrangements were needed to deal with the difficulties posed by widowed women, and in July a new Act of Parliament was passed 'to explain, amend, and extend the Provisions of an Act, passed in the last Session of Parliament, for enabling the Wives and Families of Soldiers to return to their Homes, to the Widows, Wives, and Families of Soldiers dying or employed on Foreign Service'[29] This was basically an extension of the provision which had been made to allow women who had been unlucky in the drawing of lots for foreign service to reach their homes. The new act recognized that many women, whether wives or widows, returning to Britain, were liable to be destitute and have no means of getting back to wherever they lived. As in the earlier act, the commanding office had to sign a certificate stating that the woman's husband had been a soldier and that the children, if any, were his. If a woman landed back in Britain without such a document, the general officer commanding the district could supply one after making the appropriate enquiries. As before, a magistrate would endorse the certificate and give the woman a route home. There was however a catch. The previous act had allowed two pence a mile. The local Justice could now vary the rate of allowance if he saw fit to do so, and 'to direct any such Allowance as he shall deem necessary, not exceeding Three Halfpence per Mile for each woman, and One Penny per Mile for each of her Children.' In other words, strict economy was the order of the day. The act may have been a practical response to a persistent problem, but it was not a generous one.

There were women who fell through this safety net since the rules only applied to those believed by commanding officers to be the lawful wives or widows of soldiers. There must have been large numbers of camp followers and unofficial wives of one sort or another by the war's end. In August 1815, Ensign Bakewell was ordered to take command of a detachment of time-expired men from his own regiment, the 27th Foot, as well as some from the 4th and 29th. They were to march to Ostend to return to England. As they left Paris they were joined by 'a fair featured young lady' who begged to be allowed to accompany them. Her husband, she said, had been killed at Waterloo, though with which regiment she did not say. Young Bakewell agreed, partly to help her, and partly, as he put it very honestly, 'as a distraction for myself.'[30] When they reached the port, she seems to have vanished. Perhaps she was just a follower.

Officers like Gleig and Grattan, who might be thought to have had a somewhat cavalier attitude to the rapid remarriage of soldiers' widows, probably underestimated the genuine grief many bereaved women felt, whatever their prospects of remarriage, or indeed their social standing. Perhaps they were simply unable understand the real emotions the 'other ranks' were capable of. In any case, the fact was that officers' ladies were equally capable of being overwhelmed with grief at the death of a husband and then transferring their affections to another in very short order.

Soon after the Battle of Salamanca, Captain Ross-Lewin of the 32nd had returned to a billet he had previously occupied in the city with the family of a miller. No sooner had he arrived when two English ladies were brought in. One was the wife of a captain who had

---

[29] 52 Geo III cap120. *An Act to explain, amend, and extend the Provisions of an Act passed in the last session of Parliament, for enabling the Wives and Families of Soldiers to return to their Homes, to the Widows, Wives, and Families of Soldiers dying or employed on Foreign Service.*

[30] Robertson (ed.), *The Exploits*, p.169.

fallen in the battle, the other was married to a lieutenant who was missing, though known to be wounded. The captain's wife, very young and beautiful, Ross-Lewin noted, was totally overcome with grief, and in a state of violent hysterics. Her grief was so awful that even the miller and his family, and the man who drove the mules which turned the mill wheel, were overcome with emotion. Ross-Lewin organized rations for the ladies' servants, and as the paroxysms of grief began to subside, made an offer of his services. He was therefore surprised in the morning to discover that both the ladies had left in a carriage for another billet. He was even more astonished a few days later while walking in the town square 'when the first object that arrested my attention was the lady who had caused us so much uneasiness, leaning on a young commissary with two gold epaulettes, and evidently enjoying excellent spirits. She set off with this gallant on the following day for Rodrigo.'[31]

One of the officers in the force which landed on the continent for the abortive Walcheren campaign in 1809 was Sir Richard Henegan, the military commissary in charge of the field train, responsible for the movement of artillery and the supply of ammunition for the guns. His point of view was therefore somewhat different from that of the average regimental officer.

Henegan came to know an officer he identifies only as Major B of an undisclosed regiment, whom he portrays as a paragon of all the military virtues, and a devoted, even doting, married man. The gallant major fell victim to the infamous Walcheren fever, which carried off so many of the British force. He fought for life for some days, lamenting the fact that he would never see his wife, who was in England, again. On the evening of the seventh day, when it became clear that the major was dying, Henegan resolved to sit the night with him and dismissed the attendants. In the small hours the door burst open and the major's wife, who had been told of her husband's condition, and managed to cross the Channel despite the wartime conditions, burst into the room. There was a flicker of recognition and the major died. After a display of bitter anguish the widow decided to return to England with the little boy she brought with her – the image of his father. It was what happened afterwards that shocked and upset Henegan. 'Would that truth permitted me here to devote one bright page to the constancy of woman's love…but truth forbids it.' The fact was that on the passage back to England, the lady met with an Irishman, a captain in another regiment, who wooed her like a second Desdemona, so Henegan thought, with tales of his past deeds and sufferings, 'and on my return to England, at the close of the year, the first news I heard was that she was about to surrender to the Hibernian Captain her liberty and the revered position as the widow of the gallant Major B.'[32]

When Lieutenant General Abercromby's force sailed for Egypt in 1801, to wrest it from the French army left behind by Napoleon, the regimental women went with the troops as usual. When the expedition reached Malta however, Abercromby decided that Egypt was not a place for wives, and ordered that they should be sent home 'except such as were absolutely necessary to supply the hospitals with nurses.' A rare case, it seems, when this was actually planned. Two transport vessels were accordingly fitted out, and some 300 women sailed for England, including those of the 54th. Unfortunately, being without convoy, they

---

31 Wardell (ed.), *With the Thirty Second*, p.188.
32 Henegan, *Seven Years Campaigning*, vol.1, p.81.

were captured by the French and taken into Marseille. The authorities there found the large number of women an embarrassment however, and sent them on, in a cartel, to Minorca. The island was at that time garrisoned by British troops including the Ancient Irish, a fencible infantry regiment raised in Dublin in 1799 and commanded by Colonel Thomas Fitzgerald. Fencibles were normally for home service only, but the Ancient Irish had volunteered for service abroad. In due course news reached the women that all their men had been killed in action or had died of the plague in Egypt. So, believing themselves to be widows, the women of the 54th married the men of the Ancient Irish, more or less *en masse*, shortly before the regiment was itself posted to Egypt. This time, all the women were allowed to accompany the men, and Captain Harley of the 54th described what happened when they arrived:

> It was truly laughable to witness the meeting of the women with their former husbands, when this corps [the Irish] landed in Egypt; there were a thousand expostulations and recriminations on both sides, loud and angry, but the matter was finally settled by all the former husbands, save one, refusing to take back their wives; and that one belonged to our regiment, and ever afterwards lived a miserable life, from the manner in which his comrades treated him.[33]

Campaigning far from home for years on end, and with no system of home leave, it was inevitable that Wellington's troops, including the officers, should miss female company. As Moyle Sherer of the 34th put it, whenever there was a prolonged halt and army formed an encampment or went into billets, the officers might be able to purchase various comforts from the sutlers who rapidly appeared, but still 'felt two serious wants…books, and the society of women.'[34] This yearning for female company was certainly intensified by the beauty of the local girls, which seems to have reached legendary proportions. Young Lieutenant Blakeney of the 1/28th, described Portugal as the land 'where dwell the brown maids with the lamp-black eyes.'[35] While Robert Porter, a more mature man, who was shortly to march into Spain with Moore's army, wrote to a friend from Lisbon of 'the romance-famed females of this country.'[36] Walter Henry, surgeon to the 66th Foot, was even more enamoured of the Spanish girls, and even 30 years later could not help flights of romantic fancy, and wondered how he had survived with his heart intact:

> For my own individual part, all I can say is, that they are such semi-divinities … they skim over the ground so aerially, and wear the basquina and dear little mantilla so gracefully, and their Cinderella shoes so daintily, and manoeuvre their fans so coquetishly, and have such magnificent eyes and lovely shapes; and talk so endearingly, and lisp so prettily, and smile so affectionately, and waltz so charmingly…[37]

---

33 Harley, *The Veteran*, vol.1, p.149.
34 Sherer, *Recollections*, p.98.
35 Blakeney, *A Boy*, p.209.
36 Porter, *Letters from Portugal*, p.43.
37 Henry, *Events*, vol.1, p.56.

On those occasions when it was possible to invite the local population to a social gathering, it does not seem to have been the girls' waltzing ability which caught the imagination of most young British officers, so much as their wild and uninhibited dancing to guitars and castanets. For some officers the thought that the fact these attractive young women should not only be caught up in the war itself, but that some of them might even be suffering from the effects of British action, was disturbing. One officer who was particularly worried about this was the Honourable Edward Charles Cocks, then a captain in the 16th Light Dragoons. In a letter to his cousin, Thomas Somers Cocks, written on 9 July 1810, while the French were besieging Ciudad Rodrigo, he expressed his fears for the Spanish girls trapped inside the walls: 'It is a heartbreaking thing to us to remain inactive spectators of this gallant defence, especially as some of the prettiest girls in Spain are in the town. What care we should take of them if we had them here. We would build them such nice huts! And keep them so warm at night!'[38]

In the absence of other female company, nunneries and convents exercised an almost magnetic attraction for British officers, a feeling intensified by their regret that so much youth and beauty should be shut away from the world in the service of what most of them held to be an idolatrous religion. Nobody put it better than young George Bell of the 34th, writing of the years 1811 and 1812: 'How many of those poor girls were forced into convents by the aid and advice of crafty priests, where their young hearts were blighted for ever! I often had conversations with them through their iron gratings, hearing them wailing and lamenting their unhappy fate, and pining for liberty.'[39] How British officers longed to liberate them. Moyle Sherer recalled how he and others frequented the gratings of a nunnery in Portalegre, and how much the sisters seemed to enjoy the attention.

> A military band was often brought down to the outer court of their sacred prison, for their amusement, and some of the officers would sit for hours in the convent parlours, talking with the nuns, whom a double row of thick gratings, so contrived that you could only shake hands in the space between the two rows, separated from their gay inamoratos.[40]

Some of the nuns were young and pretty, and one was said to be passionately in love with a British officer, but she died, and he was much affected by her loss. Sherer considered her death a mercy, since had she lived she would either have suffered the misery of hopeless love, or have been compelled to relinquish her religion and her country.

Captain Stothert, adjutant of the 3rd Guards, wrote something very similar in a letter from Vizeu to a friend in March 1810 when he said how the British officers preferred the grating of the local Benedictine nunnery to the attractions of the countryside. So much so that 'a regard for the eternal welfare of the nuns had induced the venerable bishop to express

---

38 J. Page (ed.), *Intelligence Officer in the Peninsula. Letters and Diaries of Major the Hon. Edward Charles Cocks 1786–1812* (Tunbridge Wells: Spellmount, 1986), p.63.
39 Stuart (ed.), *Soldier's Glory*, p.18.
40 Sherer, *Recollections*, p.98.

his displeasure to the Lady Abbess at their frequent visits.[41] Not that this had any effect. Wellington's officers were drawn to the nunneries like moths to a flame, and Lieutenant Colonel von Arentschildt of the King's German Legion was even said to have 'secured' a nun from a convent at Rio Mayor, which had been sacked by the French, and was keeping her as his mistress, and teaching her to ride.[42]

Liaisons with local girls were not always without difficulties and even risks. Francis Larpent, the army's Judge Advocate General was at headquarters at Frenada in March 1813 while Wellington was preparing for the great advance to Vitoria and had no need of distractions. One day a furious Portuguese woman, wife of a hidalgo, came to headquarters to complain that her daughter had run off with a British officer. Wellington ordered that the officer in question should be handed over to the Portuguese authorities, but when it appeared that the pair had actually married, he was obliged to rule that he could not interfere. The woman had to accept that but went off saying that she would have the priest who married them transported, and that she would kill her daughter if she managed to find her.[43] Sometimes indeed there was violence, as in the case of the Honourable Captain Gore of the 94th, brother to the Earl of Arran. He had eloped with a Spanish lady from Vitoria, and in order to get her back a party of Spanish troops stormed his billet and he was shot dead.[44] Violence could also occur between the Spanish women themselves. William Swabey, a lieutenant in E Troop of the Royal Horse Artillery, found himself quartered on a Spanish family at Villa Franca in the summer of 1812, and was deeply attracted to their 16-year-old daughter, Johanna. He could not help himself, or as he put it 'to live in the same house and not to have a tenderness for this fair one would indeed have argued an insensibility which no officer of my age could have been guilty of.' He was in no doubt that she would have put on a uniform, mounted a horse and ridden away with him had he sworn never to desert her, but he was unable to deceive her. The difficulty was that the girl had a cousin, Azulia, who naturally was 'surpassingly beautiful', and the two girls became jealous of each other. While Swabey was talking to Azulia one day, Johanna rushed into the room with a knife and stabbed her. The wound was not serious, but Swabey found himself the centre of an angry family vowing vengeance against him. He was lucky to be able to ride away with his skin intact.[45]

Sometimes these amorous adventures descended into farce. In 1813, before the advance to Vitoria, a group of officers was billeted in the house of a hidalgo near Reynosa, including Robert Blakeney, who later recounted the story. The owner's two nieces were also in the house, they were the daughters of a dignitary in the Catholic church then away at Madrid. One of the officers, a lieutenant in the artillery, fell for one of these girls, and 'the fair Iberian heroically determined to knit her fate with that of her lover' and agreed to elope with him. The other officers agreed to assist by providing spare clothing to disguise the girl as a man, including a pair of 'doeskin inexpressibles', a jacket, riding boots and a hat. The plan was

---

41 W. Stothert, *A Narrative of the Principal Events of the Campaigns of 1809, 1810 and 1811 in Spain and Portugal* (London: Martin, 1812), p.155.
42 Schaumann, *On the Road*, p.281.
43 Larpent (ed.), *Private Journal*, p.80.
44 Haythornthwaite, *Armies*, p.195.
45 Whinyates (ed.), *Diary*, p.115.

that the pair were to leave at dawn on the day appointed, and to lull any suspicions the officers threw a party to which the family were invited and plied with quantities of mulled wine fortified with brandy. Unfortunately, this had the effect of making some of the family sick, and in the early light of dawn the lovers were discovered by one of the aunts accompanied by a group of servants. The girl was promptly marched back into the house, while the officers, protesting their honourable intentions, were left to slink away more than a little crestfallen and embarrassed.[46]

Farce could however turn into something close to tragedy. Sergeant Donaldson of the 94th had a friend named Henry who fell head over heels for a young Portuguese girl named Maria. In the winter after the retreat from Madrid the army was in cantonments for six months, which gave Henry, who spoke some Portuguese, time to become well acquainted with some of the local families. When Maria's family got wind of Henry's intentions, he was banned from the house and the girl carefully guarded. A foreign soldier in time of war, and a heretic at that, was not all what they had in mind. Donaldson and Henry managed to see Maria by dint of scaling a garden wall, and were attacked for their trouble. Henry by this time was in such a state that he tried to shoot himself with his musket but was prevented from doing so and placed under guard. The upshot of the whole sad episode was that Maria was incarcerated in a nunnery until the British army marched away, and poor Henry was left in a state of deep depression from which it took him many months to recover.[47]

It was by no means only officers who fell for local girls. Large numbers of the men acquired Spanish or Portuguese camp-followers of one sort or another. William Grattan remarked on 'the poor faithful Spanish and Portuguese women, hundreds of whom had married or attached themselves to our soldiers, and who had accompanied them through all their fatigues and dangers.' Many of them 'had lived with our men for years, and borne their children.'[48] Few if any of these unions were marriages in any formal sense; that would have required the permission of a man's commanding officer, but many of them certainly were in simple human terms, and regarded as such by a man's comrades. There was for instance a rifleman named Mauley in the 1/95th who had lived with a Spanish woman almost the whole time he had been in the Peninsula, 'who was most tenderly attached to him.' Whenever there was fighting, she would get as close to him as possible, usually on her donkey. But at the Battle of the Nivelle, Mauley was killed, and when she heard this from some of the wounded making their way back, she was distracted with grief. Leaving her donkey, she ran forward, regardless of the fact that French fire was hot and the 'balls came thick as hail.' Throwing herself across Mauley's blood-stained body, she wept and tore her hair hysterically. Everyone expected that she would be hit at any moment, till a Spanish soldier who had been a friend of Mauley's, jumped out of cover and placing himself in front of her fired away at the French as fast as he could, while keeping up a string of fearful Spanish oaths. It was a miracle that they escaped unwounded.[49]

There was 'a very handsome little Spanish girl' who had attached herself to a sergeant in the 95th named Dillon. During the fighting in the Pyrenees towards the end of the war,

---

46   Blakeney, *A Boy*, p.291.
47   Donaldson, *Recollections*, pp.187–199.
48   Grattan, *Adventures*, p.333.
49   Costello, *Adventures*, p.191.

she had somehow got herself stranded on the wrong side of the river Bidassoa, and feared to go to a bridge she could have crossed by because of the French. Rifleman Costello very gallantly swam over to get her. In her panic, the girl clung so tightly to his back that they were both nearly drowned, and would have been but for some of the other riflemen who came to the rescue. One, named Kelly, dived deep for the girl, and dragged her unconscious to the bank.[50]

Whether Dillon married the girl, Costello did not say. Sometimes there were real offers of marriage, as Benjamin Harris, also of the 95th, discovered shortly after the Battle of Vimeiro, early in the war. After the battle, the British army was withdrawn to the area near Lisbon, and Harris, who was a cobbler as well as a shepherd by trade, was employed mending the company's boots in a local shoemaker's workshop. The master shoemaker had a daughter, Maria, 'a very handsome dark-eyed Spanish girl, and as a matter of course I fell in love.' Harris having picked up a little of the language, and the mother having a few words of English, they managed to communicate quite well, and one evening the woman, without much ceremony, offered her daughter to Harris as his wife. The family would even hide him when the army marched. 'The offer was a tempting one; but the conditions of the marriage made it impossible for me to comply, since I was to change my religion, and desert my colours.'[51] So Harris promised to try to obtain his discharge whenever he reached England, and return and marry Maria, but he never did.

Harris may have been able to march away with his heart in one piece, but this was certainly not the case with Captain Cocks, who fell seriously and unhappily in love with a Portuguese girl. She was Josepha Siego, daughter of a wealthy peasant named Camillo, who had leased the army a quinta at Aquila. Writing to his cousin, Cocks described her as 'a little Portuguese 16 years old, with eyes black as jet, lips ripe as peaches, and teeth white as ivory and limbs for the Venus de Medici.' Unfortunately, this ravishing creature was already the intended bride of Don Julian Sanchez, one of the guerrilla leaders, and in order to escape this fate, Josepha had already attempted to run away with Augustus Schaumann of the Commissariat. Notwithstanding this, Cocks was utterly devastated when Josepha was spirited away, presumably to the arms of Don Julian Sanchez. 'She regarded me as her husband. Her departure has aroused feelings I thought my emotions had forgot, I could kill myself and everyone I meet. Heaven bless her, poor girl, wherever she is. She deserved a better fate than will now be her lot.'[52] The fact that Cocks had lost his sense of proportion, as well as the sense of propriety he would certainly have felt in a similar situation at home, gives some sense of the power of attraction the Iberian girls possessed. Cocks was no immature cornet. He was a particularly intelligent, dedicated and cultivated officer, and certainly destined for high command, and when he was killed at the siege of Burgos Wellington was personally devastated.

In some cases, these romances did result in marriage, albeit in a variety of circumstances. After the Battle of Talavera in July 1809, parts of the army were quartered in Campo Maior, including the 88th Foot, the drum-major of which regiment was a soldier named Thorpe. One of the leading citizens of the town, and the local magistrate, was Senhor José Alfonzo

---

50   Costello, *The Adventures*, p.186.
51   Hibbert (ed.), *Recollections*, p.46.
52   Page (ed.), *Intelligence Officer*, p.140.

Cherito. This gentleman had a daughter, Jacintha, and she and Thorpe fell in love. Jacintha was Cherito's only child, and being a man of considerable property and standing in the community, he did not intend her to become the wife of a British soldier. Shortly before the regiment was due to leave, the girl left the house, taking her jewels with her. Her father was furious, and going to the colonel, demanded that every possible search be made for his daughter. As the 88th paraded ready to march, a thorough search was conducted. The ox-carts carrying the sick, the baggage mules and the animals carrying the ammunition, biscuit and rum were all scrutinized, to no avail. The horses of the officers, riding at the head and tail of the column were looked at without result. That left the ranks of the men, some thousand of them, bayonets fixed and in marching order. Jacintha was not there. The colonel asked Cherito if he was now satisfied? 'I am satisfied that my daughter is not with your regiment, sir; yet I am anything but satisfied as to her fate!' was the recorded reply. The regimental band was ordered to strike up. Drum Major Thorpe twirled his staff, and the regiment swung into motion. What nobody realized was that the lad in the ranks clashing the Turkish cymbals, face blackened and in regimental uniform, was Jacintha Cherito. The 88th reached the next town, Monte Forte, at the end of the first day's march, where the padre married the girl to her drum major.

Relating these events, William Grattan said that the full story of Thorpe and his wife would fill the pages of a romance. Thorpe seems to have been determined to win promotion at all costs. At Busaco in September 1810 he was made sergeant major for his conspicuous bravery, and throughout the rest of the Peninsular War he continued to distinguish himself, so much so that after the Battle of Orthez in February 1814, he was awarded a commission. Unfortunately, at the Battle of Toulouse in April 1814, literally in the very closing moments of the war, Thorpe was as usual exposing himself to enemy fire when a round-shot struck him in the chest and cut him in two. A day later the *Gazette* carried the announcement of his ensigncy. His posthumous promotion may have been a blessing: Jacinth Thorpe seems to have been reconciled to her father, to whom she returned, and the Connaught Rangers never heard of her again.[53]

Most marriages to local women no doubt took place in much less dramatic circumstances. One such was the marriage of Sergeant William Lawrence of the 40th to a French woman. The 40th formed part of the large army of occupation in Paris in 1815 after the Battle of Waterloo and the final abdication of Napoleon, and were quartered in a barrack outside the city at St Germains. They were there for several months, and Lawrence gradually struck up an acquaintance with a woman named Clotilde who ran a market-stall near the barrack gate. Her father was a market gardener, and the stall sold fruit and vegetables as well as tobacco, spirits and other things required by the troops. Lawrence fell into the habit of visiting the stall each day, 'and thus an attachment was formed of which I am happy to say I never afterwards repented.' The courtship prospered, and the pair decided to marry. Lawrence obtained his captain's permission, and then that of the colonel, who was unable at first to understand why he wished to marry a Frenchwoman, but, as he said, she would do to teach the soldiers French, and advised Lawrence to wait until the regiment returned to England. 'But having got the grant, it was a question of now or never for me; so I made

---

53 Grattan, *Adventures*, pp.334–339.

arrangements with the army chaplain, who fixed the time and we were duly united. It cost us nothing, for neither the parson nor clerk looked for any fee, neither were we troubled with any wedding-cake, but simply took ourselves off for a day's merrymaking.' Lawrence had explained that his regiment would not remain in the Paris area for long, and that they would probably be recalled to England, and the time came when the order for the move arrived, and Clotilde had to say farewell to her parents 'whom we expected never to behold again.' The 40th marched to Cambrai, where orders were received to proceed to Scotland, and the regiment marched to Calais to embark, where Lawrence and his wife got comfortable quarters. Lawrence was proud of Clotilde as a soldier's wife, and recorded 'I may say here that she had borne the marches quite as well as I did, if not in some cases better.'[54]

By far the most celebrated marriage of a British soldier and a local girl was that of Harry Smith of the 95th and Juana Maria de Los Dolores de Leon. The storming of Badajoz degenerated into an incontrollable orgy of drunken plunder, murder and rape as already described. The day after the troops had broken in, and with order had yet to be restored, Harry Smith was talking with another officer of his regiment, Captain Kincaid, when they saw two Spanish girls approaching from the direction of the ruined town. The older of the two said that her husband was a Spanish officer serving somewhere in the country, though she had no means of knowing whether he was alive or dead. Her house in the town was a wreck, but they had escaped the drunken violence of the troops with nothing worse than the loss of their earrings, which had been torn out of their ears, leaving blood trickling down their necks. They were lucky to have escaped being raped. The older woman's greatest worry was for the welfare of her young sister, and they had come to throw themselves on the protection of any British officer who would shield them. They need not have worried. Both officers were instantly smitten with the younger sister, who was only 14 years old. 'A being more transcendently lovely I had never before seen' wrote Kincaid. Her face was 'so irresistibly attractive, surmounting a figure cast in nature's fairest mould, that to look at her was to love her – and I did love her; but I never told my love, and in the meantime another, and a more impudent fellow stepped in and won her!'[55]

The other fellow was of course Harry Smith, who later quoted these words in his autobiography. At the age of 24, he was simply bowled over, and helplessly in love. He married Juana almost at once, despite the fact that his fellow officers ribbed him that marriage would impair his efficiency and sense of duty. Unfortunately, he did not record the details of the actual marriage ceremony. It may be that the Reverend Charles Frith, who was the only Anglican chaplain for whom Wellington had any respect did the deed, if Juana agreed. Or perhaps Smith consented to be married by a local priest according to the Catholic rite.

His new wife could not ride, which would have made it hard for Juana to keep up on the march, but Smith had a spare saddle changed into a side-saddle by a soldier in the horse artillery, and she slowly learned to master a horse. After the Battle of Salamanca in July 1812, Smith found her a horse named Tiny, which she rode for the rest of the Peninsular War. Juana went everywhere with her Enrique, as she called Harry, and became a well-known and popular figure in the army. If Smith's autobiography is to be believed, the entire

---

54 Bankes (ed.), *Autobiography*, pp.225–231.
55 Kincaid, *Adventures*, p.287.

division loved her, and she rode amongst the men laughing and talking to them on the march. 'Blackguards as many of the poor gallant fellows were, there was not a man who would not have laid down his life to defend her, and among the officers she was adored, and consulted on all occasions of baggage-guard, etc.'[56] Her story was certainly widely known, and Wellington himself seems to have a soft spot for her, and would refer to her familiarly as Juanita.

Harry Smith and Juana were the exception to the rule. For the most part, these encounters probably left nothing more than a romantic glow to warm the hearts of young men far from home and on dangerous service, and perhaps they were not uncommon. Moyle Sherer for instance fell for the daughter of the family he was billeted on at Merida, she was of course possessed of a wonderful figure and beautiful face. When the time came for the troops to leave, Sherer simply mounted his horse, and the girl, whose name he did not give, 'leaned gracefully over the balcony, and kissed her hand to us as we rode off, wishing us success and honour in war, with all the noble enthusiasm which stamps the Spanish heroine.'[57] Johnny Kinkaid had a similar brief encounter shortly after landing at Lisbon in 1810 which he did not easily forget.

> Passing through the streets on some errand I looked up, and saw a young girl, dressed in white, who was loveliness itself! In the few words which passed between us, of lively, unconstrained civility on her part, and pure confounded gratitude on mine, she seemed so perfectly after my own heart, that she lit a torch in it which burnt for two years and a half.[58]

Kinkaid at least managed to speak to the girl he admired. Captain Leach, also of the 95th, was not so lucky. In Segovia, in August 1812, he saw a girl who bowled him over. Her costume, her face and figure, her eyes, her dainty feet and movements all combined in 'an infinity of female graces happily blended, formed a whole which I have never surpassed.' Unhappily, he 'had not the felicity even of exchanging words with her' as the column marched on, but he never forgot her, and almost 20 years later, when he sat down to compile his memoirs, he could still write that the 'years have not erased from my memory her countless charms.'[59]

Perhaps Lieutenant Woodberry, whose diary reveals a keen interest in attractive local girls, was not far from the mark when he observed 'Spanish ladies have a charm that is dangerous even to describe.'[60]

---

56   Smith, *Autobiography*, vol.1, p.75.
57   Sherer, *Recollections*, p.69.
58   Kincaid, *Adventures*, p.4.
59   Leach, *Rough Sketches*, p.279.
60   Glover & York (eds), *With Wellington's Hussars*, p.182.

12

Going Home

> *Farewell and adieu you fair Spanish ladies*
> *Farewell and adieu you ladies of Spain,*
> *For we've received orders to sail for old England*
> *And we may ne'er see you fair ladies again*[1]

On 6 April 1814 Napoleon signed his first act of abdication, but Wellington had no means of knowing this, and launched what turned out to be the final major battle of the Peninsular War, the assault on Toulouse, on the 10th. It was not until the 12th, just after he had entered the city, that the news reached him when Colonel Frederick Ponsonby galloped in from Bordeaux. Later that night Colonel Cooke, who had left Paris at midnight on the 7th, arrived with the official despatches and confirmation that the Emperor had indeed abdicated and that Louis XVIII had been restored to the throne. For the moment it appeared that the war was over.

Preparations were put in hand to evacuate France. The majority of the British troops were to be returned to Britain, though some battalions were ordered across the Atlantic, to assist in the war against the Americans which was still in progress. Whatever their destination, Bordeaux was to be the port of embarkation, and the brigades and divisions of Wellington's army now marched in that direction. The Spanish and Portuguese troops would make their way back through the Peninsula. There were in fact very few Spanish regiments left. Almost as soon as the army had crossed the frontier into France, the Spanish, despite the most stringent orders against plundering had begun to pillage French villages. It was not to be expected that men whose country and inhabitants had been subjected for years to the most terrible French depredations, would fail to take violent revenge once they were in a position to do so. But Wellington did not want to have a guerrilla war raised against him as the French had suffered in Spain, so he had ordered most of the Spanish units and their women back to Spain, retaining only the well-disciplined division under *Teniente general* Pablo Morillo. For the moment the Portuguese regiments remained with the army.

The problem of what to do with all the local women who had attached themselves to the British troops during the long war at once presented itself, and on 26 April Major General

---
1   Traditional.

the Honourable Edward Packenham, the Adjutant General, issued a general order from headquarters at Toulouse to all the divisional commanders:

> The embarkation of the British army being one of the first consequences to be expected from the successful campaign, I am desired by the Commander of the Forces to suggest to you the expediency of attempting an arrangement in behalf of the Portuguese and Spanish women, followers of the army, to enable their return to their respective homes. It is natural that this description of woman should not determine on separating from those with whom they have lived till urged to do so, yet timely decision seems to be the only means of avoiding eventual distress. Although the Field Marshal foresees the necessity of leaving the greater part of the foreign women behind, who with reasonable provision may accompany the Portuguese troops to the rear, yet I am to observe there will be no objection to a few of those, who have proved themselves useful and regular, accompanying the soldiers to whom they are attached, with a view to their being ultimately married: it will appear evident to you, however, that from the unsettled life and habits of followers of the army, such selection should be made with the greatest caution.[2]

It is clear from the tone of this order that headquarters had realized that there was going to be a major problem with the Spanish and Portuguese women, and that the Adjutant General was groping for a solution. How were officers to determine which of their men were intending 'ultimately' to marry their women-folk, some of whom had children by them? What might be the criteria for deciding which of the followers were useful and regular in their habits and suitable for selection? In fact, the onus was thrown squarely on the shoulders of the generals commanding divisions. The order went on to request that they should inform headquarters as to the plans they intended to adopt to solve the problem, with a statement of the number of local women involved. Packenham then gave the game away by asking them to 'mention if you conceive that any other general arrangement will answer better than that to which I have alluded.' And he added rather lamely that he hoped officers commanding regiments 'who have allowed women to follow their corps ... should certainly take an interest in providing for their decent departure.'

In the event, as this last comment implied, the matter had to be decided at regimental level, with no overall plan. As the army marched towards Bordeaux, there was certainly a general awareness that the moment of separation was approaching. Captain John Henry Cooke of the 43rd, one of the regiments earmarked for America, recalled that as they approached Bordeaux 'there was such an abundance of kissing, as probably the like of it was never seen before ... There was kissing in the valleys, and kissing upon the hills, and in short there was embracing, kissing and counter-kissing, from Toulouse to Bordeaux.'[3] Kissing or no, the break-up of an army which had campaigned victoriously for years across the Peninsula was a melancholy business. At Condom, the 94th had to say farewell to the Portuguese regi-

---

2   Gurwood, (ed.), *General Orders*, pp.323-324.
3   John Cooke, *A Narrative of Events in the South of France and of the Attack on New Orleans in 1814 and 1815, by Captain John Henry Cooke, Late of the 43rd Regiment of Light Infantry* (London: Boone, 1835), p.40.

ment which had been in the 3rd Division with it, and as Sergeant Joseph Donaldson put it, after long campaigning together 'a kind of friendship had thus arisen, and caused us to feel sorry at parting.'[4] As the British columns marched out of the town, the Portuguese lined the streets and cheered. The scene with the women was distressing. Orders had been issued to prevent them going any further, and many of them were running about distraught, and vainly trying to conceal themselves in the ranks.

For some, the inevitable break-up of the army happened at the small town of Bazas, on the left bank of the Garonne which the Light Division reached on 11 June. This was where the Portuguese troops were to take farewell of their British allies and turn back towards Spain and their own country. For many, this was an emotional moment, as Captain Leach of the 95th remembered. 'There was a great deal of shaking of hands, accompanied by many *vivas*; and the parting was altogether affecting.'[5] The Portuguese 1st and 3rd Caçadores had by now served as part of the Light Division for four years, and the bond of trust and comradeship was strong between both officers and men of the two countries. Surtees, also of the 95th, recorded the scene in more detail:

> Our division drew up in the morning they marched, and honoured the brave Portuguese (for indeed they had always behaved well in the field) with three cheers, as they turned their faces towards Portugal. Many were the heavy hearts in both armies on this occasion; for it is not easy to conceive how the circumstances of passing through scenes of hardship, trial, and danger together, endeared the soldiers of the two armies to each other.[6]

In some regiments, the 95th for one, the men were indeed given the option of marrying their women, and some did so, whether they had children by them or not. However, it seems that this varied from regiment to regiment. There must also have been men unwilling to marry foreign wives and take them home. Officers commanding regiments were faced with impossible choices in deciding who was, or was not, actually married, and what that actually meant. As Sergeant Donaldson sympathetically expressed it: 'The generality of them [the women] were not married, but the steady affection and patient endurance of hardship which they exhibited, in following those to whom they belonged, would have done credit to a more legal tie.'[7] So the Portuguese troops turned away on the long road home, taking most of their country-women with them, and 'the departure of the poor women caused many heavy hearts, both among themselves, poor creatures, who had a long and dreary journey before them, and among those with whom they had lived, and who had shared in all their good and bad fortune.'[8] It was not surprising that Captain Leach recorded that 'There was much weeping and wailing on the part of the signoras.'[9] Indeed, it was too much to bear for a few British soldiers who chose another option altogether: desertion. Rifleman Edward Costello

---

4 Donaldson, *Recollections*, p.231.
5 Leach, *Rough Sketches*, p.369.
6 Surtees, *Twenty-Five Years*, p.316.
7 Donaldson, *Recollections*, p.232.
8 Surtees, *Twenty-Five Years*, p.317.
9 Leach, *Rough Sketches*, p.370.

wrote that 'Many of the men of our regiment, bound by the charms of the Signorettas, who had followed their fortunes throughout the war, took the opportunity to desert their country's cause, to take up that of their dulcineas.'[10] Two of his own company did so, taking their rifles and equipment with them, and were never seen or heard of again. Other diarists and memoir writers are silent on this subject, but there appears to have been a spike in desertions at this time, partly owing to men not wishing to be sent to the war in America, and in part to an unwillingness to the separated from their Spanish and Portuguese wives.[11]

The army did not simply abandon the Spanish and Portuguese women with no means of support for the trek home. The 'reasonable provision' referred to by the Adjutant General was regularised in a further order to divisional generals issued on 16 May, by which time the extent of the problem had probably become clearer. It had been decided that in view of the possible difficulties in Spain, the Portuguese women were to be issued with specially printed passports which would make their long journey official and enable them to draw rations on the way. They were to be attached to one of the various Portuguese regiments also marching back home. This was to be done officially, with the women entered on the regimental returns. The passports were to be signed by a senior officer, and this was intended to ensure that the women were indeed supplied on their long march.[12] Later, similar arrangements were made for the women of the King's German Legion returning to the Low Countries. These arrangements also applied to the many Portuguese men and boys who had attached themselves to British soldiers as servants.

It was clear that these women faced an immensely long and difficult journey, and that very many of them had not a penny to their names, and despite the fact that the British troops had not been paid for seven months, and the officers were mostly in the same state, a subscription was raised and a small sum of money shared out between the women.[13] A friend of William Surtees, who was an officer in the Portuguese service, later told him that the women marched at the same time as his own regiment, in a column some 800 or 900 strong. They were organized into companies, and commanded by a major, with captains in charge of individual companies, all of whom were married men, with their families with them. These officers were responsible for drawing the rations for each company, which was an excellent scheme. However, many of the women became totally undisciplined, leaving the column whenever they pleased. Few, said Surtees' correspondent, reached Portugal in the order in which they started.[14] This was hardly surprising. After seven years of war, murder, atrocity and counter-atrocity, many no doubt wondered whether they had a home to return to, or any friends and relations left alive to welcome them back.

Some of the Portuguese and Spanish women managed to stick to the army until it reached Bordeaux, and the moment of embarkation arrived and they were finally abandoned. It was a bitter scene, and described with his usual eloquence by William Grattan of the Connaught Rangers. These women, he wrote:

---

10   Costello, *The Adventures*, p.206.
11   Andrew Bamford, *Sickness, Suffering and the Sword* (Norman: University of Oklahoma Press, 2013), p.256.
12   Wellington (ed.), *Supplementary Despatches*, vol.XIV, p.522.
13   Grattan, *Adventures*, p.334.
14   Surtees, *Twenty-Five Years*, p.317.

A long column of troops marching into the distance. Two of the women, one smoking a pipe, tramp along with their children while two more are sharing a donkey. Aquatint by Thomas Rowlandson, 1798. (Anne S.K. Brown Military Collection, Brown University)

… had followed their husbands through the hottest of the battlefield; had staunched their wounds with their tattered garments, or moistened their parched lips, when without such care death would have been certain; they had, when such aid was not required, devoted days and nights in rendering those attentions which only they who had witnessed them can justly appreciate. Yet these faithful and heroic women were now, after all these trials, to be seen standing on the beach, while they witnessed with bursting hearts the filling of those sails, and the crowding of those ships, that were to separate them for ever from those to whom they had looked for protection and support.[15]

The British women on the other hand (other than those whose regiments were posted to America) went with their units on board transports bound for Britain or Ireland where they often found familiar faces, regiments or brigades having served together. It was a rough voyage. 'The waves rose high, and the ship tossed dreadfully. Food and drink on board

---

15 Grattan, *Adventures*, p.334.

were detestable; disorder and confusion reigned everywhere ... women and children wailed ...'[16] In other words, it was a normal journey, but there seem to have been compensations on arrival in England if the experiences of the 23rd were anything to go by. The battalion embarked 788 strong at Pauillac in the Gironde estuary on 14 June accompanied by their women and children. Landing at Plymouth, they were cheered and feted by the population who of course imagined that the long wars were over. They then marched along the south coast towards the new barracks at Gosport where they were to be stationed, and in almost every town they passed through they were treated to lavish amounts of food and drink – rather too much drink in fact. 'At length, however, these hospitable potations interfered so much with the men's marching that the Officers began to put a stop to them.'[17] It is safe to assume that the women were in the same condition.

What nobody imagined in 1814 was that Napoleon would escape from his exile on Elba, return to France, re-raise his army, and that at the end of the Hundred Days, the war would be fought to its bloody finale at Waterloo in June the following year. When the final campaign opened, stringent orders were issued in an attempt to restrict the number of women crossing to Belgium. Despite this, considerable numbers of wives did manage to accompany the troops assembling around Brussels. This did nothing to help the army in dealing with the difficulties of the many women who were shortly to find themselves newly-made widows. Waterloo was fought on 18 June, after which the Allied forces advanced towards Paris. On 2 July, when the British army was near St Denis, the Adjutant General wrote to Lieutenant Colonel James, back in Brussels, who was anxious about what should be done with the women still in the city, instructing him that the Commander-in-Chief's orders were that 'the widows of the soldiers killed in action are to be embarked from the port of Ostend; and that with respect to any allowances to be given them, his Majesty's Regulations on this head are to be adhered to.'[18] This meant that they were to be issued with rations to see them back to England and allowances to reach their homes.

There was one small concession. At the start of the campaign, Wellington had tried to restrict the number of women to four per 100 men. A fresh general order issued at Paris on 28 December 1815 stated that in future rations for six women, the usual number, would now be allowed per 100 soldiers, but that it was made clear that this included non-commissioned officers and drummers. At the same time, supernumerary women were to be sent packing back to England. Officers commanding regiments were 'desired to avail themselves of the opportunity offered by the embarkation of the troops at Calais to send to England all the women who cannot be maintained with their regiments, granting them the certificates required by the Regulations, provided that benefit was not accorded to them on their regiments coming to the continent.'[19] These, in other words, were women who had not come over officially, but who had contrived to get across the Channel by means of their own.

Naturally enough, there were individual circumstances which resulted in some unofficial bending of the rules. One such case concerned Jack Parsons, a kind-hearted, generous and good humoured private in the 73rd. Like so many of the men, Jack had a problem with

---

16 Schaumann, *On the Road*, p.412.
17 Crook (ed.), *The Very Thing*, p.128.
18 Wellington (ed.), *Supplementary Despatches*, vol. XIV, p.569.
19 Gurwood (ed.), *General Orders*, p.455.

A British bivouac in Paris. The women may be British wives, or possibly French prostitutes. Engraving by Jean Baptiste Genty, 1815. (Anne S.K. Brown Military Collection, Brown University)

drink, and frequently found himself in the guard room or doing extra drill or guard duty. Early in the campaign, while in Antwerp, Jack had formed a warm attachment to pretty Flemish girl named Theresa. Unofficial though this liaison was, it had a very steadying effect on Jack's conduct, and the girl 'conducted herself with so much propriety, that the officers suffered her to accompany the regiment.' Jack Parsons, like many others, had a premonition he would be killed, and on the morning of Waterloo went to his captain, saying that he wished to make a will – just a request that the arrears of his pay should be given to Theresa. The dream he had had proved all-too prophetic, for Jack was indeed killed. Theresa was distracted with grief, but the other men looked after her, and she marched with the regiment to Paris. There, while they were encamped in the Bois de Boulogne, some benevolent Parisian ladies interested themselves in her plight, and found her a decent position as a servant to a respectable French family.[20]

A fresh problem soon presented itself. After the fall of Paris and the banishing of Napoleon to St Helena, the British regiments remained spread out in northern France and settled down as part of the Allied Army of Occupation. Under these peaceful circumstances, it was hard for both the soldiers and their wives to accept that more women than usual could not be allowed across the narrow seas. Men began to write to their wives in Britain, so

---

20   Selby (ed.), *Recollections*, p.84.

tantalizingly close, asking them to come over to France despite the difficulties placed in their way. One such was Troop Sergeant Major James Page of the 1st Dragoon Guards, who noted in his diary in January 1816 'My wife has not joined me yet, nor cannot till I get her a passport. She came as far as Dover, but was obliged to return, no more soldiers' wives being allowed to come over; the Duke of Wellington will allow only six to every hundred men.'[21]

It was ironic that the army's own highly efficient postal system probably contributed to the high command's problem. In May 1795 an Act had been passed that allowed soldiers, NCOs and seamen to send and receive personal letters at the especially low postage rate of one penny, to be paid on posting.[22] In order to qualify, the sender's name, rank and unit had to be written on the outside of the letter, which also had to be signed by the commanding officer. Troops had first been able to take advantage of this during the 1799 campaign in Holland, and when the war in the Peninsula began, the penny post was extended to Spain and Portugal. When the Waterloo campaign opened, an Army Headquarters Post Office was established in Brussels, but after the battle it was moved first to Paris and then in 1816 to Cambrai. The mail itself was despatched to England through a packet agent at Ostend.[23] So it was that on 13 May 1816 another general order was issued for Headquarters on the subject:

> The Field Marshal having received intimations of the distress which the wives of soldiers experience, arising from the imprudence of their husbands in writing to them to come out to this country, desires that officers commanding regiments will in the most pointed manner caution the non-commissioned and soldiers against inducing their wives to come out to the regiments without the permission of the commanding officers thereof.[24]

The order went on to say that women should if possible be prevented from embarking at Dover, or 'should they by clandestine means get across the water' they should be arrested by the French police and sent back to Dover. Officers sailing with detachments of troops from England were to report to the assistant quartermaster general at Calais on any women who did manage to slip aboard ship and to ensure that none of these ladies actually disembarked in France.

The efficiency of the army's postal service, and the good use to which it was put by the troops and their wives, may be judged from the correspondence of Sergeant William Tennant of the 3/1st Guards and his wife Ann. Tennant was a pay sergeant. He and Ann had been married only a year, and she was living with her parents at Presteign in Radnorshire. Between 12 April 1815 and 22 August 1816 there are 19 letters from William, and although only one of Ann's survives, it is possible from the references in his part of the correspondence to know that she wrote 18 in reply. It is also possible from the dates mentioned to see how long it took for Ann's letters to reach France from Wales. The longest interval was 12

---

21 Glover (ed.), *The Waterloo Archive*, vol.III, p.22.
22 35 Geo III cap.53. Cited in P.B. Boyden, *Tommy Atkins' Letters* (London: National Army Museum, 1990), p.4.
23 Boyden, *Tommy Atkins' Letters*, p.4.
24 Wellington (ed.), *Supplementary Despatches*, vol.XI, p.552.

days, and the shortest five. The average was a week. All William's letters were signed on the outside by one of his officers in the prescribed manner.

It is a deeply affectionate correspondence, and full of interesting detail. Ann has made her way from the regimental depot in London back to her parents' house by coach. She has ridden on the outside during the day, but managed an inside place at night. She has nailed his trunk down securely; he remits money to her via the regimental headquarters. Ann is pregnant and William is anxious – is she well? She gives birth safely to a little boy and they are both happy. He is made a colour-sergeant and he tells her about the Waterloo medal. He is worried that he has not heard from her for a while. Should the baby be inoculated? And so it goes on, full of domestic detail between man and wife, but the real burden of these letters, and the worry of Wellington's headquarters, is that Sergeant Tennant, like many other soldiers, wanted to get his wife over to France to be with him. They had been married 12 months and separated for nine of them. By 11 November the battalion had moved into barracks in Paris, and Sergeant Bell's wife had managed to reach the city with their two children. Whether this was official, we are not told. It seems possible that some commanding officers may have turned a blind eye on some occasions. If for example the wife concerned arrived as a visitor, found her own lodgings and was not on the strength in order to draw rations, there was probably little that could be done. By mid-February the following year, the battalion had moved to Cambrai. The barracks had good accommodation for the men, but not for the NCOs. Two of the sergeants did have their wives with them, but both couples had to share the same room. William himself was crammed into a small room with three other NCOs, and told Ann, who had sent him a lock of their baby's hair, that she would have to stay in Wales a bit longer. Rumours circulated that the battalion would be relieved in the summer, but these came to nothing. As spring turned to summer, he wrote several times that he could not face another winter without her, but then began to have agonies of doubt about whether she really wanted to come, given the problems of accommodation. By the end of June William had decided on desperate measures, perhaps without the knowledge of his commanding officer, and told Ann 'you may expect an order in a few days.' She was to travel light to London, settle her financial affairs at headquarters, and then present herself to the French ambassador to obtain a passport. Ann was to wear her very best clothes, and to invent a story as to why she needed to cross to France. On no account to say that she was a soldier's wife, or the passport would be refused. She was then to make her way to Dover, make the crossing, and catch a diligence to Cambrai. All this, with a small child, must have seemed a daunting prospect. On 7 August William wrote that the battalion was staying put at Cambrai, and that Ann would soon 'receive some orders most likely concerning your march.' On the 22nd her sent her two pounds, and said that his next letter 'will be an order for you to join your regiment in France,' but there the letters end and, tantalizingly, we shall never know whether Colour Sergeant Tennant managed to get his wife and child over to join the Army of Occupation.[25]

For women returning to Britain with their husbands, the normal life of the regiment probably continued. But things could be very hard for those returning as widows. Catherine

---

25 Nottinghamshire Archives: M24, 298: Letters of Sergeant William Tennant 1/3rd Guards and his wife Ann.

Exley thought she was a widow, and it was not until some time later that she learned that her husband had been captured, and not killed, at the Battle of Maya in the Pyrenees. She had accumulated a sum of money from doing laundry work for officers' wives, and the officers of her regiment, the 34th, had also collected a subscription for her, so when she reached England she was able to pay her way. On the transport home she had fallen in with another returning woman and, when they landed at Falmouth, Catherine offered to pay their fares to London, by waggon. She did not record how long this gruelling journey took, but what happened after she reached London provides a vivid illustration of the bureaucratic difficulties faced by women in her position. When she went to the regimental agent in Pall Mall, expecting to collect three guineas from the regimental fund, she was refused because the colonel, despite his kindness to her in other respects, had forgotten to write the necessary authorization. The agent gave her a paper instead, which she was told to take to the Lodge coffee house. It was an order for £25 to which widows were entitled whose husbands had been killed in action.

Again she was thwarted. Instead of the money, she was handed a paper which she was told had to be signed by the clergy or magistrates of her home parish before the money could be released. So, on 5 November 1814, Catherine paid for a place in a waggon bound for Leeds. They travelled day and night in bitter stormy weather and arrived at Leeds on the 12th, by which time she had been a full week on the road, in winter, without proper accommodation for herself and her child. Such a homecoming must have been a frequent experience, and women in such a frustrating predicament can only have felt that officialdom was conspiring to deprive them of their entitlements.[26]

Some men and women certainly had quite different kinds of experiences. One of the regiments posted home after the allied occupation of France came to an end was the 42nd Foot, the Black Watch. They sailed from Calais to Ramsgate in the summer of 1816. It was cold on deck but fetid below, and one of the men, James Anton, left a portrait of one of the regiment's Irish women, apparently enjoying the experience:

> Here, full of harmless gaiety, sits Kate, the wife of Edward M'Kay; time had not yet put an aged wrinkle on her brow, and with pleasant cheerful countenance and handsome person, she is gifted with that readiness of reply ... Kate was what we call an old campaigner; that is she had seen more than one campaign, and could take her own part with any woman on board.[27]

Having landed, the 42nd marched to Sandwich, then via Deal and Dover to Hythe, where they spent two weeks refitting. The regiment was then ordered to proceed to Edinburgh. This was a journey frequently made by sea to Leith, but in this case, the highlanders were to march. They first moved to Chelmsford via Ashford and Chatham, presumably crossing the Thames at Gravesend, where they again spent a fortnight in the barracks. They were then given their route north. Proceeding towards Cambridge in two divisions, a day apart, they made for Huntingdon. Perhaps it was the bonnets and kilts, or maybe it was relief that

---

26 Probert (ed.), *Exley Diary*, p.45.
27 Roy, 'Memoirs', p.118.

the interminable war was over, but whatever it was, the 42nd were royally treated along their route. Church bells were rung, refreshments were provided, and in Cambridge each man was given a donation equivalent to two days' pay. In Huntingdon, they were halted by a gentleman who wished to ply them with food and drink even before they entered the town, and as they did so, the church bells were pealed. There was also a present of money, not only for the soldiers but for their women as well, which as far as the second division was concerned, came to two pounds each, an unusually generous gesture. This 'was handed over by Col. Dick to Lieut. F., but this gentleman perhaps despised any ostentatious display of what he might have considered charity, and I never heard of its distribution.'[28] It is impossible to imagine that such a hardy bunch of regimental women, old campaigners, many of them, would have put up with this. It seems that the hospitality of the people of Huntingdon was by no means unique. Another private soldier of the 42nd recorded that 'such a march could not be in any other country but in England among the kind hearted inhabitants to their soldiers in every town, one excepted. Even the women were not forgotten.'[29]

Joining the Great North Road, the 42nd made their way northwards to Durham and then Sunderland, somewhat off the route. It may have been the intention to embark the regiment at Sunderland and complete the journey by sea, but if it was the plan was abandoned and the long march went on. First to Berwick, then across the border to Haddington and so to Edinburgh, where they marched up to the castle. Anton does not record how long the journey took, but this was the reality for a marching regiment of foot. Including the detour to Hyde, they had marched something in the order of 580 miles, their women and children with them.

A similar feat was performed by Sergeant William Lawrence and his wife at much the same time. Lawrence's regiment, the 40th, had been posted to Glasgow on its return at the end of the allied occupation of France, and while there Lawrence received news from Dorset that his father was seriously ill. He was granted six weeks' leave. The first part of the journey south they made by sea to London, and then onwards overland to the south-west. When the time came to begin to return to Glasgow, Lawrence intended to walk to Bristol and then find a ship going to Scotland, but on reaching Bristol no vessel was to be found, 'so my wife who was an excellent walker proposed going all the way by road; and accordingly on the following day we started, doing generally two stages a day, through Gloucester, Worcester, Manchester, and Carlisle, and so to Glasgow, a long and tedious march.'[30] Lawrence was rather proud of Clotilde's marching ability. Sometimes she could out-march him.

There must have been plenty of homecomings which were not altogether happy. Husbands and wives, especially if they were illiterate, separated for years and not knowing whether the other was dead or alive, must often have become total strangers. Edward Costello described vividly the predicament in which one of his comrades found himself when they returned to England in July 1814. The other rifleman, whom he identified only as a sergeant with the initial S, had been with the battalion ever since Moore's disastrous Corunna campaign.

---

28   Anton, *Retrospect*, p.245.
29   Roy, 'Memoirs', p.118.
30   Bankes (ed.), *Autobiography*, p.242.

He was now on his passage homeward to his wife, to whom he had been married for ten or eleven years, and whom, some months after the wedding, he was obliged to leave with her friends at Portsmouth to rejoin his regiment, then going abroad; by some unaccountable circumstances, incidental to long campaigns, he never had received any tidings of or from her; and he consequently was now very uncertain as to where he should find her, or whether she was living or dead.[31]

As soon as they landed at Spithead, the sergeant asked Costello to go with him to find his wife. They searched the town in vain, until at last in the high street, where a crowd of women had gathered around the two riflemen, an old woman on crutches told them to try a house near the post office. The house turned out to be a small but well-built cottage. The sergeant rapped on the door, which was answered by a girl about 10 years of age. 'Does Mary S live here?' asked the soldier. 'Yes' replied the child, 'that's my name.' The sergeant promptly picked up the astonished child and dashed into the house, exclaiming 'Where's your mother?' to be confronted with a whole family of children. Then his wife appeared, and promptly fell into hysterics. By this time the child who had answered the door had gone out and returned in a few moments with a well-made man who appeared to be a carpenter. 'The facts' as Edward Costello put it, 'were stubbornly plain to every one.' The two husbands squared up to each other, each expecting to be attacked, and then the woman having collected herself, 'clung, as if for refuge, to the carpenter.' The situation was now clear enough to the soldier, and he took the skipping rope which the little girl held in her hand, and threw it lightly over his wife's neck.

> 'Now,' said he, in a somewhat collected tone, 'Now Mr Carpenter, as it appears that Mary, who was my wife, has decided on her choice, suppose we have a bargain on the matter? It's no use our skirmishing about in this manner any longer; (and I have no doubt of your abilities,)' pointing to the children, who crowded round the parents and opposite the sergeant, 'With Mary's consent, as she seems to prefer your manner of doing business, suppose we clinch the bargain with a sixpence and take her to you altogether?'[32]

The carpenter handed over the sixpence, and the rifleman, drawing aside his sash reached into his pocket for a guinea, which he tossed into his daughter's lap.

The two soldiers went into a nearby pub, where the sergeant ordered sixpence worth of liquor, and a drink for Costello. Having drunk like a man who had thirsted for a week, the sergeant adjusted his uniform, rubbed his hands together, a 'strutted up the street as if nothing whatever had annoyed him.'

Another example of the difficulties caused by the re-appearance of a husband long assumed to be dead concerned Rachel Heap of Halifax. She had not heard of her husband for years, and had assumed that he had been killed in the war. In need of a man to support her, in 1802 she had taken up with one Samuel Lumb, and had born him three children.

---

31   Costello, *The Adventures*, p.207.
32   Costello, *The Adventures*, p.207.

However, Heap did return from the wars (neither the year nor his regiment are known), and whether surprised by this development or not, agreed to sell Rachel to Lumb, though we are not told for how much, and delivered her to him in a halter at Halifax Cross. Heap did not die until 25 years later, but when he did, Rachel married Lumb, though he was by that time 83.[33] Rachel Heap and her husband had presumably not been able to write to each other during the long years of separation. Perhaps neither of them was literate; or possibly they were unable to pay for postage.

When the immediate euphoria which greeted the news of Waterloo had subsided, the cost of the battle began to be realized. The butcher's bill was terrible. Casualties in the Allied army as a whole amounted to roughly 23 percent. In some of the British regiments they were twice that. The Household Cavalry Brigade for example suffered some 48 percent casualties, and the 3rd British Infantry Division suffered 47 percent losses in killed, wounded and missing. The public response to this was rapid and to the point. Two organizations were set up in London to raise a nationwide subscription for the relief of the wounded and their families, and for the wives and children of the dead. The Westminster Waterloo Association was set up with its headquarters in the Thatched House Tavern, the name by which it became generally known. The Waterloo Subscription, which became the larger of the two charities, was set up at the City of London Tavern. The Waterloo Subscription printed a circular, signed by J. L. Welford, the secretary, for distribution to parishes across the country, dated 4 July 1815, very soon after the battle, pointing out that the great victory had been gained by 'the unexampled cost of Human Life' and outlining their suggest plan of action:

> The Committee for conducting the Subscription for the benefit of the Families of the Slain, and of the numerous severely Wounded of the British Army, convinced that you will find pleasure in every proper means to promote this good work, have directed me to call your attention to the propriety of convening a public meeting of the Inhabitants, or of taking such other steps as you may deem most proper to procure the assistance of all classes to the laudable purposes of this just, and necessary act of liberality, and beneficence.[34]

Some communities had already anticipated these developments. In Dorchester for example, the mayor, George Strickland, had called a meeting to decide what was to be done as early as Monday 3 July. It was resolved 'That a General Subscription be opened for the Relief and Benefit of the Widows and Families of the brave men who fell, and of the wounded Sufferers of the British Army, under the command of the illustrious WELLINGTON, in the splendid and memorable Victory at Waterloo.'[35] A committee was appointed and arrangements made for the collection of subscriptions at the local banks and the library, and the whole scheme was widely advertised in the press both locally and nationally.

---

33 R. Palmer, *The Rambling Soldier* (London: Penguin, 1977), p.251.
34 Huntingdonshire Record Office: HRO 109/2: List of Subscribers to the Waterloo Subscription for the parish of Buckden.
35 *The Times*, 21 July 1815.

Across the country, the response to these appeals, at first a trickle, rapidly became a flood, a sense of elation at the great victory mingling with profound relief that the long war was over, and pity for the victims who had paid a terrible price. *The Times* was soon publishing long lists of contributions. Groups of friends organized balls, theatricals, concerts, door-to-door collections, lectures and raffles. Towns, colleges, coffee houses, cathedral chapters, ships' crews and organizations of many kinds made donations, and numbers of wealthy or prominent people made individual contributions. Sir Walter Scott, one of the earliest battlefield tourists, published his poem *The Field of Waterloo* in October. The first edition of 6,000 copies sold out at a shilling each, and Scott donated the money for the relief of soldiers' widows and orphans.

By far the largest contributors were the parishes up and down the land. Particularly effective were charity sermons, and the clergy had a busy time of it that August, and although the anguish of the wounded soldiers was not forgotten, the emphasis was often on the sufferings of the widows and orphans. Having dwelt on the triumph of British arms, and the terrible cost, the vicar would paint a heart-rending picture of the plight of the bereaved. 'Whilst we exult and rejoice … how many a wife has heard the doleful tidings of her husband's death, and perchance will never smile again' enquired the Reverend Daniell at St Mary's, Whitechapel. 'How many an orphan looks in anxious expectation, but looks in vain, for his sire's return?' He went on to tell his congregation that they owed a debt of gratitude, and of justice, to themselves, to the fallen and to posterity 'to heal and assuage the wounds and the sufferings, which this memorable day has inflicted!'[36] In the small communities of Swanington and Wood Dalling in Norfolk, the message was the same. John Vickers, who preached his sermon in both churches, said of the widows and orphans that 'their very condition gives them peculiar claims upon our kindness. Every unhappy Woman bereaved of her Husband, in our service, on that memorable day, is now anxiously looking to receive from us, in some degree, the protection she has lost.' It was the Christian duty of his listeners to do something to help these thousands of unhappy widows who 'were watering their couches with their tears.'[37]

Appeals of this kind had a wonderful effect. So eloquent was the Reverend Daniell that his parishioners had the sermon printed and sold at one shilling a copy in aid of the subscription. They also collected £73 1s 3d at the church door. In the case of the parish of St Nicholas, at Great Bookham in Surrey, a sermon was followed up with a door-to-door collection by the churchwardens. They raised £34 13s 6d in sums which ranged from the Hon. Marmaduke Downey's £5 to Mrs Pelham's sixpence.[38] In Huntingdonshire, the subscription from the parish of Buckden ranged from the Bishop of Lincoln's £21 to a shilling given by five small girls 'from their rewards at school.'[39] So it went on week after week through the summer

---

36 M.Daniell, *Waterloo Subscription. A Sermon, to recommend the same, preached at St Mary's church, Whitechapel 13 Aug 1815* (London: Rivingtons, 1815).
37 J.Vickers, *A Sermon, of which the Substance was delivered in the Parish Churches of Swanington and Wood Dalling in the County of Norfolk, on the Twentieth and Twenty-seventh August 1815 in aid of the Waterloo Subscription by John Vickers MA. Rector of Swanington and Vicar of Wood Dalling* (Norwich: Bacon, 1815).
38 Surrey History Centre: BKG/8/5: Account book of the parish of St Nicholas Great Bookham listing donations to the Waterloo Subscription.
39 Huntingdonshire Record Office: HRO 109/2: List of Subscribers.

months of 1815 until the flow began to slacken in the autumn, although contributions were still being received in the new year.

By the summer of 1816, the Thatched House subscription had raised more than £100,000 and the Waterloo Subscription more than £275,000, the equivalent of perhaps £11 million in current values. On the first anniversary of the battle, the committee of the Waterloo Subscription issued a statement outlining how they intended to proceed with the disbursement of the monies. They pointed out that initially their concern had been to relieve the immediate suffering of the widows and orphans of the killed, but that to begin with, nobody had had any idea of the amount which might be raised, or of the claims which might be made on it. A year on, the position was clearer, and they could now explain to the public how the money was to be distributed.

The committee had decided that a system of annuities would be preferable to cash payment. This it was believed, would 'shield the orphan from neglect or oppression, to rear to maturity in moral and industrious habits the children of the killed, to guard the weak against the dangers of their own improvidence, and to secure the unprotected widow against the impositions of fraud.' Widows in general were to be granted life annuities, and their children were to receive annuities to the age of seven, and then an increased amount at 14 adequate for their maintenance and education. Thereafter they would receive help to find a livelihood, and at the age of 21, or earlier in the case of girls marrying, 'a further benefaction in money, provided that they shall not have forfeited their claim by misconduct.' The children of officers were to receive annuities until they reached the age of 21, at which age, or earlier if a girl married, a further sum of money 'determined by the rank of the deceased parent' would be allowed. Orphans would receive allowances 'proportionate to their rank, and to the circumstances of their aggravated calamity.' Disabled officers, NCOs and privates were to receive a life annuity, though the officers could opt for a lump sum payment. Wounded officers were to receive a cash payment, and severely wounded privates and NCOs 'likewise a pecuniary gratuity' on discharge.[40]

How was this to work in practice? By 15 September 1816 the committee of the Waterloo Subscription had drawn up a set of regulations, the first of which stated that all applications were to be made by letter, and that personal requests could not be attended to. A distinction was also drawn between the widows and dependents of dead officers, and those of NCOs and privates. An officers' widow was simply required to write to the committee stating her circumstances and the number and ages of her children. She was required to produce a marriage certificate, but if for any reason she was unable to do so, her situation 'may be made known and recommended to the committee by any respectable person.' There were no further restrictions. It was not quite so simple for the widows and children of NCOs and privates who had been killed. Whether from an assumption that many of these women would not have been literate enough to put their plight on paper, or a suspicion that they could not quite be relied on to be honest, they did not have to write personally. Instead, they had to be recommended to the committee either by the minister of the parish in which they lived, or by a magistrate, together with a marriage certificate and a statement of the number and ages of the children. Nor was this the only difference. Whereas an officer's widow was

---

40 *The Times*, 18 June 1816.

able to receive a direct payment from the fund, this was not the case for the other ranks. 'Relief will be afforded to widows when they arrive at their fixed place of settlement: the Relief will be placed in the care of the Minister of the Parish, or of some respectable person, to be given in such portions and at such times as may be most useful and beneficial to them.' However paternalistic this may sound, it undoubtedly sprang from the genuine and sensible desire on the part of the committee to protect a widow's best interests in line with their stated intentions.[41]

Occasionally the Duke of Wellington himself became involved in the case of a destitute widow. In August 1816 he received a letter from a Mrs St Aurin, the mother of Captain St Aurin, who had been killed at the Battle of Orthez. 'She has written to me a most dismal letter respecting herself, her widowed daughter-in-law, and two orphan female children.' Writing to Major General Sir Henry Torrens, the Military Secretary at Horse Guards, the Duke wondered 'Could you do anything for this family? Could the widow get a commission for sale? Could the children be put on the Compassionate list?'[42] Torrens' reply is unfortunately not recorded.

The Waterloo Subscription was not the only source of support for bereaved wives. In Scotland there was also the Kinloch Bequest. 'William Kinloch, Esq. late of Calcutta, in the province of Bengal' died in July 1812, leaving a will dated 7 March of that year. He had made a fortune in India, and left an annuity to his mother, legacies to friends and relations and the generous sum of £3,000 to the poor of the parish of Arbuthnot in the county of Kincardine. The residue of his estate however, a sum in excess of £76,000, was to placed in the 'British funds at interest' as a fund to relieve 'poor and indigent Scotchmen', and in particular those who had been maimed or disabled serving their country in the army or navy.

There was a court case to determine exactly who was to be responsible for administering this fund, and it was decided that The Scottish Hospital was the appropriate institution. It was decided that the fund should be used to assist 'all poor and disabled Scots in distress, who may have lost their legs, arms, eyesight, or have been otherwise maimed or wounded in the service of their country; as also from all commissioned and warrant officers, provided that they be really poor.' In-pensioners at Greenwich or Chelsea were excluded from the bequest, as they were already amply provided for, as were persons with an income of more than £20 a year. The sum to be paid to any individual was not to be more than £8 or less than £4 a year. This was to give the executors some flexibility in terms of an applicant's age, infirmity, illness or mutilation. The money would be paid out twice a year. The real intention of the bequest was to assist old soldiers. However, it was also decided that on the death of an old soldier, the outstanding half-yearly allowance would be paid to his widow or orphaned children so that they too could benefit.[43]

There was also His Majesty's Royal Bounty, which was a fund out of which widows, and children of officers, not other ranks, killed in action could be paid an annual allowance. The awards were not only for Waterloo but earlier actions as well, an enlightened concession for the time. Occasionally, other dependents were able to claim – sisters, mothers, and in at

---

41 Waterloo Subscription Regulations, City of London Tavern, 15 September 1816.
42 Wellington (ed.), *Supplementary Despatches*, vol.XI, p.460.
43 The Scottish Corporation, *Kinloch Bequest in Trust to the Scottish Hospital for Specific Purposes* (London: publisher unknown, 1818).

least one case an aged father. In these sad cases, the slain officers must have been the sole means of support. It was also a reflection of the times that the allowances were on a scale of seniority: the more senior the officer, the larger the sum allowed annually would be. Winifred Hawtyn, also widowed at Waterloo, got £80 because her husband was a major, while Phillipa Paterson whose husband, a lieutenant colonel had been mortally wounded at Vittoria, was awarded £150 'in consideration of his meritorious services and of the distressed situation in which she and her child are left.' Most women received more modest allowances, and the records certainly give the lie to any idea that officers were always affluent, and their families were necessarily better off than those of the non-commissioned ranks. Ann Casson, widow of Captain Thomas Casson of the 32nd, who was killed at Quatre Bras, was awarded £60 per annum 'in consideration of her being left with four children, in indigent circumstances.' Mary Buckley also had 'four infant children in distressed circumstances'. Her husband fell fighting with the 1st Foot at Waterloo, and she also received £60 a year. Deborah Potter got £60 per annum as her husband, Captain Leonard Potter of the 28th had died at the storming of Badajoz. Catherine Cuddy only received £40, 'she being left with three children totally unprovided for' because William Cuddy, who had been killed at Bergen-op-Zoom was only a lieutenant. Captain Thomas Irwin of the 88th lost his life at Fuentes de Oñoro and Mary Ann, his wife, was awarded £50. Mary Kennedy got £60 per annum as her husband, Captain Courtney Kennedy of the 9th Foot had been killed at Burgos, 'in consideration of her distressed circumstances.' The list was a long one, and makes melancholy reading.[44]

---

44 *Journal of the House of Commons* (1817), vol.12, pp.528.

13

Survivors

Thus the war terminated, and with it all remembrance of the veteran's services.[1]

So it was that after 22 years of almost continuous warfare, peace returned. The great majority of the wives and widows of both officers and private soldiers slipped into obscurity and often poverty. Their wartime experiences were forgotten or unknown to all save a few relatives and friends. Like most ordinary people of the past, they are lost to our view.

From time to time certainly, the names of old army wives did come to public attention. On 11 September 1874 for instance, the *Monmouthshire Merlin* reported the death of 98-year-old Mrs Sunderland, the widow of the late quartermaster of the Royal Horse Artillery. She was a true daughter of the regiment, having been born in 1776 at the Woolwich barracks, and marrying her husband, a serving artilleryman, when she was 19. She had been with him during the Peninsular campaigns, and also at Waterloo. She was not the only one. The *Merlin* reported on the 20th of the same month that there were three old women living in the workhouse over the age of 100. The eldest was believed to be 108, and told everyone in a 'chirping voice' that she also had been with her husband on the field of Waterloo. The old ladies were treated to a carriage ride round the town.[2]

Some women, especially officers' wives, were able to settle back into a secure and comfortable way of life. One such was Wilhelmina Smellie. She was the daughter of a Dutch mercantile family who married Peter Smellie when he was in a diplomatic post in Ceylon. In 1801, he decided to join the 51st Foot as an ensign. They returned with the regiment to Europe, and Peter served as a lieutenant in the Peninsular War. He was severely wounded at the failed storming of San Cristobal, Badajoz in June 1811. By the Waterloo campaign he had risen to the rank of captain. It appears that Wilhelmina accompanied her husband in the field during the war in Spain and Portugal, because three of their children were born at that time – in 1809, 1811 and 1812. They must have been conceived on campaign. A period of leave, unlikely in itself, could hardly account for such a rate of child-bearing.

After the end of the Napoleonic Wars, the Smellies returned to Edinburgh, where in 1821 Peter was appointed Comptroller of Stamps and Revenues in Scotland. This enabled them to buy 20 Ann Street, a very fashionable address. Portrait painter Henry Raeburn lived

---

1 Napier, *History of the War*, vol.VI, p.656.
2 *Monmouthshire Merlin*, 11 & 20 September 1874. Information from Mike Tanner, Pontypool Museum.

at number 27, and family tradition has it that he painted a group portrait of the family, which suggests that the Smellies were living in affluence rather than mere comfort. Peter Smellie died in 1829, aged about 49, possibly with his health undermined by his war wound. Wilhelmina went to live with her parents-in-law on the family estate at Addiewell House where she appeared in the 1841 and 1851 census returns. She died at a house in Portobello on 5 May 1858, and is buried in lair 50 of West Calder churchyard, West Lothian. She was certainly a Peninsular wife who spent her later years in very easy circumstances.[3]

The redoubtable Mrs Dalbiac was another such lady, or would have been had she lived long enough to enjoy the long peace. The Dalbiacs returned to England in 1812 and James did not see active service again. In 1822 he was promoted to brigadier general and spent two years in India in command of the Goojerat district of the Bombay army. Given their deep attachment and her adventurous spirit, it seems certain that Susanna went with him. In 1814 they had bought Moulton Hall in North Yorkshire, but Susanna did not live to enjoy the way of life this might have implied, or to see her daughter married to the Duke of Roxburghe, as she died in 1829 at the age of 45. Perhaps her constitution had been undermined by the rigours of campaigning. She was buried in St Michael's, Kirklington. The memorial erected by her distraught husband records that she united

> ... to a most affectionate disposition and to a fortitude of mind almost without parallel, an uncompromising rectitude of purpose in every important act of her life. Amongst numerous proofs of self-devotion she displayed the singular firmness of accompanying her husband through several campaigns under the Duke of Wellington, and was present at the Battle of Salamanca on the 22nd July 1812.

Lieutenant General James Dalbiac, as he became, soldiered on without her for another two decades, until he died in 1847 and was laid beside her in the same vault.

For most veterans, however, the peace did not promise a secure and comfortable life. The Britain to which the victorious troops, their wives or widows returned was not the land fit for heroes they might have expected. It was a country entering a severe post-war depression. The booming wartime economy collapsed just as tens of thousands of demobilized troops and sailors were returning to seek jobs. As unemployment rose, agricultural prices fell and the corn laws were introduced to keep prices up in the interests of domestic producers. Matters were made worse by the disastrous harvest of 1816. Hunger followed as the poor were scarcely able to buy bread. There were riots, and *habeas corpus* was suspended.

At the other end of the social and economic spectrum from the Dalbiacs were women such as Ellen Donaldson, wife and widow of Sergeant Joseph Donaldson of the 94th. Donaldson was a man who with luck might have been able to provide his wife and family with a good living. After the end of the Napoleonic Wars, he secured employment with the East India Company in Glasgow, and began to write his *Recollections of the Eventful Life of a Soldier*, which appeared in some ephemeral format. He used the small income from this to help him study anatomy and medicine, and after receiving his discharge from the Company in 1827, 'he was enabled, on the trifling proceeds of his literary labours, and by dint of

---

[3] Information supplied by David Patterson from a family archive.

severe economy and close application, to take the degree of surgeon.' Perhaps he thought this remarkable achievement the royal road to a substantial income, but despite trying his skills in Scotland and London, he died in Paris in October 1830, aged 37, leaving his wife and family unsupported in Glasgow. In March 1838, presumably through the good offices of a friendly editor, his *Recollections* were republished in book form as a means of raising funds for them.

> His widow ... still lives, the sole support of three surviving children. Since her husband's death, and for some years previous, Mrs Donaldson has suffered severe privation and poverty. The sole dependence to which she and her family can look forward with hope, is the recorded Recollections of her husband's misfortunes, which are now published for her behoof.[4]

At least Ellen Donaldson's husband had come home from the wars in one piece. Maria Jackson was not so fortunate. Thomas Jackson was badly wounded fighting with the Coldstream Guards at Bergen-op-Zoom in 1814, and when Maria found him in the Guards' hospital in York Street in London, he was a changed man – minus one leg, ill and emaciated. That kind of discovery was too much for some of the wives, but Jackson recorded that his wife, 'being a woman of superior mind, after the first momentary shock at the visible alteration in my appearance, recovered herself, and, with more than feminine fortitude, forgot her own feelings in her solicitude for my welfare ...' Maria had need of all the fortitude she could muster in the coming months. Despite having only one leg, the Commissioners of the Board at Chelsea considered that Jackson could still earn a living at his old trade of buckle-making, and awarded him only a shilling a day pension. So, Maria cut the gold lace from his sergeant's jacket, which she sold, together with the chain and tassels from his shako, for the useful sum of 30 shillings. They then managed to return to Walsall, where Thomas tried to resume his old trade, but times were hard in the post-war world, and Maria had had a baby. They were often reduced to one meal a day, and he was even driven 'to the necessity of pledging [pawning] our clothes to buy food.'[5] Their situation did improve later when Thomas managed to secure a job as a clerk with a coal company.

Catherine Exley was another wife who faced great hardship. Sometime after she returned to her home parish, Catherine, believing herself to be a widow, received a letter from Joshua to say that he was a prisoner in France where he had been since the fighting in the Pyrenees. He was eventually sent to Bordeaux where he was able to rejoin the 34th, which then sailed for Ireland. Catherine set off to join him there and found him sick in the hospital. He was finally discharged as an invalid, and they moved back to Batley near Leeds. They managed to find a cottage but had no furniture. A local carpenter offered to let them have some on credit, but they were so poor they refused the kind offer. After some time, Joseph managed to find some employment (she does not say what it was) and she made a little money from washing, and they were able to get some bits of furniture, though not it appears, a bed, since Catherine mentions being ill and tossing and turning on a straw mattress. But her

---

4   Donaldson, *Recollections*, p.vi.
5   O'Keefe (ed.), *Narrative*, pp.92–105.

diary entries at this time are haunted by the spectre not simply of hunger, but actual starvation. She speaks of having nothing but bread and water, and in one place 'For seven days we had only seven pounds of bread for four of us.' She herself was ill, and unable to do her washing, and Joseph out of work, and when their third child was born 'the house was often destitute of a crumb of bread.' Then Joseph had a bad accident, falling through a hole in a floor, and was without work for 22 weeks. It seems that at this time the family must have been on parish relief, for she speaks of the 'Union'. 'When I was strong enough to go out to wash, I made a practice of taking home the dinner given to me, and sharing it with my husband and children, who would have otherwise had to go without a meal.' One dinner, in other words, between two adults and three children. Joseph somehow made efforts to keep a small elementary school for a while, and this brought in a pittance, but the truth was that the Exley family were saved from starvation by small gifts of money from neighbours, and on one occasion by a supply of flour, bacon, cheese and potatoes brought to them one stormy night by the a 'person who befriended us so providentially.'[6] Joseph died, a man ruined in health and strength, and perhaps in spirit, in January 1829. Catherine lived until April 1857, when she died in her 79th year. Her diary does not reveal how she supported herself after she was widowed, except by the most zealous Christian faith she had acquired soon after her return home.

Other women were left destitute through no fault of their own. One such was Elezabeth McLane (as she signed herself) whose husband had served in the 21st Foot for six years as a private and 23 as a sergeant. Lieutenant Colpeper had transferred to a West Indian regiment still owing her late husband 'one pound three shillings and four pence as appears by the Books of the Redgt.' Mrs McLean had written to the lieutenant but had never received a reply, and in desperation, in May 1800 she petitioned the Commander-in-Chief, the Duke of York: 'I hade a son in the 21st Redgt whom dyed in the Wast indias and both My Husband and son being dead I have No person to assist Me and the paymaster capt McKay ordered all My Husbands Effects to be sold to pay his funeral charge and Left Me destitute.' Mrs McLane wrote that she had heard of the Duke's humanity, and 'houping from the goodness of hart that your Royal Highness Will order this small sume to be Remited to Me at Mr Hird Mans [Manse] Dunfermilin'.[7] It seems unlikely that she ever received the money owing to her.

Actual starvation was not impossible for a soldier's widow, especially one lacking the hand of friendship which had been offered to the Exleys. On 15 August 1795, the *Cambridge Intelligencer* reported the case of a soldier's widow who killed her own child because it was starving:

> The poor woman, having lost her husband in the war, and having implored relief at several doors in vain, in the town of Liverpool, in a fit of desperation, took her child (about three years old) in the public street, and dashed its head against the wall: immediately surgical aid was called, but in vain. Upon opening the body of

---

6   Probert (ed.), *Exley Diary*, pp.50–58.
7   Buckley (ed.), *Napoleonic War Journal*, Appendix C, p.308.

the child, the surgeon gave it as his opinion, that its stomach had not received food for three days before. The miserable woman is Committed to Lancaster Castle.[8]

Neither the woman's name, nor the regiment to which she had belonged were given, but the incident was widely reported. In 1801 it became the subject of a long anti-war poem called *War Elegy* by the Presbyterian minister and poet Joseph Fawcett which perhaps helped to keep the fate of this 'daughter of despair' before the public for longer than press reports might have done.

This was an extreme case, but many old army wives had to live in very reduced circumstances. Sarah Yeomans was the widow of Sergeant Yeomans on the Royal Artillery. She had been with him during the Peninsular War, in which he had earned no less than seven medal clasps, but by January 1855 she was being recommended for a place in the Pepper Street almshouse in Chester. Her only means of support were the three shillings allowed her by the parish, of which 1s 6d went for rent. The letter of recommendation from one R. Owen to the trustees of the charity pointed out that her late husband had been highly respected by all who knew him, and in view of Sarah's record of campaigning with him in Spain, she 'has no ordinary claims on the sympathy and kindness of others.'[9] Whether or not she was given a place is not recorded. The workhouse of course was a far worst prospect, and this was what was facing Mary Stafford in July 1861. Her husband had served in the Peninsular War, and had had an army pension, but now, at the age of 63, Mary was living on four pounds of bread and a shilling a week allowed her by the parish. However, she had been told by the relieving officer that this was to stop, and that she would have to go into the workhouse at Basford in Nottinghamshire. Mary wrote to the Poor Law guardians saying that she felt that the young mothers of illegitimate children were being given preferential treatment, and asking for their assistance. One hopes she got it, but as with Sarah Yeomans, the outcome is not known.[10]

It is not surprising that some women slipped into petty crime. Ellen Robertson (also known as Roberts and Sullivan) had been twice married to soldiers. She had been with one in the West Indies in 1795. With another, a sergeant in the 58th Foot, she had been in Spain, where he had been killed. In February 1827 she found herself in the Old Bailey accused of stealing bacon from the shop belonging to one Richard Lane. The gaoler's report showed that she had been in Newgate on a previous occasion, and she was sentenced to seven years transportation. Her defence however, pleaded that she had been inebriated at the time of the offence as a result of brain damage caused by the wrong medicine being given her as a result of illness during the time of her regimental service in the West Indies. Surprisingly, this seems to have carried some weight, because in April that year Sir Robert Peel signed a warrant for her removal from Newgate to the General Penitentiary, and she was spared transportation.[11]

---

8 *Cambridge Intelligencer*, 15 August 1795.
9 Cheshire Archives and Local Studies: ZCR 193/19.
10 The National Archives (TNA): MH 12/9247/439: Letter from Mary Stafford, Basford Poor Law Union, to the Poor Law Board, f.607.
11 TNA: HO 17/35/6: Petition of Ellen Robinson.

The Ballad Singers. A disabled veteran soldier with his wife and children, playing and singing and begging for alms in the street. Aquatint, 1820. (Anne S.K. Brown Military Collection, Brown University)

Sometimes it was the old soldier who slipped into minor crime as was the case with Mary Farmer's husband. She had married James Cooper in early 1814, at Witney in Oxfordshire while he was home on leave. He had been wounded at the Battle of the Nivelle in the previous November while fighting with the 2/24th Foot. He was discharged in July 1815, probably unfit for further service. They had a daughter, Mary, who was baptized in Witney sometime that year. James was a hatter by trade, but times were hard, and he seems to have worked as a labourer, which may have been difficult with an old wound. He had been in trouble with the law before he enlisted and perhaps this was the reason. He was prosecuted at the Oxford quarter sessions in 1811 for an affray, being bound over in the sum of £10. In 1817 he was in trouble again, this time for stealing wood. None of this can have made life any easier for Mary. James died in 1842 from some form of tuberculosis and was buried at Minster Lovell. His wife survived him by 31 years, earning her living as a laundress, and living with her daughter and grandson in a property near Church Green in Witney. She may also have acted as a domestic servant to two local sisters of independent means.[12]

Charlotte Gait was another army wife who ended her life as a washerwoman. Her husband Simon had been a sergeant in the 4th Foot. Whether or not she was with the regiment during the retreat to Corunna, she was certainly with the regiment in Spain at a later date, because she gave birth to a daughter, Mary Ann, in 1811 or 1812, who in later censuses always gave her place of birth as Spain. After Simon's discharge in 1817 the family returned to Chewton Mendip in Somerset, where he took up his trade as a shoemaker. They seem to have had a thin time of it, and when Simon died in 1836 Charlotte lost his meagre pension. She may have had to rely on the support of family members, though she was able to earn some money as a washerwoman, as she is described in the 1841 census. When she died in 1849 she was laid to rest in the churchyard of St Mary Magdalene, Chewton Mendip, though she has no headstone to mark to place.[13]

In many cases women returning from the wars, whether as wives or widows, must have lived unremarkable lives, neither very poor nor well-off, but able to support themselves in a reasonable way of life. One such was Clotilde Lawrence. In the period after the war, many regiments were reduced, and Sergeant William Lawrence was one of the men selected for discharge from the 40th Foot, then stationed in Glasgow. He and the other sergeant in the same position were ordered to proceed by sea from Leith to Chatham, and thence to Chelsea, where they were to be assessed for pensions. Clotilde went with him. The Chelsea board, taking into account the wound he had received in the knee, awarded Lawrence a pension of nine pence a day. He was then given his expenses in order to return to his native Dorset, and the parish from which he originally came. These amounted to one shilling and ten pence, and three-halfpence for his wife for every 10 miles of the journey. It was about 120 miles to Studland and they walked every step of the way. Once there, he managed to find work as a farm labourer at 10 shillings a week.

Towards the end of 1819 Lawrence was recalled to the colours, joined the 3rd Veteran Battalion, and was posted to the west of Ireland on anti-smuggling duties. He was finally discharged from military service in June 1821 and sent back to Plymouth, to resume life on his pension. From Plymouth, he and Clotilde marched once again back to Studland. For some time Lawrence 'drifted about … between one or two trades, and finally took a little public-house, where I and my wife lived pretty prosperously till she died.'[14] William Lawrence was in the end obliged to give up the pub through ill-health, though he did manage to get an addition to his pension of three pence a day, so that he had a shilling to live on until he died in 1869, when he was laid next to Clotilde. Today, Lawrence's grave occupies a conspicuous place in the churchyard of the little Norman church at Studland. A large gravestone carries a full summary of his remarkable military career, at the foot of which is a note on his marriage. On the back of the slab Clotilde is remembered too:

---

12 Information from Trevor Cooper's family research.
13 I am grateful to Steve Bumstead for sharing his genealogical researches.
14 Bankes (ed.), *Autobiography*, p.249.

Ci-Gît
Clotilde Lawrence
St Germaine-en-Laye (France)
Decedee à Studland
Le 26, Septembre 1853

Ann Jeffers was the wife of John Jeffers, who had enlisted in the Royal Artillery Drivers at Musselburgh in July 1803. Their son, also John, lived to become the editor of the *Fifeshire Advertiser* in Kirkaldy, and left an account of their experience at Waterloo, where he and his mother were with the baggage, and apparently employed assisting the wounded and dying as described earlier. John Jeffers was discharged from the army at Chatham in November 1818. He received a pension of 8d a day from the Board of Ordnance, as well as sum of marching money. This took the family back to Leith, though whether they went by sea, or like William Lawrence and his wife, covered the distance on foot, is not known. Jeffers died (date unknown) and left Ann a widow. In Edinburgh, she met and married another soldier, Sergeant Wilson. Mrs Jeffers Wilson, as she now called herself, died in Newhaven, Edinburgh, 26 February 1843, aged 57.[15]

Another wife we can catch a glimpse of is Mary Watts. She was an Irish girl, her maiden name being Foster. Richard Watts had joined the 1st Dragoon Guards in 1800 at Nottingham, the regiment being stationed in Ireland at the time. Here Richard and Mary met, and they were married on 5 July 1813. After Napoleon's escape from Elba, the 1st Dragoon Guards were posted to Belgium, and Mary, who was pregnant with their first child, was lucky in the ballot, and went with them. Richard fought at Waterloo, and it is thought Mary helped with the wounded. The regiment was in Paris as part of the Army of Occupation, and here their first child, William, was born in October 1815.

The regiment eventually returned to England, and over the next few years the couple had several more children at the various places where they were stationed. Richard was promoted Troop Sergeant Major, but he died of cholera in Brighton on 6 August 1833, while Mary was carrying their eighth child. The regimental muster book records that she was given £1 4s 9d to get her back to Leicester, which was where Richard had come from, and there she gave birth to her last child. She apparently received little help from her husband's siblings, but despite this she managed to earn a reasonable living. In the 1841 census, Mary is listed as a schoolmistress, so she must have had some education. She continued to live in Leicester, where, in 1843 she married again, to James Summers, a saddle maker. Mary also earned money as a glove maker. Summers died in 1875, leaving Mary a widow for the second time. She died in 1879, and is buried in Welford Road cemetery, Leicester, leaving 43 grandchildren and a least five great-grandchildren.[16]

Elizabeth, whose maiden name was Wadhams, was born on 31 March 1794 in Northampton, and married William Law in January 1814. William was a corporal in the 2/95th based at Shorncliffe. In May 1815 they sailed with the battalion to Belgium. William fought at both Quatre Bras and Waterloo, where he lost his left arm when a musket ball hit

---

15   Personal communication from Andrew Campbell based on his family research.
16   J.M. Hynds has generously provided the fruits of his research into their family history.

him above the elbow. Elizabeth had remained in Brussels and was serving as a nurse in the Jesuits' hospital where she cared for the wounded coming in from the battle fields. She had no idea of what had happened to her husband. By great good luck, William was sent to the same hospital, where Elizabeth found him, quite by chance, sitting up with his mutilated arm. She was 21 at the time, and had only been an army wife for a year, so she certainly was not a hardened old campaigner, and one can perhaps imagine her feelings. William was discharged from the 95th in October 1815, and the couple returned to Northampton, where they started a family. William had an army pension but found a job as a lace-maker despite the fact that he had only one arm. Somehow or other they managed to prosper in a modest way, and opened a grocer's shop from which they retired in 1861. William died in November 1869. Elizabeth lived on with one of her daughters until her own death in November 1872, aged 78.[17]

Margaret Urquhart's life was rather different. She was born as Margaret Fraser between 1781 and 1784 in either Rathven or Fordyce, in Banffshire. She married Thomas Urquhart in about 1807. He came from Hillhead of Turriff, where he had been born in 1787 or 1788. He enlisted in the 1/10th Foot at about the time of their marriage, probably in Aberdeen. The battalion was posted almost at once to Sicily, and Thomas and Margaret, who was lucky with the drawing of lots, are thought to have gone out to the Mediterranean with a draft in April of the following year. The battalion did garrison duty in several parts of the island, and Thomas and Margaret were Messina when their son Adam was born. The Macduff baptismal register has the following entry for 1808: 'Adam Lawful Son of Thos Urquhart private in 10th Regt of Foot and Margaret Fraser his wife was born and baptised July 3rd in the Isle of Sicily by the Chaplain to the brigade before witnesses.' In July 1812 it was decided to transfer the troops in Sicily to southern Spain, where an inconclusive campaign was waged for the next two years. In January 1814 Thomas was hospitalized, presumably from a wound, because he was later a recipient of monies from the Kinloch Bequest. Margaret was probably nursing him. The regimental muster and pay book for 24 March 1815 states that Thomas was discharged on 24 January that year, having completed his period of service. He and Margaret had been with the battalion for seven years of active service.

By April 1815 the couple were in England, and made their way back to Scotland. However, they had not had enough of the military life, and Thomas re-enlisted in the 71st, the Highland Light Infantry, at Aberdeen on 3 November. They then marched with a party of other recruits to Glasgow, taking a very leisurely 14 days to cover the 149 miles. The Urquharts had missed the campaign of Waterloo, but in February 1816 set out with a draft to join the first battalion of the 71st which was stationed between Douai and Calais as part of the Army of Occupation. Sometime during 1816, in France, Margaret gave birth a little girl, and they named her after her mother. The 71st remained in France until October 1818, when they were posted home, reaching Dover on 29 October. With the coming of peace, the regiment's establishment was reduced and Thomas was discharged. For some reason, Thomas Urquhart did not receive an army pension, though he did get one from the Kinloch Bequest for wounded Scottish soldiers.

---

17   I am grateful to Philip Martin for sharing information from his family archive.

The couple returned to Scotland and settled at Macduff, where Thomas became a labourer. In September 1819 their second son, Thomas, was born. By 1841 the Urquharts had moved to Netherbrae and had taken a lease on a croft. The 1851 census shows them still there with six acres and Thomas in receipt of the Kinloch Bequest. Margaret was there with their daughter, grandchildren and a nephew. Thomas died at Netherbrae on 13 June 1859 aged 71, and was buried in the kirkyard at Turriff. The family continued to farm the croft, and the 1864–1865 valuation roll shows 'Widow Thomas Urquhart and Son' leasing the croft. In the 1861 census Margaret was described as 'Farmer's Mother.' Margaret died at Netherbrae on 13 June 1867 aged 84, and is presumably buried (there is no record) with Thomas at Turriff. She had certainly lived on to a ripe old age, in peace and if not in prosperity, at least with a reasonable standard of living, and surrounded by her family.[18]

Catherine Peplow also seems to have lived her life out in reasonable comfort. Her husband, William, was a watchmaker from Wellington, in Shropshire, who took it into his head to enlist in the 90th Foot in 1812. He was discharged in 1818 after a series of postings around Britain and Ireland, and returned to Wellington where he was able to set up in business as a clock and watchmaker. Despite the difficult economic conditions, the business thrived, which was just as well as they had 13 children to feed, and in the 1871 census they are listed as having a housekeeper. Ann died in 1884 aged 84.[19]

At least two army wives were accorded memorials in stone commemorating their endeavours at Waterloo. Jenny Jones met her first husband, Lewis Griffiths, who came from Tal y llyn, when he was serving with the Merionethshire Militia. She was only 14 years old and he was 19, and there is no record of the marriage. In April 1814, Griffiths volunteered into the line, and joined the 23rd Foot, the Royal Welch Fusiliers. The regiment was posted to Belgium in March 1815 and Jenny went with them, by which time she had a child. Lewis was wounded in the battle and Jenny nursed him back to health. Griffiths was discharged in April 1821, apparently with no pension. The couple returned to Tal y llyn where he worked in a quarry until he was killed in an accident in 1837, by which time they had six offspring. Jenny later remarried, worked in a laundry, and possibly as a teacher. She died on 11 April 1884, and was buried on the 15th in the Tal y llyn parish church.[20] A stone cross was erected by a friend which suggests that she must have been a valuable and perhaps well-known member of the community. The inscription reads:

> Sacred to the memory of
> Jenny Jones
> Born in Scotland June 1789
> Died at Tal y llyn April 11 1884
> She was with her husband of the
> 23rd Royal Welch Fusiliers
> At the Battle of Waterloo
> And was on the field three days

---

18   Graham Robertson has kindly shared the fruits of his family research.
19   Information provided by Sarah Riley based on her genealogical research.
20   'Jenny Jones,' *Royal Welch Fusiliers Museum*, <https://royalwelchfusiliersmuseum.blogspot.com/2016/06/jenny-jones-at-waterloo.html>, accessed 8 February 2022.

The other Waterloo heroine was Ann Winzer, (née Keates) who like Clotilde Lawrence, is buried in a Dorset graveyard, in this case Piddlehinton. She and her husband James came from Dorchester, where they married in April 1811. Soon after this James enlisted. Ann was with her husband at Waterloo, possibly with their four-year-old son, where she nursed some of the sick and wounded. At the close of the war James' regiment was posed amongst other places to Gibraltar, where Ann remained for four years. He then appears to have been discharged, possibly wounded, because he was made an out-pensioner of the Royal Hospital at Chelsea, and they returned to Dorchester in 1824, where they remained until 1861, when they moved a short distance to Piddlehinton. James worked as a journeyman plasterer. Ann died two years before her husband on 28 November 1873, aged 82. Their joint gravestone bears a testimonial to her goodness, noting that 'She was a Waterloo heroine who assisted at that famous battle AD 1815 by aiding and assisting the sick and wounded' as well as mentioning her subsequent services, but that is not all. The inscription goes on to say 'She received a pension through the instrumentality of Colonel Astell with that of many other officers by whose kindness this stone is raised as a tribute of respect to a long life spent in true and faithful service.' Charles Astell had bought the West Lodge in Piddlehinton in 1862, shortly after Ann and James moved to the village themselves. Ann must have been seen as a notable and worthy character, and with a reputation for goodness which caused a group of officers to go to the trouble and expense of having such a gravestone erected for the wife of a private soldier.[21]

Another heroine with a gravestone to commemorate her deeds was Agnes Retson of the 94th Foot. Like the Donaldsons of the same regiment, Agnes and her husband James returned to Glasgow at the war's end. Miraculously, Agnes had survived her gallant part in the defence of Fort Matagorda at Cadiz in 1810. James died in 1834, and Agnes managed to support herself by acting as a sick nurse. By 1844 however, she had been reduced to pauperism, at one time living in the old lunatic asylum before moving with the other inmates to the new hospital. Somehow, her plight became known, and a committee of officers, perhaps from the old 94th, launched an appeal on behalf of 'this truly valiant and deserving, though sadly neglected woman.' Most donations came from the army, though both Queen Victoria and the dowager Queen Adelaide were also contributors. The appeal raised enough money to secure Agnes an annuity of £30 a year, so restoring her independence. As she no longer had a home of her own, she elected to stay at the hospital, paying for her keep. After setting aside sufficient money to pay her own funeral expenses, she left the rest to charity.

Agnes died on Christmas Eve 1856, at the good age of 85, and she was laid to rest beside her husband in Glasgow's Southern Necropolis, where their grave may still be seen. It bears the following inscription: 'In memory of James Retson, late sergeant 94th Regiment, who died on the 24th day of October 1834, aged 63 years, of Agnes Harkness, his wife "The Heroine of Matagorda" who died 24 December 1856 aged 85 years.'[22]

---

21 'Ann Winzer,' *The Keep Museum*, <https://www.keepmilitarymuseum.org>, accessed 6 March 2019. In 2000 an appeal was launched for the restoration of the headstone, which was re-dedicated.
22 'Famous Scots – Agnes Harkness', *Find a Grave in Scotland*, <http://www.findagraveinscotland.com/grave/famousgrave/125508>, accessed July 2022.

Agnes Retson had the unique and somewhat dubious distinction of being celebrated in one of William McGonnagal's doggerel poems, *A Humble Heroine,* which had the merit of bringing her adventures to a wider audience.

One exception to this pattern of normal civilian life after the long war was predictably perhaps, Juana Smith. Harry went on to hold a series of military and administrative posts in the ever-expanding empire, steadily rising in rank, and her life was anything but routine. In 1825 they were sent to Nova Scotia, and from there to Jamaica where they managed to survive an outbreak of yellow fever. The next posting was to South Africa where a native war had to be contained. Then, in 1840 Harry having been appointed Deputy Assistant Quartermaster General to the Queen's army in India, they sailed for the east, narrowly surviving a storm which they thought was going to be the end of them. It was in India that Harry Smith began to come to the attention of the public, with the outbreak of the first Sikh war, in the early stages of which Juana is said to have followed the army on elephant-back. In 1846, Harry defeated a much larger Sikh army at Aliwal. This earned him a baronetcy and the thanks of both houses of Parliament, and the sobriquet 'The hero of Aliwal' By 1847 Sir Harry and Lady Smith were back in South Africa where he had been appointed Governor of Cape Colony. This proved to be controversial appointment, and in due course he was recalled, but not before Juana had left her mark. Ladysmith in Natal is named after her.

On their return to England in 1852 Harry was promoted Lieutenant General, but died in London the following year, aged 73. According to his wish, his body was brought home to Whittlesea, the out-of-the-way little town where he had been born. Juana retired for some years to Hastings, and then to Cadogan Place in London. Compared with many army widows, she was in an affluent position. Parliament voted her a pension of £500 in recognition of her husband's services, which enabled her to be generous to members of Harry's family. When she died in 1872, she too was buried at Whittlesea, next to her Enrique, whose memory she cherished to the last.

Their joint tomb is not in the churchyard, but in the cemetery, some way from the town centre. It is not easy to find, next to the hedge on the far side from the road. It is a white granite table-tomb, surrounded by black cast-iron railings. Around the plinth are carved the names of Harry Smith's many battles, and on one side a bronze bearing a tribute by the Duke of Wellington. On one end is a smaller bronze plaque:

> Also of
> Juana Maria de los Dolores de Léon
> Relict of
> The Late Lieut. General
> Sir Harry G W Smith Bt. GCB
> Died Oct 10th 1872
> Aged 75 years

And there she lies, under the wide fenland sky, a long way from the bloody battlefields of Spain. She did however achieve a kind of literary after-life. Romantic fiction seldom meets historical fact, but in 1940 Georgette Heyer published a novel called *The Spanish Bride.* Closely based on Smith's autobiography, it follows in detail Harry's impulsive marriage to the beautiful young Juana and their experiences during the Peninsular War. A true story of love and war must have seemed particularly apt to readers in the midst of another and even greater struggle.

There was one other army wife whose life story was turned into a novel, albeit in very different circumstances. In 1853 the Reverend Richard Cobbold published a book entitled *Mary Anne Wellington, The Soldier's Daughter, Wife and Widow*. Mary Anne was a real daughter of the regiment. Her father was an artilleryman, and when in December 1805, at the age of 16, she was married in the garrison chapel at Gibraltar to Thomas Hewitt of the 48th Foot, she was described as 'belonging to the Royal Artillery.'

Disentangling facts from a novel is problematic, but it seems that Mary Anne joined her husband's regiment in Spain at about the time of *Maréchal* Massena's retreat from the Lines of Torres Vedras. She was at the Battle of Albuera where she assisted with the wounded, and at Salamanca also. She was taken ill at Abrantes where she gave birth to a baby, which died after only two months. She was on the long march which culminated in the Battle of Vitoria and with the 48th during the battles in the Pyrenees. After the end of the war in the Peninsula, they were embarked for Ireland. The 48th were then sent to New South Wales, where Anne and Thomas had several children before returning to England. They then settled in Ten Bell Lane in Norwich where they lived in very poor circumstances on Thomas's pension until his death in 1844. Mary Anne was then dependent on her two daughters, who were employed as stay-makers. Things went from bad to worse when one of them became ill and unable to work. Their landlord was a kindly man and advised Mary Anne to apply for relief from the local board of guardians – the last refuge of the poor and one usually resisted until there was no alternative. After an interview, she was granted three shillings a week. Later, she petitioned both the Duke of Wellington and Queen Adelaide, the Queen Dowager for help, apparently with some success.

It was at this point that Richard Cobbold became interested in her case. The Reverend Cobbold was the rector of Wortham in Suffolk. A hunting parson he may have been, but he also had literary leanings and was known for having written several books for charitable purposes. On account of this, in August 1845 he received a letter from William Freeman, one of the Norwich magistrates, drawing his attention to the plight of Mary Anne: 'I enclose the memorial of a woman, whose life I think would make an interesting volume, if you would see her, and hear her statements. Her address is Ten Bell Lane, Pottergate Street, just below St Giles's Church, in this city.' So Cobbold set to work, and having interviewed Mary Anne, turned her life story into a novel complete with a great deal of imagined dialogue and invented characterisation. He also chose to use her maiden name in the title, the most famous name imaginable at the time, and no doubt good publicity. At any rate his efforts were a considerable success, and raised some £600. Mary Anne was able to live out her days in reasonable comfort.[23]

Cobbold's book raised considerable local interest in the widow's case and had an unexpected outcome. Anthony Sands, a Norwich artist, decided to paint her portrait. Today it hangs in the Northampton art gallery. It is a small picture, fitting perhaps for its humble subject. She wears a dark dress and white lace collar and cap and is fingering what appears

---

23 Richard Cobbold, *Mary Anne Wellington. The Soldier's Daughter, Wife and Widow* (Ipswich: publisher unknown, 1853) I am indebted to Susan Bickley for putting me on Mary's track.

to be a watch on a pink ribbon. In the background hangs a large picture in which, appropriately, a battle or siege seems to be taking place. Despite the plump cheeks it is an alert and rather quizzical face with a sharp nose and watchful eyes, and perhaps a suggestion of mild surprise at finding herself sitting for her portrait.[24]

The great majority of the thousands of women who accompanied the British troops during the long conflict with France have marched away leaving no account of their lives or record of their passing. Mary Ann Wellington was probably unique in having her portrait painted, and she is the only private soldier's wife with whom we can actually come face to face. We know the names of a few score more, but can hear only a distant echo of a handful of voices. They were women of their time and place, and displayed the strengths and weaknesses of the army of which they were a part. Trying to catch a glimpse of them, we may be amused by their humour or their stratagems for outwitting authority. We may look askance at their plundering or be repelled by the callousness with which they looted the dead while admiring the courage with which they rescued and tended the wounded, sometimes under fire. We may deplore their drunkenness and disobedience, but we marvel at their toughness and their powers of endurance, living in the open in all weathers. Frequently hungry and sometimes starving, their clothing often in rags, they endured the traumas of childbirth and widowhood in foreign fields with a hardihood which baffles the modern imagination. Marching endless miles with their few worldly possessions, braving the dangers of sickness, drowning or capture, they were fiercely loyal to their men and the regiment which was their only home. They were indeed the women who followed the drum.

---

24 'Mary Anne Wellington (b.1789)', Art UK, < https://artuk.org/discover/artworks/mary-anne-wellington-b-1789-49983/>, accessed 3 November 2018.

Bibliography

Manuscript Sources

Cheshire Archives and Local Studies
ZCR 193/19: Letter concerning Sarah Yeomans and almshouse vacancy 1855
DTM72: Tomkinson Family of Willington Hall papers: 16th Light Dragoons regimental order book April–August 1815

East Riding Archives
DDHV/73/5: Letters to Thomas Norcliffe from Thomas Bollard 1807–1820

Huntingdon Record Office
HRO 109/2: List of subscribers to the Waterloo Subscription for the parish of Buckden

Lancashire Infantry Museum, Preston
846/3.2.13: Regimental order book and court martial book 1808–1814
846/3.1.132: Wives' punishment book, 82nd Foot

The National Archives
HO 17/35/6: Papers regarding trial and sentence of Ellen Robinson for stealing bacon, 1827
MH 12/9247/439: Letter from Mary Stafford seeking parish relief, 1861

Nottinghamshire Archives
M24, 298-24, 320: Letters of Sergeant William Tennant 1/3rd Guards and his wife Ann

Private Collection
Peninsular Letters of Norcliffe Norcliffe, 4th Dragoons, and of Colonel and Mrs Dalbiac

Surrey History Centre
SHC BKG/8/5: Account book for the parish of St Nicholas, Great Bookham, listing donations to the Waterloo subscription

Primary Printed Sources

Adye, R. W., *The Bombardier, and Pocket Gunner* (Boston: Larkin, 1804)
Albemarle, George Thomas Kepple, 6th Earl of Albermarle, *Fifty Years of My Life* (London: Macmillan, 1879)
Anderson, J., *Recollections of a Peninsular Veteran* (London: Arnold, 1913)
Anglesey, Marquess of (ed.), *The Capel Letters* (London: Cape, 1955)
Anon., 'Table talk of an Old Campaigner' *United Services Journal and Naval and Military Magazine*, 1834, part 3, pp.50–57
Anon., *General Orders for Troops Destined for Continental Service* (London: Adjutant General's Office, 1807)
Anon., *General Regulations and Orders for the Army* (London: Adjutant General's Office, 1811)
Anon., *Journal of an Officer in the Commissariat Department of the Army* (London: Porter, 1820)
Anon., *Journals of the House of Commons Volume 72 Jan to Dec 1817* (London: House of Commons, 1817)
Anon., *Kinloch Bequest in Trust to the Scottish Hospital for Specific Purposes* (London: Scottish Corporation, 1818)
Anon., *Leaves from the Diary of an Officer of the Guards* (London: Chapman, 1854)
Anon., *Letters from Flushing; containing an account of the Expedition to Walcheren, Beveland and mouth of the Scheldt. By an Officer of the Eighty-First Regiment* (London: Phillips, 1809)
Anon., *Memoirs of a Sergeant late of the 43rd Light Infantry, previous to and during the Peninsular War, including an account of his Conversion from Popery to the Protestant Religion* (Stroud: Nonsuch, 2005)
Anon., *Memoirs of a Sergeant of the 5th Regiment of Foot Containing an Account of His Service in Hanover, South America and the Peninsula* (Ashford: Elliott, 1842)
Anon., *Military Memoirs of an Infantry Officer 1809–1816* (Edinburgh: Anderson, 1833)
Anon., *Narrative of a Private Soldier in His Majesty's 92nd Regiment of Foot Written by Himself* (Uckfield: Naval & Military, nd.)
Anon., *Personal Narrative of a Private Soldier who served in the Forty-Second Highlanders for Twelve Years, during the Late Wars* (London: Allman, 1821)
Anon., *Rules and Regulations for the Cavalry* (London: Adjutant General's Office, 1795)
Anon., *Twelve Years' Military Adventures in Three Quarters of the Globe, or, Memoirs of an Officer* (London: Colburn, 1829)
Anon., *Vicissitudes in the Life of a Scottish Soldier Written by Himself* (London: Colburn, 1827)
Anton, James, *Retrospect of a Military Life during the most eventful periods of the Last War* (Edinburgh: Lizars, 1841)
Atkinson, C.T. (ed.), 'Letters of Major-General Sir F P Robinson', *Journal of the Society for Army Historical Research*, vol.34, (1956), pp.153–170
Bankes, G.N. (ed.), *The Autobiography of Sergeant William Lawrence* (London: Sampson Low, 1886)
Batty, R., *Campaign of the Left Wing of the Allied Army in the Western Pyrenees and the South of France, in the Years 1813–14* (London: Murray, 1823)
Bell, George, *Rough Notes of an Old Soldier During Fifty Years' Service* (London: Day, 1867)
Bell, Mrs Arthur (trans. & ed.), *Memoirs of Baron Lejeune* (London: Longmans, 1897)

Birks, M. (ed.), *The Young Hussar. The Peninsular War Journal of Colonel Thomas Wildman of Newstead Abbey* (Brighton: Book Guild, 2007)

Blakeney, Robert, *A Boy in the Peninsular War* (London: Murray, 1889)

Blathwayt, George W., 'Account of Lt. George William Blathwayt 23rd Light Dragoons', in G. Glover (ed.), *The Waterloo Archive* (Barnsley: Frontline, 2011), vol.3, pp.70 –76.

Blenkinsop, Dr., *Memoirs Written by Himself* (London: Bentley, 1852)

Bogle, J., and Uffindell, A. (eds), *A Waterloo Hero. The Reminiscences of Friedrich Lindau* (London: Frontline, 2009)

Brown, Robert, *Impartial Journal of a Detachment from the Brigade of Foot Guards, commencing 25th February 1793, and ending 9th May 1795* (London: Stockdale, 1795)

Brown, S. (ed.), *The Autobiography, or Narrative of a Soldier* (Solihull: Helion, 2017)

Buckham, E., *Personal Narrative of Adventures in the Peninsula During the War 1812-1813* (London: Murray, 1827)

Buckley, R N. (ed.), *The Napoleonic War Journal of Captain Thomas Henry Browne 1807-1816* (London: Bodley Head, 1987)

Burghclere, Lady, *A Great Man's Friendship. Letters of the Duke of Wellington to Mary Marchioness of Salisbury 1850-1852* (London: Murray, 1927)

Burroughs, G.F., *A Narrative of the Retreat of the British Army from Burgos* (Bristol: Egerton, 1814)

Butler, R., *Narrative of the Life and Travels of Sergeant Butler Written by Himself* (Edinburgh: Brown, 1823)

Cadell, Charles, *Narrative of the Campaigns of the Twenty Eighth Regiment since their return from Egypt in 1802* (London: Whittaker, 1835)

Cassels, S.A.C. (ed.), *Peninsular Portrait 1811-1814 The Letters of Captain William Bragge Third (King's Own) Dragoons* (London: Oxford University Press, 1963)

Chandler, D., 'The Journal of Edward Heeley, servant to Lieutenant Colonel Sir George Scovell, KCB, Assistant Quartermaster General to the British Army in the Campaign of 1815', *Journal of the Society for Army Historical Research,* vol.64, (1986) pp.94–142

Chelsea Pensioner, *Jottings from my Sabretasch* (London: Bentley, 1847)

Cobbold, Richard, *Mary Anne Wellington. The Soldier's Daughter, Wife and Widow* (London: Coburn, 1846)

Cooke, John H., *A Narrative of Events in the South of France and of the Attack on New Orleans in 1814 and 1815* (London: Boone, 1835)

Cooper, John S., *Rough Notes on Seven Campaigns in Portugal, Spain, France and America* (Carlisle: Smith, 1869)

Costello, Edward, *The Adventures of a Soldier* (London: Colburn, 1841)

Crook, J. (ed.), *Incidents in the Life of an Old Fusilier. The Recollections of Sergeant Richard Roberts of the 23rd Foot* (Huntingdon: Trotman, 2011)

Crook, J. (ed.), *The Very Thing. The Memoirs of Drummer Richard Bentinck Royal Welch Fusiliers 1807-1823* (Barnsley: Frontline, 2011)

Daniel, John E., *Journal of an Officer in the Commissariat Department* (London: Porter, 1820)

Daniell, M., *Waterloo Subscription. A Sermon, to recommend the same, preached at St Mary's Church, Whitechapel 13 August 1815* (London: Rivingtons, 1815)

Dobbs, John, *Recollections of an Old 52nd Man* (Waterford: Palmer, 1863)

Donaldson, Joseph, *Recollections of the Eventful Life of a Soldier by the late Joseph Donaldson, Sergeant in the Ninety-fourth Scots Brigade* (Edinburgh: Tait, 1838)

Duncan-Jones, C.M. (ed.), *Trusty and Well Beloved. The Letters Home of William Harness an Officer of George III* (London: SPCK, 1957)

E. Gillet (ed.), *Elizabeth Ham by Herself 1783-1820* (London: Faber, 1945)

Eaton, Charlotte ('An Englishwoman'), *Narrative of a Residence in Belgium during the Campaign of 1815 and of a Visit to the Field of Waterloo* (London: Murray, 1817)

Esdaile, C., & Reed, M. (eds), *With Moore to Corunna. The Diary of Ensign Charles Paget, Fifty Second Foot* (Barnsley: Pen & Sword, 2018)

Fergusson, William, *Notes and Recollections of a Professional Life* (London: Longman, 1846)

Fernyhough, Thomas, *Military Memoirs of Four Brothers by the Survivor* (Staplehurst: Spellmount, 2002)

Fletcher, I. (ed.), *A Guards Officer in the Peninsula. The Peninsular War letters of John Rous, Coldstream Guards, 1812-1814* (Tunbridge Wells: Spellmount, 1992)

Fletcher, I. (ed.), *For King and Country. The Letters and Diaries of John Mills, Coldstream Guards, 1811-14* (Staplehurst: Spellmount, 1995)

Fletcher, I. (ed.), *In the Service of the King. The Letters of William Thornton Keep, at Home, Walcheren, and in the Peninsula, 1808-1814* (Staplehurst: Spellmount, 1997)

'Flexible Grummet', 'Leaves from my Log-Book No 1', *United Services Journal and Naval and Military Magazine*, 1834, part 1, pp.484–497

Gleig, G.R. (ed.), *The Hussar* (London: Colburn, 1837)

Gleig, G.R. (ed.), *The Light Dragoon. The Story of Private George Farmer 11th Light Dragoons, 1808-1836* (London: Routledge, 1850)

Gleig, G.R., *The Subaltern: A Chronicle of the Peninsular War* (London: Blackwood, 1823)

Glover, G. (ed.) *The Waterloo Archive* (Barnsley: Frontline, 2010–2014)

Glover, G. (ed.), *A Narrative of the Battles of Quatre-Bras and Waterloo with the Defence of Hougoumont* (Huntingdon: Trotman, 2006)

Glover, G. (ed.), *A Scots Grey at Waterloo. The Remarkable Story of Sergeant William Clarke* (Barnsley: Frontline, 2017)

Glover, G. (ed.), *An Eloquent Soldier. The Peninsular War Journals of Lieutenant Charles Crowe of the Inniskillings 1812-1814* (Barnsley: Frontline, 2011)

Glover, G. (ed.), *Ensign Carter's Journal 1812. The Peninsular War Diary of Ensign John V Carter 30th (Cambridgeshire) Regiment of Foot* (Huntingdon: Trotman, 2006)

Glover, G. (ed.), *Eyewitness to the Peninsular War and the Battle of Waterloo. The Letters and Journals of Lieutenant Colonel the Honourable James Stanhope 1803 to 1825* (Barnsley: Pen & Sword, 2010)

Glover, G. (ed.), *The Military Adventures of Private Samuel Wray, 61st Foot 1796-1815* (Huntingdon: Trotman, 2009)

Glover, G. (ed.), *The Recollections of Lieutenant John Hildebrand 35th Foot in the Mediterranean and Waterloo Campaigns* (Barnsley: Frontline, 2016)

Glover, G., and Yorke, C. (eds), *With Wellington's Hussars in the Peninsula and Waterloo. The Journal of Lieutenant George Woodberry, 18th Hussars* (Barnsley: Frontline, 2018)

Glover, M. (ed.), *A Gentleman Volunteer. The Letters of George Hennell from the Peninsular War 1812-1813* (London: Heinemann, 1979)

Graham, W., *Travels Through Portugal and Spain during the Peninsular War* (London: Phillips, 1820)

Granville, Countess (ed.), *Private Correspondence 1781–1821* (London: Murray, 1916)
Grattan, William, *Adventures with the Connaught Rangers* (London: Arnold, 1902)
Green, John, *The Vicissitudes of a Soldier's Life or a series of occurrences from 1806 to 1815* (Louth: Green & Jackson, 1827)
Greenwood, A. (ed.), *Through Spain with Wellington. The letters of Lieutenant Peter Le Mesurier of the 'Fighting Ninth'* (Stroud: Amberly, 2016)
Gurwood, J. (ed.), *General Orders in Portugal, Spain and France from1809 to 1814 and the Low Countries and France 1815* (London: publisher unknown, 1832)
Gurwood, J. (ed.), *The General Orders of Field Marshal the Duke of Wellington in Portugal, Spain and France from 1809 to 1814, in the Low Countries and France in 1815, in France, Army of Occupation from 1816 to 1818* (London: Parker, 1837)
Hale, James, *Journal of James Hale, late Sergeant in the Ninth Regiment of Foot* (London: Longman, 1826)
Hall, Basil, *Fragments of Voyages and Travels* (Edinburgh: Cadell, 1831)
Hamilton, Anthony, *Hamilton's Campaign with Moore and Wellington During the Peninsular War* (Staplehurst: Spellmount, 1998)
Harley, J., *The Veteran, or Forty Years in the British Service* (London: Colburn, 1838)
Harrington, P. (ed.), *With the Guards in Flanders. The Diary of Captain Roger Morris 1793–1795* (Warwick: Helion, 2018)
Hathaway, E. (ed.), *A True Soldier Gentleman. The Memoirs of Lt. John Cooke 1791–1813* (Swanage: Shinglepicker, 2000)
Hawker, Peter, *Journal of a Regimental Officer during the Recent Campaign in Portugal and Spain under Viscount Wellington with a Correct Plan of the Battle of Talavera* (London: Johnson, 1810)
Head, George, *Memoirs of an Assistant Commissary-General* (London: Murray, 1837)
Henegan, R.D., *Seven Years Campaigning in the Peninsula and the Netherlands 1808-1815* (Stroud: Nonsuch, 2005)
Henry, Walter, *Events of a Military Life* (London: Pickering, 1843)
Hering, J.F., *Journal of an Officer of the Kings German Legion* (London: Colburn, 1827)
Hibbert, C. (ed.), *A Soldier of the Seventy-First* (London: Leo Cooper, 1975)
Hibbert, C. (ed.), *Recollections of Rifleman Harris* (London: Leo Cooper, 1970)
Hibbert, C. (ed.), *The Wheatley Diary* (London: Longmans, 1964)
Hunt, Eric, (ed.), *Charging against Napoleon. Diaries and Letters of Three Hussars 1808–1815* (London: Leo Cooper, 2001)
Jackson, B, *Notes and Reminiscences of a Staff Officer* (London: Murray, 1903)
Jeffery, R.W. (ed.), *Dyott's Diary 1781–1845. A Selection from the Journal of William Dyott, sometime General in the British Army and Aide-de-Camp to His Majesty King George III* (London: Constable, 1907)
Johnston, Archibald, 'Journal of Sergeant Archibald Johnston of the 2nd Royal North British Dragoons' in G. Glover (ed.), *The Waterloo Archive* (Barnsley: Frontline, 2010), vol.1, pp.33–57
Johnston, S.H.F, 'Letters of Lieutenant John Carss 2/53rd', *Journal of the Society for Army Historical Research*, vol.26, (1948), pp.2–17
Jones, L.T., *An Historical Journal of the British Campaign on the Continent in the Year 1794 with the Retreat Through Holland in the Year 1795* (London: Swinney, 1797)

Kelly, S. (ed.), *The Life of Mrs Sherwood* (London: Darton, 1854)
Kincaid, John, *Adventures in the Rifle Brigade and Random Shots from a Rifleman* (London: Maclaren, 1911)
Kussmaul, A. (ed.), *The Autobiography of Joseph Mayett of Quainton 1783–1839* (Buckingham: Buckinghamshire Record Society, 1986)
Landman, G.T., *Recollections of my Military Life* (London: Hurst, 1854)
Larpent, G. (ed.), *The Private Journal of Judge Advocate Larpent attached to the Head-Quarters of Lord Wellington during the Peninsular War from 1812 to its close* (London: Bentley, 1854)
Leach, J., *Rough Sketches of the Life of an Old Soldier* (London: Longman, 1831)
Leeke, William, *The History of Lord Seaton's Regiment (the 52nd Light Infantry) at the Battle of Waterloo* (London: Hatchard, 1866)
Leslie, C., *Military Journal of Colonel Leslie, KH, of Balquhain Whilst Serving with the 29th Regt. in the Peninsular and the 60th Rifles in Canada etc 1807–1832* (Aberdeen: Aberdeen University Press, 1887)
Leslie, J. (ed.), *The Dickson Manuscripts being the Diaries, Letters, Maps, Account Books With various other Papers of the Late Major-General Sir Alexander Dickson* (Woolwich: Royal Artillery Institution, 1908)
Liddell Hart, B.H. (ed.), *The Letters of Private Wheeler 1809–1828* (London: Michael Joseph, 1952)
Londonderry, Charles W.V., 3rd Marquess of, *Story of the Peninsular War* (London: Colburn, 1848)
Longford, Lord, (ed.), *The Packenham Letters 1800 to 1815* (London: Bumpus, 1914)
Lowry Cole, M., and Gwynn, S. (ed.), *Memoirs of Sir Lowry Cole* (London: Macmillan, 1934)
MacCarthy, J., *Recollections of the Storming of the Castle of Badajoz to Which are Added Memoirs of the Battle of Corunna* (London: Clowes, 1836)
Mackinnon, Henry, *A Journal of the Campaign in Portugal and Spain from the Year 1809 to 1812* (Bath: Duffield, 1812)
Macready, Edward N., 'Letter of Ensign Edward Neville Macready to his father' in G. Glover (ed), *The Waterloo Archive* (Barnsley: Frontline 2010), vol.1, pp.161–163
Malcolm, J., 'Reminiscences of a Campaign in the Pyrenees and South of France in 1814' in Anon. (ed.), *Memorials of the Late War* (Edinburgh: Constable, 1828), pp.232–307
Malmesbury, Earl of (ed.), *A Series of Letters of the First Lord Malmesbury His Family and Friends from 1745 to 1820* (London: Bentley, 1870)
Maxwell, W.H. (ed.), *Peninsular Sketches by Actors on the Scene* (London: Colburn, 1845)
McGrigor, James., *The Autobiography and Services of Sir Jas. McGrigor, Bart, Late Director General of the Medical Department* (London: Longman, 1861)
McGuffie, T H. (ed.), *Peninsular Cavalry General (1811–13) The Correspondence of Lieutenant-General Robert Ballard Long* (London: Harrap, 1951)
Mclean, H., *An Enquiry into the Nature and Causes of the Great Mortality among the Troops at St Domingo* (London: Cadell, 1797)
Mercer, Cavalié, *Journal of the Waterloo Campaign kept throughout the Campaign of 1815* (London: Greenhill, 1985)
Miller, Benjamin., *The Adventures of Sergeant Benjamin Miller Whilst Serving in the 4th Battalion of the Royal Regiment of Artillery 1796 to 1815* (Uckfield: Naval & Military, nd.)
Mockler-Ferryman, A.F. (ed.), *The Life of a Regimental Officer During the Great War 1793–1815. Compiled from the correspondence of Col Samuel Rice, 51st Light Infantry* (London: Blackwood, 1913)

Monick, S. (ed.), *Douglas's Tale of the Peninsula and Waterloo by John Douglas, former Sergeant, 1st Royal Scots* (London: Leo Cooper, 1997)

Moore Smith, G.C., (ed.), *The Autobiography of Lieutenant-General Sir Harry Smith* (London: Murray, 1901)

Neale, Adam, 'The Spanish Campaign of 1808' in Anon. (ed.), *Memorials of the Late War* (Edinburgh: Constable,1831), vol.1, p.141–231

Neale, Adam, *Letters from Portugal and Spain* (London: Phillips, 1809)

Nicol, D., 'The Unpublished Diary of Sergeant Daniel Nicol', in M. MacBride (ed.), *With Napoleon at Waterloo* (London: Griffiths, 1911), pp.9–70, 86–114

O'Keefe, E. (ed.), *Narrative of the Eventful Life of Thomas Jackson Militiaman and Coldstream Sergeant, 1803–15* (Solihull: Helion, 2018)

O'Neil, Charles, *The Military Memoirs of Charles O'Neil* (Worcester: Livermore, 1851)

Ompteda, L., *In the King's German Legion. Memoirs of Baron Ompteda, Colonel in the King's German Legion During the Napoleonic Wars* (London: Grevel, 1894)

Page, J. (ed.), *Intelligence Officer in the Peninsula. Letters and Diaries of Major the Hon Edward Charles Cocks 1786–1812* (Tunbridge Wells: Spellmount, 1986)

Patterson, John, *Camp and Quarters. Scenes and Impressions of Military Life* (London: Saunders & Otley, 1840)

Patterson, John, *The Adventures of Captain John Patterson of the 50th or Queen's Own Regiment from 1807 to 1821* (London: Boone, 1837)

Porter, Robert K., *Letters from Portugal and Spain written during the March of the British Troops under Sir John Moore* (London: Longman, 1809)

Probert, R. (ed.), *Catherine Exley's Diary. The Life and Times of an Army Wife in the Peninsular War* (Kenilworth: Brandram, 2014)

Robertson, D., *The Journal of Sergeant D Robertson, Late 92nd Foot* (Perth: Fisher, 1842)

Robertson, I. (ed.), *The Exploits of Ensign Bakewell. With the Inniskillings in the Peninsula,1810–11* (Barnsley: Frontline, 2012)

Robinson, E., 'Peninsular Private. The account of John Macfarlane of the 71st (HLI)', *Journal of the Society for Army Historical Research*, vol.32, (1954), pp.4–14

Roy, R.H., 'Memoirs of Private James Gunn', *Journal of the Society for Army Historical Research*, vol.49, (1971), pp.90–120

Sabine, S. (ed.), *Letters of Sir Augustus Simon Frazer, KCB, Commanding Royal Horse Artillery under Wellington, Written during the Peninsular and Waterloo Campaigns* (London: Longman, 1859)

Schaumann, A., *On the Road with Wellington. The Diary of a war commissary in the Peninsular Campaigns* (London: Heinemann, 1824)

Selby, J. (ed.), *Recollections of Military Service in 1813, 1814, and 1815* (London: Longmans, 1967)

Sherer, Moyle, *Recollections of the Peninsula* (Staplehurst: Spellmount, 1996)

Shipp, John, *Memoirs of the Extraordinary Military Life of John Shipp, late Lieutenant in His Majesty's 87th Regiment* (London: Hurst, 1829)

Simmons, George, 'Journal of First Lieutenant George Simmons', in G. Glover (ed.), *The Waterloo Archive* (Barnsley: Frontline, 2012), vol.4, pp.201–223

Sorell, T.S., *Notes on the Campaign of 1808–1809 in the North of Spain* (London: Murray, 1828)

Steevens, Charles, *Reminiscences of my Military Life from 1795 to 1815* (Winchester: Warren, 1878)

Stevenson, John, *A Soldier in Time of War; or, the Military Life of Mr John Stevenson* (London: Brittain, 1841)

Stewart, D., *Sketches of the Character, Manners and Present State of the Highlanders of Scotland with details of the Military Service of Highland Regiments* (Edinburgh: Constable, 1822)

Stothert, W., *A Narrative of the Principal Events of the Campaigns of 1809, 1810, and 1811 In Spain and Portugal* (London: Martin, 1812)

Stuart, B. (ed.), *Soldier's Glory being 'Rough Notes of an Old Soldier'* (London: Bell, 1956)

Surtees, William, *Twenty Five Years in the Rifle Brigade* (London: Muller, 1973)

Teague, J. & D. (eds), *Where Duty Calls Me. The Experiences of William Green in the Napoleonic Wars* (West Wickham: Synjon, 1975)

Thompson, W.F.K. (ed.), *An Ensign in the Peninsular War. The letters of John Aitchison* (London: Michael Joseph, 1981)

Thorpe, Samuel, *Narrative of Incidents in the Early Military Life of the late Major Samuel Thorpe* (London: Seeleys, 1854)

Timewell, J., 'Diary of a Private Soldier in the Peninsula War', *Macmillan's Magazine*, vol.77, (1897), pp.3–8

Tomkinson, W., *The Diary of a Cavalry Officer* (London: Macmillan, 1894)

Vansittart, J. (ed.), *Surgeon James' Journal 1815* (London: Cassell, 1964)

Verner, W. (ed.), *A British Rifle Man. Journals and Correspondence during the Peninsular War and the Campaign of Wellington* (London: Black, 1899)

Verner, W., 'Reminiscences (1782-1871) Seventh Hussars', *Journal of the Society for Army Historical Research,* Occasional Publication No.8, (1965)

Vickers, J., *A Sermon, of which the Substance was Delivered in the Parish Churches of Swanington and Wood Dalling in the county of Norfolk on the Twentieth and Twenty-seventh August, 1815 in aid of the Waterloo Subscription by John Vickers MA Rector of Swanington and Vicar of Wood Dalling* (Norwich: Bacon, 1815)

Ward, B.R. (ed.), *A Week at Waterloo in 1815. Lady De Lancey's Narrative Being an Account of how she nursed her husband, Colonel Sir William Howe De Lancey, Quartermaster-General of the Army, mortally wounded in the great battle* (London: Murray, 1906)

Ward, Mrs., *Recollections of an Old Soldier: A biographical sketch of the late Colonel Tidy, CB. 24th Regt.* (London: Bentley, 1849)

Wardell, J. (ed.), *With the Thirty-Second in the Peninsula and other Campaigns* (Dublin: Hodges,1904)

Warre, E. (ed.), *Letters from the Peninsula 1808–1812* (London: Murray, 1909)

Wellington, 2nd Duke of (ed.), *Supplementary Despatches, Correspondence and Memoranda* (London: Murray, 1858–1872)

Whinyates, F.A. (ed.), *Diary of Campaigns in the Peninsula, for the Years 1811, 12 and 13* (Woolwich: Royal Artillery Institute, nd.)

Whinyates, F.A. (ed.), *Letters Written by Lieut.-General Thomas Dyneley CB RA, while on Active Service Between the Year 1806 and 1815* (Huntingdon: Ken Trotman, 1984)

Wilson, R.T., *Narrative of the Expedition to Egypt under Sir Ralph Abercrombie* (London: Dutton, 1803)

Wollocombe, R.H. (ed.), *With the Guns in the Peninsula. The Peninsular War Journal of 2nd Captain William Webber, Royal Artillery* (London: Greenhill Books, 1991)

Wood, George, *The Subaltern Officer. A Narrative* (London: Prowett, 1825)

Wood, S.C.I. (ed.), *Reminiscences 1808–1815 Under Wellington* (London: Simkin, 1901)
Woodford, L.W. (ed.), *A Young Surgeon in Wellington's Army. The Letters of William Dent* (Old Woking: Unwin, 1976)
Wylly, H.C. (ed.), *A Cavalry Officer in the Corunna Campaign 1808–1809. The Journal of Captain Gordon of the 15th Hussars* (London: Blackwood, 1913)

Secondary Printed Sources

Anon. *Records of the 54th West Norfolk Regiment* (Roorkee: Thomason, 1881)
Bamford, A., *Sickness, Suffering and the Sword* (Norman: University of Oklahoma Press, 2013)
Boyden, P B., *Tommy Atkins' Letters* (London: National Army Museum, 1990)
Bromley, J. & D., *Wellington's Men Remembered. A Register of Memorials to Soldiers who Fought in the Peninsular War and at Waterloo* (Barnsley: Pen & Sword 2011)
Burley, R.D., *An Age of Negligence? British Army Chaplaincy, 1796–1844* (M.Phil thesis, Birmingham University, 2013)
Clammer, D., 'Soldiers and Civilians. Troops in Dorset 1793–1805', *Journal of the Society For Army Historical Research*, vol.93, (2015), pp.214–230
Condon, M E., 'Living Conditions on Board Troopships during the war against Revolutionary France 1793–1802', *Journal of the Society for Army Historical Research*, vol.49, (1971), pp.14–19
Davies, Godfrey, *Wellington and His Army* (Oxford: Blackwell, 1954)
Esdaile, Charles J., *Women in the Peninsular War* (Norman: University of Oklahoma Press, 2014)
Fuller, J.F.C., *Sir John Moore's System of Training* (London: Hutchinson, 1924)
Gardyne, C.G., *The Life of a Regiment. The History of the Gordon Highlanders from its Foundation in 1794 to 1816* (Edinburgh: Douglas, 1901)
Geggus, D., 'Yellow Fever in the 1790s: The British Army in Occupied Saint Domingue', *Medical History*, 23, pp.38–58
Glover, Michael, *The Peninsular War 1807–1814, A Concise Military History* (Newton Abbot: David & Charles, 1974)
Glover, Michael, *Wellington's Army in the Peninsula 1808–1814* (Newton Abbot: David & Charles, 1977)
Glover, Richard, *Britain at Bay* (London: Allan & Unwin, 1973)
Haythornthwaite, Philip J., *The Armies of Wellington* (London: Arms & Armour, 1994)
Hibbert, Christopher, *Corunna* (London: Pan, 1961)
Howard, Martin R., *Death Before Glory! The British Soldier in the West Indies in the French Revolutionary & Napoleonic Wars 1793–1815* (Barnsley: Pen & Sword, 2015)
Knight, R., *Britain Against Napoleon. The Organization of Victory 1793-1815* (London: Penguin, 2014)
Lin, P.Y.C.E., 'Caring for the Nation's Families: British Soldiers' and Sailors' Families and The State 1793–1815', in A. Forrest, K. Hagemann, and J. Rendall (eds), *Soldiers, Citizens and Civilians: Experiences and Perceptions of the French Wars 1790–1820* (London: Palgrave Macmillan, 2008)
Longford, Elizabeth, *Wellington, The Years of the Sword* (London: Weidenfeld & Nicholson, 1969)
Mackinnon, D., *Origins and Services of the Coldstream Guards* (London: Bentley, 1833)

McAulay, K.E., and Robertson-Kirkland, B.E., '"My Love to the War is Going": Women and Song in the Napoleonic Era', in P. Hore(ed.), *The Trafalgar Chronicle* (London: Seaforth, 2018), pp.202–212

Napier, W.F.P., *History of the War in the Peninsula and the South of France* (London: Murray, 1832–40)

Oman, Charles, *Wellington's Army, 1808–1814* (London: Arnold, 1913)

Palmer, Roger, *The Rambling Soldier* (London: Penguin, 1977)

Page, F.C.G., *Following the Drum. Women in Wellington's Wars* (London: Deutsch, 1986)

Southey, Robert, *History of the Peninsular War* (London: Murray, 1823–1832)

Steppler, G.A., 'British military law, discipline and the conduct of courts martial in the Later eighteenth century', *English Historical Review*, vol.102, pp.859–886

Trimble, W.C., *The Historical Record of the 27th Inniskilling Regiment* (London: Clowes, 1876)

Vine, P.A.L., *The Royal Military Canal* (Newton Abbot: David & Charles, 1972)

Ward, S.P.G., *Wellington's Headquarters. The Command and Administration of the British Army during the Peninsular War* (Oxford: Oxford University Press, 1957)

Weller, J., *Wellington in the Peninsula 1808–1814* (London: Vane, 1962)

Online Sources

Army Children's Archive, 'Waterloo Veterans: the army children of Waterloo', <www.tacadrum.blogspot.com/2015/06/waterloo-veterans-army-children-of.html>, accessed 2 July 2019

Art UK, <https://artuk.org>, accessed 3 November 2018

Bennett, B.T., 'British War Poetry in the Age of Romanticism, 1793 – 1815', <romantic-circles.org/editions/warpoetry/index.html>, accessed 7 November 2020

Guilfoyle, M., 'Elizabeth Watkins, Waterloo Veteran', <www.foblc.org.uk/2010/07/Elizabeth-watkins-1810-1904.html>, accessed 2 July 2019

Howard, Martin R., 'Walcheren 1809: a medical catastrophe', British Medical Journal, <https://doi.org/10.1136/bmj.319.7225.1642>, accessed 2 February 2019

Hazzard, K., 'Working Women's Clothes, 1810-1820', <https://www.95th-rifles.co.uk/civilian-clothing/working-women-clothes-1810-1820/>, accessed 3 February 2019

Keep Museum. Dorchester, <https://keepmilitarymuseum.org>, accessed 16 March 2019

Major, Joanne, 'Margaret Tolmie – another "Waterloo Child"', All Things Georgian, <https://Georgianera.wordpress.com/2015/06/18margaret-tolmie-another-waterloo-child>, accessed 3 July 2019

Royal Welch Fusiliers Museum, <https://royalwelchfusiliersmuseum.blogspot.com/2016/06/jenny-jones-at-waterloo.html>, accessed 8 February 2022

The Heroine of Matagorda – Find a Grave in Scotland, <https://www.findagraveinscotland.com/grave/famousgrave/125508>, accessed 6 June 2022

Index

The Women

Allen, Mrs 27, 109, 192
Anton, Mary 79, 81, 119, 190, 217–218
Ashton, Mrs 135–136

Carsons, Nelly 90, 110
Cochan, Mrs 162, 192–193
Cowell, Mrs 84, 90, 112
Currie, Mrs 22, 93

Dalbiac, Susanna 78, 151–152, 163, 170, 226
De Lancey, Lady Magdalene 174
Deacon, Mrs 152–153
Donaldson, Ellen 226–227

Eaton, Charlotte 145, 149
Exley, Catherine 27, 37–38, 83, 97, 99, 101, 107–108, 115, 118, 147, 171, 195, 217, 227–228

Fisher, Mrs 176, 178

Gifford, Mary 167–168
Grey, Mrs 93, 150
Griffiths, Jenny 28, 234

Harness, Bessy 15–16
Howans, Mrs 22, 139–140
Howley, Mrs 158–159

Jeffers, Ann 164, 232

Lawrence, Clotilde 205–206, 218, 231–232, 235

M'Dermot, Nance 22, 167, 196
Maguire, Mrs 22, 59
Maibee 22, 157
Maloney, Mrs 137, 142
Mrs Morris 79–80
Muttlebury, Mrs 172–173

Parsons, Theresa 213–214
Pullen, Mrs 143–144

Quinn, Elinor 195–196

Retson, Agnes 22, 156, 235–236

Scovell, Mary 75, 94, 99
Sherwood, Mrs 24, 39, 43, 50–51, 67, 191
Skiddy, Mrs 100, 119, 182
Smellie, Wilhelmina 225–226
Smith, Lady Juana 151–152, 173, 206–207, 236

Tennant, Ann 38, 215–216
Thorpe, Jacinth 204–205
Tolmie, Eliza 22, 152–153

Urquhart, Margaret 114, 233-234

Wellington, Mary Anne 237

General Index

Abercromby, Lieutenant General Sir Ralph 15, 60, 64, 80, 199
Albuera, Battle of 38, 94, 107, 154, 237
Alexandria 16, 60, 120
Anderson, Captain Joseph 55, 195
Astorga 125, 128, 130
Aytoun, James 20, 196

Badajoz 97, 102, 108, 110, 116, 151, 158, 160, 165, 168–169, 181, 196, 206, 224–225
Baird, Lieutenant General Sir David 123–126, 128–129, 139
Bakewell, Ensign Robert 26, 109, 176, 198
Belgium 17, 28–29, 38, 145, 152–153, 164, 172, 213, 232, 234
Bell, Ensign George 68, 93, 100, 119, 151, 169, 182, 201
Bentinck, Drummer William 87, 89, 101–102, 191
Blakeney, Lieutenant Robert 93, 131–132, 134, 200, 202
Blathwayt, Lieutenant George 74–75
Board of Ordnance, corps of; **Royal Artillery** 40, 51, 54, 91–92, 94, 105, 163, 229, 232, 237
Royal Horse Artillery 18, 29, 64, 68, 71, 84, 99, 111, 122, 172, 202, 225
Bowles, Captain George 27, 51–52, 66
British Army, cavalry regiments of; **1st Dragoon Guards** 99, 215, 232; **2nd Dragoons** 18, 22, 43, 153, 168, 170, 173; **4th Dragoons** 78, 151, 170; **11th Light Dragoons** 18, 159, 176; **12th Light Dragoons** 68, 120; **15th Hussars** 128, 134, 139; **16th Light Dragoons** 151, 163, 201; **18th Hussars** 33, 48, 66, 79–80, 101, 127, 178, 184, 193; **20th Light Dragoons** 20, 84, 168, 185
British Army, infantry regiments of; **1st Guards** 38, 118, 195, 215; **Coldstream Guards** 26–27, 40, 66, 95, 155, 159, 161, 183–184, 227; **3rd Guards** 26, 77, 120, 146, 154, 201; **1st** 24, 27, 44, 88, 105, 109, 155, 157, 180, 191, 224; **4th** 20, 22, 59, 231; **7th** 49, 112, 147, 158, 187; **9th** 15, 30, 55, 80, 83, 95, 118, 140, 165, 178, 224; **14th** 38, 147; **20th** 15, 131, 137; **22nd** 120, 178; **23rd** 28, 32, 56, 60, 87, 90, 101, 105, 179, 234; **25th** 53, 58, 60, 104; **27th** 26, 28, 60, 109, 113, 176, 198; **28th** 32, 35, 57, 93, 131, 157, 167, 200; **29th** 18, 68, 92; **30th** 58, 93, 96, 146, 150; **32nd** 48, 86, 96, 106, 198, 224; **34th** 27, 37, 68, 78, 83, 91–93, 100, 108, 115, 118, 147, 151, 169, 182, 195, 200–201, 217, 227; **39th** 18, 97; **40th** 42, 52, 55, 180, 205–206, 218, 231; **42nd** 20, 59, 62, 79, 88, 107, 119, 134, 137, 141–142, 145, 155, 167, 190, 195, 217–218; **43rd** 18, 29, 32, 43, 79, 129–130, 136–137, 140, 159, 165, 209; **45th** 69, 89, 97, 161, 163, 170; **47th** 84, 112; **48th** 122, 237; **50th** 14, 47, 133, 141; **51st** 17, 22, 118, 157–158, 166, 192, 196, 225; **52nd** 69, 98, 100, 124, 130, 137–138, 140, 153; **53rd** 24, 39, 43, 50–51, 66–67, 191; **54th** 40, 105, 199–200; **58th** 20, 196, 229; **61st** 51–52, 59, 196; **64th** 53, 62; **66th** 105, 117, 158, 200; **67th** 32, 39; **68th** 45, 61, 89, 98, 184, 192; **71st** 16, 72, 126, 136, 143, 159, 196, 233; **73rd** 37, 54, 78, 86, 152, 213; **77th** 26, 32; **80th** 15, 43, 106; **81st** 14, 46, 49, 106; **82nd** 30, 57, 108, 176; **85th** 22, 24, 32, 34, 146, 193, 196; **88th** 26, 48, 57, 69, 73, 90, 94–95, 110, 115, 158, 164, 169, 193, 196, 204–205, 211, 224; **91st** 106, 140; **92nd** 26, 37, 78, 100, 105, 114, 132, 139, 153; **94th** 22, 24, 43, 50, 73, 87, 112, 116, 148, 154, 156, 165, 175, 202–203, 209, 226, 235; **95th** 16–17, 22, 28, 34, 44–45, 54, 72–73, 87, 95, 99, 102, 104, 107–108, 129–130, 140, 143, 147–148, 151, 153, 155, 164, 168, 173, 196, 203–204, 206–207, 210, 232–233
British Army, foreign corps of; **King's German Legion** 51, 57, 103, 115, 118, 159, 185, 202, 211
Browne, Captain Thomas Henry 55, 60, 62, 72, 90, 163–164, 169, 171, 186, 191, 194
Burgos 70, 94, 100, 112, 121, 126, 154, 157–159, 184–185, 204, 224
Busaco, Battle of 52, 184, 205
Butler, Sergeant Robert 24, 27, 100, 106, 109, 192

Cape of Good Hope 15, 59, 120
Ciudad Rodrigo 43, 68–70, 72, 85, 87, 92, 101, 112, 154, 159, 161, 164–165, 193, 201
Clay, Private Matthew 135, 145–146, 155
Cooke, Lieutenant John 32, 208–209
Cooper, Sergeant John 147–148, 187, 230
Copenhagen 57, 77, 143

INDEX

Cork 55, 61, 78, 196
Corunna 15–16, 21, 34, 70, 122–123, 125–131, 133, 135, 137–141, 143, 145, 155, 160, 180–181, 218, 231
Costello, Private Edward 72, 153–155, 164, 196–197, 204, 210, 218–219
Craufurd, Brigadier General Robert 130, 139–140
Crowe, Lieutenant Charles 29, 60–61, 113, 176–178

Dalbiac, Colonel James 78, 151
Donaldson, Sergeant Joseph 24–25, 43, 50, 87, 112–113, 115–116, 149, 156–157, 165, 175, 203, 210, 226–227, 235
Dyneley, Captain Thomas 71, 99
Dyott, Lieutenant Colonel William 53, 60

Egypt 15–16, 20, 54, 60, 64, 105, 120, 193, 199–200

Frazer, Major Augustus 68, 71, 111, 115, 125, 128, 172

Gibraltar 39, 45, 48, 54–55, 59, 62, 92, 105, 114–115, 164, 235, 237
Gleig, Lieutenant George 24, 32, 34–35, 146, 167, 193, 198
Grattan, Lieutenant William 90, 95, 110, 112, 159, 169, 193, 198, 203, 205, 211
Green, Private John 45, 89
Green, Private William 87, 95, 108, 140, 160, 168
Guernsey 32, 39, 43
Gunn, Private James 59, 62

Hale, Sergeant James 55, 140, 165
Hamilton, Sergeant Anthony 129, 136
Harley, Captain John 40–41, 112, 200
Harness, Major William 15–16, 43, 106, 164
Harris, Private Benjamin 102, 130–131, 139–140, 143–144, 162–163, 192–193, 204
Henegan, Sir Richard 51, 55, 63, 91, 166, 199
Hennell, Lieutenant George 79, 159
Henry, Surgeon Walter 117, 158, 200
Hill, Lieutenant General Sir Rowland, Lord 22, 70, 75, 92–93, 150, 187
Hythe 20, 34–35, 143, 217

India 15, 20, 24, 27, 39, 43, 51–52, 105–106, 109, 178, 191, 196, 223, 226, 236

Jackson, Sergeant Thomas 40, 153, 227
Jersey 24, 27, 37, 48, 50, 57
Johnston, Sergeant Archibald 43, 168

Landmann, Captain George 48–49, 149–150, 160, 163, 168, 170
Larpent, Francis 75–76, 85, 94, 202
Lawrence, Sergeant William 42, 52, 205–206, 218, 231–232, 235
Le Mesurier, Lieutenant Peter 15, 68, 80, 83, 92, 95, 178, 187–188
Leach, Captain Jonathan 69, 102, 104, 162, 207, 210
Leslie, Lieutenant Charles 41–42, 55, 68, 77, 92, 109, 186
Lisbon 27, 50–52, 55, 64, 66, 85, 93–94, 107–109, 112–113, 115, 119, 121–124, 128, 180–181, 193, 200, 204, 207

Mackinnon, Major General Henry 66, 69
Macready, Ensign Edward 96, 146
Malcolm, Lieutenant John 20, 145
McGrigor, Surgeon Dr Sir James 57–58, 181
Mercer, Captain Cavalié 29–30, 64
Miller, Sergeant Benjamin 54, 59, 105, 115, 142, 198–199
Moore, Lieutenant General Sir John 14, 17, 46, 59, 66, 70, 100, 122–124, 126–128, 130–131, 136, 138, 141–142, 145, 181, 193, 200, 218
Morris, Sergeant Thomas 54, 78–80, 152

Nive, Battle of the 79, 119
Nivelle, Battle of the 108, 166, 192, 203, 230
Nova Scotia 32, 53, 55–56, 62, 179, 194, 236

O'Neil, Private Charles 35, 57, 94, 169
Orthez, Battle of 79, 154, 158, 178, 205, 223
Ostend 27–29, 57, 64, 198, 213, 215

Patterson, Major John 14–16, 47, 50, 133
Plymouth 32, 57, 142–143, 213, 231
Portsmouth 24, 28, 32, 38, 42–43, 50–51, 61, 68, 143, 219

Quatre Bras, Battle of 58, 146–147, 152–154, 164, 167, 172, 197, 224, 232

Ramsgate 14, 26, 42, 50, 191, 217
Roliça, Battle of 149, 163, 170

Ross-Lewin, Captain Harry 48, 71, 83, 96, 106, 198–199
Royal Navy 25, 47, 64, 140

Salamanca 66, 68, 70, 72, 83–84, 87–88, 90, 94, 100–102, 113, 118, 124, 126–127, 148, 163, 170, 182, 237
Salamanca, Battle of 73, 78, 101, 151, 157, 159, 163, 169, 187, 191–192, 198, 206, 226
Schaumann, August 63, 84, 87, 116, 129, 132, 135–136, 140, 184, 204
Sherer, Captain Moyle 78–79, 91–92, 200–201, 207
South America 20, 42
Spithead 29, 52, 59, 219
Steevens, Captain Charles 15, 131, 136–137
Surtees, Quartermaster William 16, 34, 54, 73, 147, 196, 210–211
Swabey, Lieutenant William 84, 122, 202

Talavera, Battle of 66, 87, 95, 103, 109, 170, 204
Thornton Keep, Ensign William 26, 32, 54
Toulouse, Battle of 89, 101, 148, 158, 163, 167, 195, 205, 208–209

Villafranca 125, 130–133
Vimeiro, Battle of 102, 150, 160, 193, 204
Vitoria, Battle of 66, 73, 79, 97, 101–102, 148, 166, 171, 184, 192, 237

Walcheren 14, 26, 30, 42, 44–45, 49, 58, 106, 143, 155, 197, 199
Waterloo, Battle of 17, 20–22, 27, 43, 52, 58, 64, 74, 77, 96, 99, 108, 145, 148–149, 152–153, 155, 157, 164, 166–167, 170–174, 176, 186, 188, 196, 198, 205, 213–216, 220–225, 232–235
Webber, Captain William 86, 88, 91–92, 94, 184
Wellington, Field Marshal Sir Arthur Wellesley, Duke of 27–28, 64, 68, 70, 72, 74–75, 81, 86, 88–95, 100–101, 106, 113, 116, 145, 154, 157, 159–160, 169, 172, 174, 181–182, 184–185, 187–188, 197, 200, 202, 204, 206–208, 213, 215–216, 220, 223, 226
Wheeler, Private William 17, 66, 108, 157, 166, 192
Woodberry, Lieutenant George 48, 50, 66, 79–80, 178, 184, 207
Wray, Private Samuel 52, 59

Yarmouth 37, 54

From Reason to Revolution – Warfare 1721-1815

http://www.helion.co.uk/series/from-reason-to-revolution-1721-1815.php

The 'From Reason to Revolution' series covers the period of military history 1721–1815, an era in which fortress-based strategy and linear battles gave way to the nation-in-arms and the beginnings of total war.

This era saw the evolution and growth of light troops of all arms, and of increasingly flexible command systems to cope with the growing armies fielded by nations able to mobilise far greater proportions of their manpower than ever before. Many of these developments were fired by the great political upheavals of the era, with revolutions in America and France bringing about social change which in turn fed back into the military sphere as whole nations readied themselves for war. Only in the closing years of the period, as the reactionary powers began to regain the upper hand, did a military synthesis of the best of the old and the new become possible.

The series will examine the military and naval history of the period in a greater degree of detail than has hitherto been attempted, and has a very wide brief, with the intention of covering all aspects from the battles, campaigns, logistics, and tactics, to the personalities, armies, uniforms, and equipment.

Submissions

The publishers would be pleased to receive submissions for this series. Please contact series editor Andrew Bamford via email (andrewbamford@helion.co.uk), or in writing to Helion & Company Limited, Unit 8 Amherst Business Centre, Budbrooke Road, Warwick, CV34 5WE

Titles

No 1   *Lobositz to Leuthen: Horace St Paul and the Campaigns of the Austrian Army in the Seven Years War 1756-57* (Neil Cogswell)

No 2   *Glories to Useless Heroism: The Seven Years War in North America from the French journals of Comte Maurès de Malartic, 1755-1760* (William Raffle (ed.))

No 3   *Reminiscences 1808-1815 Under Wellington: The Peninsular and Waterloo Memoirs of William Hay* (Andrew Bamford (ed.))

No 4   *Far Distant Ships: The Royal Navy and the Blockade of Brest 1793-1815* (Quintin Barry)

No 5   *Godoy's Army: Spanish Regiments and Uniforms from the Estado Militar of 1800* (Charles Esdaile and Alan Perry)

No 6   *On Gladsmuir Shall the Battle Be! The Battle of Prestonpans 1745* (Arran Johnston)

No 7   *The French Army of the Orient 1798-1801: Napoleon's Beloved 'Egyptians'* (Yves Martin)

No 8   *The Autobiography, or Narrative of a Soldier: The Peninsular War Memoirs of William Brown of the 45th Foot* (Steve Brown (ed.))

No 9   *Recollections from the Ranks: Three Russian Soldiers' Autobiographies from the Napoleonic Wars* (Darrin Boland)

No 10 *By Fire and Bayonet: Grey's West Indies Campaign of 1794* (Steve Brown)

No 11 *Olmütz to Torgau: Horace St Paul and the Campaigns of the Austrian Army in the Seven Years War 1758-60* (Neil Cogswell)

No 12 *Murat's Army: The Army of the Kingdom of Naples 1806-1815* (Digby Smith)

No 13 *The Veteran or 40 Years' Service in the British Army: The Scurrilous Recollections of Paymaster John Harley 47th Foot – 1798-1838* (Gareth Glover (ed.))

No 14 *Narrative of the Eventful Life of Thomas Jackson: Militiaman and Coldstream Sergeant, 1803-15* (Eamonn O'Keeffe (ed.))

No.15 *For Orange and the States: The Army of the Dutch Republic 1713-1772 Part I: Infantry* (Marc Geerdinck-Schaftenaar)

- No 16 *Men Who Are Determined to be Free: The American Assault on Stony Point, 15 July 1779* (David C. Bonk)
- No 17 *Next to Wellington: General Sir George Murray: The Story of a Scottish Soldier and Statesman, Wellington's Quartermaster General* (John Harding-Edgar)
- No 18 *Between Scylla and Charybdis: The Army of Elector Friedrich August of Saxony 1733-1763 Part I: Staff and Cavalry* (Marco Pagan)
- No 19 *The Secret Expedition: The Anglo-Russian Invasion of Holland 1799* (Geert van Uythoven)
- No 20 *'We Are Accustomed to do our Duty': German Auxiliaries with the British Army 1793-95* (Paul Demet)
- No 21 *With the Guards in Flanders: The Diary of Captain Roger Morris 1793-95* (Peter Harington (ed.))
- No 22 *The British Army in Egypt 1801: An Underrated Army Comes of Age* (Carole Divall)
- No 23 *Better is the Proud Plaid: The Clothing, Weapons, and Accoutrements of the Jacobites in the '45* (Jenn Scott)
- No 24 *The Lilies and the Thistle: French Troops in the Jacobite '45* (Andrew Bamford)
- No 25 *A Light Infantryman With Wellington: The Letters of Captain George Ulrich Barlow 52nd and 69th Foot 1808-15* (Gareth Glover (ed.))
- No 26 *Swiss Regiments in the Service of France 1798-1815: Uniforms, Organisation, Campaigns* (Stephen Ede-Borrett)
- No 27 *For Orange and the States! The Army of the Dutch Republic 1713-1772: Part II: Cavalry and Specialist Troops* (Marc Geerdinck-Schaftenaar)
- No 28 *Fashioning Regulation, Regulating Fashion: Uniforms and Dress of the British Army 1800-1815 Volume I* (Ben Townsend)
- No 29 *Riflemen: The History of the 5th Battalion 60th (Royal American) Regiment, 1797-1818* (Robert Griffith)
- No 30 *The Key to Lisbon: The Third French Invasion of Portugal, 1810-11* (Kenton White)
- No 31 *Command and Leadership: Proceedings of the 2018 Helion & Company 'From Reason to Revolution' Conference* (Andrew Bamford (ed.))
- No 32 *Waterloo After the Glory: Hospital Sketches and Reports on the Wounded After the Battle* (Michael Crumplin and Gareth Glover)
- No 33 *Fluxes, Fevers, and Fighting Men: War and Disease in Ancien Regime Europe 1648-1789* (Pádraig Lenihan)
- No 34 *'They Were Good Soldiers': African-Americans Serving in the Continental Army, 1775-1783* (John U. Rees)
- No 35 *A Redcoat in America: The Diaries of Lieutenant William Bamford, 1757-1765 and 1776* (John B. Hattendorf (ed.))
- No 36 *Between Scylla and Charybdis: The Army of Friedrich August II of Saxony, 1733-1763: Part II: Infantry and Artillery* (Marco Pagan)
- No 37 *Québec Under Siege: French Eye-Witness Accounts from the Campaign of 1759* (Charles A. Mayhood (ed.))
- No 38 *King George's Hangman: Henry Hawley and the Battle of Falkirk 1746* (Jonathan D. Oates)
- No 39 *Zweybrücken in Command: The Reichsarmee in the Campaign of 1758* (Neil Cogswell)
- No 40 *So Bloody a Day: The 16th Light Dragoons in the Waterloo Campaign* (David J. Blackmore)
- No 41 *Northern Tars in Southern Waters: The Russian Fleet in the Mediterranean 1806-1810* (Vladimir Bogdanovich Bronevskiy / Darrin Boland)
- No 42 *Royal Navy Officers of the Seven Years War: A Biographical Dictionary of Commissioned Officers 1748-1763* (Cy Harrison)
- No 43 *All at Sea: Naval Support for the British Army During the American Revolutionary War* (John Dillon)
- No 44 *Glory is Fleeting: New Scholarship on the Napoleonic Wars* (Andrew Bamford (ed.))
- No 45 *Fashioning Regulation, Regulating Fashion: Uniforms and Dress of the British Army 1800-1815 Vol. II* (Ben Townsend)
- No 46 *Revenge in the Name of Honour: The Royal Navy's Quest for Vengeance in the Single Ship Actions of the War of 1812* (Nicholas James Kaizer)
- No 47 *They Fought With Extraordinary Bravery: The III German (Saxon) Army Corps in the Southern Netherlands 1814* (Geert van Uythoven)

No 48 *The Danish Army of the Napoleonic Wars 1801-1814, Organisation, Uniforms & Equipment: Volume 1: High Command, Line and Light Infantry* (David Wilson)

No 49 *Neither Up Nor Down: The British Army and the Flanders Campaign 1793-1895* (Phillip Ball)

No 50 *Guerra Fantástica: The Portuguese Army and the Seven Years War* (António Barrento)

No 51 *From Across the Sea: North Americans in Nelson's Navy* (Sean M. Heuvel and John A. Rodgaard)

No 52 *Rebellious Scots to Crush: The Military Response to the Jacobite '45* (Andrew Bamford (ed.))

No 53 *The Army of George II 1727-1760: The Soldiers who Forged an Empire* (Peter Brown)

No 54 *Wellington at Bay: The Battle of Villamuriel, 25 October 1812* (Garry David Wills)

No 55 *Life in the Red Coat: The British Soldier 1721-1815* (Andrew Bamford (ed.))

No 56 *Wellington's Favourite Engineer. John Burgoyne: Operations, Engineering, and the Making of a Field Marshal* (Mark S. Thompson)

No 57 *Scharnhorst: The Formative Years, 1755-1801* (Charles Edward White)

No 58 *At the Point of the Bayonet: The Peninsular War Battles of Arroyomolinos and Almaraz 1811-1812* (Robert Griffith)

No 59 *Sieges of the '45: Siege Warfare during the Jacobite Rebellion of 1745-1746* (Jonathan D. Oates)

No 60 *Austrian Cavalry of the Revolutionary and Napoleonic Wars, 1792–1815* (Enrico Acerbi, András K. Molnár)

No 61 *The Danish Army of the Napoleonic Wars 1801-1814, Organisation, Uniforms & Equipment: Volume 2: Cavalry and Artillery* (David Wilson)

No 62 *Napoleon's Stolen Army: How the Royal Navy Rescued a Spanish Army in the Baltic* (John Marsden)

No 63 *Crisis at the Chesapeake: The Royal Navy and the Struggle for America 1775-1783* (Quintin Barry)

No 64 *Bullocks, Grain, and Good Madeira: The Maratha and Jat Campaigns 1803-1806 and the emergence of the Indian Army* (Joshua Provan)

No 65 *Sir James McGrigor: The Adventurous Life of Wellington's Chief Medical Officer* (Tom Scotland)

No 66 *Fashioning Regulation, Regulating Fashion: Uniforms and Dress of the British Army 1800-1815 Volume I* (Ben Townsend) (paperback edition)

No 67 *Fashioning Regulation, Regulating Fashion: Uniforms and Dress of the British Army 1800-1815 Volume II* (Ben Townsend) (paperback edition)

No 68 *The Secret Expedition: The Anglo-Russian Invasion of Holland 1799* (Geert van Uythoven) (paperback edition)

No 69 *The Sea is My Element: The Eventful Life of Admiral Sir Pulteney Malcolm 1768-1838* (Paul Martinovich)

No 70 *The Sword and the Spirit: Proceedings of the first 'War & Peace in the Age of Napoleon' Conference* (Zack White (ed.))

No 71 *Lobositz to Leuthen: Horace St Paul and the Campaigns of the Austrian Army in the Seven Years War 1756-57* (Neil Cogswell) (paperback edition)

No 72 *For God and King. A History of the Damas Legion 1793-1798: A Case Study of the Military Emigration during the French Revolution* (Hughes de Bazouges and Alistair Nichols)

No 73 *'Their Infantry and Guns Will Astonish You': The Army of Hindustan and European Mercenaries in Maratha service 1780-1803* (Andy Copestake)

No 74 *Like A Brazen Wall: The Battle of Minden, 1759, and its Place in the Seven Years War* (Ewan Carmichael)

No 75 *Wellington and the Lines of Torres Vedras: The Defence of Lisbon during the Peninsular War* (Mark Thompson)

No 76 *French Light Infantry 1784-1815: From the Chasseurs of Louis XVI to Napoleon's Grande Armée* (Terry Crowdy)

No 77 *Riflemen: The History of the 5th Battalion 60th (Royal American) Regiment, 1797-1818* (Robert Griffith) (paperback edition)

No 78 *Hastenbeck 1757: The French Army and the Opening Campaign of the Seven Years War* (Olivier Lapray)

No 79 *Napoleonic French Military Uniforms: As Depicted by Horace and Carle Vernet and Eugène Lami* (Guy Dempsey (trans. and ed.))

No 80 *These Distinguished Corps: British Grenadier and Light Infantry Battalions in the American Revolution* (Don N. Hagist)

No 81 *Rebellion, Invasion, and Occupation: The British Army in Ireland, 1793 -1815* (Wayne Stack)

No 82 *You Have to Die in Piedmont! The Battle of Assietta, 19 July 1747. The War of the Austrian Succession in the Alps* (Giovanni Cerino Badone)

No 83 *A Very Fine Regiment: the 47th Foot in the American War of Independence, 1773–1783* (Paul Knight)

No 84 *By Fire and Bayonet: Grey's West Indies Campaign of 1794* (Steve Brown) (paperback edition)

No 85 *No Want of Courage: The British Army in Flanders, 1793-1795* (R.N.W. Thomas)

No 86 *Far Distant Ships: The Royal Navy and the Blockade of Brest 1793-1815* (Quintin Barry) (paperback edition)

No 87 *Armies and Enemies of Napoleon 1789-1815: Proceedings of the 2021 Helion and Company 'From Reason to Revolution' Conference* (Robert Griffith (ed.))

No 88 *The Battle of Rossbach 1757: New Perspectives on the Battle and Campaign* (Alexander Querengässer (ed.))

No 89 *Waterloo After the Glory: Hospital Sketches and Reports on the Wounded After the Battle* (Michael Crumplin and Gareth Glover) (paperback edition)

No 90 *From Ushant to Gibraltar: The Channel Fleet 1778-1783* (Quintin Barry)

No 91 *'The Soldiers are Dressed in Red': The Quiberon Expedition of 1795 and the Counter-Revolution in Brittany* (Alistair Nichols)

No 92 *The Army of the Kingdom of Italy 1805-1814: Uniforms, Organisation, Campaigns* (Stephen Ede-Borrett)

No 93 *The Ottoman Army of the Napoleonic Wars 1798-1815: A Struggle for Survival from Egypt to the Balkans* (Bruno Mugnai)

No 94 *The Changing Face of Old Regime Warfare: Essays in Honour of Christopher Duffy* (Alexander S. Burns (ed.))

No 94 *The Changing Face of Old Regime Warfare: Essays in Honour of Christopher Duffy* (Alexander S. Burns (ed.)

No 95 *The Danish Army of the Napoleonic Wars 1801-1814, Organisation, Uniforms & Equipment: Volume 3: Norwegian Troops and Militia* (David Wilson)

No 96 *1805 – Tsar Alexander's First War with Napoleon* (Alexander Ivanovich Mikhailovsky-Danilevsky, trans. Peter G.A. Phillips)

No 97 *'More Furies then Men': The Irish Brigade in the service of France 1690-1792* (Pierre-Louis Coudray)

No 98 *'We Are Accustomed to do our Duty': German Auxiliaries with the British Army 1793-95* (Paul Demet) (paperback edition)

No 99 *Ladies, Wives and Women: British Army Wives in the Revolutionary and Napoleonic Wars 1793-1815* (David Clammer)